THE FINANCIAL SYSTEM
AND THE COORDINATION
OF ECONOMIC ACTIVITY

THE FINANCIAL SYSTEM AND THE COORDINATION OF ECONOMIC ACTIVITY

Robert E. Krainer

New York
Westport, Connecticut
London

Library of Congress Cataloging in Publication Data

Krainer, Robert E.
  The financial system and the coordination of
economic activity.

  Bibliography: p.
  Includes index.
  1. Finance. 2. Macroeconomics. I. Title
HG174.K69   1985   339.5'2   84-17988
ISBN 0-275-90130-0 (alk. paper)

Library of Congress Catalog Card Number: 84-17988
ISBN: 0-275-90130-0

First published in 1985

Praeger Publishers, 521 Fifth Avenue, New York, NY 10175
A division of Greenwood Press, Inc.

Printed in the United States of America

∞

The paper used in this book complies with the Permanent
Paper Standard issued by the National Information Standards
Organization (Z39.48-1984).

10 9 8 7 6 5 4 3 2

For L.R.K., E.H.K., and L.A.K.

Preface

This book is devoted to the study of various aspects of financial economics. It is therefore reasonable to begin by defining finance, for as we will see in the course of this work the word admits several interpretations which in turn will establish the boundaries of the subject matter. Today the word finance is generally taken to mean the obtaining of funds or capital for purposes of spending on goods and services. Thus we speak of a firm financing its plant and equipment and inventories with debt and equity securities, and much of traditional micro financial economics is concerned with the present values investors place on these securities. However, the word itself can be traced back to Middle English where it had a slightly different meaning: namely, referring to ending, settlement, payment, and ransom. What is interesting is that this meaning of the word emphasizes the conclusion of an economic transaction, whereas current usage tends to emphasize the beginning or present. In this book we will also consider the Middle English sense of the word in the course of our discussion, and develop a financial economics around this interpretation. When using the word finance in this sense it becomes apparent that financial economics includes a study of the contractual arrangements that characterize organized economic activity within the institutional framework of the firm. In such a society many individuals contribute different factor services to the production process for purposes of creating an output, and the study of finance will include an analysis of the different contractual arrangements that define the distribution of output to these different input contributors. As such the subject matter of finance in this work will include the study of input- and output-sharing arrangements for all factor contributors, and not just those for the capital input as in the conventional treatment.

Finance as a study of input- and output-sharing arrangements will be one of the principal themes running throughout this work. The associated theme will be that the subject matter is somewhat broader than the limits suggested by the traditional treatment. In this connection Professors Modigliani and Miller (1958) took a giant step forward when they integrated what up to that time was considered to be two separate subjects in finance, namely, the study of investment principles and business finance. Something similar is required today to join together the micro and macro aspects of the subjects. Curiously, the constituent parts are already there, although they tend to be studied separately. Thus the interaction of firm investment decisions and individual portfolio decisions simultaneously determines the capital market value of the firm (the subject matter of finance in schools of business administration) and the level of output and employment (the subject matter of finance in departments of economics) in the economy. This, of course, is the classical Keynesian IS-LM description of product and financial market equilibrium. Both the micro and macro aspects of finance in this scheme embody the current interpretation or definition of finance as a study in the raising of funds or capital. This particular usage of the term was useful in highlighting the nature and significance of demand in the economy. In this work we will see that the payment or settlement interpretation that directs our attention to the contractual arrangements within the firm will help us understand the nature and significance of supply in the economy; a subject that is attracting more attention from academic and applied economists.

In some ways the life cycle of an individual and a body of unified knowledge such as financial economics are similar. When we are young we innocently accept everything and think that everything is for the best in the best of all possible worlds. This is the classical world of perfect certainty and perfect exchange markets that produces a Pareto efficient allocation of resources which in turn includes an optimal level of employment as well as unemployment for the entire economy. The invisible hand is very much at work in this world, and the attempt to improve on it by outside intervention, either by some government or company financial manager, was thought to be irrelevant at best or perhaps even harmful. Youth, however, eventually gives way to adolescence, and this is the period of rebellion. Here the truths of an earlier day are treated with derision and there is a desire to change everything. The adolescence of the micro and macro aspects of financial economics are strikingly similar. In the macro branch of the subject, market imperfections and uncertainty were presumed to preclude the full and efficient utilization of society's resources. The invisible hand must be restrained by the very visible hand of the state. Consequently the economy must be consciously directed, and this direction must come from the hands of some party that presumably represents the interests of all members of society. To be sure, some members of society will gain while others lose as the result of a given course of action, but the political arena of the ballot box was thought to be the best way to resolve these conflicts. In micro finance, adolescence was reflected in the belief that clever financial management by someone could improve on the invisible hand allocation of consumption and investment in the economy. Here, too, the result is obtained because of market imperfections. The allocation between consumption and investment and the distribution of investment throughout the different sectors of the economy can then be improved by such schemes as packaging the returns on physical assets in terms of different types of securities. The adolescence stage in both micro and macro financial economics can be characterized as one where financial policy has an impact on such real magnitudes as employment, output, investment, consumption, and the distribution of income.

Sadly, for an individual the zeal of adolescence yields to old age. Here as in youth we come to accept everything often because we have no choice, but also partly because the experience of adolescence has not lived up to our expectations. The world is a bitter and mean place in which to live, but unfortunately, conscious intervention often seems to produce this very result or at least contribute to disappointing outcomes. Like Whittier we say: "For of all sad words of tongue or pen, the saddest are these: It might have been!" In finance the answer to what "might have been" is the theory of rational expectations and the rebirth of the perfect market hypothesis, or at least a markets-are-perfect-enough hypothesis. Here financial management—be it of the government or private firm variety—is irrelevant. What happens in the input and output markets will be translated into the financial market independent of the financial policies of both firm and government. Financial managers in the private and public sectors might just as well sit back in rocking chairs and watch the real magnitudes of the economy go by. What then will be the next stage? For an individual human being we know part of the answer. For financial economics this chapter has yet to be written. In what follows we hope to offer a few suggestions.

Acknowledgments

One of the more pleasant tasks confronting any author is acknowledging the personal and professional support provided by the many individuals that invariably contributes in one way or another to the completion of a book. On the personal front this typically takes the form of an apology to one's spouse and children for dropping out of family life during the evenings and on weekends. In this connection I need not apologize in the usual way to my wife Lynne nor our three children John, Elizabeth, and Katherine for any undo neglect when gathering and assimilating the subject matter of this book. Work never stood in the way when it came to hockey, soccer, baseball, swimming, and other pleasurable activities that allow parents to become children once again. Like many husbands and fathers I have always taken seriously the duty of coach, adviser, and critic in these and other family activities. Of course it is arguable that less parental guidance and more gathering and assimilating for this work would have contributed more to the felicity of the family and perhaps this book, and for this reason an apology might still be very much in order. If so, I apologize.

The upshot is that this work has been in process since 1974 when I spent the year in Oxford as a visiting fellow at the Centre for Management Studies and as a member of Common Room at Brasenose College. In particular, the material now in Chapters 9–11 first appeared in shorter form under the title "Firm Adjustment and Macro-Economic Equilibrium" in 1974 only to be revised in 1976 to "Efficient Capital Markets, Firm Adjustment, and Macro-Economic Equilibrium," and finally back in Oxford in 1978 as "On the Role of a Capital Market in the Determination of Macroeconomic Equilibrium." To both of these foundations in Oxford (particularly the Centre for Management Studies) and the Graduate School of Business at the University of Wisconsin–Madison I owe a great debt of gratitude for the research support that enabled me to complete this book. In addition, financial support from the Earhart Foundation in 1974, 1978, and 1984 is gratefully appreciated.

Many people on both sides of the Atlantic have offered me free advice on this project. In Oxford the ideas in this book were first presented in the M.-Phil. Seminar in Finance in 1978, and this was followed by a graduate course in Financial Economics at the University of Wisconsin–Madison in 1979. In addition, a series of lectures based on the material of this book was presented in 1979 at the Bedriftsøkonomisk Institute in Oslo. To the students and faculty members of these three institutions I would like to express my thanks for their critical comments, many of which were incorporated in subsequent revisions. In particular I would like to acknowledge the helpful advice of the late Norman Leyland and Peter Sinclair of Brasenose College in Oxford, the late Harry G. Johnson of the University of Chicago, Robert M. Solow and Fischer Black of M.I.T., and Donald D. Hester, James Johannes, Donald A. Nichols, J. David Richardson, and Donald R. Schuette of the University of Wisconsin–Madison. They are in no way responsible for any errors that might remain in this book.

My greatest debt, however, is to Charles Thompson of the Oxford Centre for Management Studies, who in 1974 and 1978 discussed the issues in this book with me on an almost daily basis. He, more than anyone, provided encouragement in the early stages of this project when many of the ideas were slowly and imperfectly taking shape. Books are very much like children in that beyond a certain point both lead lives that are in some measure independent of their parents. Mr. Thompson helped me decide when that point had been reached. Pushing from the opposite direction were Knute Reichel and Robert Dammon (the latter now at Carnegie-Mellon University) who provided research assistance above and beyond the call of duty. Both in their own way taught me a great deal about financial economics in general and this book in particular. Patricia McSherry typed the manuscript with an efficiency and good cheer that was contagious. If I had done my job as well as she did hers, this book would have been finished much sooner. My wife Lynne and Betsy Brown of Praeger read the entire manuscript and greatly improved the presentation. Family friends and relatives who were a constant source of moral support included Mr. E. H. H. Graf and my Uncle Leo. I hope this book measures up to the goals they have often set before me. Finally I would like to thank my mother and father to whom this book is dedicated for their fine example as parents, and for teaching me above all things that family comes first.

Contents

PART IV
THE FINANCIAL ECONOMICS OF A PARTNERSHIP ECONOMY

List of Tables and Figures

Tables

Figures

THE FINANCIAL SYSTEM
AND THE COORDINATION
OF ECONOMIC ACTIVITY

—1—

Introduction

One of the important prerequisites for the good life, according to that shrewd observer of the human condition Charles Dickens, is when a husband earns £20/0/0 in a year and his wife and children spend but £19/19/6. What he and the rest of the community do with their six pences constitute the subject matter of micro and macro financial economics. Comedy and tragedy abound in both the study and practice of financial principles, and the general objective of this work will be to trace certain micro and macro adventures taken by this and other six pences in their journey throughout the economy.

Consider in this connection the principal areas of study in financial economics. The savings of a household must be invested in something. Thus, portfolio theory is intended to provide our humble Dickensian householder with prudent advice as to how single pounds, shillings, and pence can best be invested for a future consumption within whatever environment nature and man see fit to provide. And yet Dickens was only half right in extolling the virtues of individual savings, for the study of macro financial economics tells us that in order to ensure the felicity of an entire society, there must be those who are prepared to spend £20/0/6 in real terms when earning £20. In other words, failure to keep the six pence saved by our prudent householder circulating in the expenditure stream may result in the temporary unemployment of society's human and nonhuman resources, and thereby render it impossible for some families to earn £20 in some future time period. The subject matter of corporation finance is partly concerned with the different types of financial contracts that firms can issue in order to attract the six pence saved by our household, and thereby return the six pence to the expenditure stream. These financial contracts in turn are issued and traded in an economy-wide capital market, and that branch of financial economics known as capital market theory studies the institutions and efficiency of that

1

market. In principle, allocational efficiency has always been presumed to be an important goal for a market economy. On the other hand, in actual practice we often observe trade restrictions between countries, and these restrictions distort the allocation of resources within a country. The existence of these numerous trade restrictions in market economies reminds us that individuals or small groups of individuals have economic objectives, too, which generally center around their position within the distribution of society's income. In a U.S. type of democracy there is ample evidence to suggest that these individuals are often able to achieve or partly achieve these income objectives in the political arena when they fail in the economic arena.[1] Neither micro nor macro financial analysis has much to say about these positional struggles between different individuals within a society, and one of the specific objectives of this book will be to study this aspect of economic life, including the role financial contracts play in resolving these conflicts.

As a branch of economics, finance has had a moderately long history punctuated with more than its share of important controversy. The macro side of the subject has been the handmaiden to politics at least since the work of John Maynard Keynes in the 1930s. Government financial policy (e.g., monetary policy, government expenditure and tax policy, and government debt management policy) in many of the models inspired by Keynes' original work was presumed to play an important role in the political authority's attempt to achieve certain economy-wide goals (such as full employment) that the sum total of private market participants were thought unlikely to attain in the pursuit of their individual self-interests. According to this influential school of thought there was such a thing as an optimal financial policy that government could pursue, and the culmination of this view was put forth by such writers as Tinbergen (1952), Phillips (1958), and Mundell (1962), all of whom suggested that a number of political/economic goals such as the elimination of involuntary unemployment, high inflation, and the attainment of some target level of international reserves or relative exchange rates could be achieved or optimally traded off against one another by the skillful manipulation of monetary and fiscal instruments. Only comparatively recently has the effectiveness of discretionary government financial policy been questioned and then only within the context of a full information and market clearing long-run equilibrium. A great deal of professional effort now goes into the study of just how long that long run might be, and whether it is long enough to allow any scope for an active government financial policy in the interim.

The micro side of the subject has had a similar history although, because of its micro nature, it tended to attract less attention. For a long time the subject was characterized by a description of the institutions and instruments that made up the financial system of a capitalist economy. With that description of institutions and instruments there gradually evolved the belief that certain ways of financing private productive activity might be better than others, and eventually scholars and practitioners attempted to rationalize and formally theorize that belief. In the 1950s there occurred a major revolution in the study of micro finance, namely, the rediscovery of how powerful the twin assumptions of perfect (including complete) capital markets and homogeneous rational expectations are when it comes to deriving propositions concerning the financing of productive activity. With this rediscovery the old beliefs regarding optimal financial policies for corporations were, by and large, set aside, at least in academic circles. Thus throughout the 1960s and early 1970s business students were taught in their morning finance courses that discretionary financial management can accomplish little or nothing. And yet in their afternoon macroeconomic courses they were told that government financial policy could potentially achieve some optimal (social-welfare maximizing) combination of employment and inflation in the economy. No doubt this difference in opinion made the taking of examinations in both areas more difficult, but it certainly did not stop practicing financial managers from taking the questions and issues of financial management seriously, for they still continued to devote time and resources to formulating what they believed to be optimal financial strategies. Eventually scholars attempted to rationalize and theorize about this kind of behavior by opening their models to such complications as the corporate and personal income taxes, bankruptcy costs, and the various forms of moral hazards and agency costs that arise in modern corporations where factor ownership is separated from control. Curiously, at about the time micro financial economists were re-evaluating their irrelevancy propositions in corporation finance, macro financial economists were increasingly coming to question the efficacy of government financial policy in light of the widespread stagflation that was experienced in many of the Western market economies during the 1970s. As might be expected this continual vacillation in professional opinion in both areas over the past 30 years has not gone unnoticed and undoubtedly has shaken the confidence of many financial economists in terms of what they think they can contribute to discussions of financial policy. Moreover, the general public and those in policymaking authority seem less willing to seek the advice of financial economists. One noteworthy example of this state of affairs was that hardly any academic economists participated in the formulation and implementation of the so-called "supply side" view of economic policy that propelled Ronald Reagan by a landslide majority vote to the presidency of the United States in 1980. While these policies have not proven to be conspicuously successful (in terms of reducing unemployment and the government deficit), it is nonetheless true and virtually without precedent that academic economists played no role in their formulation. A further indication of this disarray is the contentious tone that now pervades

the professional literature, possibly signalling the creation of a new generation of academic schoolmen. How long these trends will continue into the
1980s is difficult to say, but as long as they do, financial economists will
remain part of the silent majority when it comes to formulating and imple-
menting corporate and government financial policies.

In reviewing these broad developments it is immediately apparent that
there are a number of important similarities between certain topics that pertain to policy issues in both branches of financial economics. In light of these
similarities it is indeed strange that the development of ideas and models in
both micro and macro financial economics have, by and large, proceeded
independently of one another.[2] This would seem to be unfortunate, for one
would suspect that the formulation of models bearing on the question of
discretionary financial management at the firm and government level would
be closely related.

One of the objectives of this work will be to integrate certain aspects of
micro financial theory into macro financial analysis to a greater extent than
has heretofore been the case. In pursuing this integration we will broaden the
scope of financial economics, and in the process develop a somewhat different view of how individual agents resolve the uncertainties that exist in the
environment, which in turn will lead to a very different view of the firm than
the one that underlies conventional economics. The conventional view and
our own are developed in Chapters 2–11 as they relate to the financial policy
issues around which our discussion is organized.

In Chapter 2 we begin our inquiry where all studies in financial economics must begin; namely, with a description of Irving Fisher's (1930)
model of consumption and investment in an environment characterized by
perfect certainty and perfect exchange markets. It is here that we first en-
counter the classical view of the firm and the famous separation principle
wherein households can separate their optimal consumption decisions from
their investment decisions thanks to a perfect capital market. Separation
simplifies the decision problems confronting individual households in that
the amounts of consumption and investment can be decided on their own
intrinsic merits and are independent of one another. As we will see throughout this work, Fisher's separation principle has come to have a profound effect on the subsequent development of micro financial theory. When there is
separation of one sort or another, discretionary financial management tends
to be irrelevant. Chapter 3 extends the Fisher model of consumption and
investment by describing a general equilibrium of production and distribution in a society comprised of differentiated input contributors such as
workers and capitalists. All the well-known classical propositions are shown
to hold in this general equilibrium, including the full utility maximizing utilization of human and nonhuman resources. It is also shown that noncompetitive pricing practices in the labor market will influence the level of employ-

ment and output in the direction indicated by the classical school of economic thought. And yet from our point of view the main objective of this chapter is to describe the input-sharing and output-sharing arrangements among the different factor contributors within the classical conception of the firm and the role these arrangements play in the equilibrium allocation for the economy.

In Chapter 4 we continue our study of the coordinating role of the financial contract system but within an environment characterized by uncertainty. The particular framework of analysis used here is the well-known and now much-maligned capital asset pricing model (CAPM). While the primary objective of this model was originally to describe relative rates of return on risky assets, it can also be used to describe factor (investment) allocations across risky sectors in the economy. These allocations in turn will imply a unique risk/return trade-off for all savers in this economy, and the trade-off will come to represent one of the key prices in the economic system. In addition, the model is of interest in terms of the input/output-sharing arrangements that characterize firms in this economy. Once again—as in the case of the Fisher model discussed in Chapter 2—discretionary financial management at the micro level is rendered nugatory as a result of a separation property and the types of input/output-sharing arrangements that coordinate production in a CAPM economy. At the economy-wide level this separation property and view of the firm precludes the development of involuntary unemployment of factor inputs in the system and eliminates the income redistribution consequences of unexpected inflation: two problems that continue to plague actual market economies. The end result is that the CAPM tends to have some of the normative implications of the classical macroeconomic model discussed in Chapter 3.

Our study of the financial system within the CAPM framework continues in Chapters 5 and 6, in which we explore several different macroeconomic issues. Chapter 5 surveys the literature concerned with the efficient allocation of investment in a CAPM economy. This issue nicely illustrates the somewhat unusual view of the firm that is assumed within the CAPM set-up. The savings side of the economy is, for all intents and purposes, socialized in that all household savings are turned over to two mutual funds: one that invests in the riskless sector of the economy and the other in the risky sector. But what about the investment side of the economy? If investment demand comes from individually unique firms that base their investment decisions on maximizing the capital market value of the firm, then it turns out that these unique firms will demand less investment than the Pareto efficient level. But are unique firms (unique in the sense that their future outputs are imperfectly correlated with other firms in the economy) compatible with the CAPM set-up? For example, if firms are so small that they tend to be nonunique (i.e., their future outputs tend to be perfectly correlated with the outputs of all other firms in the economy, which is nothing more than the perfect competition assumption applied to an uncertain environment), then firms will demand the Pareto efficient level of investment. In other words, the efficiency of investment allocation in the CAPM critically depends upon the uniqueness of firms in the sense discussed above. In Chapter 6 we use the CAPM to evaluate certain forms of government regulation of the investment market in terms of efficient investment allocation. More particularly we study the effects of government restrictions on foreign investment and the effects such restrictions may have on the efficiency of investor diversification as reflected in the risk/return trade-off available to savers in the capital market. Of course it is obvious that any government restriction (be it aimed at foreign or domestic investment) in the investment market will reduce the diversification possibilities of investors and thereby cause a reduction in the risk/return trade-off. What is somewhat surprising is how difficult it is to empirically verify this straightforward implication of CAPM (or any portfolio theory, for that matter) with real-world capital market data. An empirical test of the effects foreign investment restrictions have on the risk/return trade-off is carried out in Chapter 6 with U.S. capital market data, and the results are found to be consistent with capital market theory.

In Chapters 2–6 the consumption/investment model of Fisher and the CAPM are studied within an environment in which production is carried out under conditions of constant returns to scale, and exchange takes place in perfect markets. Moreover, in the CAPM set-up it is assumed that every household will diversify their savings across all the different types of financial contracts issued by all the different firms in the economy. One implication of this diversification is that there tends to be little disagreement among investors as to how the firm should be managed; namely, all investors would direct the managers to carry out production decisions that maximize the share valuation of the firm. Product market decisions that maximized the share valuation of the firm would not differentially affect the welfare of individual investors in the CAPM framework. With these assumptions it is hardly surprising that unexpected inflation and involuntary unemployment of factor services do not emerge as major economic problems as they have in actual market economies. It was only quite natural, then, that more practical economists would begin to look elsewhere for model economies that could generate these kinds of outcomes. One of the first attempts to specifically model the involuntary unemployment outcome was the income/expenditure model of John Maynard Keynes (1936). What is somewhat curious is that the IS-LM version of this model parallels certain aspects of the Fisher consumption/investment model and the CAPM. The key idea is that the simultaneous attainment of the equilibrium conditions in both the market for new output (i.e., the investment equals savings condition or intertemporal consumption plan) and the market for the riskless asset (i.e., the demand for money equals the supply of money condition or the portfolio allocation plan) determines the risk premium in the capital market, and the level and distribution of output and employment in the consumption and investment goods markets.[3] However, when this income/expenditure model was expanded to incorporate a description of output price determination or the inflationary process, troubles began to develop. These troubles and a description of the income/expenditure model are presented in Chapter 7. There it is observed that the model can explain employment/output levels or the level of output prices, but not both.

Part of the difficulty, in our opinion, is that the implied micro structure of firm behavior in both the income/expenditure model and the CAPM prevent us from fully understanding price and output determination in market economies. This shortcoming in turn is the result of two closely related implicit assumptions shared by both models. The first important implicit assumption centers around the equity type of financial contract that all capitalists are presumed to receive in exchange for their capital input. These equity contracts by and large preclude managerial decisions (e.g., pricing, production, and financing decisions) from affecting the distribution of income among different capitalists in the same firm. The end result is that while some capitalists have larger ownership shares in firms than others, all accept the objective of managing the firm so as to maximize the capital market value of the equity.[4] There is, in other words, no conflict of interest among different capitalists in the system, and the only risks they face (and share together) are those imposed by nature. Redistributions of incomes resulting from changes in the inflation rate simply do not occur in these models. Since inflation has no effect on investor welfare in the basic IS-LM and CAPM models, it is hardly surprising that neither provides a micro description of price determination. The second and related common assumption is that both model descriptions of the economy originally tended to fix supply and concentrated almost exclusively on aggregate demand. While almost nothing has been done in the macro literature regarding the first assumption concerning contract form, a great deal has been done to incorporate the supply side of the economy, particularly in the non-CAPM descriptions of macroeconomic equilibrium. A short and somewhat selected review of professional opinion regarding the supply side of the economy is presented in Chapter 8. The main conclusion of that chapter is that professional opinion is very much divided. In fact, it is this division of opinion that motivates us to offer our own theory of supply and supply adjustments for a market economy.

That theory of supply adjustment or the business cycle (which is based on nominal contracting among different agents) is developed in Chapters 9, 10, and 11, and a variety of empirical tests of the theory are presented in Chapter 12. It is at this point in our work—more than any other—that micro financial concepts can be most fruitfully incorporated into a macroeconomic analysis. Unfortunately the CAPM form of micro financial analysis, with its assumptions of equity contracts and separation, will not be well suited to play a role in this integration. Our own work assumes production is financed by a diverse group of capitalists with different investment requirements, and consequently there will be more than one type of financial contract or claim to the firm's end-of-period income. When this is the case, these different capitalists holding these different contract forms will have an incentive to participate in the management of the firm, for conflicts will surely arise in terms of future pricing, production, and financing decisions. The end result is that capitalists will no longer agree that equity value maximization should exclusively guide the management decisions of the firm, which in turn will result in a nonseparation between financing and operating decisions within the firm. Our characterization of supply adjustments over the business cycle will then be to find the combination of pricing, employment, output, and financing decisions that coalesce the interests of all the different factor input contributors to the firm, and thereby provide a rationalization for initiating productive activity within the firm in the first place. In this connection it is important to remember that any theory of supply adjustment over the trade cycle must be consistent with a rationalization of initiating productive activity within the institutional framework of the firm when input contributors are diverse and hold different financial contract forms. Moreover, these short-run cyclical supply adjustments take place in Western market economies within a long-run framework in which these different financial contract forms continue to survive. Thus, business cycle theory must provide an explanation for the repeated use of these different contract forms.

In concluding this introductory chapter, it is important to remind the reader that any attempt to integrate *certain* parts of micro and macro financial economics can easily be misinterpreted as an attempt to integrate the entire body of knowledge in these two areas. It is clear that this work cannot and does not attempt to accomplish that formidable if not impossible task. We therefore want to make it abundantly clear at the outset that our review of the traditional micro and macro financial economics is not intended to be a complete survey of all that has been learned in these two areas. Essentially we review those parts of the literature in both branches of financial economics that enable us to present the theory of supply adjustment and the business cycle contained in Chapters 9–11, and to compare that theory to the more conventional theories discussed in Chapters 7 and 8. Our choice is quite personal and perhaps arbitrary; no doubt others might have chosen differently. In any event, and in this connection, it should be pointed out that we do not discuss such topics in micro financial analysis as: time-state preference theory, option pricing theory, capital budgeting theory, agency theory, taxation issues, and the growing number of nonstatic theories of asset pricing. In the macro financial area we do not discuss the vast literature dealing with consumption, investment, money demand, interest rates, and the labor market. These omissions are not meant to imply that important progress has not been made in these areas (it has) but, our personal opinion about which topics in micro and macro finance will be useful in presenting and developing our theory of the business cycle.

Our work begins with the Fisher model of consumption and investment in the ideal environment of perfect certainty and perfect exchange markets. The simple CAPM and IS-LM models represent extensions of Fisher's model to an uncertain environment and contain similar views of the nature and role of financial contract forms in guiding productive activity within the firm. Our own model assumes different contract forms, and from these different contract forms we develop a somewhat different view of the firm and a different theory of the business cycle. It is now time to begin this work, and in Chapter 2 we take up the consumption/investment model of Fisher along with its associated description of the contract forms that define the firm.

Notes

1. For a further elaboration of this theme, see Thurow (1980).

2. While we are unaware of any work that systematically integrates company and government finance issues in a macroeconomic model, some individuals have worked separately on both topics. Perhaps the best known is F. Modigliani whose work up to now in micro finance was most closely associated with the financial policy ineffectiveness school of thought, but whose work in macro finance is closely associated with the advocacy of a discretionary monetary and fiscal policy.

3. The third market incorporated in the IS-LM version of the income/expenditure model is the market for risky securities. Equilibrium in the market for new output and the safe asset automatically implies equilibrium in the market for risky assets, and hence the usual practice is not to analyze this market for risky assets explicitly.

4. The problems of equity value maximization have not gone unnoticed in the micro finance literature. For a sample of opinion regarding the question of when equity value maximization is or is not in the interest of all shareholders, see Leland (1974), Ekern and Wilson (1974), Grossman and Stiglitz (1977), and Grossman and Hart (1979).

Part I

The Financial Economics
Of Perfect Certainty

—2—

The Microeconomic Foundations of Finance Theory: The Fisher Model

Introduction

When men and women discovered long ago that under certain circumstances it might be better to take the time to fashion sticks and stones into cutting instruments to till the soil or chase the stag, capital theory was born. When later we discovered that it was still better to get many like-minded individuals doing the same thing together in a joint endeavor, capitalism and finance theory were born. Now the existence of roundabout techniques of production does not in itself imply any particular legal form of the ownership of the joint productive endeavor known as the "firm." Firms have been owned and operated both for the primary benefit of certain individuals unaffectionately known as capitalists, or for all individuals euphemistically known as society. What system of ownership prevails in a given society at a given point in time will generally turn on philosophical considerations. It is doubtful that arguments of economic efficiency are of overriding importance. The socialist, when told that an unbridled free market system may lead to a more efficient allocation of scarce resources than a socialist system, will invariably reply that there is more to life than static allocational efficiency, and in this the socialist is surely right. Thus, notwithstanding the presumed efficiency of a free market system, many socialists oppose the private ownership of land and capital on the grounds that such ownership differentiates individuals in society, and such differentiation is itself inherently evil. They will argue, as Marx (1961, pp. 152–153, 298, 595, and 698) has argued, that capitalists accumulate capital in order to differentiate themselves socially from those who do not or, more probably, cannot accumulate capital. How different this view is from the underlying philosophy that pervades the writings of Irving Fisher (1907, 1930) and other neoclassical economists who view capital as an

13

innocent means to an end, namely, that of securing a future consumption or standard of living. Here capital is not viewed as an insidious divider of society into social classes but instead as a means for distributing consumption over time in much the same way that squirrels save nuts in autumn in order to avoid starvation in winter. If consumption is viewed as the end of all economic activity then why should we not allow individuals to freely order consumption over their lifetime in a way that affords them the greatest satisfaction?

Every person who might by chance read this book has at least once asked and answered this important question. For our part we will merely assume that consumption is the bottom line insofar as economic activity is concerned and that individuals strive to order their consumption opportunities—both at a point in time and over time—within the framework of a free market economy. For the most part we will not be concerned about how an individual or society divides its consumption between this or that particular commodity at any point in time, but instead how it divides its consumption opportunities over successive time periods. In addition we will not have much to say here about how those consumption opportunities are technologically created, but once created or potentially created, how they will be distributed over the lifetime of an individual. At the level of society as a whole—a topic we take up in more detail in Chapter 3—much of what we will have to say bears on the important question of the intergenerational distribution of income. Our study, in other words, will be directed towards the social role of a capital market; the market used by individual households for distributing their consumption or standard of living over time.[1] This is the stuff of financial theory and analysis as it is taught and practiced in capitalist societies.

Our point of departure in this chapter will be the well-known two-period, one good, perfect foresight, and perfect market paradigm originally developed by Irving Fisher but extended and passed on to the current generation of economists by Jack Hirschleifer (1958). We shall see that even in such a simplified world as this, the capital market plays an extraordinary role in widening the opportunities of households in their attempts to achieve the greatest possible satisfaction over their two-period life, given the limitations of their endowment[2] and transformation opportunities. In the next section we will introduce the subject by discussing in some detail the economic environment presumed to exist, namely, perfect certainty. We do this because perfect certainty is a strong assumption and consequently needs a certain amount of explaining away. And yet we will see that this strong assumption is worth the price in terms of getting at the essentials of the allocation problem facing individuals. We then analyze economic activity within this perfectly certain environment from the point of view of the primary agents in this economy: households. In particular we will concern ourselves with a description of how households convert endowments of resources into a standard of living over time. A capital market is then introduced into the analysis in order to facilitate the spreading of consumption over time. The fourth section continues the story by introducing the notion of a firm into the analysis, that is to say, the joint ownership of a productive opportunity set by two or more households. Actually we will see that the introduction of the firm, as the vehicle by which households own and operate productive opportunity sets, makes little difference in how this economy functions, partly because of the rather fanciful environment we have imposed onto the analysis. One example of this deals with the financing decisions of the firm. When the capital market is perfect, how the firm finances a given production plan is irrelevant. This will be the first of several irrelevance propositions that follow from a complete and perfect capital market. Finally, we conclude the chapter by presenting a short summary of the main results and point the way to the subject matter taken up in Chapter 3.

The Environment

Perfect Certainty

Living in an age in which the dollar price of gold and silver can double in the course of 60 days, one might well ponder the wisdom of basing so much of our economic and financial analysis on the assumption of perfect certainty. Yet as incredible as that assumption might seem today, it is important not to lose sight of the fact that perfect certainty, like the labor theory of value, has rendered some useful service in the understanding of the economic system. Moreover, just because the environment is uncertain does not mean investment return (the key variable along with tastes and technology in the model presented below) is not an important consideration in the intertemporal allocation problem. In this connection it is instructive, if not amusing, to reflect on the provocative challenge the mathematician Stanislaw Ulam was recorded to have thrown up to the social sciences in general and economics in particular: "Name me one proposition in all the social sciences which is both true and nontrivial." While the recorder of this tale sadly confessed that at the time he was unable to successfully respond to this challenge (remember it had to be nontrivial to a genius), many years later he thought the principle of comparative advantage might come close.[3] In this connection it is interesting to recall that the principle of comparative advantage, like other important propositions in economics, was developed without any reference to uncertainty. Thus while perfect foresight does not characterize the actual environment we live in, its tractability as well as its robustness in analyzing a broad range of problems has enabled economists to clarify a number of economic issues at least to a first approximation.

What then will perfect certainty mean in our discussion of the neoclassical theory of intertemporal choice? We will take this term to mean that of all possible environments that might unfold in the second of our two periods, the consumer-investor will be presumed to know the particular environment that will actually prevail. Among other things this will mean that every household will know the initial endowment, current consumption; productive opportunities, borrowing and lending opportunities, and future consumption of all other households in the system. The implication of households possessing all this knowledge is that *ex-ante* plans are equivalent to *ex-post* results. What this allows consumer-investors to do at the inception of their economic lives is to wind up the clock, so to speak, by planning their consumption for all future periods. All they do then is sit back, relax, and presumably enjoy life to the extent permitted by their endowment.

Another important characteristic of perfect foresight is that there are no surprises with respect to the fulfillment of contracts between individual households within the firm. Thus, the problems often associated with the nonfulfillment of contracts—such as the various forms of bankruptcy—are avoided in a world of perfect certainty. As a result, there is no redistribution of wealth or consumption goods other than that given by the optimal consumption plans of households over the two periods, and those plans are known to every participant in the economy. The more a man or woman eats today, the less they will eat tomorrow. The fulfillment of contracts and the absence of surprise turns out to be one of the important distinctions between a certain and an uncertain economic environment, for in an uncertain environment potential nonfulfillment of contracts will magnify the risk imposed by nature. It is no wonder then that the combination of perfect certainty and perfect exchange markets provides an ideal environment in which to study, if not carry out, economic activity.

Additional Assumptions

In addition to the assumption of perfect foresight, there are a number of other assumptions that should be mentioned in order to complete our discussion of the economic environment. Since these assumptions are quite standard in the microeconomic and finance literature we will merely list them at this point and reserve the right to discuss them more fully below if and when the occasion merits.

The first and perhaps most important assumption is that society is comprised of rational economic agents in the sense that each individual prefers more wealth to less wealth at any given point in time. Rational choice implies that the individual can compare the desirability of alternative combinations of dated consumption plans as well as be consistent in ordering these alternative consumption plans. The latter characteristic is generally called the transitivity axiom of rational choice and is useful when discussing the more general n-good and n-period household allocation problem, while the former characteristic is called the comparability axiom. The final two axioms that will be presumed to govern household choice pertain to the shape of the individual's indifference curve, the curve which in our case expresses the various combinations of period 1 and period 2 consumption that yield a constant level of satisfaction or utility measured in some relevant way. These axioms restrict the individual's indifference curve to a continuous and convex one, implying that when moving along a given curve from any arbitrary point, the individual must not only give up one dated consumption bundle in order to obtain another, but also that the terms of trade between the two bundles will continuously change, becoming higher for the bundle being given up and lower for the bundle being obtained. These assumptions are respectively known as the axioms of nonsatiation and convexity. In what follows we will use these assumptions when describing household preferences.

The next set of assumptions deal with market institutions and participants. Central among these will be the assumption of a complete and perfect capital market entailing two important properties. The first property is that at any point in time (in this particular discussion, the beginning of our two time periods) there is only one price at which households can trade present for future consumption. This price is known as the rate of interest or yield on a capital market instrument, and the important point is that in a world of perfect certainty it is the same for all participants in the capital market. This is the financial version of the law of a single price and provides us with one of the main building blocks of capital market theory. The second property is closely related; namely, the transactions of any particular household or firm have no effect on the price or interest rate prevailing in the capital market. As we will see on many occasions below, the twin assumptions of rationality and perfect capital markets are the alpha and omega of finance theory and generate a number of important as well as controversial implications for the theory of financial policy.

Finally, we will assume our world to be free of a number of analytically troublesome drains such as transaction costs and government spending and taxation. The entire analysis will focus on a private and costless exchange economy.

With this listing of the necessary and simplifying assumptions we can now proceed to a discussion of the allocation problem confronting the individual household. In the following section the problem is analyzed without the social contrivance of firms; each household is presumed to be in possession of a productive opportunity which enables it to transform a present endowment into various combinations of present and future consumption. In the first part of that section it is assumed that households are "islands unto themselves;" that is to say, there is no financial market for the exchange of intertemporal claims on consumption, and the only exchange possible is with nature. In the second part we come close to the general idea of a firm by allowing individuals not only to engage in productive transformations, but also to exchange claims or promises to deliver dated consumption goods with other individuals in a perfect capital market. Firms as a joint endeavor among individuals and a legal entity, however, are still presumed not to exist. Our discussion of the allocation problem continues in the fourth section when firms as a legal-contract-creating entity are explicitly incorporated into the analysis. There we will see that our assumptions of perfect certainty, rationality, and perfect capital markets render the distinction between firms and households as owners of productive opportunity sets as one that is essentially meaningless. This absence of any distinction turns out to be an important implication of the theory of finance both in its certain and uncertain versions. The message we will present in a subsequent chapter is very different, and consequently the introduction of the firm here and the associated contracts they give rise to will begin to give us an appreciation of the inherent conflicts among input contributors in capitalist societies. We will now move on to the Fisher-Hirschleifer solution of the household allocation problem.

The Consumption-Investment Decision of Households

Productive Opportunities without an Exchange Market

In this connection consider the proverbial agricultural economy where each individual household has an initial endowment of grain which can be consumed as bread immediately or planted and consumed as bread in the next period. In this economy each person will, according to our previous assumptions, attempt to maximize the utility of consumption for both periods subject to the limitations imposed by the initial endowment and the productive opportunity to transform current grain, as seed, into future grain. This they will do through some judicious allocation of the initial endowment between current consumption and current investment which in turn will yield a desired future consumption.

The details of the allocation can easily be described pictorially—thanks to Hirschleifer—and are presented in Figure 2.1. Following the Hirschleifer notation, K_0 and K_1 will be taken to represent grain available for present and future consumption, respectively. In the simplest case the initial (and only) endowment point is presented along the K_0 axis and for this particular household is given by the distance OA.[4] In addition, the productive possibility facing this investor for converting current grain into future grain is represented by the straight line AB which indicates that the investment is subject to constant returns. With this particular endowment and productive possibility, the

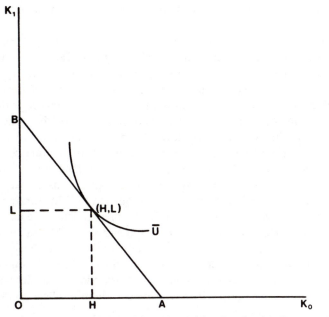

Figure 2.1. Intertemporal Consumption with a Productive Opportunity

consumer-investor would maximize intertemporal utility by equating his or her personal terms of trade between current and future consumption (given by the slope of the indifference curve $\bar{U}$) to the terms of trade given by the constant slope of the productive opportunity line AB.[5] In the example considered in Figure 2.1 the solution would entail immediate consumption of OH and investment of AH which in the second period would yield a consumption of OL.

Productive Opportunities with a Capital Market

Next consider a slightly more complicated case, one where in addition to a productive opportunity as a means for converting a present endowment into future consumption, the consumer-investor also has an opportunity to exchange dated consumption claims with other consumer-investors in a capital market.[6] At the outset it should be noted that exchange in the capital market (i.e., borrowing and lending) cannot create consumption goods in either period; only initial endowments—which can be thought of as a carryover from previous production—and subsequent production can create consumption goods. Yet, while borrowing and lending do not create consumption goods, their very existence enables the individual to generally achieve a higher level of intertemporal utility for any given endowment and productive opportunity set.

This of course is one of the great themes in literature, although to hold the readers' attention the author almost always imposes an uncertain environment on the story. For example, had Tom Jones known with perfect certainty that in the end he would be in possession of both Squires Western and Allworthy's capital, he could have easily used the capital market of that day to enhance his and Mr. Partridge's current consumption which, in the course of the tale, had fallen to a very low level. However, he was not certain and he was surely wise not to exchange the mere prospect of a future consumption for a sure present consumption since the laws of the land in that day strongly mitigated against the creation of risky debt contracts as evidenced by the public hanging of the Reverend Dodd at Tyburn in 1777 for forging a bond in the name of the Earl of Chesterfield, his former student. The authorities of that day were evidently unmoved by Samuel Johnson's plea for clemency partly based on the argument that respect for religious authority would be diminished. Nor does it seem that they embraced the view sometimes put forth in finance theory that the creation of risky debt securities will expand the opportunity set of portfolio investors and therefore be a good thing for society.

But here we are analyzing a certain world, and these surprises, which delight the reader of fictional capital market literature, never occur. To continue our analysis of the household allocation problem in this surpriseless world with a capital market, it will now be convenient to assume the traditional concave productive opportunity which asserts that investment is subject to diminishing returns. A productive opportunity with this characteristic is displayed as curve AB in Figure 2.2, along with two linear capital market lines AC and DE. The constant slope of the capital market line indicates that the consumer-investor can trade present for future and future for present consumption bundles at the same rate of interest. As before, the objective of the individual, whose indifference curve is given by $\bar{U}$ in the figure, is to try to reach as high a capital market line as possible given some initial endowment and productive opportunity.[7] In this case the household invests AJ (AH in productive opportunities, lending HJ on the capital market to other households) and consumes OJ in the current period. In the next period the consumer-investor would consume OL, OP of which comes from the productive investment undertaken in the first period, and PL from lending to other households in the capital market.

Suppose instead that our hypothetical investor's intertemporal utility function dictated current consumption of OA, thus indicating a point of tangency between an indifference curve and capital market line DE southeast of F, say at point N. This solution—more consumption today and less tomorrow than that given at point G—would yield investment of AH combined

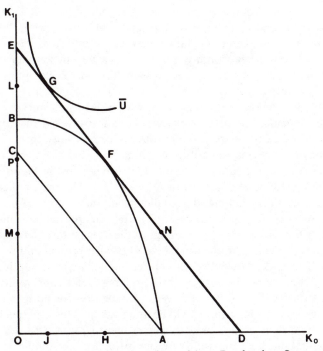

Figure 2.2. Intertemporal Consumption with a Productive Opportunity and Financial Opportunity

with borrowing of *HA* on the capital market in order to restore current consumption to the amount given by the initial endowment point *OA*. This debt obligation of *HA* is then discharged in the next period when out of a total income of *OP* generated from the productive investment, the amount *PM* is paid to the lender, leaving *OM* available for consumption.

Notice that in the two cases considered in Figure 2.2—first the lending case involving less current and more future consumption, and then the borrowing case of more current and less future consumption—the amount of productive investment remained the same, namely, *AH*. What this means in effect is that consumption and investment decisions are in fact separate decisions at the household level. The allocation problem facing the consumer-investor can then be broken down into two separate decisions: first, make those productive investment decisions that place the household in question on the highest possible capital market line, and second, lend or borrow in the capital market with other households in order to obtain the combination of K_0 and K_1 that maximizes the utility of consumption over the two time periods. This illustrates one of the important social roles of a capital market, namely, to allow the individual economic agent the freedom to focus atten-

tion and efforts on productive activity independent of how the fruits of that
activity are to be realized in terms of intertemporal consumption. In this way
a capital market makes an important contribution to the efficient allocation
of resources in a market economy over time. As we will see later on, when
this separation is not attainable, resources will no longer be optimally allocated in a market economy.

Finally it should be mentioned that within this framework it would be
possible to consider the effects on the allocation process resulting from
changes in: the rate of interest, the productive opportunity curve, and individual tastes for present and future consumption. In this connection consider a reduction in the rate of interest. This is described in Figure 2.3 by a
shift in the capital market line from DE to $D'E'$. The shift indicates that
now today's resources command a smaller premium in terms of tomorrow's
resources than was formerly the case. Whether any particular household is
better off or not as a result of the change in the interest rate cannot be determined without reference to the household's taste for present and future consumption. Those like Micawber who prefer immediate consumption will be
better off, while those like Scrooge who prefer to defer consumption to the
indefinite future will be worse off. What can be said for both, however, is
that more productive investment will be undertaken. This is indicated in the
figure by the expansion in productive investment from AH to AH'. Variations in capital market rates will therefore influence the volume of produc-

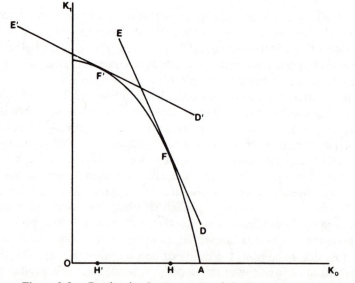

Figure 2.3. Productive Investment and the Rate of Interest

tive investment in a society. Nevertheless it still remains true that for the individual household, consumption decisions remain separated from investment decisions when the economy possesses a perfect capital market.[8]

Firms

What are firms and why do they exist? Much has been written on this subject (see Alchian and Demsetz [1972] for a selected survey of developments in this area) but one common general theme seems to center around the efficiency of specialization in production. Within this general theme we will emphasize the cooperative aspects between different individuals in productive activity, both in terms of creating and distributing an output. Firms, then, are the institutional vehicles by which two or more individuals together produce an output and then distribute the monetary proceeds from the sale of that output. We choose to emphasize this aspect of firm activity because the focus of the material presented in subsequent chapters will be on the potential conflicts between different suppliers of factor inputs and the attempt to resolve the conflicts through the use of securities and other forms of contracts along with management practices. In the present context of certainty and perfect markets, these conflicts do not exist. They do not exist because the output-sharing rule is fixed by the rate of interest or the market terms of trade between present resources and future income. In this world managers are instructed to convert present resources into future income up to the point where the present value of the resources is maximized, which is the same thing as reaching the highest capital market line attainable with the given productive opportunity in Figure 2.2.

The allocation process in the presence of a firm is described geometrically in Figure 2.4. In quadrant 1 we have our hypothetical individual i with an initial endowment of OA in the first period. This particular consumer-investor could exchange present for future consumption in the capital market along the line AC, and somewhere along that line there would be a tangency with his or her indifference curve $\bar{U}$, and that tangency would define the optimal current and future consumption for that person. Next let us suppose that individual i and at least one other person (not shown in the figure) develop together a productive opportunity like BF in quadrant 3 and call that productive opportunity firm j. It can readily be seen from the figure that this productive opportunity provides a more favorable trade-off between present and future consumption over the interval BH than the trade-off available to individual i in the capital market. Moreover, note that our individual i will, for reasons outside the scope of this analysis, supply OA (or 50 percent) of the total resource cost BH of the productive opportunity with the remainder being supplied by the codevelopers of the project. All devel-

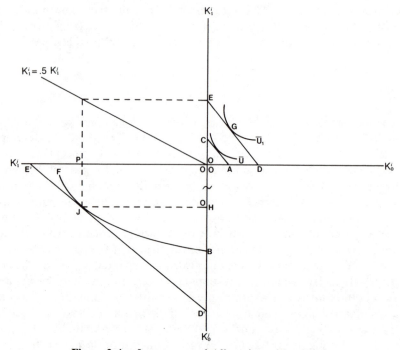

Figure 2.4. Intertemporal Allocation with a Firm

opers (including i) who hold a pro-rata share in the project would therefore see to it that firm j would make productive investments of BH, which in turn would yield a total return of OP in period 1 consumption. Since in this example individual i supplied one-half the inputs to firm j, he or she would be entitled to one-half the period 1 output. In Figure 2.4 that amount is OE along the K_1 axis. Of course any banker or lender (precluded by assumption from developing project j) could see that our consumer-investor i has a good thing going in project j and would be prepared to lend a maximum of OD in current consumption goods against his or her share of the future output generated by firm j.[9] This possibility allows individual i to trade along capital market line DE rather than AC which represented his or her intertemporal opportunities in the capital market. The opportunity of investing in firm j, therefore, enables i to achieve a higher level of utility as indicated by the new tangency at point G between the indifference curve $\bar{U}_1$ and capital market line DE. This new higher level of utility, however, could only be achieved if firm j maximized the present value of productive opportunity BF, just as was the case in Figure 2.2 for the individual household. Accordingly, the introduction of firms does not seem to alter the implications of the allocation process from what they were in the second part of the previous section. In particular, we still have separation between consumption and productive investment decisions.

Let us amplify this important point in a slightly different way by asking the following question: Does firm control over the productive opportunity set preclude any individual consumer-investor like i from attaining any desired intertemporal consumption pattern subject, of course, to the limitations imposed by the initial endowment, capital market opportunities, and the productivity of project j? In other words does the fact that firm j undertakes the productive investment preclude i from trading intertemporal consumption along the capital market line DE in quadrant 1 of Figure 2.4? When the question is put this way it is closely related to the dividend policy question analyzed by Miller and Modigliani (1961). Miller and Modigliani have shown that with perfect capital markets in the sense used here, the individual as partial owner of the firm can obtain any desired pattern of consumption—subject to the endowment and opportunity constraints—independent of whether the firm finances its current productive investment with internal or external equity.[10] Their argument is simple. If the particular dividend paid by a firm to an investor in any particular time period is less than the investor's desired consumption, then that investor could sell (borrow) some portion of his ownership claim on the firm to make up the difference and thereby obtain the desired consumption. Conversely, if the same dividend paid by the firm results in claims on current consumption in excess of that desired by the investor, there is no law that precludes the investor from reinvesting the excess on the capital market. In other words, in both cases the consumer-investor can adjust his or her particular consumption-investment plan by appropriate lending or borrowing on the capital market and need not rely on the firm producing just the right dividend. In terms of Figure 2.4 our investor i could finance his or her share of company j either from the initial endowment (in which case he or she would finance their current consumption by borrowing OA) or by borrowing OA on the capital market (in which case he or she would use their initial endowment to finance their current consumption of OA).

The dividend or financing irrelevance proposition—the first of several irrelevance propositions to be encountered in financial economics—is clearly the direct and immediate result of the separation property discussed in the previous section. If productive investment decisions are separated from consumption decisions because individuals can attain any desired combination of present and future consumption by appropriate lending or borrowing on the capital market (and subject to the endowment and opportunity constraints) then dividend or financing policy is irrelevant by definition. In other words, dividend policy can only be relevant in the type of world described in Figure 2.1 where the consumer-investor possesses a productive opportunity for converting present into future consumption but no capital market in which to lend or borrow. In this world consumption and investment at the household level are not separated in the sense that the individual must settle for an allocation of present consumption and investment that happens to coincide with his or her intertemporal ordering of present and future consumption. The existence of a capital market as described in Figures 2.2 and 2.4 allows for more flexibility in that the household's position can be adjusted in terms of intertemporal consumption via borrowing and lending, and is not wholly dependent upon the productive opportunity itself nor how that opportunity is financed.

At this point an interesting question that might be raised is whether the dividend irrelevance proposition would hold for an entire economy. In other words, if it is true, as suggested above, that an individual firm maximizing the capital market value of its productive opportunity set can pursue a dividend policy independent of the optimal intertemporal consumption plan of one of its shareholders, is it then not the case that all firms in the economy can ignore the intertemporal consumption plans of all households? The answer is "no" when firm managers act in the best interests of their shareholders. The reason the answer is "no" is that the individual firm and household are assumed to be mere chips in a vast ocean of capital market wealth. Hence, both firm and investor are presumed to be able to engage in capital market transactions without affecting the rate of interest. But this is not the case when all firms and investors are taken together. This is the difference between partial and general equilibrium analysis. Whenever the aggregate investment plans of firms and the aggregate period 1 consumption plans of households fail to equal the current social endowment, then something must give in the system. That something of course would be the rate of interest in a competitive economy and that price would continue to adjust until all households' planned consumption and firms planned investment exactly exhausted the current social endowment. Only then would we have equilibrium in the capital market. Thus, we can conclude that for any given set of productive opportunities and preferences for present and future consumption for the entire economy, there will, in equilibrium, be one and only one optimal transfer of resources from the firm to the household sector. Any other attempted transfer would set in motion the equilibrating mechanism of changes in the rate of interest. In this sense one can speak of an optimal aggregate dividend and the nonseparation of consumption and investment decisions in equilibrium.

We have seen, then, that in the ideal world of certainty and perfect capital markets, whether a particular firm finances a desirable investment project with internal or external equity is seemingly irrelevant. Initial endowments and borrowings on the capital market are indistinguishable sources of funds. In an uncertain world, funds can be obtained on the capital market in two forms: debt or priority securities and equity securities; and firms can use both sources in financing their productive opportunities. As we have already mentioned, the distinction between debt and equity securities in a certain world is meaningless since there is only one trade-off between present and future consumption available in the capital market. Yet it was over the question of whether there was an optimal combination of debt and equity securities to finance a given production plan in an uncertain environment that Modigliani and Miller (1958) reminded financial economists of the deep significance of the Fisher-Hirschleifer analysis. Here, too, it was observed that when capital markets were perfect, firm investment decisions could be separated from the consumer-investor's portfolio decision, and the debt-equity decision becomes irrelevant. This, however, is getting somewhat ahead of our story, and we will defer further discussions until Chapter 4.[11]

Summary and Conclusions

What are the lessons to be learned from the two-period model presented in this chapter? They are the lessons learned by post-war Germany and Japan and the athlete Johan Cruyff, whose income and consumption were not perfectly synchronized through time. This is the social significance of a capital market; it facilitates the spreading of consumption over time intervals not perfectly matched by the generation of income. Saving and investment in this paradigm are means to an end, namely, the attainment of a future consumption. Yet as we observed earlier, this is not the only social view of the saving-investment process. Socialists have long argued that the objective, if not the effect, of the saving-investment process is a kind of ossification of social classes. Can it really be the case, they would ask, that the spreading of lifetime consumption motivates the Rockefellers, Mellons, Fords, and Gettys in their saving-investment decisions? The class conflicts envisioned by socialists are somewhat hard to see in the two-period model of Fisher and Hirschleifer presented here, but in Chapter 3 we will extend the model and see that these conflicts between the cooperating factors of production are ever present.

The capital market, like any market, is a social contrivance of profound importance. It is an integral part of the Western economic system of production and distribution. Like all private markets, however, the capital market is only open to those who are in possession of an endowment. Those without an endowment are ignored. All societies recognize this fact in varying degrees and have accordingly modified their economic systems, usually by creating a public sector.

A second significant lesson pertains to the separation property between individual consumption and productive investment decisions. This is a partial equilibrium proposition in the sense that it takes the productive opportunity and financial opportunity (or interest rate) as given to the individual household. Under these conditions individual consumer-investors exploit their productive opportunities to the maximum (i.e., attain the highest possible capital market line or line of highest constant present value) independent of their own personal consumption preferences. Optimal consumption over time, in turn, is then secured with capital market transactions in the form of borrowing and lending. In this way society (those with endowments) obtains the maximum benefits from its productive investments without having to depend on the consumption preferences of the owners of the productive opportunity sets.

By explicitly introducing firms into the analysis a variant of the second lesson unfolds; namely, if the firm follows an optimal policy of maximizing the present value of the productive opportunity set, then the financing of the investment plan becomes a mere detail. This was seen to be the direct implication of the separation of consumption from investment decisions resulting from a perfect capital market. At the aggregate level, however, it was observed that in equilibrium there was one best transfer of resources from the firm to the household sector for a given distribution of endowments, tastes, and technology. In this sense aggregate consumption is not separable from aggregate investment, and both are simultaneously determined along with the interest rate in a general equilibrium.

Finally, by admitting firms to the analysis we introduce the idea of a contract between the different suppliers of factor inputs including managers. In a perfectly certain world, where there exists only one trade-off between present and future consumption in equilibrium, there is not much that can be said about such contracts except that all input contributors agree that managers should maximize the present value of the firm's resources. It is within the framework of an uncertain economic environment that contracts and conflicts become important in the course of the management of the firm. How well these man-made contracts resolve the underlying conflicts between the various input contributors will determine the kinds of economic institutions that we will bequeath to our grandchildren. This will provide the motivation for our study of contracts and all that follows in this work.

Notes

1. The contribution of capital and labor services to the production process is not the only means by which any given generation (young or old) can obtain a claim to consumption goods. Both voluntary (e.g., bequests) and involuntary (e.g., social security receipts and taxation) transfers are alternative means by which the intergenerational distribution of consumption is determined. In what follows we will

not have much to say about these kinds of transfers although they have been studied by academic financial economists within the framework of the two-period consumption-investment model presented below.

2. The endowment can take the form of present and/or future resources (i.e., anything of value such as time in the form of labor services or capital goods) distributed in some way over the two periods. To facilitate the discussion it might be convenient to think of the resource as being grain which can be converted into a consumption good (bread and cake) or used as a capital good in the form of seed.

3. See Samuelson (1969, p. 9). On the other hand, it should be noted that Max Planck, the originator of quantum theory, once told Keynes (1956, p. 327) that in his student days he considered a serious study of economics but rejected the idea on the grounds that the subject was too difficult.

4. The analysis has been extended (see Hirschleifer, 1970) to include cases where the endowment is only available in the future (e.g., a bequest) or some combination of the present and future. These extensions, however, will not be important for our purposes.

5. The allocation problem described in Figure 2.1 can be written out in a simple arithmetical form. Consider first the productive opportunity set and let:

E = the initial endowment;
X = the proportion of the endowment invested in the productive opportunity;
$(1 - X)$ = the proportion of the endowment spent on current consumption;
ρ = the rate of return earned on the productive opportunity or real investment;
K_0 = current consumption;
K_1 = future consumption.

Now current and future consumption can be expressed as:

(i) $K_0 = (1 - X)E$

(ii) $K_1 = (1 + \rho)XE$

Rearranging (i) and (ii) yields:

(iii) $XE = E - K_0$

(iv) $XE = K_1/(1 + \rho)$

which is the saving-investment identity. Equating (iii) and (iv) and rearranging yields:

(v) $K_1 = (1 + \rho)E - (1 + \rho)K_0$

the equation of the straight line in Figure 2.1 that describes the possible intertemporal patterns of current and future consumption given this particular endowment and productive opportunity. The slope of this line, $-(1 + \rho)$, defines the trade-off between present and future consumption offered by nature in productive investment. All we need now is some description of our consumer-investor's personal trade-off between present and future consumption in order to effect a solution to the allocation problem. To get this we need to define, in a general way, an indifference or constant utility curve which can be written as:

(vi) $U(K_0, K_1) = \bar{U}$

where $\bar{U}$ represents a fixed amount of utility or satisfaction somehow measured. Taking the total differential of (vi) and rearranging yields:

(vii) $dK_1/dK_0 = -(\partial U/\partial K_0)/(\partial U/\partial K_1) < 0$

which is the slope of the indifference curve $\bar{U}$. The numerator and denominator of the right-hand side of (vii) are, respectively, the marginal utility of current and future consumption, and the ratio is known as the marginal rate of substitution of K_0 for K_1. The solution to the allocation problem is then obtained when the consumer-investor equates his or her personal terms of trade between K_0 and K_1 to the terms of trade offered by nature: i.e.,

(viii) $dK_1/dK_0 = -(\partial U/\partial K_0)/(\partial U/\partial K_1) = -(1 + \rho) < 0$

6. By admitting borrowing or lending on the capital market, the productive opportunity sets owned by households look more and more like firms. In fact they are firms—one-owner firms. Below we will use the word "firm" to describe a productive opportunity owned by two or more consumer-investors.

7. Each of the infinitely many parallel capital market lines represent lines of so-called constant present value. Accordingly, an endowment point on a higher capital market line represents a superior position in terms of the basic objects of choice, K_0 and K_1, than endowment points along a lower capital market line. The term "constant present value" indicates that any point along a given capital line has the same value today as any other point on that line. In this connection recall (v) in note 5. If we solve (v) for E, the initial endowment point, we obtain:

(i) $E = K_1/(1 + \rho) + K_0$

which is the line of constant present value when ρ is taken to be the interest rate.

8. When market imperfections (e.g., transaction costs) exist there could be two or more capital market lines with different slopes facing the individual: (1) a relatively steep line (high rate of interest) when the individual borrows, and (2) a gently sloped line (low rate of interest) when the individual lends. With imperfections, then, there is no separation between consumption and investment decisions.

9. Our individual i is not unlike a certain quarterback at one of our large Midwestern universities some years ago who discovered that he, too, was in possession of a lucrative productive opportunity set in the form of a professional career in football, and used that future opportunity to obtain a somewhat immodest current consumption. Unfortunately, the capital market he tapped was somewhat imperfect in that it comprised the alumni of that university. Regrettably, the story had a disappointing conclusion in that the university was placed on probation by the NCAA, the team precluded from participating in postseason football games which are keenly scouted by professional teams, and as a result the quarterback never did realize the future benefits attributed to his productive opportunity set. This little episode illustrates both the practical significance of the Fisher-Hirschleifer analysis and the problems that arise when capital assets or factor inputs are exchanged at nonmarket prices.

10. This is in contrast to the so-called traditional view that individual consumption-investment plans are partially constrained, in any given period of a multi-period setting, to the actual dividend payment made by the firm. If this were so then there would be, in principle, one best dividend policy from the point of view of the shareholder, and a firm manager in the role of agent should provide that dividend policy. The traditional view, in other words, takes the position that the capital market value of a firm's securities is determined not only by the productive opportunities available to the firm, but also by the particular means the firm chooses to distribute the benefits derived from those opportunities, just as well-furnished retail outlets are presumed to enhance the value of any given commodity, say fine French wine. The Miller-Modigliani view, on the other hand, holds that it is the product or returns that confer value while the packaging is irrelevant.

11. It is easy to see that other financial policy questions—such as the merging of two or more firms together into a single ownership entity, or the construction of an optimal portfolio of securities for a financial institution or individual—that seem to occur in the financial system and are reported in the financial press do not arise in an economy where the future is known with perfect certainty along with the single interest rate. It is only within the context of an uncertain economic environment that we can, perhaps, rationalize the benefits of merger, debt-equity combinations, and household ownership of different kinds of securities. These topics will be taken up in Chapter 4 and others to follow, but the issues themselves can now be more fully appreciated having once traversed the ideal environment considered in this chapter.

—3—

The Macroeconomics
of the Fisher Model

Introduction

By and large, the consumption-investment paradigm developed in Chapter 2 has found its greatest application as a vehicle for analyzing individual investment decisions. For example, the formation of capital expenditure plans for business firms and governmental departments as well as the selection of security portfolios for individual households are normative propositions regarding economic behavior that are built upon the ideas underlying the intertemporal consumption-investment model. Many more examples from the fields of business finance and investments could be cited.[1] It would therefore be no exaggeration to claim that this paradigm, with its emphasis on separation, represents the substructure for much of the work that continues to be done in micro financial economics.

In this chapter we will attempt to extend the paradigm in a somewhat different direction from that taken by the traditional micro theory of finance. That direction will consist of analyzing the social or macro implications of the model. To be sure, important work such as the time-state preference theory and the two-parameter capital asset pricing model has already proceeded in the direction of general equilibrium under uncertainty, and a number of issues have already been clarified, particularly those dealing with risk bearing. Yet it must be acknowledged that the consumption-investment model of Fisher as well as the time-state preference and two-parameter models of general equilibrium have not, by and large, been directed toward those economic issues such as inflation and unemployment that are inextricably linked to the political process of a society.[2] In contrast, the macroeconomic models of Keynes and the quantity theory of money are much more closely identified with political action and governmental decisions.

Before beginning, however, it is instructive to pause momentarily and consider why we have a micro and macro (as distinct from general equilibrium) development of economic ideas in the first place.[3] In this connection we should remember that it was once said that "supply creates its own demand." This observation was offered as a fundamental proposition in macroeconomics and was the implication of the microeconomics of that time. That fundamental proposition was seriously challenged by Keynes who believed that the microeconomics of that day was incapable of explaining the worldwide depression in the 1930s. Keynes in fact not only challenged the validity of that fundamental proposition, but also the approach economists would take toward their subject. In his view demand in the form of a social problem creates its own supply of economic explanations and solutions, and if the conventional explanation is found wanting then a new one must be manufactured. In this spirit modern macroeconomics was incorporated into the subject matter of economics.

With these social problems and the proposed economic explanations came political solutions. Yet to implement a solution it is generally the case that the economic explanation or model must be kept relatively simple and focus attention on a few key variables and relationships, therefore ruling out general equilibrium descriptions of the economy. This is necessary because the proposed solutions to economic problems are generally implemented by nonprofessional economists who must, at least to some degree, be made to understand them in the context of the particular problem. In fact a good measure of the early success of the income-expenditure and quantity theory of money models must be attributed to their ability to generate an intuitively plausible and understandable explanation of employment and inflation with a limited number of economic relationships.[4] For this reason policy-oriented macroeconomics tends to be partial equilibrium analysis rather than general equilibrium analysis, and this has constituted the standard criticisms made against these types of models. Policy prescriptions and empirical tractability would then appear to be the *raison d'etre* for the partial nature of macroeconomic models. Moreover, those individuals charged with the conduct of macroeconomic policy have sometimes (usually when all seems to be going well with the economy) been accorded an important rank within society. This rank in turn has been known on occasion to reinforce the power of policy, if not in reality at least within the mind of the policymaker. If, as Lytton Strachey tells us in his delightful sketch of the eminent Victorian Cardinal Manning, the nineteenth-century Pope Pio Nonno could humbly declare, "Before I was Pope I believed in infallibility, now I can feel it," how much more so could a modern day central banker say the same thing about monetary policy?

At this point we might ask what real-world problems can be addressed with the consumption-investment model of Fisher and Hirschleifer. In a perfectly certain environment with perfect exchange markets it would appear on the surface that involuntary unemployment cannot emerge as an important social problem even if we introduce labor as a separate factor of production. Perhaps that is why Keynes struck off in a different direction. Nor does it seem obvious that unexpected inflation can be studied fruitfully within the consumption-investment paradigm outlined in Chapter 2 since there is no uncertainty, much less a money-type commodity, in the system. Since unemployment and inflation are considered the two most pressing macroeconomic problems in market economies, it is hardly surprising that the consumption-investment model has received scant attention in macroeconomic analysis.[5]

Yet it would seem that the two-period model should have something to offer as a framework for analyzing certain contemporary economic problems. After all, unemployment and inflation are social problems primarily because they affect the volume and distribution of consumption among the various economic classes in a society and not because they are intrinsically bad in their own right. Socialists have long recognized the conflict inherent in cooperative production as it applies to the distribution of the social output. Their solution is to socialize the means of production. Moreover, the union movement, as it developed in Europe and North America, viewed the securing a "fair share" of the social output for labor as one of its objectives. We believe that the consumption-investment model described in Chapter 2 has much to say about the distribution of income within a market economy, and our objective in this chapter will be to indicate the direction this extension of the paradigm might take.[6] Finally, this extension will lay the foundation for the theory of input/output sharing presented in Chapters 9 and 10.

An Aggregate Consumption-Investment Model

Some Simplifying Assumptions

Before proceeding further it will be useful to set forth a number of assumptions that will both simplify the analysis and yet highlight the point we think the model addresses. With regard to the economic environment we will again assume a two-period (present and future) perfectly certain world with perfect exchange markets. However, unlike our previous discussion we will now assume the existence of two productive inputs: capital in the form of a single good and labor services in the form of the expenditure of human time.[7] We will defer until later any discussion on how the two factor inputs are combined to produce the single output and how that output, in turn, is distributed among the social classes.

The next set of assumptions pertain to the ownership of the two factors of production. In order to emphasize the point we think is important, it will be assumed that all individuals live two periods in this society: the first as a worker and the second as a capitalist.[8] Between the two periods each individual has offspring who in turn become workers in the next period. Consequently, for any given time period there are two generations providing factor inputs to the production process: young laborers providing labor services and their parents or retired workers providing capital services as a result of previous accumulation.[9] Moreover, to simplify the exposition we will further assume that the current consumption of goods by young workers is provided by their parents and thus constitutes part of the consumption of capitalists. Thus, current consumption of goods by the working class is predetermined and not a choice variable under their control. Finally, each outgoing generation of capitalists passes on a bequest to their children who the become the incoming generation of capitalists (at which time they, too, have offspring), and in this way the process repeats itself.

What are the objects of choice for capitalists and workers in this artificial economy? For the current generation of capitalists (the previous generation of laborers) it will be the same as it was in Chapter 2, namely, an initial endowment of the single good which in turn represents the labor income from the previous period plus any bequest from their parents. The capitalists can either consume this good or invest it in the current period production process for purposes of obtaining a future income and the passing on of a bequest. The choice, in other words, is between more consumption today or more (via bequests) tomorrow. As before, it will be assumed that both objects of choice are subject to diminishing marginal utility, and hence the indifference curve for a representative capitalist will be convex. Since we are interested in describing certain features of a general equilibrium for the economy and with the simple geometry used in Chapter 2, it will be useful to make whatever assumptions are necessary in order to arrive at a convex social indifference curve for all capitalists in the system.[10]

Consider next the current generation of workers who in turn will be tomorrow's capitalists. Young workers possess an initial endowment of time—their consumption of goods is provided by their parents. This endowment of time can either be consumed during the period as leisure or invested as labor services in the production process, thereby producing a future income and membership in tomorrow's capitalist class. In addition, it will be assumed that current leisure and future income are subject to diminishing marginal utility, and hence the representative worker's indifference curves are convex. Finally, we will again feel free to invoke those assumptions that permit an aggregation of the individual worker's indifference curve to arrive at a convex social indifference curve for the entire working class.

Production and Distribution

Perfect Factor Substitution

With this description of the environment and the two types of participants in this society we can now move on to consider the conditions of production as well as a description of the resulting general equilibrium. How
then are labor and capital inputs combined today to produce an output tomorrow? This question is answered by the production function, and the aggregate function we intend to explore in our discussion of the production and
distribution of the social output is the additively separable constant elasticity
of substitution function (hereafter, CES) developed by Arrow, Chenery,
Minhas, and Solow (1961). This function can be written as:

$$Q_1 = \gamma[\delta I_0^{-\rho} + (1 - \delta) N_0^{-\rho}]^{-1/\rho} \tag{3.1}$$

where

Q_1 = the aggregate physical social output produced at the end of period 1,
  or what is the same thing, the beginning of period 2;
γ = the scale parameter[11];
I_0 = the investment input in the current period;
N_0 = the labor input in the current period;
δ = the distribution parameter[12];
ρ = the substitution parameter[13] which lies on the interval: $-1 \le \rho \le \infty$.

The CES function is a technological relationship between inputs and
output and is consistent with profit-maximizing behavior by firms in perfect
exchange markets. In addition, the output-sharing rule between the owners
of the two factor inputs is based on the marginal productivity of the factor
inputs; that is, the rental income of a factor input contributor depends on
that factor input's marginal product. Since we are primarily interested in the
production and distribution of society's output at the end of the period, we
will not emphasize the fact that production functions are generally thought
to be the property of a firm or group of individual firms in a particular sector. In one sense this is more or less in keeping with the theory presented in
Chapter 2 where the distinction between firm ownership and individual ownership of the productive opportunity set was irrelevant for the purpose of
determining the intertemporal consumption of households. Thus it might be
helpful to view the productive sector of the economy as one large firm to
which the two social classes or copartners sell labor and capital services.
        One of the attractive features of the CES production function is its
flexibility. To both ease into a discussion of production and distribution and

to facilitate a comparison with the allocation problem considered in Chapter 2, it will be convenient to begin by analyzing one of the limiting cases of the CES function; namely, the case when $\rho = -1.0$, and to make things easy for the geometry, a distribution parameter of $\delta = 0.5$. In this case both labor and capital are perfect substitutes for each other (or can be thought of as the same factor input supplied by two different groups), and thus the allocation problem reduces to one where each class or generation decides separately how much of their initial endowments are to be spent on current enjoyments and how much is to be invested in the firm in productive activity to create a future output. The solution to this problem follows the same lines as the solution offered in Chapter 2, namely, each group equates the slope of their respective productive opportunity curve to the slope of their indifference curve. Solving this problem for both groups will define today's consumption of leisure by the young and goods by the old as well as the amounts of labor services and capital goods invested in the productive process. The output is then produced (according to (3.1)) and distributed tomorrow to each group of individuals based on their individual contributions to the total inputs. Any individual contributing α percent of the inputs would be entitled to α percent of the produced output. In this way the economic destiny of each class or generation in terms of intertemporal consumption is squarely in the hands of that class given an initial endowment and production technology. In this day of economic interdependence such an outcome would be welcomed by many.

As we mentioned above, one of the main reasons for considering a CES production function with substitution parameter $\rho = -1.0$ and distribution parameter $\delta = 0.5$ is that it facilitates a geometry similar to that used in Figure 2.1.

In this connection consider the description of the economy presented in Figure 3.1. In quadrants 2 and 4 we present the relevant indifference curves and productive opportunity curves for the working and capitalist classes, respectively. Thus the left horizontal axis in quadrant 2 measures the total amount of time T at the disposal of the new generation of workers which must be allocated in the first period between leisure L and productive employment N. As we move from left to right on this axis, work is being substituted for leisure. The right vertical axis in turn measures the labor income received in the second period q_1^N in exchange for the expenditure of N_0 units of productive labor today. In quadrant 2 we have drawn the relevant linear productive opportunity curve facing the new generation of workers that indicates the amount of future income or output that can be generated with any given expenditure of labor time employed. That this productive opportunity curve is linear is due to the twin assumptions of constant returns to scale and the fact that both factor inputs are perfect substitutes for each other.[14] Finally, a convex social indifference curve $\bar{U}^W$ is presented in the body of the quadrant, indicating diminishing marginal utility to current leisure and

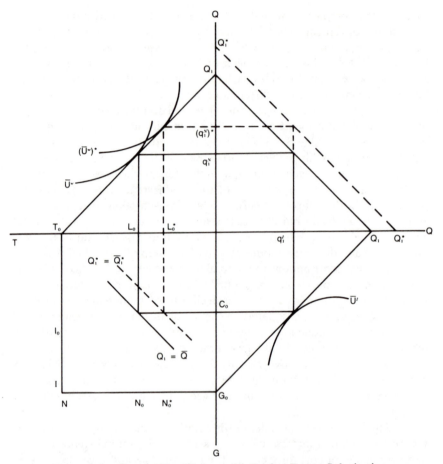

Figure 3.1.   General Equilibrium with Perfect Factor Substitution

future income for the entire working class. The solution to the allocation problem confronting workers is then obtained in the usual way by equating the terms of trade offered by nature in the conversion of leisure into future income—the constant slope of the productive opportunity curve—to the personal trade-off between leisure and future income represented by the slope of the indifference curve. The solution to this problem will define a unique amount of current leisure consumed L_0 and productive labor invested N_0 as well as the assured future income q_1^N going to the working class as a result of this employment.

Similarly, in quadrant 4 we describe the allocation problem confronting the current generation of capitalists. Thus the lower vertical axis measures the initial endowment of goods G owned by capitalists (obtained from past labor income or bequests) which can either be consumed in the current period or invested in the productive process as a capital input. As we move from the bottom toward the top of the vertical axis, investment spending I_0 is being substituted for consumption spending C_0. The top right-hand horizontal axis measures the future income q_1^i generated from this investment which in turn becomes available for consumption and investment in the next period. In the body of this quadrant we again display a linear productive opportunity curve and a convex social indifference curve $\bar{U}^I$ for the entire class of investors. The linear productive opportunity curve defines the constant terms of trade with nature whereby capitalists can convert present goods via investment into future goods, and like the labor productive opportunity curve, it is determined by technology. The convex indifference curve defines the tastes of the capitalist class by presenting the various combinations of present consumption and future income that yield a constant level of satisfaction. Thus capitalists solve their allocation problem in the same way as workers by equating the constant slope of their productive opportunity curve to the slope of their indifference curve. This solution determines the equilibrium levels of current consumption C_0 and investment I_0 and the future income q_1^i generated by that investment.

It is also possible to construct the isoquants for this stylized economy from the information presented in quadrants 2 and 4. The aggregate isoquant for this world is presented in quadrant 3 where the lower horizontal axis measures the labor input while the left-hand vertical axis measures the capital input. These inputs are the complements of leisure and consumption presented in quadrants 2 and 4. As we mentioned before, this particular limiting case of the CES production function implies that labor and capital are perfect substitutes in production. In terms of the isoquants these assumptions regarding the substitution and distribution parameters imply that they will be straight lines with slope equal to negative unity.[15] We can also see in quadrant 3 that production in this economy is carried out with N_0 units of labor services and I_0 units of investment or capital services which in turn generate an aggregate future output of $\bar{Q}_1 = Q_1$.

This aggregate future output of $\bar{Q}_1 = Q_1$ is also displayed in quadrant 1. On the vertical axis, q_1^N of the total output Q_1 goes to workers while q_1^i on the horizontal axis goes to capitalists. The ray q_1^N/q_1^i represents a measure of the distribution of future income between the two economic classes, and for this particular investment of labor and capital and parameterization of the CES function, the future income will be shared equally by both participants. This need not be the case even within the context of our stylized example. For example, if the young become more industrious and supply a greater quantity of labor to the firm (say to N_0^* while the capital input remains unchanged), the total level of output would rise to $Q_1^* Q_1^*$, and labor's share of that output would rise to $(q_1^N/q_1^i)^*$. In this connection note also that the isoquant in quadrant 3 will shift to the northeast of the initial isoquant, indicating a higher level of future output in the amount of $Q_1^* = \bar{Q}_1^*$.

The artificial economy presented in Figure 3.1 is, admittedly, an oversimplification of an actual economy. Yet it does have the advantage of permitting a straightforward and simple geometric description of an intertemporal general equilibrium, and this general equilibrium in turn highlights the factors bearing on the class distribution of income. The new generation of workers enter the economy with time and the old generation of workers (the new generation of capitalists) with goods. Each social class or generation equates its personal terms of trade between current enjoyments (leisure and consumption of goods) and future income to the terms of trade offered by nature in the form of their respective productive opportunity curves. The resulting optimization performed by both groups determines the consumption of current leisure and goods as well as the investment of labor services and capital goods. In addition, the model determines the level of future output and the division of that output among the two classes that cooperate in its production. Finally, we observe that in the context of this particular economy there is—apart from the question of initial endowments—little scope for class or intergenerational conflict in the important sense that each class or generation is free to pursue its economic interests unfettered by the activities of the other class. Every person in this economy reaps only where they have sown, either in the form of the sweat of their brow or the sweat of their abstinence. For an incurable romantic this artificial economy might represent the best of all possible worlds. Having worked through this simple case we now move on to consider an artificial economy that is somewhat closer to that of the real world.

Imperfect Factor Substitution

The weight of ordinary experience and professional economic opinion both suggest that production is not governed by the relationship underlying the general equilibrium presented in Figure 3.1 but rather by one where the productivity and hence income of any factor input or class is partly determined by the usage of the other factor input or class. One function that has this property is the well-known Cobb-Douglas function, itself a special case (i.e., one where $\rho = 0$) of the CES function.[16] The Cobb-Douglas production function can be written as:

$$Q_1 = AI_0^\delta N_0^{(1-\delta)} \tag{3.2}$$

With this production function and the kind of environment assumed in this chapter, the future income of any class is given by the product of the factor usage in production and the marginal physical product of the factor.

These future incomes for both social classes can be written in the following way:

$$q_1^I = (\partial Q_1/\partial I_0)I_0 = \delta Q_1 \tag{3.3}$$

$$q_1^N = (\partial Q_1/\partial N_0)N_0 = (1 - \delta)Q_1 \tag{3.4}$$

Interdependence of factor or class income in (3.3) and (3.4) can be seen by noting that anything that changes Q_1 on the right-hand side of either expression (such as the utilization of the other factor input) will change the income for the class.

This type of interdependence in factor incomes complicates the geometric description of a general equilibrium compared to the case of independence considered in Figure 3.1. The problem is that the total future income of a particular social class depends not only on the extent to which that factor input is used in the production process, but also the extent of the participation by the other cooperating input. Thus a particular expenditure of labor services will yield a varying amount of future income to the working class depending upon the amount of capital services that accompany it to the production process. Fortunately our assumption of certainty will enable us to circumvent this problem, and below we will present a description of a general equilibrium for an economy in which inputs are converted into output by a Cobb-Douglas function.

Toward this end consider the second model economy described in Figure 3.2. The production function[17] for this economy takes the specific form:

$$Q_1 = (I_0 \cdot N_0)^{1/2} \tag{3.5}$$

All four quadrants of Figure 3.2 are defined in terms of the same variables as those described in Figure 3.1; that is, quadrants 2 and 4 describe the allocation problem facing workers and capitalists, quadrant 3 presents the convex isoquant for this economy,[18] and quadrant 1 describes the total future income generated from production as well as its distribution between the two social classes.

From Figure 3.2 we see that both classes can only invest their respective factor service subject to diminishing returns, other things remaining equal. For this reason all productive opportunity curves in quadrants 2 and 4 that transform current inputs into future output are concave. Four such productive opportunity curves are presented for both social classes, with higher curves indicating a greater fixed quantity of the other factor input. Thus, for labor, each successively higher productive opportunity curve describes the possibility of converting time in the form of labor services into a future income when there are successively greater amounts of a fixed level of invest-

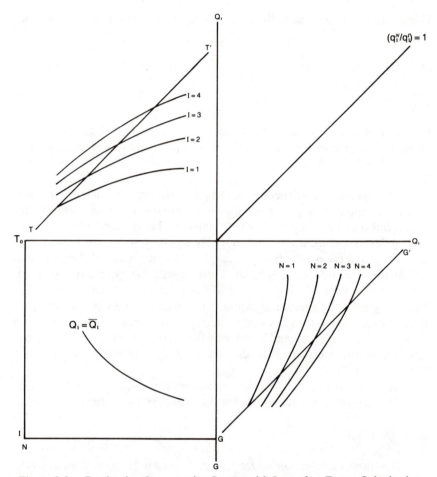

Figure 3.2.   Productive Opportunity Curves with Imperfect Factor Substitution

ment or capital services; that is, for $I_0 = 1$, $I_0 = 2$, and so forth. A similar description applies to the four concave productive opportunity curves confronting capitalists, but this time for different levels of the labor input. Note also that when both factor inputs are increased at the same rate along TT' and GG', the total future output will rise by that same rate, thus indicating that the Cobb-Douglas function is a constant return to scale function. This can be seen by observing that similar points on the two diagonal lines of TT' in quadrant 2 and GG' in quadrant 4 intersect on the 45° line in quadrant 1, implying that both workers and capitalists receive the same future income since $q_1^N/q_1^I = 1.0$. For this particular parameterization ($\delta = 0.5$) of the function, both social classes will always receive the same total income regardless of whether the factor allocations fall along TT' and GG' or not. However, when the allocations lie along TT' and GG' the ratio of output per unit of input (a rate of return) will be identical for both factor contributors. On the other hand, when the allocations of inputs lie above or below GG' and TT', these rates of return will be higher or lower for the two groups of input contributors. For example, consider the productive opportunity curve for labor when $I_0 = 2$ and labor services invested in production is $N_0 = 4$. From Table 3.1 we can see that total future output in this case is roughly $Q_1 = 2.828$ which is shared equally between capitalists and workers. Note, however, that the rate of return for capitalists is $R_I = 1.4145/2 = 0.707$, whereas for laborers it is $R_N = 1.414/4 = 0.354$. If capitalists could be induced to invest one more unit of capital, the rate of return (or wage rate) would rise to $R_N = 1.732/4 = 0.433$, provided they continued to invest four units of labor services to the production process. Clearly, labor's best friend is capital (one does not observe labor unions opposing capital import, but they do, in general, oppose capital export), and capital's best friend is labor (managers of firms rarely oppose immigration) in this world of interdependence.

In describing the actual general equilibrium for this economy, we must introduce some measure of preferences which again will take the form of a social indifference curve for the two classes or generations in the society. As in Figure 3.1 it well be assumed that these indifference curves are convex.

Figure 3.3 presents a hypothetical general equilibrium for this model economy based on the data presented in Table 3.1. As we mentioned above, the diagonal lines TT' for workers in quadrant 2 and GG' for investors in quadrant 4 describe the paths of constant returns to scale for the production function given in (3.5). Note that both TT' and GG' approach but do not touch the left-hand horizontal and bottom vertical axes, thus indicating that a positive output requires positive inputs of both factors. It was also observed above that equivalent movements along these paths generated equal rates of

Table 3.1.   Production in a Simple Cobb-Douglas Economy*

Investment Input	Labor Input: N_0					
I_0	1	2	3	4	5	6
1	1.000	1.414	1.732	2.000	2.236	2.449
2	1.414	2.000	2.449	2.828	3.162	3.464
3	1.732	2.449	3.000	3.464	3.873	4.243
4	2.000	2.828	3.464	4.000	4.472	4.899
5	2.236	3.162	3.873	4.472	5.000	5.477
6	2.449	3.464	4.243	4.899	5.477	6.000

*$Q_1 = (I_0 N_0)^{1/2}$ $\{I_0, N_0 = 1, 2, \ldots, 6\}$

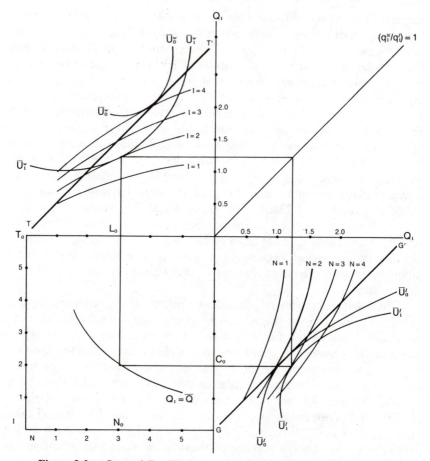

Figure 3.3.   General Equilibrium with Imperfect Factor Substitution

returns earned by both factor inputs. Consequently, allocations off these scale paths result in differential rates of return for the two groups: higher rates for the factor in short supply and lower rates for the relatively more plentiful factor input.

The solution to the allocation problem for both social classes is obtained when the fixed and observable convex indifference curves for the two classes just touch a fixed and observable concave productive opportunity curve that is consistent with the decision of the other factor input.[19] To illustrate this consistency requirement, note that in Figure 3.3 the indifference curve $\bar{U}_0'$ for capitalists is just tangent to the constant returns to scale line GG' for the particular productive opportunity curve where $N_0 = 2$, and that tangency—which in a certain world is known to both classes—indicates that two units of investment will be tentatively supplied to the production process, provided workers supply at least two units of labor services. A glance at quadrant 2, however, indicates that the worker's first choice is to supply four units of labor services since their indifference curve $\bar{U}_0^W$ is tangent to TT' at a point where they would willingly supply $N_0 = 4$. This tangency, however, occurs on a productive opportunity curve that requires capitalists to supply four units of capital. If capitalists could be induced to supply $I_0 = 4$ then workers would supply $N_0 = 4$, and the produced output according to Table 3.1 would be $Q_1 = 4$ to be equally divided between the two classes ($q_1^N = q_1^I = 2$) with both groups earning the same rate of return $R_N = R_I = 0.5$ on their input contribution.

But capitalists cannot be induced to supply the requisite four units of investment. To be sure, there is an indifference curve associated with the supply of four units of capital, but that curve intersects GG' and lies below the one that will tentatively bring forth two units of investment. Hence, there is no incentive for capitalists to move from their position of supplying $I_0 = 2$. If anyone must move, it will have to be the workers. Workers could, of course, supply two units of labor services, in which case output for the next period would be $Q_1 = 2$ with both classes receiving $q_1^N = q_1^I = 1$ and earning an identical rate of return of $R_N = R_I = 0.5$. Yet this solution is not particularly attractive to workers, for they can raise their utility in this example by supplying three units of labor services to the production process. This can be seen in the figure by observing that the indifference curve associated with the labor supply of $N_0 = 2$ on the productive opportunity curve for $I_0 = 2$ would lie below the indifference curve $\bar{U}_1^W$ which is associated with the labor supply of $N_0 = 3$. Moreover, this decision by workers to supply $N_0 = 3$ of labor services to the firm will still not budge capitalists from their initial decision to supply $I_0 = 2$ units of capital, for as we have drawn their indifference curves, any movement from this position would result in a loss in utility for the capitalist class. Production in this model economy, then, will be carried out with $N_0 = 3$ and $I_0 = 2$, and the produced output will be roughly $Q_1 = 2.45$. Workers' income will be $q_1^N = 1.225$ in this equilibrium and their rate of return $R_N = 0.408$, while capitalists will collect the remainder or $q_1^I = 1.225$ and a rate of return of $R_I = 0.613$ on their investment. Note that in this allocation the capitalists obtain a larger future income ($q_1^I = 1.225$) than the 1.000 units of future output associated with the tangency of their indifference curve $\bar{U}_0^I$ and the constant returns to scale path GG' on the productive opportunity curve for $N_0 = 2$. This free gift of income from workers to capitalists (for supplying $N_0 = 3$ rather than $N_0 = 2$ units of labor services) was again perfectly foreseen by both participants to production and is associated with a higher level of utility, $\bar{U}_1^I$, than the utility associated with $\bar{U}_0^I$. In effect, capitalists are able to attain a level of utility above that given by the constant returns to scale path GG'. What does this mean? It simply means that capitalist's marginal product or rate of return is higher when two units of capital services are invested in production than say three or four units. In other words, there is value in terms of the rate of return in being the relatively scarce factor of production.

Does this situation reflect exploitation? Exploitation is a word that can be defined in a number of different ways. Karl Marx chose to define it as a positive net income for the capitalist class, and many socialists today still hold to this definition.[20] On the other hand, neoclassical theory would define exploitation as any situation in which the rate of return earned by any factor or class is different from its marginal productivity. If this definition is accepted, then there is no exploitation in the economy described in Figure 3.3, whereas if the Marxian definition is accepted, then the system can be characterized by exploitation. One definition proposed by Webster's dictionary falls somewhere between the Marxian and neoclassical definitions and comes close to linking it with the grim reality of diminishing returns; namely, "coaction between organisms in which one is benefited at the expense of the other." Workers in our artificial economy described in Figure 3.3 might find it hard to disagree with this definition. Things would certainly be better for them in the next period if they and their parents could be induced to consume less and invest more, for then perhaps they would not be required to work with such a barren productive opportunity curve.

Unemployment is also an ambiguous word in this neoclassical model of general equilibrium. To be sure, anyone and everyone can work as much as he or she pleases in this system, although with other things remaining equal the fruits of this labor will decrease as more and more young workers avail themselves of this opportunity. In this sense there can be no such thing as involuntary unemployment in this economy, and the full employment output would approximate $Q_1 = 2.45$. The difference between an employment of $N_0 = 4$ (the N_0 associated with the tangency between the workers' community indifference curve $\bar{U}_0^W$ and the constant returns to scale path TT' on the productive opportunity curve for $I_0 = 4$) and the equilibrium employment of $N_0 = 3$ would represent voluntary unemployment or the demand for leisure given the market price between future income and leisure facing young workers.

Suppose, however, young workers form an association, and the association in turn pegs the rate of return on labor services at $R_N = 0.5$. At a wage rate of $R_N = 0.5$ only two units of labor services will be used in productive activity, which in combination with two units of capital will produce a future output of $Q_1 = 2$ and a total labor income of $q_1^N = 1$. It is easy to see that a price-fixing policy of this sort would not benefit the working class since in Figure 3.3 the indifference curve in quadrant 2 for the pegged price solution ($N_0 = I_0 = Q_1 = 2$, $q_1^N = q_1^I = 1$, $R_N = R_I = 0.5$) would intersect the scale path TT' and lie everywhere below the indifference curve $\bar{U}_1^W$ associated with the equilibrium market solution. In an interdependent society the utility-maximizing factor allocation cannot be attained by price fixing. We might add that if the reduction in employment from the market equilibrium level of $N_0 = 3$ to the pegged price equilibrium of $N_0 = 2$ is not equally shared by all young workers (i.e., some lucky workers are employed at a wage rate of $R_N = 0.5$ while others are unemployed and earning nothing), then the resulting unemployment in the system would be considered involuntary, at least by those workers who are out of work.[21]

These remarks are probably sufficient to illustrate that words like exploitation and unemployment are not unambiguous in the context of the equilibrium model presented in Figure 3.3 but instead can only have meaning within a social context. As such, these words are political in nature. This is why exploitation and unemployment are primarily treated as political problems. In this chapter we have constructed an aggregate neoclassical model to illustrate the potential conflict between different groups in society over the distribution of future income. Unemployment and changing rates of inflation are political issues in that they affect the distribution of income and consumption within a society, and as such they should be studied within the context of economic models that emphasize the distributional aspects of the problem. This will be our approach to these problems in Chapters 9 and 10, and the approach is very much influenced by the aggregate neoclassical model presented in this chapter. Having introduced this idea we can now summarize the results and implications of the discussion in this chapter.

Summary and Conclusion

In this chapter we have extended the two-period consumption-investment model to provide a complete description of factor allocation, income determination, and income distribution in an environment characterized by perfect certainty and perfect exchange markets. In this model workers contribute time while capitalists contribute goods. Both are partners in one enterprise. In the process of maximizing their respective utilities an allocation occurs which determines the amount of leisure and work by the young and the amount of consumption and investment by the old. These inputs of labor and capital, along with a production function, determine the amount of future output and the distribution of that output between young workers and their parents, the current generation of capitalists.

Two particular cases of the constant elasticity of substitution production function were considered. The first case was described in Figure 3.1 and was characterized by the fact that output generated by any one factor input was independent of the usage of the other factor input. The economic interpretation of this case was that both factor inputs were perfect substitutes for each other. In this world we only reap where we have sown. The second case was described in Table 3.1 and Figures 3.2 and 3.3, and had the property that output or income earned by one factor of production was dependent upon the utilization of the other factor input. In this case both factors of production were imperfect substitutes for one another. As we observed, men and women in this world may reap where, in a certain sense, they have not sown, and vice versa.

The output-sharing rules underlying the two numerical examples of firm production were seen to be based on productivity; that is to say, each social class was paid a remuneration for its factor service based on its marginal product. These distribution rules or financial relationships were in turn embedded in the tangencies between the two productive opportunity curves and indifference curves and defined the trade-offs between current enjoyments (leisure and current consumption) and future income for workers and capitalists.

It is of interest to note that in this neoclassical world of perfect foresight and perfect exchange markets, income redistributions through involuntary unemployment (or unexpected inflation, for that matter) simply do not occur. Moreover, they do not occur for the reason summarized in the extreme version of Says Law, namely, a supply of a factor input implies a demand for the future output. Anyone can work in this society and receive the marginal product income for his or her effort. This proposition, however, can only hold true in a world of constant returns characterized by perfect certainty and perfect markets where every participant knows the utility function, endowment, and productive opportunities of every other participant in the economy. Uncertainty and imperfect markets are the only factors that can account for the income redistributions associated with unemployment and inflation. In the neoclassical world studied in this chapter the only problem encountered arose from interdependent factor productivity and the harsh reality of diminishing returns in the Cobb-Douglas case. At this point we reminded ourselves that to allow marginal productivity to completely determine the distribution of income was essentially a political assumption which is not strictly adhered to in actual economies. Granting this assumption, there was nothing to guarantee that the preferences for current enjoyments and future income for the two social classes would result in an allocation falling on the constant returns to scale paths TT' and GG' in Figure 3.3. When the allocations were off these paths it simply meant that one of the factors of production or social classes desired to supply a greater quantity of their input to the firm than was consistent (in the sense that both preferences would lead to allocations lying along TT' and GG') with the known preferences of the other cooperating factor of production. The end result was an equilibrium allocation that entailed a higher level of current enjoyments and a lower level of future output than the one that would have emerged if the preferences of the two classes were consistent. In the one case considered, workers were unable to achieve an allocation lying along the constant returns to scale path TT', but instead achieved an allocation interior to that frontier. By the same token the older generation of capitalists received a future income that, together with their current consumption, placed them on an indifference curve beyond the frontier of their scale path GG'. However, this numerical example was presented for illustrative purposes only and was not intended to be a statement about the actual position of workers and capitalists with respect to the scale paths TT' and GG'.

Finally, the reason we study any paradigm is because it promises to be useful in explaining some important economic phenomena. The Keynesian income-expenditure theory, for example, attempts to rationalize the relationship between the autonomous and induced expenditures made over time in a society, and how that society might come to experience an unemployment equilibrium due to an insufficiency of aggregate demand. The theory of rational expectations attempts to explain unemployment in terms of forecasting errors by rational (but mistake-prone) economic agents. In this chapter we have seen that the two-period consumption-investment model can also account for an equilibrium characterized by unemployment, but here the unemployment arises from an attempt to peg the price or rate of return of a factor input at a level different than the free market price. What is more important is that the consumption-investment model penetrates to the heart of the problem in a way that the income-expenditure or rational expectations theories cannot, namely, by directing our attention to the input/output-sharing arrangements in production within an interdependent market economic system. In Chapters 9 and 10 we will pursue this line of inquiry further and explore the cyclical fluctuations in unemployment and inflation but within the context of an uncertain environment. Before we can do this, however, we must first discuss economic activity and factor allocation in an uncertain environment. This will be the subject matter of Chapters 4–6.

Notes

1. Including those parts of finance dealing with capital structure and dividend policy. In addition, Hirschleifer's (1958) reformulation of Fisher's theory was directed toward reconciling the contending views in the capital budgeting literature as to whether the lending or borrowing rate was the appropriate rate to use when appraising capital projects.

2. There are some exceptions to this assertion that should be mentioned at this point. One exception centers around the financing of government expenditures; another on whether a government-mandated social security system fundamentally alters the composition of national output between consumption and investment. Both questions were at the center of a great national debate in the early 1980s, and

both have been analyzed by academic financial economists within the Fisher-Hirschleifer framework. A partial listing of the important references here might include Samuelson (1958), Diamond (1965), Cass and Yaari (1966), Feldstein (1974), Miller and Upton (1974), Barro (1974), and Buiter and Tobin (1980). Finally, Lucas (1972) has used this general framework to analyze Phillips-type relationships between prices and outputs in an economy subject to uncertainty. It would therefore be unfair to claim that intertemporal consumption-investment models have never been used to address public policy issues.

    3. John Maynard Keynes was one of the most prominent economists who separated macroeconomics from microeconomics or value theory. It has been suggested by a friendly interpreter (see Harrod 1951, p. 324) that Keynes made little attempt to fully understand the value theory of his time but instead rushed headlong into the task of developing an economics that was more responsive to the social problems of the day. Be that as it may, it is nonetheless true that much effort has been expended by the economics profession on providing a micro foundation for his income-expenditure theory in an equilibrium as well as a disequilibrium context. This model and the quantity theory of money description of macroeconomic activity will be discussed in Chapter 7.

    4. In the *IS-LM* description of the model, we see how the interplay of income and balance-sheet items simultaneously determines the level of real output and the price of financial assets in the system. Moreover, it is important to note that the development of this theory was contemporaneous with the development of national income and product accounts which facilitated the interpretation of the theory and provided the basis for empirical work.

    5. Although certain ideas of Fisher, such as the distinction between real and nominal interest rates, play an important role in monetarist models of macroeconomic activity. In this connection see Friedman (1974).

    6. Keynesian and monetarist models, while interesting for many purposes, are not particularly useful for analyzing the class distribution of income which ultimately becomes the important social issue associated with changing rates of inflation and unemployment. The reason for this is that they focus on aggregate demand and ignore, to a certain extent, the interaction between capitalists and workers on the supply side and how that interaction determines the supply of output as well as the distribution of the claims against that output. This, as we will see below, is the focal point of analysis in the two-period consumption-investment model. Throughout this chapter we will classify individuals as either workers or capitalists, and analyze the factors determining the distribution of income between these two classes. This we do because workers and capitalists supply specific factor inputs to the production process or firm in this society, and we are interested in how they share the produced output. In this connection we fully realize that individuals can be classified in a number of different ways (e.g., old versus young or rich versus poor, neither of which falls exactly in the capitalist-worker classification) and that all social problems do not necessarily collapse to the distribution of income between workers and capitalists. Notwithstanding this qualification, it is still interesting to study the sharing of input and output among workers and capitalists.

7. As in Chapter 2, this one good could be consumed or invested in the productive process. Similarly, time can be expended in productive labor or consumed as leisure.

8. The growth of pension funds and various deferred annuity plans are rapidly making this assumption (that each individual passes through both the working class and capitalist class) the reality. If these trends continue there will probably be some fundamental changes in the direction taken by trade unions. How, for example, will trade unions negotiate a current wage settlement when yesterday's workers are increasingly coming to represent the other side of the wage bargain? Moreover, what will it mean for a union to obtain a retirement income for the current generation of workers if subsequent labor negotiations are permitted to renegotiate the agreement tomorrow? How will labor unions confront this dilemma? In this connection we would also expect the structure of decisionmaking authority to change within the union. In many unions retired workers have a vote along with active workers in the election of union officials who in turn formulate and negotiate the wage contract. In the majority of cases, however, only active workers can ratify a negotiated agreement. If these trends continue we would expect retired workers to also vote on the ratification of a labor agreement. Thus, the class distribution of income as well as the management of the firm will increasingly come to be determined by the union as the representative of both active and retired workers. Such trends are presently observable in Europe and Japan, and with time will be observable in North America. Therefore, regarding the future, we are mildly optimistic that many of the social tensions associated with unemployment, strikes, and unexpected inflation that accompany the division of the national income in industrial societies will, in the course of time, moderate as institutions like trade unions evolve in response to certain structural changes taking place in the class ownership of factor inputs.

9. This rosy view of the source of endowments is not shared with socialists. According to Marx (1961, pp. 713–760) the endowment of capitalists was obtained by conquest, enslavement, robbery, murder, and the enclosure of farm lands.

10. For a description of these conditions, see Gorman (1953) and Samuelson (1956).

11. This parameter converts units of input into units of output. When $\gamma = 1.0$ the production function is in its standardized form and output Q_1 is in standardized units.

12. With given factor proportions and a given elasticity of substitution, the distribution of income between capitalists and workers is given by the distribution parameter δ and $(1 - \delta)$.

13. The substitution parameter ρ is uniquely linked to the so-called elasticity of substitution parameter σ by the formula $\rho = (1/\sigma - 1)$ and provides a measure of the degree of substitutability between factor inputs. The higher the σ (in the limit, $\sigma \to \infty$) or the closer ρ approaches -1.0, the more perfectly one factor substitutes for the other. Conversely, a low σ (in the limit, $\sigma \to 0$) or $\rho \to \infty$ implies that the two factors can only be combined in a unique way, the so-called fixed coefficient case. Finally, in between the two limiting cases we have the Cobb-Douglas case where $\sigma = 1.0$ and $\rho = 0$. In this case, factor inputs are imperfect substitutes for one an-

other. For a further discussion of these various cases, see Intriligator (1971), pp. 186–189).

14. An alternative interpretation is that there is only one factor input which is supplied to the firm by two different investors.

15. To see this, differentiate (3.1) to obtain

(i) $dQ_1 = \gamma\{-1/\rho[\delta I_0^{-\rho} + (1 - \delta)N_0^{-\rho}]^{-(1+1/\rho)}\}$

$$\times\ \{-\rho\delta I_0^{-(1+\rho)}dI_0 - \rho(1 - \delta)N_0^{-(1+\rho)}dN_0\}$$

which can be rearranged to:

(ii) $dI_0/dN_0 = -[(1 - \delta)/\delta]\ [I_0/N_0]^{(1+\rho)} = -1.0$

when $dQ_1 = 0, \rho = -1.0, \delta = 0.5$, and $\gamma = 1.0$, which is the straight line $Q_1 = \bar{Q}_1$ in quadrant 3 in Figure 3.1.

16. Consider the general form of the CES function for $\gamma = 1.0$.

(i) $Q_1^{-\rho} = \delta I_0^{-\rho} + (1 - \delta)N_0^{-\rho}$

Differentiating (i) yields:

(ii) $-\rho Q_1^{-(1+\rho)}dQ_1 = -\rho\delta I_0^{-(1+\rho)}dI_0 - \rho(1 - \delta)N_0^{-(1+\rho)}dN_0$

or

(iii) $dQ_1/Q_1^{(1+\rho)} = \delta\ dI_0/I_0^{(1+\rho)} + (1 - \delta)\ dN_0/N_0^{(1+\rho)}$

Letting $\rho = 0$ (the Cobb-Douglas case) and integrating (iii) yields:

(iv) $\log Q_1 = \delta \log I_0 + (1 - \delta) \log N_0 + \log A$

where A is the constant of integration. This is the Cobb-Douglas function in logarithmic form which can be written as:

(v) $Q_1 = A I_0^{\delta} N_0^{(1-\delta)}$

which is (3.2) in the text.

17. We waive the question of whether the conditions for aggregation are satisfied for this production function. While it is true that the Cobb-Douglas function is additive separable in the logarithms of the variables, the resulting aggregate function does not satisfy the marginal productivity conditions as noted by Walters (1963). As we mentioned above, it will be useful to visualize production as being carried out by one large firm.

18. The isoquants for this case turn out to be rectangular hyperbolas. To see this consider Equation ii in note 15 which describes the isoquants for the CES production function.

(i) $dI_0/dN_0 = -[(1 - \delta)/\delta]\ [I_0/N_0]^{(1+\rho)}$

When $\rho = 0$ we have the separable differential equation which in turn can be written as:

(ii) $dI_0/I_0 = -[(1 - \delta)/\delta]\ [dN_0/N_0]$

Integrating (ii) and then exponentiating yields:

(iii) $I_0 = CN_0^{-\left(\frac{1-\delta}{\delta}\right)}$

where C is some constant. When $\delta = 0.5$ (the case considered in Figures 3.2 and 3.3) we get the equation for a rectangular hyperbola, namely,

(iv) $I_0 = C/N_0$

19. In a perfectly certain world all parties that supply factor inputs can see with unfailing accuracy not only the different productive opportunity curves but also the fixed family of indifference curves for both classes and hence the general equilibrium. Without the assumption of perfect foresight, which requires all participants to be like the Shadow and look into the innermost recesses of each others' souls, both social classes would be tempted to withhold their input to the firm until the other factor made the extent of its participation known, and in this way convert the problem to one of allocation under uncertainty. Attempts to solve such a problem along game theory lines by developing intertemporal strategies for both classes would be complicated by the fact that every individual in this society spends only one period in each social class. An alternative assumption that would produce the same result is that one class (capitalists, in this case) makes its investment commitment to the firm first, and then the other class supplies its factor input so as to maximize utility.

20. Oscar Lange (1935) offered the argument which in effect rejects the labor theory of value underlying the original argument of Marx. It is suggested that while capital is productive there is no reason why individual capitalists should own it and obtain an income from it.

21. This is the type of unemployment that could arise in a noncompetitive classical system. The monopoly (union) solution always involves a higher price (wage rate) and lower quantity (employment). The classical remedy is then simple: break up the monopoly and restore competition which in turn will reduce wage rates and increase employment. This analysis and remedy were vigorously attacked by Keynes (1936, pp. 4–22).

Part II

The Financial Economics Of Risk And Uncertainty

—4—

The Capital Asset Pricing Model

Introduction

Up to this point in our inquiry we have discussed a number of interesting economic propositions revolving around the subject of intertemporal consumption within the framework of a perfectly certain environment and with perfect exchange markets. In this environment the individual household faced the problem of converting some initial endowment into a desired sequence of consumption over time with the help of a productive opportunity and a capital market. Clearly this environment and the Fisher model of intertemporal consumption have taken us a long way toward an understanding of the social role of a capital market in a capitalist society. Yet in an uncertain world there will be additional lessons to learn concerning the social role of a capital market. One immediate lesson concerns the sharing of risk and return among different investors for a given risky productive opportunity. In this environment it is possible for risk and return to be shared among investors in a way different from that given by their contribution of inputs to the productive process. This differential sharing of risk and return, that typically characterizes bond and stock financing of a given productive opportunity set, will be reflected in differential rates of return on these capital market instruments; something that did not nor could not occur in a certain environment. Contracts like those embedded in bonds and stocks will therefore come to play an important role in the allocation of the social endowment. In this chapter our main objective will be to describe a model of investment allocation across productive opportunity sets, and then explore—within the context of the model—a number of financial-policy-related issues.

In approaching this objective we must remember at the outset that there are a number of issues of interest to both policymakers and scholars that do not require a complete description of capital market equilibrium. For example, Modigliani and Miller (1958, 1969) and Miller and Modigliani (1961) have considerably enhanced our understanding of the implications of capital market equilibrium for certain financial decisions without describing, in any precise way, just how that equilibrium is determined. Their analysis for an uncertain world in many ways parallels the analysis of Fisher. Both used a partial equilibrium construction. Yet in an uncertain environment there are many expected trade-offs between present and future consumption in the capital market, whereas in a certain world there is only one. To deal with this problem Modigliani and Miller (hereafter, MM) developed their justly famous risk class, a classification scheme whereby all firms in a particular class are deemed to be perfect investment substitutes. Armed with the risk class concept they demonstrated the power of arbitrage in a taxless[1] and transaction costless world. The policy implication of their analysis was that the financing of a firm's given production plan and an individual's consumption and personal investment plan were irrelevant.[2] What is somewhat remarkable is that over time the implications of their analysis have come to represent the criterion upon which more general models of capital market equilibriums are now judged. If a particular model of capital market equilibrium fails to generate the MM results, that model will surely be relegated to the scrap heap of rejected economic theories, or at least so it would seem at present. Consequently, from the policymaking point of view one can go a long way within the MM partial equilibrium framework.

In this chapter we will not follow the MM path, partly because our interest in subsequent chapters will be in economy-wide or social issues, whereas their approach is more fruitful for understanding the problems confronting an individual firm. Our interest then will be in a model of capital market equilibrium, and the model we dwell on below is the well-known and now much maligned two-parameter capital asset pricing model (hereafter, CAPM). This model constitutes an important extension of the Fisher paradigm and has something important to say about the allocation of investment across different firms under uncertainty.[3] Furthermore, as we will see below, this model also satisfies the Fisher-MM criterion that, in equilibrium, financing is separable from individual investment and consumption decisions and hence irrelevant. Financing is therefore not a problem in this model, but it is not for that reason that we choose to devote an entire chapter to its development. Our ultimate aim will be to show just where the model could be potentially useful and where it might not be useful in answering a wide range of practical questions.

The CAPM, like every other economic model, is not universally applicable to all possible problems and issues in financial economics. For example, in order to avoid merely describing a general equilibrium, the model is forced to make a number of strong assumptions, several of which preclude any interesting analysis of the types of contracts that can be created when the environment is uncertain.[4] To be sure, it is possible to differentiate broad categories of financial contracts such as debt and equity, but the distinctions between these contracts becomes meaningless within the CAPM in the sense that no one could differentiate an equilibrium where production was financed with both debt and equity contracts from an equilibrium where production was financed exclusively with equity. If someone was interested in the question of why production is financed with debt and equity securities, and what difference this would make for managing the firm—if this indeed is a question worth asking—he or she would be required to look elsewhere for an answer. On the other hand, if that someone were interested in those issues concerning the risk-return trade-off for an economy, he or she would find the CAPM immensely useful. In any event, the model's shortcomings as well as its strengths will enhance our understanding of market processes, and for that reason is worth studying.

Accordingly, the plan of this chapter will be as follows. In the next section we undertake a description of the economic environment within which the model will subsequently be developed. In the third section we present the model. Since the model is well known to financial economists, our discussion here will be relatively brief. The fourth section continues the analysis by describing a number of interesting implications of the model that bear directly on certain aspects of financial policy. Moreover, we remove the assumption of perfect markets and observe the effect on certain aspects of financial policy. Finally we conclude the chapter by summarizing the results. The model is rich with possibilities—several of which will be pursued in subsequent chapters—but it also has its limitations. What is important is that we understand where these limitations are important and hence the implications likely to be incorrect, and where the limitations are less important and the implications of greater interest.

The Environment

In the perfectly certain environment considered in Chapters 2 and 3, all participants in the economy were presumed to know each other's endowments, tastes, opportunities, and the state of the world in the second period. Accordingly, *ex-ante* plans were always fully realized as *ex-post* results. In this environment every household could plan their two-period lifetime consumption-investment strategy in the first period and then sit back and watch their intertemporal consumption (including bequests) unfold. Life in this environment held no surprises. Since there were no surprises in this kind of world there emerged only one trade-off between current and future consumption in the capital market: the risk-free rate of interest.

Life, however, is uncertain and the problem confronting the individual consumer-investor is how to live happily in a world where "the best laid plans of mice and men often go astray." Financial economists have formulated a number of best-laid plans for men and women to follow in an uncertain world, but plans and results are often different. This is, perhaps, the most important thing to remember throughout our discussion of financial decision-making under uncertainty; namely, that it only refers to the act of planning and not the actual outcome, although it is presumed that how well we plan will have some effect on how little we are likely to go astray. A second but more controversial point worth bearing in mind when plans can go astray is embodied in Wordsworth's "Sonnet on Inside King's College Chapel": " . . . high Heaven rejects the lore/of nicely calculated less or more." By this we mean that in practice, procedures for actual planning in an uncertain world cannot be nicely calculated less or more. Not everyone will agree with this view, but as we will shortly see it is the view taken by the CAPM.

At this point we must mention again that it is not our intention to provide a complete description of the consumption-investment decision under uncertainty. The topic is vast and many of the issues have not been satisfactorily resolved even among professional economists. Consequently, all we will do here is state some selective results that will be useful for our purposes in this and subsequent chapters.[5]

To begin with, we will again consider a two-period (today and tomorrow), one-good world where the one good can either be consumed today or invested to yield a consumption or bequest tomorrow. However, unlike our previous discussion, we will now assume that the individual household has already decided, by one means or another, how much of its initial endowment will be allocated to current consumption and how much to saving and investment.[6] Our focus of attention, then, will be on the question of how households should allocate their savings among the various investment opportunities available. This is the so-called portfolio problem first described by Keynes (1936, p. 166). To make things simple we will assume that there are two broad categories of investment opportunities: riskless investments that convert the present input into a known future output and risky investments that convert a current input into an uncertain output in a sense to be defined below. In other words, single project firms purchase the single good from households and pay for it by issuing various types of claims to the future output.

Let us take a closer look at the firms in this economy. For the group of firms in the riskless sector, tomorrow's output is known with perfect certainty just as it was in previous chapters. For the second group of firms the exact amount of future output for any given level of input is unknown. Nevertheless our investors do know something or at least are prepared to act as if they know something. We will assume they know enough about the firm's activities and future states of nature to assign a subjective probability distribution to the unknown future output.[7] In order to simplify matters further we will assume these probability distributions to be fully described by their means and standard deviations.[8] Thus, while the actual *ex-post* investment outcome of firms in the risky sector is unknown, it is presumed that households take means and standard deviations into account in some way when making portfolio decisions.[9]

To sum up, then, the environment that seems to be emerging is the following. First there is at least one firm or production process in this economy where households can exchange their initial endowment of the input good for a second-period output on terms that are fixed and known to all market participants. The return on investment in this sector is therefore riskless.[10] Moreover, it will also be assumed that production in this sector is governed by constant returns to scale. Second, there are also a number of other firms in this economy for which initial inputs can be converted into a probability distribution and from this into an actual second-period output drawn from the first-period probability distribution. This first-period distribution was assumed to be fully described by the mean and standard deviation. Since the actual outcome is unknown, investment returns for these firms are considered risky and uncertain. In addition it will also be assumed that production is governed by stochastic constant returns to scale[11] in this sector. Finally, all households are assumed to be risk averse in the sense that in order to induce them to hold increasing amounts of risk, they must be compensated with ever-increasing amounts of return. Risk aversion implies that the consumer-investor's indifference curves will be convex in return/risk space.[12]

With this description of the economy it will now be useful to state the portfolio selection rule first proposed by Markowitz (1952) (1959). This rule states that if mean return is regarded as desirable and variance of return as undesirable, then an efficient portfolio of risky securities (i.e., an allocation of inputs to the risky sector) is one where for a given mean return the accompanying variance is the smallest possible; or alternatively, for a given variance of portfolio return, the mean return will be the largest possible. The Markowitz rule was originally offered as a practical guide for portfolio construction in actual securities markets and is nothing more than a procedure recommended to the individual investor with given expectations on return distributions for choosing among alternative portfolios. What it tells the investor is simply that some portfolios are better than others and that attention should be focused on the better portfolios while all others should be rejected out of hand. It does not, however, tell the investor which of the better portfolios should actually be selected. This is left up to the individual investor. But it does tell us that once an investor picks a given level of risk, for whatever reason, there is much to be said for the criterion of picking the portfolio that maximizes mean or expected return for that level of risk. What does not seem particularly sensible is to pick the portfolio that only provides the third or fourth best return attainable for that level of risk. While all this may seem obvious, we will see in the next section that this Markowitz rule, with some additional assumptions, provides a theory for the pricing of risky claims to future output. Moreover, this theory, unlike some other theories, offers the possibility of empirical testability as well as serving as an input in the testing of other theoretical and policy propositions in economics.

The Capital Asset Pricing Model

Once Markowitz developed his famous procedure for selecting port-folios in the early 1950s, it was only a matter of time before others asked what implications this rule might have for price relationships in the capital market. The question posed was both interesting and important since, at the time, it was generally felt that the biggest gap in our understanding of eco-nomic phenomena was in the investment market where the present must con-front the future through the veil of uncertainty.[13] To be sure, a theory of allo-cation under uncertainty had already been developed at that time by Arrow (1964) and Debreu (1959), but unfortunately the practical implications of that theory were somewhat limited partly because there were not many real-world counterparts to the types of securities analyzed in their model. The important insights of the Arrow-Debreu model would lie in a different direc-tion. The Markowitz approach, however, started with actual observable cap-ital market instruments and hence could reasonably be expected to provide a number of important practical insights into the operation of a modern capi-tal market. A number of these insights were developed in the middle and late 1960s under the general heading of the two-parameter capital asset pricing model.[14]

The CAPM is a theory of the price structure of risky capital assets. In principle it is a theory of valuation for all current inputs in an economy and will be treated as such in this chapter. However, any practical application of the model—particularly any empirical analysis of the sort presented in Chapter 6—will inevitably require us to back away from this idealization and restrict our attention to the capital inputs for sale on the New York Stock Exchange. A number of assumptions are generally invoked in developing the model, and some of the more important are:

1. The total amount of household saving and the division of that saving between the riskless and risky sectors are given.
2. Security markets are perfect, which is usually taken to mean:
   (a) Transaction and information costs are zero for every investor.
   (b) Taxes are ignored.

(c) Perfect substitutes in the securities market command the same capital market price.
3. All investors can lend or borrow (or go short) in the riskless sector at a known and fixed rate. By assumption, then, default on any debt contract is precluded.
4. All investors have the same two-period (today and tomorrow) horizon.
5. All investors are risk averse and construct their portfolios according to the Markowitz mean-variance rule.
6. All investors are in complete agreement as to the expected returns, variance of returns, and all pairwise covariances of returns for all claims to the second-period output in the economy. This crucial homogeneity assumption is partly the result of our previous assumption that all information is costless and available to all portfolio investors.

From these assumptions the CAPM of relative input or asset prices can be derived. Before deriving the model, however, we will present a verbal description of the theory.

To begin with, note that there is a riskless and risky sector in the economy, and the latter will generally contain a number of different projects or firms. Now, from assumption 6—regarding investor agreement on the probability distribution of returns, including their interrelationships in terms of pairwise covariances or correlations—it is obvious that every individual investor will (indeed must) group the risky firms in exactly the same way and according to the Markowitz rule. The Markowitz rule by itself, however, will not define a unique grouping or portfolio of risky firms but rather a set of such portfolios all with the property that for a given level of risk (measured by the standard deviation of return) there is no other portfolio or allocation of inputs among risky firms that would have a higher expected return. Once a rate of return is specified in the riskless sector (assumption 3) we then obtain a unique mean-standard deviation efficient allocation of inputs which when combined into a portfolio will, in general, be held by all households in the economy.[15] Call this unique mean-standard deviation allocation or portfolio, the market portfolio. This market portfolio will then have the property of providing the investor with the most favorable trade-off between risk (the standard deviation of return on the market portfolio) and excess expected return (the difference between the expected returns on the market portfolio of risky firms and the rate of return earned in the riskless sector); a property that would seem commendable when allocating inputs among different risky firms when investors are risk averse. The unmistakable implication, then, is that with homogeneous expectations all investors will hold the same market portfolio of claims to the second-period output, and that market portfolio will provide the most favorable trade-off between risk and return attainable in this economy. In fact, this trade-off is such an important economy-wide price it has been given a special name: the market price of risk reduction.

When an equilibrium is attained and a market price of risk reduction is established in the capital or input market, how will individual portfolio investors differ? The only way they can differ within the framework of CAPM is in terms of the strength of their risk aversion, which, in turn, is reflected by how they combine the projects in the riskless and risky sectors in achieving some personally desired combination of risk and return in their portfolio. There are only three ways the individual consumer-investor can combine the riskless and risky sectors. First, it is possible for the investor to place his or her saving entirely in the market portfolio of risky firms to be spread across all firms in that sector. This investor would be neither a lender nor a borrower to the riskless sector. In the second case the investor would lend a portion of his savings to the riskless sector and invest the remainder in the market portfolio or risky sector. This investor would be deemed more risk averse than the investor in the first case. Finally, an investor could borrow (or sell short) from the riskless sector and, together with an initial amount of saving, plunge into the risky-market portfolio. This investor would be considered the least risk averse.

To sum up, then, individual differences between households are reflected in their borrowing or lending status but not in how they group firms in the risky-market portfolio. With homogeneous expectations, all investors combine varying amounts of borrowing or lending in the riskless sector with the same market portfolio (or allocation of investment across risky firms) in order to obtain some desired combination of risk and return on their personal portfolio.[16] The only task CAPM must perform is to describe the procedure by which the individual risky firms in the market portfolio are valued or weighted, one relative to another. This procedure is to weight the individual firms in the market portfolio in such a way as to maximize the social risk-return trade-off or market price of risk reduction.

There are two forms of the model: one expresses the interrelationships between risky assets in terms of expected rates of return; the other, in terms of their monetary or resource valuations. We will follow convention and first develop the rate of return formulation. In this connection the following notation will be used.

$E(\tilde{R}_M)$ = the expected rate of return on the market portfolio containing all the risky firms in the economy.

R_F = the rate of return prevailing in the riskless sector.

$\sigma(\tilde{R}_M)$ = the standard deviation of the rate of return on the market portfolio of risky assets.

$E(\tilde{R}_j)$ = the expected rate of return on risky firm j.

$\sigma^2(\tilde{R}_j)$ = the variance of the rate of return on firm j.

$\mathrm{cov}(\tilde{R}_j, \tilde{R}_M$ = the covariance of the rate of return on firm j and the rate of return on the market portfolio.

w_j = the weight or proportion firm j represents relative to the market portfolio, i.e., $w_j = P_j/P_M$.

$E(\tilde{X}_j)$ = the second-period expected output of firm j.

$E(\tilde{X}_M)$ = the second-period expected output on the market portfolio containing all risky firms in the economy.

$\text{cov}(\tilde{X}_j, \tilde{X}_M)$ = the covariance between the second-period outputs of j and M.

$\sigma(\tilde{X}_M)$ = the standard deviation of the second-period output of the market portfolio.

P_j = the first-period known price or valuation placed on firm j.

P_M = the first-period valuation placed on the market portfolio.

As we mentioned above, the objective of all like-minded investors in this system will be to maximize the expected rate of return on the market portfolio of risky assets per unit of market portfolio risk. This is accomplished by all investors optimally adjusting the weights w_j on the individual risky firms so that in equilibrium the risk-return trade-off or market price of risk reduction is maximized.[17]

Following Lintner (1965), the problem is to maximize the market price of risk reduction.

$$\frac{E(\tilde{R}_M) - R_F}{\sigma(\tilde{R}_M)} = \frac{\sum_{1}^{N}{}_{j} w_j E(\tilde{R}_j) - R_F}{\left[\sum_{1}^{N}{}_{j} w_j^2 \sigma^2(\tilde{R}_j) + 2\sum_{1}^{N-1}{}_{j} \sum_{j+1}^{N}{}_{k} w_j w_k \text{cov}(\tilde{R}_j, \tilde{R}_k)\right]^{\frac{1}{2}}} \tag{4.1}$$

subject to $\Sigma_j w_j = 1.0$. This is accomplished by differentiating (4.1) with respect to w_j and setting the result equal to zero.

$$\frac{\partial[(E(\tilde{R}_M) - R_F)/\sigma(\tilde{R}_M)]}{\partial w_j} = [E(\tilde{R}_j) - R_F][\sigma^2(\tilde{R}_M)]^{-\frac{1}{2}} - \frac{1}{2}[\sigma^2(\tilde{R}_M)]^{-\frac{3}{2}} \tag{4.2}$$

$$[2w_j\sigma^2(\tilde{R}_j) + 2\sum_{j \neq k}{}_{k} w_k \text{cov}(\tilde{R}_j, \tilde{R}_k)]$$

$$[\Sigma_j w_j E(\tilde{R}_j) - R_F] = 0$$

Solving for $E(\tilde{R}_j)$ and defining $S_M = [E(\tilde{R}_M) - R_F]/\sigma(\tilde{R}_M)$—the market price of risk reduction—yields the expected rate of return on firm j when j is held in a market portfolio; namely,[18]

$$E(\tilde{R}_j) = R_F + S_M[\text{cov}(\tilde{R}_j, \tilde{R}_M)/\sigma(\tilde{R}_M)] \tag{4.3}$$

Note that in the equilibrium relationship for the individual firm described in (4.3), R_F, S_M, and $\sigma(\tilde{R}_M)$ are aggregate market variables and only faintly related to firm j itself.[19] The only firm-specific variable on the right-hand side is $cov(\tilde{R}_j,\tilde{R}_M)$ which is the risk firm j brings to the market portfolio. Thus the CAPM indicates that in equilibrium the expected rate of return on project j is related to the risk it contributes to the market portfolio of risky projects. This is the fundamental insight provided by portfolio theory; namely, the relevant risk that goes into the equilibrium determination of the expected rate of return on asset j is the risk it contributes to the market portfolio of risky assets. This is in contrast to the older view, which suggested that the return on an asset was related to the risk attached to that asset considered in isolation. If risky assets are held in a portfolio then this older view would appear to be incorrect. In fact it is the central normative message of portfolio theory that much of the risk attached to an individual asset when held in isolation can be removed by the simple expedient of holding that asset in a portfolio. Diversification, then, is a kind of social insurance scheme in that it eliminates certain socially unnecessary risks from the economy, although in actual economies transaction costs and other impediments may prevent this idealization from being fully attained.

Consider next the equilibrium relationship between risk and return for the market portfolio itself. This relationship is obtained by summing the individual equations expressed in (4.3) for all j firms in the risky sector.

$$\Sigma_j w_j E(\tilde{R}_j) = E(\tilde{R}_M) = R_F + S_M \sigma(\tilde{R}_M) = R_F + S_M[\sigma^2(\tilde{R}_M)/\sigma(\tilde{R}_M)] \quad (4.4a)$$

or

$$E(\tilde{R}_M) - R_F = S_M \sigma(\tilde{R}_M) \quad\quad\quad\quad\quad\quad\quad\quad\quad\quad\quad (4.4b)$$

Equation (4.4) describes the market identity that holds in equilibrium, given the definition of S_M.

The final job before us in this section is to convert the equilibrium rate of return expressions given in (4.3) and (4.4) into their monetary value certainty equivalents.[20] For firm j we obtain the following expression.[21]

$$P_j = \frac{1}{1 + R_F}\{E(\tilde{X}_j) - S_M[cov(\tilde{X}_j,\tilde{X}_M)]/\sigma(\tilde{X}_M)\} \quad\quad (4.5)$$

Likewise for the entire risky sector we obtain[22]:

$$P_M = \frac{1}{1 + R_F}\{E(\tilde{X}_M) - S_M \sigma(\tilde{X}_M)\} \quad\quad\quad\quad\quad\quad (4.6)$$

Both expressions convey the notion that investors price up expected returns at $1/(1 + R_F)$, a positive capitalization rate, indicating expected return is favorably regarded by investors, while pricing down the relevant risk by the negative capitalization rate $-S_M/(1 + R_F)$, which indicates investors are unfavorably disposed to this dimension of investment return.

Both R_F and S_M are important prices in the economic system. The risk-free rate has already been discussed in Chapters 2 and 3, and we will therefore focus our attention here on S_M, the market trade-off between risk and return. As we mentioned above, S_M is the market price of risk reduction in that it informs the household of the price they must pay in terms of forgone excess returns—returns over and above the riskless rate—in order to reduce the risk of their individual portfolios, by a given arbitrary amount. Like any other price, S_M must evolve out of the interplay of the supply and demand for the productive factor input in the economy. Up to this point in our development of the CAPM it has been assumed that the supply of this input is fixed and the job is merely one of allocating the fixed input across the risky sector to the individual risky firms.

Suppose, however, we use the CAPM within a partial equilibrium context. It then may be the case that the model can provide some first-order approximations to some important questions bearing on supply and demand for inputs in general. For example, with regard to supply it would seem, other things remaining equal, that a change in S_M would have some predictable effect on how households might allocate their savings between the riskless and risky sectors, much like a change in the rate of interest would affect savings in a certain world. Likewise, with respect to the demand for inputs in the risky sector, firms would be more willing to create new risky projects if somehow the creation of these projects would contribute to a higher or more favorable economy-wide trade-off between risk and return in the new equilibrium. Yet it must be remembered that these observations are merely interesting hunches that might have some empirical validity, for, strictly speaking, they cannot be deduced within the CAPM developed up to this point. If we wish to explore these and other interesting issues within the context of this model, it is obvious that we must be prepared to forsake certain implications of its general equilibrium nature. It should not be surprising that applied research in financial markets has proceeded in this direction, and a number of issues have already been and continue to be analyzed by financial economists. In Chapters 5 and 6 we will use the CAPM in this same spirit in order to explore several issues that might be of concern to government policy-makers. In order to prepare the way for this work we will now consider several implications of the model bearing on financial management. These implications, in turn, will provide the motivation for developing an alternative model of capital market equilibrium in Chapter 9.

Policy Implications of the Capital Asset Pricing Model

Before concluding this chapter it will be useful to consider several financial policy implications of the model, policy issues that have been keenly debated by both academics and practitioners in the field for some time. In the course of this discussion we will soon discover the limitations of the model for purposes of analyzing those financial issues centering around wealth redistribution among the input contributors.

The financial policy issues we will now discuss have been treated in the literature as two separate issues, but as we will see they are essentially two sides of the same coin. The first to be considered is whether the merger of two or more firms into a single entity can ever provide a lasting benefit to the stockholders of the separate firms. The second issue concerns the relative merits of financing the productive inputs of the individual firms with various combinations of debt and equity securities. In approaching the second question we first consider the problem in which the debt securities in question are riskless and then proceed to the case of risky debt. The consideration of risky debt raises, for the first time, the question of nonfulfillment of contracts in the economy and the implications, if any, for the real investment decisions of firms. Yet, as we will see, the CAPM is remarkably resilient to imperfections of this sort. Whether it should be, of course, is another question, which one must decide for oneself.

First consider the question of merger, but where the merger has no effect whatsoever on the operating efficiency of the separate firms. Since the productive opportunity sets in the CAPM are really individual projects with their own distributions, the problem really is to determine the collection of projects that constitute what we recognize to be a firm. In the absence of scale economies (a subject we take up in Chapter 5) or other operating considerations, it is clear that within the framework of the CAPM there is no optimal way of combining projects into security-issuing firms.[23] What this simply means is that if the individual firms or projects are already in the market portfolio before the merger, then they will still be in after the merger with no effect whatsoever on the risk-return trade-off on the market portfolio. If neither the risk nor return on the market portfolio is altered as a result of the merger, then surely we must expect the current valuation on that portfolio to remain unchanged since, as we observed in equation (4.6):

$$P_M = \Sigma_j P_j = \frac{1}{1 + R_F} \left\{ \Sigma_j E(\tilde{X}_j) - S_M \left[\frac{\Sigma_j \text{cov}(\tilde{X}_j, \tilde{X}_M)}{\sigma(\tilde{X}_M)} \right] \right\} \qquad (4.7)$$

In other words, merger does nothing to aggregate expected return and risk in the system, and since all investors hold this market portfolio, no one is made better off as a result of the combining of two or more firms. Thus, within the framework of CAPM as developed up to this point, there is no one best $E(\tilde{X}_j)$ for project j. This, of course, should not be surprising since individual firms have no particular importance in a world where every investor holds the market portfolio; or what amounts to the same thing, each individual investor holds the same proportion of the total stock in every risky firm. If we tend to flinch at this result it is only because deep down in our hearts we do not believe that all households invest in the market portfolio. Notwithstanding this somewhat unbelievable assumption, there still is little evidence that mergers provide lasting benefits for outside shareholders of the raiding company.[24]

A second issue that has been analyzed within the CAPM framework is whether a given stock of productive inputs will command different capital market valuations depending upon the types of securities used in the financing.[25] This is an ancient but still-debated issue, and earlier in this chapter we discussed MMs side of this argument. Recall that they concluded—on the basis of a number of similar assumptions used to develop CAPM—that the debt-equity mix used to finance a given stock of inputs had no effect on the market valuation placed on these inputs.[26] Moreover, the convincing demonstration they provided for their view turned out to be independent of how investors actually valued capital market claims. In other words, whether investors used a two-parameter or three-parameter or n-parameter model to value securities was immaterial for their debt-equity proposition just so long as in equilibrium, perfectly correlated outputs command the same capital market price. Consequently, if the debt-equity irrelevance proposition is true, independent of how valuations are rationally determined in the capital market, then surely the proposition will be just as true in the two-parameter model described in this chapter.[27]

The fact that varying mixtures of common stock and safe debt will have no effect on firm or project valuation should by now not be surprising when equilibrium valuations are described by the CAPM. The reason it should not be surprising is the same as that offered in the discussion of the merits of nonsynergistic merger; namely, the underlying aggregate expected return and risk on the market portfolio are unaffected by these kinds of policies, and it is the market portfolio which is held by all investors. To see this, combine the separate firms in the riskless and risky sectors in the following way:

$$(P_F + P_M) = \frac{1}{1 + R_F}\{[X_F + E(\tilde{X}_M)] - S_M\sigma(\tilde{X}_M)\} \qquad (4.8)$$

where P_F and X_F represent the aggregate current and second-period valuations, respectively, of firms in the riskless sector. Now suppose firm f in the riskless sector F (financed with safe bonds) and firm j in the risky sector or market portfolio M (financed with common stock) decide to merge. Will this merger affect the right-hand side of equation (4.8)? In this connection, remember that R_F is the given rate of return on a riskless productive opportunity governed by constant returns to scale. Moreover, we know that adding the constant x_f to the random variable $\tilde{X}_M$ will have no effect on the risk in the system as measured by $\sigma(\tilde{X}_M)$, since adding or subtracting a positive constant to a random variable leaves any parameter associated with the second moment of the distribution unchanged. Consequently the only effect of the merger is on the first term on the right-hand side of equation (4.8) where X_F falls by the amount x_f and the total output in the risky sector rises to $E(\tilde{X}_M) + x_f$.[28] The end result is that the right-hand side of (4.8) remains unchanged, and we can safely conclude that the merged value of a safe and risky project is not greater than their separate values considered in isolation. What the CAPM indicates is that if there are riskless and risky projects coexisting in the economy, there is no need to merge them into a single entity in order to obtain their combined patterns of returns over future states of nature since it is possible to hold both in a portfolio. Moreover, if they were combined in a single firm, then spinning off the riskless project would also have no effect on the aggregate amount of risk and return generated in the economy and therefore would not change the opportunities available to portfolio investors.

What does all this have to do with the debt-equity controversy? Simply this: both MM and CAPM assume an economy where riskless and risky projects coexist. They must coexist since both riskless and risky rates of return coexist in their systems. The question then becomes whether it makes any difference—in terms of opportunities available to portfolio investors in the system—if: (1) a single firm owns both types of projects; and (2) if the claims to the future outputs are called debt (for the safe project), and equity (for the risky project), or just equity for both projects. Consequently, if it is true that portfolio investors' opportunities in some sense expand when each individual firm finances its projects with one unique combination of safe debt and risky equity, then the unmistakable implication is that there is one best way to combine the given riskless and risky projects in the economy into the legal entities known as firms. This, on the other hand, is nothing more than the merger question, and within the framework of CAPM there can be no one best way of combining projects into firms. Of course this does not necessarily mean that methods of financing production and the combining of projects to form firms is necessarily irrelevant, since ultimately these are empirical questions. Rather, our discussion merely points out that the indeterminacy of forming optimal combinations of projects into firms is the logical implication of the assumption set used to develop CAPM and that the debt-equity controversy is nothing more than this same question regarding the uniqueness of the individual firm.

Yet if we were to ask flesh-and-blood managers if these financial decisions are irrelevant, they would invariably say "no." Moreover, if we even casually perused the popular financial press we would soon discover that a great deal of attention is devoted to company financial matters that we have just shown to be irrelevant. What is the matter here? Are managers and financial writers ignorant or do they see, or think they see, something that is not seen by our CAPM? It is probably safe to conclude that managers and financial writers are not ignorant. Rather, they look around and see a somewhat different environment, or set of assumptions that characterize the environment, than we have assumed in our development of the CAPM. Basically they believe they see a world in which certain financial decisions can, and will, have an effect on the operating decisions of the firm, and this we carefully avoided in our CAPM world. Whether their view or that of CAPM is a more accurate view of actual financial markets and business behavior is an empirical matter, but this in turn is nothing more than a statement about the questions posed to the model. In this connection we must never lose sight of the fact that just because a model is useful in thinking about some questions and issues—such as the social risk-return trade-off—it need not be equally useful in analyzing every conceivable issue in financial economics.

With regard to the CAPM this would seem to be the case for all those questions and issues centering around financial failure in its various forms.[29] Financial failure is not a problem in most equilibrium versions of the theory of finance. On the other hand, it is perceived to be a very real problem for business managers personally and the health of the economy in general. Like civil war and revolution, society can only tolerate small doses of financial failure. We will now attempt to interpret both contending positions starting first with the modern theory of finance.

Toward this end we will begin by assuming that there are no costs associated with financial failure in its various forms. What this means is that lawyers and accountants are not required to adjudicate disputes between creditors and stockholders who supply the initial inputs. In addition it will also mean that the human and nonhuman assets that constitute the firm can be sold in a perfect secondhand market and that the capital market value and secondhand asset value of the firm are one and the same at every point in time. With these assumptions it is possible to show that even in the presence of potential financial failure the choice of a capital structure is irrelevant. There are two closely related arguments that lead to this conclusion and both are worth considering.

One of the arguments is articulated in a paper by Stiglitz (1974) and has the merit of not imposing a specific valuation model on the analysis. He poses the following interesting problem. Suppose there is an all-equity firm with a given production plan that is part of a given general equilibrium. Suppose, furthermore, that for some reason the firm wishes to alter its capital structure to include debt obligations which in certain future states of the world will not be fulfilled due to an insufficiency of funds. Thus the new financing plan carries with it the possibility of financial failure. Will this new financing plan result in a capital market valuation for the firm's given production plan different from the initial plan of all equity. "No," argues Stiglitz. "No" because any discrepancy in the market valuations of the two financial plans would provide an incentive for some financial intermediary to step in and buy the securities of the so-called inferior financial plan (equity and risky debt) and issue on its own account securities of the so-called superior financial plan (equity securities) and pocket any difference in market valuations for the firm as a pure profit. Any individual investor could then buy the equity securities of the intermediary and obtain the same pattern of returns over all future states of the world that he could when holding the equity of the firm in question in the initial general equilibrium. If financial intermediaries were costless to organize and operate this would indeed be an effective force in insulating the market value of production plans from the associated financial plan. Moreover, even in the presence of operating costs there must be something to this viewpoint given the rapid growth rate of financial intermediaries in the United States during this century, as documented by Goldsmith (1958) and emphasized in the writings of Gurley and Shaw.[30] In fact the general line of this argument can be traced back to Gurley and Shaw where they clearly spelled out the view that the *raison d'etre* of financial intermediaries was to convert the relatively unattractive features of bonds and stocks of operating firms (primary securities, in their terminology) into a relatively attractive financial package for individual investors.[31] It was an important insight by Stiglitz to see that their argument would render financial planning irrelevant in an equilibrium context.

The CAPM itself might be invoked to demonstrate the irrelevancy of financial policy in the presence of costless financial failure. After all, if the debt securities of a firm are risky they, too, will be included in the market portfolio of risky securities and priced in equilibrium according to the expected return and risk they contribute to the market portfolio. Thus if B_j represents today's price on risky bonds and D_j tomorrow's investment proceeds from holding these bonds, then:

$$B_j = \frac{1}{1 + R_F} \left\{ E(\tilde{D}_j) - S_M \left[\frac{\mathrm{cov}(\tilde{D}_j, \tilde{X}_M)}{\sigma(\tilde{X}_M)} \right] \right\} \qquad (4.9)$$

Since the structure of the market portfolio (in terms of the weight of the individual risky securities) is identical for all investors, we have the result that every investor owns the same fraction of any firm's risky debt as he or she does of that firm's risky equity. Thus, if investor i owns α percent of the stock of firm j, then he or she will own α percent of the risky debt. The end result is that every stockholder in a particular firm owes the debt to himself, and the differences between debt and equity become meaningless. If the differences between debt and equity are meaningless in this framework of analysis, then surely financial failure is not a problem.

Finally, we can even go one step further and argue that CAPM can accommodate certain costs associated with financial failure, such as legal and accounting costs. After all, these costs appear elsewhere in the economy as expected returns and portfolio risks on law and accounting firms and thus do not represent a drain to the system. Thus, as long as we own the law and accounting firms and as long as they are correctly priced according to the CAPM valuation equation, financial policy even in the presence of costly financial failure is still irrelevant.

Modern portfolio theory presents a picture of a very congenial world. Bondholders and stockholders as input contributors march into an unknown future arm in arm, sharing in whatever pleasant or adverse outcome nature may throw their way. In this world of complete diversification it would be unthinkable for the left hand (the hand holding α percent of the firm's risky bonds) to declare bankruptcy on the right hand (the hand holding α percent of the firm's stock). Moreover, if the left hand would, for some unknown reason, stoop so low, then everyone would eventually be saved by owning α percent of the financial undertakers of the system: the law and accounting firms. While this scenario surely does not describe class conflict among investors in modern capital markets, it does point the way towards a better future. Diversification is a powerful concept and movements in that direction would do much to reduce the socially unnecessary risks that exist when diversification tends to be incomplete.

Thus portfolio theory describes an ideal environment for the sharing of the risks and returns associated with capitalist production. On the other hand, our skeptical manager and financial writer see a different environment where, among other things, bondholders and stockholders in any given firm tend to be separate individuals. In their view it is incredible to think that individuals hold a market portfolio. Moreover, they would list such factors as transaction costs, differing expectations concerning the return distributions for all firms in the economy, differing investment horizons, and tax considerations as reasons for the fact that the structure of portfolios will differ for individual investors. These institutional factors—reinforced in many instances by legal restrictions—would tend to segment the capital market in the sense that any given portfolio investor will have a net position in either the stocks or bonds of a particular firm and hence a different perspective on the management of the firm's productive resources. This is why bankruptcy is so much feared and sensationally reported in the financial press. It represents a visible point of conflict between those who supply the inputs to firm production in exchange for different types of claims to the second-period output. This is why bondholders and stockholders will, in general, differ in terms of their perspectives on how the firm should be managed, and this is also why managers are always constrained in their operating decisions when production is financed with debt and equity.

Ultimately, the belief by practical managers that financing and operating decisions are interdependent must rest on market imperfections of one sort or another. Among other things it implies that a given *ex-post* return will be given different interpretations depending upon the firm's capital structure.[32] In particular, this means that those outcomes that threaten to disturb the existing bondholder-stockholder relationship are of more concern than that same outcome when there is no bondholder-stockholder relationship simply because there are no (or fewer) bondholders. These information imperfections would then have to extend to the output and input markets of the firm. For example, when a firm lands in a state of financial distress, the event is conveyed very quickly to the product markets. Suppliers (including personnel) may not provide inputs on the same terms as they did before the financial distress. Likewise, customers may not purchase the firm's products at the same prices they did before the financial difficulty, particularly if they require servicing in the future. Thus, when the market for information is imperfect, financial distress and failure provide a blunt and important signalling function for customers and suppliers alike. In this way the financial decisions of yesterday might affect the operating decisions of today. In this kind of world the firm has a reputation to maintain and this reputation can change over time just as it can for an individual. In a world of perfect information we would neither observe slander (who would believe it?) nor the resulting libel suits. Similarly for firms, the distinctions between the various categories of financial distress that threaten bondholder-stockholder relationships would have no differential effect on the firm's operations, irrespective of the debt-equity decision, when all markets are perfect. Yet both are observed in practice as well as the large conflict-resolution industry (law and accounting firms) they give rise to, and if these conflicts are thought to be worth studying they will have to be explored within a different framework than that provided by CAPM.

Before leaving our discussion of the CAPM we might pause and ask whether this model could serve as a useful artificial economy in which to study the problems and issues associated with inflation and unemployment, for that, after all, is the ultimate objective of our inquiry. Recall again from our previous discussions that the principal evils of unanticipated inflation and involuntary unemployment lie in their income and consumption distribution consequences. The unemployed agent for some reason seems to be precluded from participating in productive activity, and the end result is that total production and consumption are below their potential levels. Yet what is even more important from the individual perspective is that the involuntarily unemployed agent observes his or her share of consumption falling drastically relative to the consumption of employed agents, and when this happens on a relatively large scale, political adjustments have historically taken place. With regard to unanticipated inflation the distributional consequences are somewhat different. Here the problem is one in which the consumption possibilities of employed agents are distributed in a way that does not necessarily reflect their factor input contribution or technological risk confronted, but instead partly reflects the kinds of contracts they make with one another when cooperating in productive activity in an economy where contracts are denominated in money. Here, too, there have historically been limits within which this kind of redistribution can take place without evoking a political adjustment.

In the CAPM set-up presented in this chapter unemployment and inflation do not seem to be the social problems they appear to be in actual economies, judging from political and popular journalistic discussions. It is instructive to see why this is the case. To begin with, in the model presented above, there were no barriers to investing resources in either the riskless or risky sectors. This, in fact, was an important assumption underlying the model. The end result is that the resources of agents are never involuntarily unemployed in the CAPM world nor will their allocation be inefficient. As we will see in Chapter 5, this result is due to the assumptions of perfect markets and constant returns to scale in production. Moreover, with respect to the distributional impact of inflation, this model assumed that input contributors received pro-rata claims to the end-of-period output in both the riskless and risky sectors. Thus, an agent providing α percent of the inputs to both of these sectors will surely receive α percent of the combined realized output in the next period—no more or less. It is impossible in this world to contribute α percent of the input to the risky sector and receive less or more than α percent of the output, depending upon whether the claim held by the input contributor is fixed or variable in terms of money (which incidentally we have not shown exists in this model) and whether the money price of output unexpectedly rises or falls. This is because the input contributors hold both debt- and equity-type contracts in the same proportions if they coexist, and consequently there can be no redistributions of real returns based solely on contract forms.[33] If the distributional consequences of unemployment and inflation are thought to be important then it would seem that a different class of artificial model economies will be required. A number of such model economies will be presented in Chapters 7–10.

Summary and Conclusions

In this chapter we have described one possible extension of the two-period model into an uncertain economic environment, namely, the capital asset pricing model. On the basis of certain assumptions the model suggests that the portfolio of an individual investor could be separated into a riskless component (which differs in magnitude across investors for reasons of differences in wealth and risk aversion) and a risky component (which in *structure* will be identical for all investors).[34] This important separation property not only implies an equilibrium trade-off between risk and return, but also what has come to be called a "closed-form" expression describing how individual risky assets should relate to one another. Recently a great deal of academic and applied research has been concerned with the question of just how good a job CAPM can do in describing relative valuations of individual assets or portfolios of assets. Unfortunately the social risk-return trade-off generated by the model has received less attention in the literature, and to partly repair this omission we intend to devote the next several chapters to several issues in applied economics where this economy-wide price plays an important role.

The two-parameter model provides some useful insights into a number of interesting economic phenomena. To begin with, the portfolio approach provides a rationalization for diversification. The objective of this diversification is to obtain the largest possible portfolio return for a given amount of portfolio risk, an eminently sensible objective for households that are risk averse. An important implication of this portfolio view of investment behavior is that the valuation of an individual risky asset is related to the risk that asset contributes to the overall portfolio of risky assets and not just to the risk of the individual asset standing in isolation.

A second implication of the model suggests that nonsynergistic mergers of projects or firms can be expected to have no effect on market valuations because individual portfolio investors can—and clearly do, in the CAPM— perform the mergers themselves. The other way of addressing this issue is that what constitutes the firm as a collection of projects is unspecified in this theory. In perfect markets it is the projects themselves that command value in the capital market, and how those projects are put together to form security issuing firms is irrelevant. It is so irrelevant that portfolio investors will not, according to the theory, pay a premium in the market place to have managers perform this task for them.[35]

Finally, the model suggests that under a broad range of assumptions the financing of a given stock of productive capital, as between debt and equity securities, is irrelevant. In this conection we showed that for the case of riskless debt this was equivalent to the above-described merger question, namely, the merging of a riskless project and a risky project. This type of merger was shown not to expand the opportunity set confronting portfolio investors, and hence the combined values, in principle, must equal the sum of the individual values of the projects. Moreover, the same implication emerges when the debt securities are risky and even when there are costly penalties associated with the realization of the risk, just so long as the penalties do not leave the system.[36] Here we personally feel the theory shows some signs of stress in the sense that the model was not designed with this question in mind. To the extent that bankruptcy is associated with wealth redistribution within a single firm, the CAPM with separation does not seem to be the appropriate analytical vehicle. In this same vein, inflation, insofar as it redistributes wealth between bondholders and stockholders within the same firm, is not a very relevant problem within CAPM. The real question, then, becomes: For what class of problems is it fruitful to use the CAPM and for what problems should we look elsewhere? This if course is up to the individual researcher, and different researchers have, in the past arrived (and will continue in the future to arrive), at different answers. If they did not there would be no fun in finance. In the following chapters we will reveal our own personal preferences.

Notes

1. Miller (1977) and Miller and Scholes (1978) have argued that government taxation will not alter these results when both corporate and personal taxes are taken into account. Their analysis assumes that investors are able to arbitrage away the presumed tax disadvantage associated with dividend payments compared to capital gains, and that the market rate of return on corporate debt must be high enough in equilibrium to offset the higher personal tax rate applied to bond income compared to the tax rate applied to stock income. The end result is that: (1) portfolio investors can blunt (and in the limit, completely negate) the government's attempt to distinguish between capital gain and dividend income; and (2) portfolio investors will price bonds and stocks so that these securities reflect the differential personal tax treatment that applies to their respective incomes so that, in an equilibrium, firms will be indifferent to financing production with debt or equity.

2. Their argument is that if two firms have identical patterns of returns (earnings before interest and taxes) over all states of the world, then they are perfect substitutes from the point of view of portfolio investment, and their capital market valuations must be identical in equilibrium. If for some reason they are not, then a profitable arbitrage opportunity exists in the marketplace, and arbitrage profits cannot exist in the market when the market is in equilibrium. To show this let:

1. $V_U = S_U =$ the value of the stock in an all equity firm.
2. $V_L = S_L + D =$ the value of the stock and debt of a levered firm.
3. $X = X_U = X_L =$ the average return (as defined above) that would accrue to those who held the securities issued by U and L in perpetuity.
4. $rD =$ the interest payments on debt securities.

Now for all those states of the world where $X > rD$, it must be the case for some individual i that a given investment in one company, say U, can be perfectly replicated in the other. Thus, if individual i owns α percent of the shares in firm U that provides an investment income of αX, then a corresponding investment of α percent in the shares and debt of company L would provide $\alpha(X - rD) + \alpha rD = \alpha X$ or the same income as in company U. Since this income is no better or worse than the corresponding income in U, the capital market valuations of the two firms must be identical.

Their dividend irrelevance proposition follows the same line of reasoning outlined in Chapter 2 for a certain world. Essentially it asserts that individual i's optimal consumption and portfolio plans at any given point in time is in no way dependent on any particular firm's dividend policy when capital markets are perfect. The reason dividend policy is irrelevant is that individual i who owns stock in firm j can declare his or her own dividend by buying or selling the appropriate number of shares in j if j's dividend policy does not meet i's consumption and portfolio requirements. In a perfect capital market, investment in j is not the indissoluble pact that Keynes thought marriage was, and investment in securities should be, but rather a union to be maintained only as long as it fulfills the consumption-investment requirements of individual i.

3. Words like firms and uncertainty are not completely unambiguous concepts in financial economics, and we shall use the terms somewhat loosely, although there will be different shades of meaning at several points in our inquiry. Roughly speaking, firms will be viewed as productive opportunity sets for converting present inputs into a multitude of possible future outputs, one of which will actually occur at a specificed date in the future. Moreover, each productive opportunity set will be owned in varying degrees by all consumer-investors in the economy. The uncertainty in the system pertains to the fact that consumer-investors today do not know which output will actually materialize tomorrow. The tradition has been to describe the multitude of possible future outputs in terms of some probability distribution and then define the economic risk of investment as some measure of dispersion of that probability distribution.

4. The contingent commodity models of Arrow (1964) and Debreu (1959) represent the most elaborate descriptions of financial contracts that have been devised by economists to date. These contracts represent a promise to deliver a specified quantity of future output given that a certain sequence of events, called states of the world, occur. When the market is complete—that is, when there are as many distinct contracts as states of the world—the financial system will be optimal in the sense that every individual consumer-investor can in effect obtain insurance for every insurable risk. This should not be construed to mean that the financial system eliminates the consequences of risk, but only that it optimally allocates it across different consumer-investors. Natural disasters, such as crop failures, will still cause people to starve. Transaction costs and the problem of "moral hazard" have been cited as reasons why we do not observe this kind of financial system in actual economies.

5. Even reference works reviewing developments in this rapidly growing area are extensive. For a sample of this literature and its controversies see Arrow (1965) (1970), Hirschleifer (1970), Jensen (1972), Fama and Miller (1972), Mossin (1973) (1977), and Dreze and Mirrlees (1974) among others.

6. The effect of uncertainty on the initial consumption-saving decision is ambiguous. For example, an increase in perceived risk on the one hand would suggest a reduction in saving (the substitution effect associated with the increased undesirability of saving), but on the other hand it might be argued that saving should rise in order

to assure some minimum future consumption (the so-called risk effect). Economic theory alone cannot tell us, in any general way, which effect will dominate. For a discussion of this issue see Sandmo (1969) (1970) (1974).

7. All uncertainties in this chapter will reside in the firms' activities and not in the condition of the household in the second period.

8. The normal distribution is fully described by its mean and variance and has a number of desirable properties as far as portfolio analysis is concerned. Strictly speaking, however, normality cannot apply in reality since the negative output that can be produced (e.g., cleanup and removal costs) is limited by the legal institution of limited liability to the households' investment in the firm. We can rescue this inadequacy by assuming the firms' output in finite time is distributed log-normally which in turn collapses to a normal distribution in the limit of infinitesimal time. In the following we shall not worry about such fine points and merely regard normality as a convenient approximation, or alternatively argue that the investor believes that the bulk of relevant information about the distribution is contained in its first two central moments. This is the kind of " . . . higher Heaven rejects the lore . . . " argument that the two-parameter CAPM is built upon.

9. Portfolio decisions are initial allocations of the investment input to various firms in the economy.

10. This investment could represent riskless storage and thus entail a cost or negative rate of return.

11. Stochastic constant returns to scale for the firm will be defined to be a situation where return and risk expand or contract at the same rate as the investment of the firm. In the CAPM model presented below the specific definition of stochastic constant returns to scale is one where the expected rate of return of firm j, $E(R_j)$, and the covariance of j's return with the returns on all risky firms in the economy, $\operatorname{cov}(R_j, R_M)$, is constant and independent of the level of j's investment.

12. Convex indifference curves in mean-standard deviation space (the measures of return and risk in the two-parameter model) have been shown by Tobin (1958) to follow from joint normality of risky asset returns or when investor utility functions are quadratic in return. Both demonstrations are relatively straightforward and can be found in the leading textbooks in finance. We will only replicate the quadratic utility demonstration of this proposition, partly because we have already commented in note 8 on some of the technical difficulties associated with normal distributions describing the return-generating process. Consider, then, the following utility of return function.

(i) $U(R) = aR + bR^2, a > 0, b < 0,$ and $R \leq -a/2b$

where $U(R) = $ the utility of return R; $a,b = $ constants. Such a function over its permissible range of Rs is concave when $U(R)$ is plotted against R. This conveys the idea of risk aversion and the diminishing marginal utility of return in that the increment in utility associated with $(R + \triangle R)$ is less than the decrement in utility associated with $(R - \triangle R)$ for any given R and equal probability of a given $\triangle R$. From the utility function described in (i) it is possible to derive an indifference curve for the consumer-investor. To do this, take expectations of (i) and add and subtract $b[E(R)]^2$ to obtain:

(ii) $E[U(R)] = aE(R) + b E(R^2) + b[E(R)]^2 - b[E(R)]^2$

or

(iii) $E[U(R)] = aE(R) + b\,\sigma^2(R) + b[E(R)]^2$

since $\sigma^2(R)$, the variance of R, is defined to be $E(R^2) - E(R)^2$. Setting (iii) equal to some constant c and differentiating with respect to $\sigma(R)$ yields the slope of the indifference curve.

(iv) $dE(R)/d\sigma(R) = -2b\sigma(R)/[a + 2bE(R)] \geq 0.$

Note that the indifference curve has a slope of zero when $\sigma(R) = 0$.

   An important criticism of the quadratic utility function is that it has been shown by Arrow (1965) and others to imply increasing absolute risk aversion; that is to say, give any investor additional wealth and he or she will revise their portfolio by reducing the absolute amount of wealth invested at risk from what it was before the increase in wealth. Most economists conclude that this odd behavior is sufficient reason to reject the quadratic utility function as an adequate reflection of investor preferences. As an approximation the quadratic has its supporters. In this connection see Samuelson (1970) for a defense when risks are small.

   13. This was evidenced by the relatively poor performance of investment equations in many of the early econometric models. The instability of the investment equation—due in large measure to uncertainty—no doubt dampened the enthusiasm for an aggressive countercyclical monetary policy. Thus Keynes (1936), in his conclusion of Chapter 12, was personally skeptical of the effectiveness of monetary policy.

   14. Early developers of the model included Treynor (1961), Sharpe (1964), Lintner (1965), and Mossin (1966).

   15. The implication of this analysis is that if any investor wants to invest any portion of his endowment in the risky sector, he is obliged to invest it in all firms in the sector and in exactly the same manner as anyone else investing in this sector. This efficient and complete diversification was not necessary when the environment was certain, for then every security on the capital market was a perfect substitute for every other security.

   16. How different this theory is from the theory of liquidity preference developed by Keynes (1936) and to be discussed in Chapter 7. In the theory of liquidity preference all market participants are speculators holding either a safe asset or a single risky security. For every individual investor there is a single trigger price on the risky security which causes his or her investments to be either the safe asset or the risky security, but not both. Whether an investor is in the risky security or not depends upon whether he or she is bullish or bearish regarding the future course of risky security prices as perceived by that investor. It is possible to draw a smooth demand curve for the safe asset by assuming a distribution of expectations among investors regarding the future course of the risky security's price. Tobin (1958) achieves the same smooth demand curve for the riskless asset by assuming risk-averse investors holding identical expectations of the risky security's future price. The main difference is that Tobin's investors diversify their holdings between the safe and risky security, whereas Keynes' investors are out and out speculators that do not diversify. Both, however, can give rise to a smooth demand function for the riskless asset as some function of future returns on the risky asset.

17. In setting these weights, portfolio investors are providing an initial allocation of the input to the firms in the risky sector. Since the analysis applies for two periods (today and tomorrow), the rate of return includes the initial investment and might more accurately be described as a holding-period rate of return; i.e., one plus the percentage rate of growth of the value of project j would represent $E(R_j)$. Fama (1970) and Merton (1973) have described the conditions which must hold in order for a household to treat a multiperiod consumption-investment problem as a sequence of single-period problems.

18. The intermediate step includes:

(i)
$$\frac{E(\tilde{R}_j) - R_F}{\sigma(\tilde{R}_M)} = -\left\{ \frac{1}{2}\left[\frac{\Sigma_j w_j E(\tilde{R}_j) - R_F}{\sigma^2(\tilde{R}_M)} \right] [2w_j\sigma^2(\tilde{R}_j) \right.$$
$$\left. + 2\sum_{\substack{k \\ j \neq k}} w_k \text{cov}(\tilde{R}_j, \tilde{R}_k)] \right\} [\sigma(\tilde{R}_M)]^{-1}$$

recalling that $\Sigma_j w_j E(\tilde{R}_j) = E(\tilde{R}_M)$ yields the result in equation (4.3). Moreover, the second-order condition for a maximum is satisfied since:

(ii)
$$\frac{\partial^2\{[E(\tilde{R}_M) - R_F]/\sigma(\tilde{R}_M)\}}{\partial w_j^2} = -\frac{S_M}{\sigma(\tilde{R}_M)}\left\{ \frac{\sigma^2(\tilde{R}_j)}{\sigma(\tilde{R}_M)} \right\} < 0$$

19. Firm j, remember, is a constituent part of the market portfolio M and hence its return and risk is embedded in S_M. Strictly speaking the relationships described in (4.3), and later in (4.4), are equilibrium relationships that only hold in equilibrium.

20. Since we do not have money in this economy the term will be taken to mean quantities of the single good.

21. In this connection define: $\tilde{X}_j = P_j(1 + \tilde{R}_j)$, $\tilde{X}_M = P_M(1 + \tilde{R}_M)$, $\text{cov}(\tilde{X}_j, \tilde{X}_M) = P_j P_M \text{cov}(\tilde{R}_j, \tilde{R}_M)$, and $\sigma(\tilde{X}_M) = P_M \sigma(\tilde{R}_M)$, remembering that the Ps are fixed prices while the $\tilde{X}$s and $\tilde{R}$s are random variables. Putting these definitions into (4.3) yields:

(i)
$$\frac{E(\tilde{X}_j) - P_j}{P_j} = R_F + S_M\left[\frac{\text{cov}(\tilde{X}_j, \tilde{X}_M)}{P_j\sigma(\tilde{X}_M)} \right]$$

which in turn can be rewritten as (4.5). As we mentioned in note 11, stochastic constant returns to scale at the firm level is defined to be a situation where $E(\tilde{R}_j)$ and $\text{cov}(\tilde{R}_j, \tilde{R}_M)$ are invariant with respect to the usage of the factor input. What this means is that the firm produces risk and return in fixed proportions.

22. Summing over equation (4.5) we obtain:

(i)
$$\Sigma_j P_j = \frac{1}{1 + R_F}\left\{ \Sigma_j E(\tilde{X}_j) - \frac{S_M[\Sigma_j \text{cov}(\tilde{X}_j, \tilde{X}_M)]}{\sigma(\tilde{X}_M)} \right\}$$

or

(ii)
$$P_M = \frac{1}{1 + R_F}\left\{ E(\tilde{X}_M) - S_M\left[\frac{\sigma^2(\tilde{X}_M)}{\sigma(\tilde{X}_M)} \right] \right\}$$

which is (4.6) in the text.

23. This is the uncertain environment analog of the indeterminable size of the individual firm with constant returns to scale when the environment is certain. In both cases total output (expected output in the uncertain world) is determinable, but how that output is shared between the different firms requires a richer set of assumptions.

24. For some of the more relevant papers dealing with the merger question see Levy and Sarnat (1970), Lewellen (1971), Lintner (1971), Higgins and Schall (1975), Mandelker (1974), and Grossman and Hart (1980).

25. See Hamada (1969) and Rubenstein (1973) for a discussion of this problem within CAPM.

26. When debt is riskless the problem is somewhat contrived in that what is evidently envisioned is a collection of projects within a single firm, some of which are riskless and thereby provide the basis for issuing riskless debt, while others are risky. Up to this point in our development of CAPM we have separated riskless and risky production, but now the two are to be combined in a single firm.

27. The Hamada-Rubenstein CAPM proof of this proposition runs along the following lines. Consider two firms (U an unlevered all-equity company and L a levered company) whose future outputs X are perfectly correlated over all states of nature. According to CAPM we would have:

$$\text{(i)} \quad E(\tilde{R}_U) = R_F + S_M\left[\frac{\text{cov}(\tilde{R}_U,\tilde{R}_M)}{\sigma(\tilde{R}_M)}\right] = \frac{E(\tilde{X})}{P_U}$$

and

$$\text{(ii)} \quad E(\tilde{R}_L) = R_F + S_M\left[\frac{\text{cov}(\tilde{R}_L,\tilde{R}_M)}{\sigma(\tilde{R}_M)}\right] = \frac{[E(\tilde{X}) - R_FD]}{P_L}$$

where D = the market value of debt in firm L, and all other terms are defined as above. Since the $\tilde{X}$s are the same for U and L we can solve (i) and (ii) for $E(\tilde{X})$ and equate them to get:

$$\text{(iii)} \quad P_U\left[R_F + \frac{S_M}{\sigma(\tilde{R}_M)}\{\text{cov}(\tilde{R}_U,\tilde{R}_M)\}\right] =$$
$$P_L\left[\frac{S_M}{\sigma(\tilde{R}_M)}\{\text{cov}(\tilde{R}_L,\tilde{R}_M)\} + R_F(P_L + D)\right]$$

Moreover,

$$\text{(iv)} \quad \text{cov}(\tilde{R}_U,\tilde{R}_M) = \frac{1}{P_U}\text{cov}(\tilde{X},\tilde{R}_M)$$

$$\text{(v)} \quad \text{cov}(\tilde{R}_L,\tilde{R}_M) = \frac{1}{P_L}\text{cov}[(\tilde{X} - R_FD),\tilde{R}_M] = \frac{1}{P_L}\text{cov}(\tilde{X},\tilde{R}_M)$$

The latter is true since adding or subtracting a constant like R_FD from X does not change the distribution of $\tilde{X}$ and hence its covariance. Thus substituting (iv) and (v) into (iii) yields.

$$\text{(vi)} \quad P_UR_F + \frac{S_M}{\sigma(\tilde{R}_M)}\{\text{cov}(\tilde{X},\tilde{R}_M)\} = \frac{S_M}{\sigma(\tilde{R}_M)}\{\text{cov}(\tilde{X},\tilde{R}_M)\} + R_F(P_L + D)$$

which reduces to the MM result,

(vii) $P_U = P_L + D$

Originally the argument was advanced that this proof was in some sense more general than the MM proof which required risk classes; that is, two or more firms like U and L "whose future outputs X are perfectly correlated over all states of nature." Yet as we observed at the beginning of this note the risk class assumption is also built into this CAPM proof. Moreover, the MM proof is not constrained within the framework of any specific valuation model.

Finally, it is not at all clear what this line of reasoning has to do with the invariance issue raised by the so-called traditional school of finance, namely, that two firms whose future outputs and operating incomes are perfectly correlated over all states of nature will have different capital market valuations if their financial structures are different. In this connection we have been using X and $E(\tilde{X})$ in at least two subtly different senses in (i) and (ii) above. In one sense X is defined to be the operating income of the two firms, and risk classes were then defined in terms of these operating incomes. These operating incomes, in turn, evolve from product and factor markets. However, CAPM also uses a definition of X that is based on the capital market income of a security when that security is held for one period. This capital market income is defined to be the sum of dividends paid on the security over the period in question and the difference in the capital market price of the security over the same period. The definition of X that uses capital gains (or losses) plus dividends on securities is a very different definition than one that uses the operating incomes of firms, particularly those in a multiperiod time framework. The issue for the traditionalists is whether or not the capital market measure of X is independent of the debt-equity decisions of firms whose product-factor market measures of X are perfectly correlated over all states of nature. The CAPM proof of the invariance proposition assumes the two definitions of X are equivalent, but of course that is to assume the conclusion. In a one-period world with a beginning and an end, this is a perfectly permissible assumption. Yet this is clearly not the world that the traditionalists had in mind. For this reason we conclude that the CAPM proof presented above cannot be considered a definitive proof of the invariance proposition, at least as the proposition is conceived and argued by traditional financial economists. A one-period equilibrium model of financial markets is just not rich enough to answer this important question.

28. Of course this does not mean that the risky sector is now producing a known output, nor does it mean that production in the risky sector is not governed by constant returns to scale. These concepts apply to individual projects, whereas the words firm and merger refer to combinations of projects.

29. Financial distress and failure are really a set of issues. The term distress is usually taken to mean that the firm is unable to honor all covenants in at least one of its debt contracts at a particular point in time. The creditors are then called in to see whether the covenant in question might be modified temporarily or permanently so that the firm continues operations in much the same way except for the modification in the troublesome covenant. In addition the creditors might require certain changes in the operating policies of the firm. If the covenant in question or the changes required in operating policies cannot be satisfactorily resolved between the creditors and stockholders then ownership is transferred—where allowed by society—to the creditors. This transfer might be called financial failure in that the previous arrange-

ments between creditors and stockholders—who supplied the inputs to the productive process—have failed. Finally, the term financial disaster will be reserved to describe the actual liquidation of the firm and the disbursing of the inputs to other firms in the economy.

30. Especially in their papers (1955) (1956).

31. Gurley and Shaw spoke of direct finance (sales of bonds and stocks directly to individual investors) and indirect finance (sales of bonds and stocks to financial intermediaries who in turn issued their own securities to individual investors), and claimed that a modern capitalist society could only maintain a high level of savings if financial intermediaries continued to grow. They also argued—less persuasively, judging from their critics—that a modern capitalist economy would be more difficult, if not impossible, to stabilize through monetary policy given the growth of nonbank financial intermediaries.

32. The academic form of this argument is known as signalling. For an application in financial economics see Ross (1977).

33. This is not to say that the distribution of end-of-period consumption will be identical to the initial distribution of inputs among agents. Two agents with identical endowments of resources will generally consume different quantities of the end-of-period output if their individual portfolios are comprised of different proportions of investments in the safe and risky sectors. But here any redistribution is the result of the agents' allocation of investment inputs to the two sectors and not the contract forms of the securities.

34. The separation property does not require the existence of a risk-free asset in the system, as demonstrated by Black (1972). For the risk-free asset Black substitutes the so-called zero-beta portfolio, a portfolio whose returns have a zero covariance with the market portfolio and a minimum variance. Black achieves this interesting result by assuming a perfect short-selling mechanism in the capital market; that is, short-sellers have unlimited use of their short-sale proceeds. Many developments of the two-parameter model now proceed along the lines suggested by Black. We have chosen to proceed by assuming risk-free lending and borrowing mainly because in subsequent chapters we will be interested in the risk-return trade-off for society, and this trade-off has a natural interpretation when there is a riskless sector.

35. There is a lesson to be learned here for those who feel the Christian religion is weak because of its many separate denominations. Far from it. There are undoubtedly more churchgoers in an uncertain world when there is greater diversity in religious expression than when the modes of expression are few in number. This must be an important part of the explanation for low church attendance in those countries where one denomination enjoys a monopoly often conferred by government. Those in positions of authority who decide such issues would do well to master the theory of finance in more ways than one.

36. Although no one would argue that expending valuable resources to settle disputes—even though those resources remain in the market portfolio—is not socially wasteful.

—5—

The Allocational Efficiency
of Investment in the
Capital Asset Pricing Model

Introduction

By and large, capital market theory of the kind discussed in Chapter 4 has found its greatest application in the area of micro financial issues and problems. The literature in the 1960s and 1970s presented the closed-form solution of the CAPM as a useful paradigm in which to analyze individual portfolio strategies and company decisions such as those pertaining to what particular combination of projects constitutes an optimal security-issuing firm and whether the capital market value of a given combination of projects is in any way influenced by the choice of the claim structure between debt and equity securities.[1] One exception to this micro orientation has centered around the question of whether there is a socially efficient allocation of productive resources or investment inputs among the different risky projects *qua* firms in the economy when households make portfolio decisions according to the two-parameter model. This is the perfect academic question in that in principle perfect allocative efficiency is one of the most important attributes an artificial economy can possess, but in practice hardly anyone cares. Consequently we can expect to find disagreement.[2] The objective of this chapter will be to re-examine this issue.

Pareto Efficiency in a Certain Environment

In beginning this discussion it will be useful to describe, in a very general way, just what is meant by a Pareto efficient allocation of inputs and outputs under conditions of certainty and competitive equilibrium. Essentially, the underlying idea is that in a perfectly competitive environment with well-behaved preferences and technologies,[3] the pricing and production of particular commodities and factor inputs in the state of equilibrium fully reflects the tastes of individual households weighted by their relative endowments. This of course is what a fully coordinated price system is supposed to achieve in that the structure of output should reflect both the preferences and the economic votes of consumers. It also goes without saying that the resulting allocation is not necessarily fair in some ethical sense since that would imply, among other things, that the distribution of votes or wealth (productive inputs) in the equilibrium was fair. However, fairness cannot be objectively determined, at least by economists.

To push this idea a little further—but not so far as to introduce both an arithmetic and jargon radically different from that used up to this point in the study—consider the following simple economy. In this economy, households as producers own capital, K, and labor, L, whose services in the state of equilibrium are priced, respectively, at r and w. With these two factor inputs firms (say X and Y) produce two commodities, A and B, which in turn are priced in the consumer goods market at $P(A)$ and $P(B)$ in the state of equilibrium.[4] A Pareto efficient equilibrium in this simple economy can then be characterized by three conditions. The first is that the relative prices of the two commodities in the consumer goods market, $P(A)/P(B)$, must be such that in the resulting equilibrium there is no incentive for any two households as consumers—say m and n—to personally trade the amounts of good A and B they obtain within the equilibrium.[5] The second condition is similar but pertains to the factor input market; namely, relative prices for capital and labor services, r/w, must be such that in equilibrium there is no advantage for any two firms (say X and Y) to trade inputs K and L when the market for factor inputs is in the state of equilibrium.[6] The first two conditions, then, ensure that there will be an efficient (i.e., no trade) allocation of total output of $Q(A)$ and $Q(B)$ between individual consumers m and n in the consumer goods market, and an efficient allocation of K and L between individual firms X and Y in the factor market. The relative prices, $P(A)/P(B)$ and r/w, in equilibrium will see to that. One implication of the resulting equilibrium is that on the production side of the economy with a given initial quantity of capital and labor services relatively priced at r/w, some combinations of $Q(A)$ and $Q(B)$ make more sense than others. The notion here is similar to that underlying the Markowitz efficient set discussed in Chapter 4 where some portfolios make more sense than others; that is, the set of all feasible portfolios (or investment allocations to the risky sector) that minimize risk for a given expected return comprises the risk-return efficient set of portfolios. Similarly the set of all feasible combinations of $Q(A)$ and $Q(B)$ that maximizes $Q(A)$ per unit of $Q(B)$ (since in order to produce more A, capital and labor must be released from the production of B) constitutes the efficient set of $Q(A)$ and $Q(B)$, one of which, in equilibrium, will be produced. Economists call this efficient set or optimal combinations of $Q(A)$ and $Q(B)$

the product transformation curve or production possibilities curve since it describes the set of optimal transformations of $Q(A)$ into $Q(B)$ and vice versa for both firms X and Y.[7] With this description of the production side of the economy we can now summarize our discussion into a third and final condition required in order for an equilibrium to be Pareto efficient; namely, the slope of this product transformation curve (or the marginal rate of transforming $Q(A)$ into $Q(B)$ in production) must equal the marginal rate of substitution (the slope of the indifference curve) between A and B in consumption for both individuals m and n. What this means is the following: labor and capital are distributed among firms X and Y producing goods A and B, respectively, in such a way that the marginal rate at which these firms can transfer labor and capital from the production of A into the production of B (or vice versa) is equal to the common rate at which households m and n can substitute the two goods in consumption and still obtain the same level of utility. Satisfaction of this condition means that the economy is producing the combination of $Q(A)$ and $Q(B)$ that perfectly reflects the preferences of individuals m and n weighted by their endowments of capital and labor relatively priced at r/w. Moreover, it is obvious that when these "no trade" marginal conditions hold in a given state of equilibrium, no one individual m can be made better off without making some other individual(s) n worse off, say by redistributing the initial endowments of capital and labor.

The preceding arguments can, and have been, given a simple geometric interpretation. Towards this end consider Figure 5.1. The curve PT represents the product transformation curve or the most efficient combinations of $Q(A)$ and $Q(B)$ that can be produced with the fixed technologies of firms X and Y with the given stocks of capital and labor. The curve CC within the product transformation curve represents the so-called consumer contract curve and has the property that everywhere along the curve the marginal rate of substitution of good A for good B is identical for all consumers m and n. Along this contract curve we display two representative sets of indifference curves for individuals m and n. Note that while the marginal rates of substitution are always equal between m and n at any point along the curve, the rates themselves need not be equal between different points on the curve, and this is illustrated by the two points D and E. Now consider the production equilibrium at point F on the product transformation curve PT. Point F defines one combination of goods A and B produced in the economy, and these amounts are described by $Q(A)^*$ and $Q(B)^*$ on the horizontal and vertical axes. We now construct something called the Edgeworth-Bowley box which is represented in the figure by the rectangle $OQ(A)^* FQ(B)^*$. The Pareto efficient equilibrium associated with point F is given by point E in the box where individual m receives OG out of a possible $OQ(A)^*$ of good A and OJ out of a possible $OQ(B)^*$ of good B. Individual(s) n receive the remainder. How do we know that this particular distribution of goods between m and n repre-

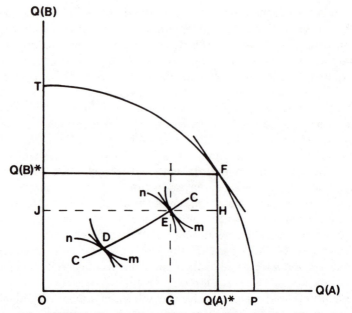

Figure 5.1. Efficient Production and Exchange in a Riskless Environment

sented by point *E* along the contract curve is the Pareto efficient distribution associated with point *F* on the product transformation curve rather than some other point, say *D*? We know this because at point *E* the marginal rate of substitution between goods *A* and *B* in consumption is equal to the marginal rate of transformation in production. At point *D* good *B* is deemed more valuable in terms of good *A* in consumption (i.e., the slope of the tangency at point *D* is less steep than at *E*) compared to the equilibrium at point *E*. If the allocation between *m* and *n* were at point *D*, more of good *B* should be produced than is currently being produced at point *F.* Hence points *F* and *D* cannot constitute a Pareto efficient production and a distribution of that production to *m* and *n* since there would be excess demand for good *B* in the consumer goods market at that equilibrium, and there can be no excess demands in the state of equilibrium.

Pareto Efficiency in an Uncertain Environment with CAPM Allocations

We must now translate this description of a Pareto efficient allocation in a perfectly competitive and certain environment into the uncertain setting in which CAPM allocates inputs and outputs. In doing this along the lines suggested in Chapter 4 it becomes immediately apparent that there are a number of differences between the two environments. The first distinction to be made in an uncertain environment is the obvious one that *ex-ante* plans and *ex-post* results will not, in general, be the same. Which allocation then should be evaluated in terms of Pareto efficiency? It would only seem reasonable to evaluate the *ex-ante* allocation of investment since this in fact is what CAPM is designed to do. The second distinction to be noted is that in the above discussion there were two inputs used to produce two outputs. In CAPM there is only one input—which for convenience we have been calling investment—and one future output. That single future output, however, has two relevant characteristics today from the point of view of individual households; namely, mean or expected aggregate output generated on the investment which is regarded as "good," and the standard deviation on the distribution generating the aggregate output which is regarded as "bad" by portfolio investors.

In this setting and with these distinctions firmly in mind we must now seek the analogues to the product transformation curve and the consumer or household contact curve. Toward this end recall that CAPM, as was developed in Chapter 4, assumes an initial allocation of household endowments to current consumption and risk-free investments. The job then is to allocate the remainder of the endowment between the different projects in the risky sector. One helpful assumption used to develop the closed-form equations of CAPM in Chapter 4 was that of homogeneous expectations regarding the joint probability density of risky individual project outputs, which in effect allows us to pretend that there is a market manager who actually makes the allocations for us. The only job before this market manager is to propose and put into effect an allocation of investment across the individual projects in the risky sector and convey this plan to household savers. With constant returns to scale describing the technology on individual risky projects, the allocation or relative weights across projects will be invariant with respect to the level of investment input advanced to the risky sector. What this allocation across projects will be depends, of course, on the rate of return in the risk-free sector, for as we observed in Chapter 4 the objective of the mutual fund manager is to maximize the risk/return trade-off for portfolio investors. Consequently, for a given level of investment input advanced to our hypothetical mutual fund, there will be a number of different optimal allocations of that investment across individual risky projects, depending upon the rate of return in the risk-free sector. The set of these different optimal plans or allocations across projects is the Markowitz efficient set, and which one is chosen in equilibrium will depend upon the rate of return in the riskless sector. Like the product transformation curve discussed in the previous section, all project allocations of investment that place the market portfolio on the Markowitz efficient frontier are potentially production efficient.

   In the perfect competition and certain world the Pareto efficient allocation of production and consumption could be characterized by an equality between the marginal rate of transforming good A for good B in production and the marginal rate of substituting good A for good B in consumption. In other words it is the allocation where the trade-off between good A and good B in production is equal to the trade-off between good A and good B in the consumer goods market place as reflected in their relative prices. Similarly we must now find that point on the Markowitz frontier where the marginal rate of transformation of market risk (i.e., the standard deviation of return generated in the risky sector) for expected market excess return in the risky productive sector equals the marginal rate of substitution of market risk for expected market excess returns in the capital market for all households as portfolio investors. Another way of saying the same thing is that the optimal allocation of the investment input across projects in the risky sector would be one where the risk/return trade-off in the capital market is exactly equal to the risk/return trade-off in the efficient production of risky output. Thus, as we stated above, once the risk-free allocation and the riskless rate of return are given, the Pareto efficient allocation to the risky sector is determined; namely, it is that particular distribution of investment input that defines the relative weights of the individual risky projects in the market portfolio. The market portfolio, in turn, is the portfolio represented by the tangency of the capital market line with the Markowitz frontier. This capital market line defines the best possible trade-off between risk and return available to households in the securities market.[8] Therefore the tangency portfolio or allocation has the property that the marginal rate of substitution between risk and return in the market for securities equals the marginal rate of transformation of risk for return in efficient risky production.
   The geometric representation of this Pareto efficient equilibrium for a given level of aggregate risky investment and risk-free interest rate is presented in Figure 5.2. The horizontal axis measures portfolio risk, $\sigma(\tilde{R})$, while the vertical axis measures excess expected portfolio return, $[E(\tilde{R}) - R_F]$, which in turn is the reward for bearing portfolio risk. The curve PT in Figure 5.2 represents the Markowitz frontier or the analogue to the product transformation curve in Figure 5.1. This curve describes the optimal trade-off between risk and return in production for a number of different risk-free rates of return. The line CML touching the Markowitz frontier at point M is the capital market line for a particular risk-free interest rate R_F, and this line describes the trade-off between risk and return in the market for securities. Point M is the market portfolio (formed by all of us or, what is the same thing, our hypothetical market manager) and this portfolio contains the optimal allocation of the investment input to the various risky projects in the economy. Of course it is important to remember that individual portfolio investors only have a claim on the market portfolio M, and the notion of a

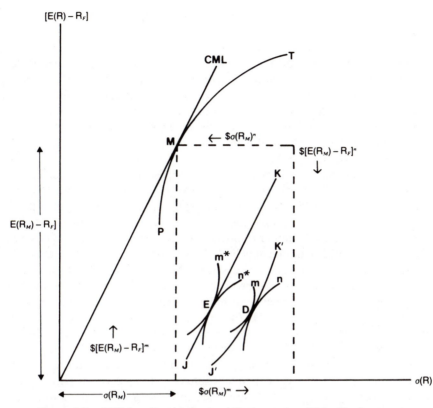

Figure 5.2.   Efficient Production and Exchange in a Risky Environment

firm is somewhat ambiguous at this point. Associated with point M will be an economy-wide quantity of risk denoted by $\sigma(\tilde{R}_M)$ and excess expected return $[E(\tilde{R}_M) - R_F]$.

So far the returns described in Figure 5.2 are percentages or rates of return. Yet to complete the analogy with Figure 5.1 it will be necessary to convert these rates of return into money (or wheat) returns and risk, which in turn can be shared among individual portfolio investors much like good A and good B were shared in Figure 5.1 between individuals m and n. This can be done once it is recognized that Figure 5.2 applies for a given level of investment (say $1) to the risky sector, and therefore the aggregate amounts of dollar risk and return become, respectively, $\$\sigma(\tilde{R}_M)$ and $\$[E(\tilde{R}_M) - R_F]$, which in turn will be shared among the different households in the economy that hold the market portfolio. With this amendment the dotted line box in Figure 5.2 becomes the CAPM analogue to the Edgeworth-Bowley box presented in Figure 5.1. The horizontal length of the box then represents the aggregate amount of dollar risk in the system, $\$\sigma(\tilde{R}_M)$, to be shared by individuals m and n, while the vertical length measures the total excess dollar returns, $\$[E(\tilde{R}_M) - R_F]$, which again must be shared between the two households. The origin for m is the lower left-hand corner of the box, while for n it is the upper right-hand corner. Moving upward from the origin for m along the left vertical axis implies m's share of aggregate dollar excess market return is rising, while moving to the right along the lower horizontal axis implies m's share of dollar market risk is rising. This holds for individual n as well. There we can see that a downward movement along the right vertical axis implies n's share of dollar excess market return is rising, while a movement to the left along the upper horizontal axis implies n is absorbing a greater share of dollar market risk. Consequently individual m's indifference curves (represented by m and m^* in the box) in money risk and return space will be convex to the lower-left-hand corner, while n's (represented by n and n^*) will be convex to the upper right-hand corner of the box. Consider next the lower left–upper right diagonal line JEK which of course must parallel the capital market line CML. This line describes the various ways in which m and n share the dollar risk and dollar excess returns generated on the market portfolio in equilibrium. An upper-right-hand movement along JEK implies m's share of the market portfolio is growing, while n's share is declining. Note also that in order for m or n to obtain α percent of the expected excess returns on the market portfolio, they must also absorb α percent of the market risk when the claim allocation lies along JEK. Claim or security allocations off JEK would imply that n, for example, could obtain α percent of $\$[E(\tilde{R}_M) - R_F]$ by absorbing something less than α percent of $\$\sigma(\tilde{R}_M)$; an impossible outcome given the proportional sharing rules that characterize securities in the CAPM.

Recall from Figure 5.1 that one of the conditions required for Pareto efficiency was that the marginal rates of substitution (the slopes of the indifference curves for our two households) must be equal for m and n. What this simply means in this context is that both m and n obtain the same trade-off between risk and return in the perfect capital market postulated by the model. Now in the box we present two allocations of risk and return between m and n where this condition is met: point E along JEK and point D along the curve $J'DK'$. Of the two points it is clear that E is both feasible and Pareto efficient, while D is not feasible. The point E is feasible in that it lies along JEK where an α percent claim to $\$[E(\tilde{R}_M) - R_F]$ is associated with an α percent absorption of $\$\sigma(\tilde{R}_M)$. The point E is also Pareto efficient since the marginal rate of substitution of risk for return available to both m and n in the capital market is equal to the marginal rate of transformation between risk and return in production at point M along the Markowitz frontier.[9] The point D along $J'DK'$ is not feasible since, at that allocation, individual n obtains α percent of $\$[E(\tilde{R}_M) - R_F]$ but absorbs something less than α percent of

$\$\sigma(\tilde{R}_M)$. The marginal conditions alone cannot decide the issue in this case since in principle there is a point along $J'DK'$ where they would be fulfilled but the allocation would not be feasible.

We therefore conclude that the CAPM allocation of investment to the risky sector presented in Chapter 4 must be Pareto efficient for two inter-related reasons. One of the reasons was discussed in note 27 in Chapter 4; namely, a perfect capital market (an assumption of CAPM) implies an equiv-alence between capital market and product market incomes, and hence the trade-off between risk and return in both must also be equal. The second and related reason is that savings and investment are internalized by the market manager in this model. This result is primarily due to the twin assumptions of homogeneous expectations on the joint probability density of the risky project outputs by households as savers and investors, and the constant re-turns to scale technology of projects in both the risky and riskless sectors. With these assumptions—and the others invoked in the development of CAPM—non-Pareto efficient allocations of the investment input cannot occur.

Why then do Jensen and Long (1972), Stiglitz (1972), Fama (1972), and Bosshardt (1983) conclude otherwise? We suspect their conclusions are the result of using the CAPM framework in a way it was originally not intended to be used, namely, to describe decentralized decision making in a market economy. In a world of homogeneous expectations, simple separation, con-stant returns to scale, and all the other assumptions invoked in the develop-ment of CAPM, it is difficult if not impossible to motivate the problems associated with decentralized decision making. Nevertheless, perhaps for the sake of realism, the above authors wish to separate production and portfolio investment decisions in their analyses of investment allocations, although as Lucas (1980) reminds us, realism in this sense can sometimes be counterpro-ductive. They pose a world in which on one side of the market stands utility-maximizing households as portfolio investors who in turn are the ultimate source of the investment input. On the other side stand these same individ-uals as owners of value-maximizing firms[10] who in turn are the vehicles by which investment inputs are converted into end-of-period outputs. In be-tween stands the capital market. Thus the world becomes artificially decen-tralized into a "we" (households as suppliers of inputs) and "they" (house-holds as demanders of inputs) group, and this artificial decentralization, of course, creates the potential for an artificial suboptimal allocation of invest-ment inputs. The so-called "they" group establishes a production plan based on observable prices in the capital market. These prices, like all prices, should reflect the relative scarcities among economic goods. The objective of this production plan, in turn, is the conventional one of maximizing the dif-ference between the capital market value of that production plan and the actual resource or investment cost of the plan. Of course, in competitive equilibrium, this difference between market value and cost both for the individual firm and all firms taken together must be zero.

In order to provide a sharper focus to some of these ideas consider the following linear production relationship proposed by Fama (1972).

$$\tilde{X}_j = A_j + B_j\tilde{\mu} + \tilde{e}_j \tag{5.1}$$

where $\tilde{X}_j$ = the random output of firm j; $\tilde{\mu}$ = a random market factor that systematically influences the output of all risky firms; $\tilde{e}_j$ = a random variable independent of $\tilde{\mu}$ and all other $\tilde{e}_k$ for firm k; i.e., a factor specific to firm j; A_j and B_j = fixed constants.

The question then becomes whether the "we" group will price this production relationship correctly in the capital market in order that the "they" group will demand the Pareto efficient level of investment input. The capital market price of this production relationship is then obtained by substituting equation (5.1) into the CAPM pricing equations (equation (4.3) or (4.5)) and becomes[11]:

$$P_j = \frac{1}{1 + R_F} \left\{ E(\tilde{X}_j) - S_M \left[\frac{\sigma^2(\tilde{e}_j) + B_j(\Sigma_k B_k \sigma^2(\tilde{\mu}))}{\sigma(\tilde{X}_M)} \right] \right\} \tag{5.2a}$$

$$P_j = \frac{1}{1 + R_F} \left\{ E(\tilde{X}_j) - S_M \left[\frac{\sigma^2(\tilde{e}_j) + \Sigma_k B_k \text{cov}(\tilde{X}_j,\tilde{\mu})}{\sigma(\tilde{X}_M)} \right] \right\} \tag{5.2b}$$

Summing over all risky firms we then obtain today's price for all risky firms in the economy.

$$P_M = \frac{1}{1 + R_F} \left\{ \Sigma_j E(\tilde{X}_j) - S_M \left[\frac{(\Sigma_j B_j)^2 \sigma^2(\tilde{\mu}) + \Sigma_j \sigma^2(\tilde{e}_j)}{\sigma(\tilde{X}_M)} \right] \right\} \tag{5.3}$$

Note from (5.2) that each firm j contributes $E(\tilde{X}_j)$ and $[\sigma^2(\tilde{e}_j) + \Sigma_k B_k \text{cov}(\tilde{X}_j,\tilde{\mu})]$ to the return and risk on the market portfolio that will be held in equilibrium by all households.

Consider next the demand for projects by households in their role as value-maximizing firms, and indicate the resource cost of these projects as I_j and $\Sigma_j I_j = I_M$ for individual projects and all projects taken together. In equilibrium it must be the case that the capital market value of the project(s) must equal the resource cost or

$$P_j - I_j = 0 \tag{5.4}$$

$$P_M - I_M = 0 \tag{5.5}$$

Following Fama, note that in order to generate $\bar{X}_j$ units of expected output, project j also generates B_j units of market factor risk and/or $\sigma^2(\tilde{e}_j)$ units of residual variance or project-specific risk. Inserting equations (5.2) and (5.3) (the CAPM valuation of the linear production relationship) into equations (5.4) and (5.5) (the value maximization rule governing investment demand) yields the two following expressions for the individual firm and all firms in the risky sector.[12]

$$\bar{X}_j[B_j,\sigma^2(\tilde{e}_j)] - (1 + R_F)I_j[B_j,\sigma^2(\tilde{e}_j)] - S_M^j \left\{ \frac{\sigma^2(\tilde{e}_j) + B_j[\Sigma_k B_k \sigma^2(\tilde{\mu})]}{\sigma(\tilde{X}_M)} \right\} = 0$$

(5.6)

$$\Sigma_j \bar{X}_j[B_j,\sigma^2(\tilde{e}_j)] - (1 + R_F)\Sigma_j I_j[B_j,\sigma^2(\tilde{e}_j)] - S_M^J \left\{ \frac{(\Sigma_j B_j)^2 \sigma^2(\tilde{\mu}) + \Sigma_j \sigma^2(\tilde{e}_j)}{\sigma(\tilde{X}_M)} \right\} = 0$$

(5.7)

where $\bar{X}_j = E(\tilde{X}_j)$; S_M^j = the marginal rate of transformation between risk and excess expected return for firm j; S_M^J = the marginal rate of transformation between risk and excess expected return for the entire risky sector.

It is then argued that in order for the investment allocation to be Pareto efficient it is necessary for the two S_Ms (which (i) is determined by B and $\sigma^2(\tilde{e})$, and (ii) are the household's marginal rate of substitution between risk and excess expected return when holding the market portfolio) to be equal.

Let us look at this matter further. The S_M^j embedded in equation (5.6) evolves from individual firm value maximization at the margin; i.e., $P_j - I_j = 0$. According to the value maximization rule no individual firm will push investment to the point where the capital market value of a project is less than its resource or investment cost, and the equilibrium S_M^j will reflect this fact. The S_M^J in equation (5.7), on the other hand, evolves from summing the differences between the individual P_js and I_js when j can only be held in the market portfolio. Note that in (5.7) the aggregate expected output and investment in the risky sector are merely the sums of individual outputs and investments of firms. This, however, is not the case with the production of aggregate risk (the third term in equation (5.7)) in the system since part of this risk is firm specific (the $\tilde{e}_j$ in equation (5.1)) and can therefore be eliminated when firm j is held in a well-diversified portfolio like the market portfolio. It is this phenomenon of risk reduction through diversification on the capital market that leads some of the above authors to conclude that the value-maximizing decisions of individual firms in the product market will lead to a misallocation of scarce investment inputs in society, for it turns out to be the case that not enough expected output and residual variance (or firm-specific risk) are produced in equilibrium in the risky sector, which in turn implies households invest too heavily in the risk-free sector. To see this, differentiate (5.6) and (5.7) first with respect to B and then $\sigma^2(\tilde{e})$ and compare the resulting S_Ms.[13]

$$S_{M,B}^j = \left(\frac{\partial \bar{X}_j[B_j,\sigma^2(\tilde{e}_j)]}{\partial B_j} - \frac{(1 + R_F)\partial I_j[B_j,\sigma^2(\tilde{e}_j)]}{\partial B_j}\right) \left(\frac{(\Sigma_k B_k)\sigma^2(\tilde{\mu})}{\sigma(\tilde{X}_M)}\right)^{-1}$$

$$= \left(\frac{\partial \bar{X}_j[B_j,\sigma^2(\tilde{e}_j)]}{\partial B_j} - \frac{(1 + R_F)\partial I_j[B_j,\sigma^2(\tilde{e}_j)]}{\partial B_j}\right) \left(\frac{(\Sigma_k B_k)\sigma^2(\tilde{\mu})}{\sigma(\tilde{X}_M)}\right)^{-1} \quad (5.8)$$

$$= S_{M,B}^J$$

$$S_{M,\sigma^2(\tilde{e})}^j = \left(\frac{\partial \bar{X}_j[B_j,\sigma^2(\tilde{e}_j)]}{\partial \sigma^2(\tilde{e}_j)} - \frac{(1 + R_F)\partial I_j[B_j,\sigma^2(\tilde{e}_j)]}{\partial \sigma^2(\tilde{e}_j)}\right) \left(\frac{1}{\sigma(\tilde{X}_M)}\right)^{-1}$$

$$< \left(\frac{\partial \bar{X}_j[B_j,\sigma^2(\tilde{e}_j)]}{\partial \sigma^2(\tilde{e}_j)} - \frac{(1 + R_F)\partial I_j[B_j,\sigma^2(\tilde{e}_j)]}{\partial \sigma^2(\tilde{e}_j)}\right) \left(\frac{1}{2\sigma(\tilde{X}_M)}\right)^{-1} \quad (5.9)$$

$$= S_{M,\sigma^2(\tilde{e})}^J$$

From (5.8) it can be seen that if the only risk generated in risky production is market factor risk, B, then individual value-maximizing decisions by firms as set forth in equation (5.4) will result in a Pareto efficient allocation of investment in the economy. In this case the marginal rate of substitution between portfolio risk and excess expected portfolio returns equals the marginal rate of transformation in production between market factor risk and expected excess returns. The "we" and "they" groups have coordinated saving and investment optimally. On the other hand, if risky firms also generate residual variance or firm-specific risk, $\sigma^2(\tilde{e})$, when producing expected output and pay attention to that risk when formulating production plans, then from (5.9) it can be seen that the marginal rate of transforming residual variance for expected excess returns in the risky sector, $S_{M,\sigma^2(e_j)}^J$, is greater than the marginal rate of substitution between portfolio risk and excess expected portfolio returns. What this means is that the risky sector can convert residual variance into excess expected returns on more favorable terms in production than households can convert risk for excess expected returns on the capital market. Society would therefore be better off if the firms in the risky sector demanded more of the investment input than the value-maximizing level indicated in equation (5.4), for the reason that the only cost associated with the increased expected output resulting from this additional investment would be an increase in residual variance, which of course households can diversify away when holding the market portfolio. Since residual variance can be diversified away on the capital market it commands no price in equilibrium and there is no incentive for its production. In this case the "we" and "they" groups are evidently unable to optimally coordinate savings and investment decisions through competitive markets and the value maximization rule.

There is even a more simple and intuitive explanation of why the Pareto efficient level of investment made by a market manager in CAPM will always exceed the decentralized level of investment when outputs are not perfectly and positively correlated among firms, and the value maximization rule governs investment demand. The fundamental idea of portfolio theory is that the whole is in some sense greater than the sum of its individual constituent parts when outputs are not perfectly correlated across firms. When there are independent elements in the production of output, and production processes can be divided as finely as we please, then the aggregate expected output in the risky sector is just the sum of the expected outputs of the individual production processes, but the total quantity of risk as represented by the standard deviation of aggregate output is less than the apparent sum of the individual project risks.[14] Stated somewhat differently, the sum of expected output (the "good" in the portfolio) grows proportionally or linearly with the number of variables or firms in the sum, but the standard deviation (the "bad" in the portfolio) grows less than proportionally (actually by the square root) with the number of variables or firms in the sum. To see how this will effect investment demand in the risky sector of the economy, imagine the two following hypothetical regimes: one like CAPM in which households can only hold firm j in a market portfolio with weight $w_j = P_j/P_M$; and the other in which households are required to hold firm j in isolation and are specifically precluded from diversifying, much less holding, the CAPM market portfolio. In other words, in the latter regime, each household can only invest in one enterprise, and hence there must be at least as many individual households as enterprises in this economy. Now if households are risk averse and if we can pretend everything else is equal in the two regimes,[15] it must be the case that the value of the market portfolio, P_M, in the first regime will always be greater than the value of the sum of individual risky firms in the second regime. This will be the case because firm valuations are simply the difference between the aggregate quantity of expected output discounted at the risk-free rate (assumed to be equal between the two regimes) and the aggregate quantity of risk (which is not the same between the two regimes, in that risk to individual households is greater in the second regime) discounted by the ratio of the market price of risk reduction, S_M, to one plus the risk-free rate. If the value of the market portfolio in the first regime is greater than the value of the sum of risky firms in the second, then by equation (5.5) the aggregate demand for investment will be greater in the first regime than in the second. There is, in other words, an important element of social insurance associated with the holding of the market portfolio that is presumed to be available to all households at zero cost, and this insurance scheme eliminates an avoidable risk in society. The existence of this insurance (which is a free good) is what differentiates the above regimes and creates differences in valuations and the level of investment. Returning to the alleged misallocation in the CAPM framework, we can now see that to the extent that value maximization in equation (5.4) directs the individual firm to take account of $\sigma^2(\tilde{e})$ when calculating its investment demand in the product market—even though households can get rid of $\sigma^2(\tilde{e})$ risk on the capital market when constructing and holding the market portfolio—the same phenomenon of underinvestment arises as it did in our second regime discussed above. This suggests that any return-generating process that implies $\sigma^2(\tilde{e})$ is a component of risk in pricing equations like (5.2) and (5.3) is inappropriate when firms are the right size and are held in a well-diversified portfolio, and below we will describe how this term is eliminated in a CAPM model of production.

The implication of the Fama analysis is that in a CAPM framework individual value-maximizing production decisions will generally fail at the margin to allocate investment inputs in a Pareto efficient manner since capital market prices observable by individual firms do not correctly reflect all scarcities in the system which, in this case, is the production of firm-specific or diversifiable risk. In discussing the causes of this market failure, Fama, along with Jensen and Long, Stiglitz, and Bosshardt, have offered the traditional reasons; namely, the product or capital market or both are not *perfectly competitive*, and there are *external economies* in production. Since both account for nonoptimal allocations in the conventional perfectly certain equilibrium, the reader is left with the impression that there is something within the CAPM and the value maximization rule applied to the linear production relationship in equation (5.1) that precludes households from obtaining the best possible societal trade-off between risk and return.

As we mentioned in the introductory section not all financial economists agree with the above conclusion. For example, Merton and Subrahmanyam (1974), in concluding their review of this literature, argue that all previous studies impose noncompetitive assumptions on their analyses and, not surprisingly, observe a misallocation of resources. The particular assumption they have in mind pertains to entry; namely, ". . . that as long as firms (entrepreneurs) are value maximizers and profit opportunities exist, then if they can enter, they will enter, and in a competitive market, entry is not restricted" (1974, p. 168). When barriers to entry are removed and the number of firms and level of investment is allowed to grow, the residual variance term that appears in an equation like (5.2) disappears and the resulting allocation of investment goes to the Pareto efficient allocation.

Merton and Subrahmanyam drive this residual variance term out of the system and achieve the efficient allocation by allowing free entry into any technology and the capital market, but the price they must pay is the assumption of a world in which the number of firms and level of investment is allowed to change without changing capital market prices such as S_M and

$(1 + R_F)$. Our grand mutual fund manager can achieve this same result with a fixed level of investment by creating an infinite number of infinitesimally small security-issuing firms. To get the flavor of this result divide equation (5.1) by N (the number of equally small-sized firms investing in technology or project j) and note that $\bar{X}_j$ for each individual firm goes to $(1/N)\,\bar{X}_j$, cov $(\bar{X}_j,\tilde{\mu})$ goes to $(1/N)\,\mathrm{cov}(\bar{X}_j,\tilde{\mu})$ but $\sigma^2(\tilde{e}_j)$ goes to $(1/N^2)\,\sigma^2(\tilde{e}_j)$. As N grows large equation (5.2b) goes to the CAPM expression,

$$P_j = \frac{1}{1 + R_F}\left\{ E(\tilde{V}_j) - S_M\left[\frac{\mathrm{cov}(\tilde{V}_j,\tilde{\mu})}{\sigma(\tilde{V}_M)}\right]\right\} \tag{5.2c}$$

where P_j = the current value of the Pareto efficient security-issuing firm; $\tilde{V}_j = (1/N)\,\bar{X}_j$; $\tilde{V}_M = \Sigma_j \tilde{V}_j$, which when inserted into (5.6) and (5.7) and differentiated as in (5.8) yields $S_M^i = S_M^j$ and the Pareto efficient allocation of the investment input. In other words, when an individual firm is small relative to the market as a whole and the only risk it generates is a market factor risk—both assumptions of which suggest that the productive sector is perfectly competitive—then the resulting allocation will be efficient, as suggested by Stiglitz (1972, p. 50).[16]

This discussion again reminds us that the firm is an artifact in the CAPM and has no meaning except that it makes a contribution to risk and return to the two funds households are allowed to hold in this world of perfect markets and homogeneous expectations. The essence of portfolio theory is that people hold portfolios and not the securities of individual firms, just as a symphonic orchestra is something different from the individual instruments of which it is comprised. In the CAPM world of Chapter 4, households are born with an endowment and possess both homogeneous expectations on the joint probability density of risky project outputs and individual preferences for risk and return. After making a current consumption decision they turn over the remainder of their endowment to a mutual fund manager, who, facing a given risk-free rate and thinking like they, spreads the investment input across the different constant returns to scale production processes in the economy in a Pareto efficient manner. In the resulting equilibrium the risk/return trade-off in the capital market is equated to the risk/return trade-off in the productive sector, as in Figure 5.2. Moreover, in equilibrating these two trade-offs, the mutual fund manager creates security-issuing firms to take on productive activity in such a way that the societal trade-off between risk and return is maximized for any given set of consumption plans and preferences. In the process of achieving this best trade-off our manager will also, through his ability to carve up a technology among firms, eliminate all production externalities. The output is then produced and distributed *ex-post* to individual households in proportion to their initial investment contri-

butions to the mutual funds. Since economic activity is internalized in
CAPM the investment allocation must always be *ex-ante* efficient just as
Robinson Crusoe's time is always *ex-ante* efficiently allocated on his island.[17]

Summary

Welfare economics in general and Pareto optimality in particular are
not what you would call your typical light table conversation economics, in
that if asked to explain in plain English the ideas underlying the marginal
conditions described in the previous two sections to your Aunt Margaret or
Uncle Leo you would be confronting one of the most difficult tasks imagina-
ble in economics. Moreover, if you ever finished, there would be some question as to whether such an exercise in eloquence was worth the effort unless
your aunt and uncle enjoyed brain-teasing exercises for their own sake. This,
no doubt, partially explains why welfare topics are generally relegated to the
end of courses and textbooks in microeconomics.

True to this tradition, in this chapter we have considered the question as
to whether the CAPM allocation of investment was Pareto efficient or not.
We have concluded that it was, given the somewhat austere assumptions used
in its development in Chapter 4. The apparent disagreement among the
scholars who have contributed to this literature is really over whether it is fair
or interesting to stick unbendingly to the CAPM assumption set. When they
do, and give up the notion of a unique value-maximizing firm in the residual
or disturbance sense of equation (5.1), all find that the resulting allocation is
optimal, although with the exception of Merton and Subrahmanyam the tendency seems to be to make this point in some obscure footnote and devote
most of the analysis to subtly violating one of the model's assumptions, perhaps in the spirit of realism. Nevertheless we hope by now it is clear that there
can be no place for realism in discussions of Pareto efficiency. With homogeneous expectations and simple separation the CAPM internalizes all economic activity, and there can be no conflict between the act of saving and
investment since the product market and capital market incomes in the system are one and the same. Moreover, if for some reason we wish to impose
the fiction of decentralized value-maximizing firms on this fictional economy, then we are equally obliged to carve up these firms into fictionally small
entities devoid of firm-specific risk, for only then can we preserve the implications of simple separation (i.e., grouping projects so as to maximize the
trade-off between risk and return), which is the heart and soul of the capital
asset pricing model.

In closing we wish to reaffirm the view that fictional economies with
fictionally small firms can be very useful when attempting to understand
how a modern market economy or perhaps a socialist economy works. Of

course there are some issues and problem areas where the model provides more usable insights than in others, and for our part we think those associated with the economy-wide risk/return trade-off or the capital market line are in this category. Others disagree, as evidenced by all the empirical research that has centered around the security market line. In Chapter 6 we will attempt to redress this balance in a very small way by looking at an economy-wide issue that can, in our opinion, be usefully analyzed within the CAPM framework.

Notes

1. We have argued in Chapter 4, and will continue to argue here, that this focus on firms is somewhat odd. In the CAPM all consumer-investors hold a claim on the market portfolio or mutual fund, and in this setting individual firms are important only insofar as they make contributions to market returns, $E(\tilde{R}_M)$, and market or portfolio risk, $\sigma(\tilde{R}_M)$. Firms in this world cannot be held in isolation, and as a result we must change our view of what a firm is and in particular what governs its behavior in the marketplace. What seems clear and will be emphasized below is that when firms cannot be owned separately but only within a market portfolio, our common sense notions regarding potential conflicts between private and social welfare must be revised. Nowhere will this be more evident than when formulating rules for optimal production decisions.

2. By and large this debate has been good-natured in that it is universally agreed that all contributors have proved something. The apparent disagreement pertains to the questions and issues that the various proofs were intended to address. Nevertheless it would not be too far off the mark to claim that Jensen and Long (1972), Stiglitz (1972), Fama (1972), and Bosshardt (1983) felt they identified different reasons why the equilibrium allocation of investment across sectors would not be Pareto efficient. Merton and Subrahmanyam (1974), on the other hand, argued that these reasons were well known in analyses of perfectly certain environments, and hence uncertainty per se cannot be the cause of any misallocation of resources in society.

3. For a more detailed description of these preferences and technologies see Chapter 10 in Intriligator (1971).

4. It is also assumed here that factor inputs are inelastically supplied and that each firm uses both capital and labor to produce good A or good B.

5. In terms of jargon this condition states that the marginal rates of substitution between good A and good B (i.e., the slopes of the indifference curves) must be the same for individuals m and n, which means they are on the so-called contract curve.

6. Again in terms of jargon this condition states that the marginal rate of technical substitution between capital and labor (the slopes of the isoquants in production) must be the same for firms X and Y, which means the two firms are on the production equivalent of the contract curve.

7. This product transformation curve is obtained from the production equivalent of the contract curve by plotting the combined outputs of A and B produced by firms X and Y that lie along this curve. The shape of this curve depends on the returns to scale as well as the relative factor intensities in the production of the two goods.

8. A particular capital market line, then, is analogous to one point on the contract curve in that the marginal rate of substitution between risk and return in the capital market is identical for all households.

9. When the market manager forms the market portfolio and allocates investment inputs across projects, the distinction between capital market and product market becomes academic and in a practical sense disappears.

10. It is important to note that we have tried to avoid using the word firm in this section. We have preferred using the word project since, as we will see below, the CAPM equilibrium imposes certain conditions on the optimal size and number of security-issuing firms.

11. The intermediate steps are as follows. From equation (i) in note 18 of Chapter 4 we have the yield form of the CAPM.

$$\text{(i)} \quad E(\tilde{R}_j) = R_F + S_M \left\{ \frac{w_j \sigma^2(\tilde{R}_j) + \sum_{k \neq j} w_k \mathrm{cov}(\tilde{R}_j, \tilde{R}_k)}{\sigma(\tilde{R}_M)} \right\}$$

where $w_j = P_j/P_M$. Converting (i) to the value form, inserting the linear production relationship of (5.1) in the text, and noting that $\sigma^2(\tilde{X}_j) = B_j^2 \sigma^2(\tilde{\mu}) + \sigma^2(\tilde{e}_j)$ and $\mathrm{cov}(\tilde{X}_j, \tilde{X}_k) = B_j B_k \sigma^2(\tilde{\mu})$ provides us with:

(ii) $P_j =$

$$\frac{1}{1 + R_F} \left\{ E(\tilde{X}_j) - S_M \left[\frac{w_j(1/P_j)\{B_j^2 \sigma^2(\tilde{\mu}) + \sigma^2(\tilde{e}_j)\} + \sum_{k \neq j} w_k(1/P_k) B_j B_k \sigma^2(\tilde{\mu})}{1/P_M \sigma(\tilde{X}_M)} \right] \right\}$$

Multiplying the numerator and denominator of the second term on the right-hand side of (ii) by P_M and observing that $P_M/P_j = 1/w_j$ and $B_j^2 \sigma^2(\tilde{\mu}) + \sum_{k \neq j} B_j B_k \sigma^2(\tilde{\mu}) = B_j(\Sigma_k B_k) \sigma^2(\tilde{\mu})$ when k includes j yields equation (5.2).

12. Incorporating these ideas into (5.2) and (5.3) we first get, for firm j,

$$\text{(i)} \quad P_j = \frac{1}{1 + R_F} \left\{ \bar{X}_j[B_j, \sigma^2(\tilde{e}_j)] - S_M \left[\frac{B_j\{\Sigma_k B_k \sigma^2(\tilde{\mu})\} + \sigma^2(\tilde{e}_j)}{\sigma(\tilde{X}_M)} \right] \right\}$$

where $\Sigma_k B_k$ and $\sigma(\tilde{X}_M)$ are taken to be fixed in value. For the entire risky sector we obtain:

$$\text{(ii)} \quad P_M = \frac{1}{1 + R_F} \{ \Sigma_j \bar{X}_j[B_j, \sigma^2(\tilde{e}_j)] - S_M[(\Sigma_j B_j)^2 \sigma^2(\tilde{\mu}) + \Sigma_j \sigma^2(\tilde{e}_j)]^{\frac{1}{2}} \}$$

According to Fama (1972, p. 517) we obtain this particular expression for P_M, since it is assumed that $[(\Sigma_j B_j)^2 \sigma^2(\tilde{\mu}) + \Sigma_j \sigma^2(\tilde{e}_j)] = \sigma^2(\tilde{X}_M)$. Subtracting $I_j[B_j, \sigma^2(\tilde{e}_j)]$ and $\Sigma_j I_j[B_j, \sigma^2(\tilde{e}_j)]$ from both sides of (i) and (ii) and setting the resulting expressions equal to zero and rearranging yields equation (5.6) and (5.7).

13. In (5.6) it is assumed that S_m, $(1 + R_F)$, $\Sigma_k B_k \sigma^2(\tilde{\mu})$, and $\sigma(\tilde{X}_M)$ are fixed, while in (5.7) it is assumed that S_M, $(1 + R_F)$, $\sigma^2(\tilde{\mu})$, and $\sigma(\tilde{X}_M)$ are fixed.

14. The latter proposition follows from the fact that $(a + b) > (a^2 + b^2)^{\frac{1}{2}}$. Moreover, when asset returns are independent and identically distributed random variables, then the aggregate expected return on the market portfolio becomes $E(\tilde{X}_M) = NE(\tilde{X}_j)$, while the standard deviation becomes $\sigma(\tilde{X}_M) = N^{\frac{1}{2}}[\sigma^2(\tilde{X}_j)]^{\frac{1}{2}}$ where N represents the number of identical firms in the risky sector. Only when asset returns are identically distributed and perfectly correlated will the standard deviation grow proportionally with the number of firms, N, in the sum.

15. In particular we are pretending that individual firm valuations in the second regime can still be valued according to equation (5.2). Moreover, throughout this discussion, we have been assuming, like Fama, that outputs are not negatively correlated between firms.

16. Of course this assumes that the $\tilde{e}_j$ in equation (5.1) is firm specific. On the other hand, if the $\tilde{e}_j$ is specific to a technology, then the number of firms investing in the technology will have no effect on $\sigma^2(\tilde{e}_j)$.

17. The CAPM is the investment allocation analogue to the nonmarket economy that characterizes much of daily household activity. Family gardening, house cleaning, and the preparation of meals are just a few examples of these kinds of activities coordinated by the mutual fund manager of the household, say the mother. Thus, in the case of gardening, the household begins with a certain quantity of seed, preferences, and the mother's expectations on the joint densities of the different food technologies. She then orders a planting among the different food technologies. In the fall she commands the realized crop to be harvested. The food is then distributed among the family members as she sees fit, although in principle it should be based on each member's relative contribution. Moreover, if she keeps bees in conjunction with her vineyard, she will not run afoul of the ownership externalities that characterize decentralized private ownership market economies. What is clear from all this is that here the household is both the producer and consumer of wholesome food products, and it would be indeed odd if the investment allocation was not *ex-ante* Pareto efficient.

—6—

An Asset Pricing Analysis
of U.S. Government Intervention
in the Capital Market

Introduction

In Chapter 4 we developed a description of how asset prices or returns might relate to one another in an uncertain environment. This theory of capital market equilibrium was based on a number of assumptions which included: (1) all investors form portfolios according to the Markowitz rule of minimizing variance for a given expected return, (2) all investors can borrow or lend any amount they desire at the riskless rate of interest,[1] (3) all investors have homogeneous expectations of the jointly normal distributions of returns on assets at the end of the single period, and finally, (4) capital markets are perfectly competitive and frictionless. The resulting capital asset pricing model or CAPM has come to be one of the leading paradigms in financial economics, and has provided a framework for analyzing a number of questions concerning the functioning of a financial system in a capitalist economy.

It is only natural, then, to ask whether there are any testable implications of this model, or whether this model might provide us with a framework for exploring other interesting issues in financial economics. For the past decade and a half finance specialists have been occupied in exploring just these issues, and as a result we certainly have a better understanding of how our financial system operates in practice.[2] For the most part the CAPM has served as a benchmark for analyzing capital market efficiency in its various forms, and the results, by and large, are consistent with the efficient market hypothesis.[3] For example, there are a number of studies that use CAPM or the related market models to show that the stock market reacts swiftly to any news that might be relevant to the fortunes of individual companies such as stock splits, mergers, changes in accounting procedures, and the reporting of accounting income, just to mention a few.[4] In addition, using the CAPM as a benchmark for determining portfolio returns, it has been observed that certain institutional investors such as mutual funds or unit trusts cannot outperform the CAPM, or at least outperform it over and above their operating expenses. From these types of empirical studies it is gradually being concluded that the capital market is remarkably efficient in that it processes information quickly and discards unimportant information, as well as the fact that there seems to be no investor having access to public information alone who can consistently earn a portfolio return in excess of the return given by the CAPM risk of the portfolio in question.[5]

Yet the empirical work that has been done to date within this framework is not above criticism. Fama (1976) and Roll (1977) have both suggested that most, if not all, of the empirical work using this model cannot be regarded as being definitive. Roll, in particular, has emphasized the paucity of testable implications of the CAPM. The only testable implication seems to be that the market portfolio is mean-variance efficient, and that a number of hypotheses previously tested—such as the linear relationship between risk and return and that beta is a complete measure of risk—are nothing more than implications of the single hypothesis that the market portfolio is mean-variance efficient. Since the market portfolio, in principle, represents a value-weighted portfolio containing *all* the assets in the system such as bonds, stocks, real estate, commodities, and any other valuable asset in the economy,[6] it has been concluded by some that there is not much of an empirical future for CAPM, and for this reason we should begin to look elsewhere for theories of asset valuation under uncertainty. The reason we should look elsewhere is that for many questions asked of the model a proxy measure of the market portfolio will generally not enable the researcher to reject the usual null hypothesis that is often posed. For example, according to Roll, when proxies for the "true" market portfolio are used to appraise the investment performance of mutual funds, it is indeed almost impossible to reject the hypothesis that institutional investors cannot outperform the market when CAPM is used as a benchmark. Thus financial economists might suspect or believe that the market is efficient, but the tests to date using CAPM cannot be regarded as conclusive.

What are we to make of this criticism and how will it affect subsequent research? Personally we doubt whether this type of criticism will bring subsequent empirical research within this framework to a grinding halt, although it will again remind us that empirical research and the formulation of theoretical models must be viewed as ongoing interrelated processes. All too often the research strategy in finance has been to formulate a theory like CAPM, develop an empirical test and a criterion for rejecting the proposed hypothesis, carry out the test and reject the hypothesis, or conclude that the evidence gathered is consistent with the proposed hypothesis; and this, presumably, is the end of the matter. The Fama and Roll criticism reminds us that test results should not end the matter. Rather, test results help us gain a better understanding of how the economy actually works, and from this better understanding we should go back and reformulate the hypothesis and repeat the process again. By successively repeating this process we obtain a deeper insight into the economic phenomena we are exploring, and this, after all, is why we study the particular phenomena in the first place. Within this methodology all empirical research plays some role in furthering our understanding of the financial system, and consequently none can be worthless, as some of the critics of CAPM have come close to contending. It will be in this spirit that for the remainder of this chapter we will construct and conduct an empirical experiment loosely based on CAPM that hopefully will shed some light on the workings of the international capital market.

U.S. Foreign Investment Restrictions: An Analysis of Their Impact on the Market Price of Risk Reduction

Introduction and Background

For the most part empirical research using CAPM has centered around the development of a standard by which investment performance might be evaluated. As such the policy payoff or implications have been directed toward in some way evaluating the investment performance of the private sector or the efficiency of the capital market. By and large the use of the model to analyze the macro implications of public policy have been ignored. Yet the market price of risk reduction, $S_M = [E(\tilde{R}_M) - R_F]/\sigma(\tilde{R}_M)$, that evolves from the model is a crucial economy-wide variable that certainly can be influenced by government policy as well as influence such important magnitudes like aggregate investment. In this chapter some of these macro or economy-wide issues will be explored within the framework of CAPM.

In this connection one area of frequent government intervention has been in the international capital market. The question of the desirability of the free flow of capital between countries has long been the subject of intense debate both at the theoretical and public policy level. Classical economic theory maintains that in a perfectly competitive and certain world, unrestricted capital flows potentially maximize economic welfare for all countries. Notwithstanding these theoretical arguments, many interest groups within a country have been historically opposed to the unrestricted movement of capital between countries and in many instances have been successful in persuading their governments to erect barriers and restrictions that limit foreign investment. One typical example of this opposition is contained in a policy study commissioned by the AFL-CIO where among other things it is concluded:

> There must be new tax measures to regulate the activities of the multi-
> national corporations. Such measures would remove the incentive to es-
> tablish production and assembly facilities abroad and create tax disin-
> centives to curb expanded production, which results in the export of
> U.S. jobs. [Ruttenberg, 1971, p. 123]

Arguments such as these have been augmented by a number of professional economists including MacDougall (1960), Kemp (1961), and others. These economists have argued that when total world investment is fixed and subject to diminishing returns in a perfectly certain and competitive environment, the profit-maximizing level of foreign investment[7] is generally excessive and hence nonoptimal from the point of view of either the creditor or debtor country considered in isolation. Consequently a creditor country could increase its national income by imposing some restrictions on the export of capital. The effect of the restriction would be to reduce foreign investment (but not eliminate it) and raise domestic investment and employment and thus domestic output. While the aggregate volume of world investment is assumed to remain unchanged in this argument, world output must clearly fall due to diminishing returns to investment in both creditor and debtor countries. In other words, the world supply of capital is inefficiently allocated between the two countries as a result of the restrictions, and therefore world output cannot be as high as it was before the restriction. The end result of the restrictions, then, is that the gain in output to the restricting country is less than the loss in output to the debtor country.[8] The policy implication that might be drawn from this line of reasoning is that the government in the creditor country should impose some sort of barrier on foreign investment that restricts it to the level that maximizes domestic national income. This barrier could take the form of a tax on investment returns earned abroad (such as the Interest Equalization Tax—hereafter, IET—enacted in the United States in 1964) or a quota on foreign investment (such as the Federal Direct Investment Program—hereafter, FDIP—enacted in the United States in 1968).

In an uncertain world where households form portfolios according to the mean-variance rule and all other assumptions of the CAPM hold, it is obvious that a restriction on foreign investment is more difficult to analyze than in the certain world of MacDougall and Kemp. To begin with, any restriction on foreign investment will change the opportunity set facing portfolio investors in the way described in Figure 6.1. There it can be seen that a downward change in the opportunity set lowers the slope of the capital market line S_M or, what is the same thing, the market price of risk reduction. The question then becomes whether portfolio investors will supply as much capital to risky firms with the new or postrestriction opportunity set as they did in the initial equilibrium or prerestriction opportunity set. Recall in this connection that MacDougall and Kemp fixed the aggregate volume of invest-

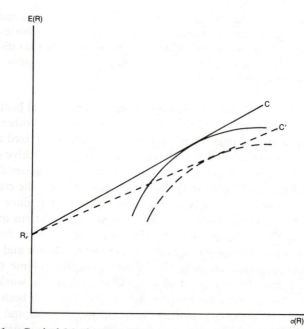

Figure 6.1. Capital Market Equilibrium and the Capital Market Line for Two Opportunity Sets of Risky Investments

ment in their analysis. Moreover, in our development of the CAPM in Chapter 5 we fixed the level of savings, although households were free to invest their savings in the riskless or risky sectors. Whether households will actually change their allocation of the capital input between the safe and risky sectors in the economy depends upon their aversion to risk (in the Arrow-Pratt sense), which in turn can be described by the curvature of the community indifference curve in expected return and risk space. In other words, any portfolio reallocation—induced by a change in the market price of risk reduction due to government restriction—will depend upon the relative strengths of the familiar income and substitution effects. While the substitution effect is predictable (a fall in the market price of risk reduction will lead households to demand more risk reduction, i.e., risk-free investments), the income or wealth effect can be ambiguous. It has been shown by Tobin (1958) and Arrow (1965) that when returns on risky assets are normally distributed and households exhibit constant or decreasing risk aversion in the Arrow-Pratt sense, the sum of income and substitution effects will be positive. Thus, in our case where the foreign investment restriction causes the capital market line to rotate to $R_F C'$ as in Figure 6.1, this amounts to saying that households in both the capital exporting and importing countries will respond by investing a smaller proportion of their endowment of productive inputs in the risky sector than was the case in the prerestriction equilibrium. The point to be noted from this discussion, then, is that anything that changes the opportunity set comprising all firms in the risky sector will generally alter the allocation of capital advanced to both the risky and riskless sector. If foreign investment restrictions cause such a change in the opportunity set facing households, then clearly this is a disadvantage that must be considered in determining whether such restrictions are in the national interest.

U.S. Foreign Investment Restrictions, Capital Market Perfection, and the Market Price of Risk: Some Empirical Results

Introduction

Unfortunately a direct test of the impact, if any, on the market price of risk stemming from a government-imposed barrier on capital export is not possible.[9] What we would like to do in principle is to run history twice over a given time period: the first time without investment restrictions and the given economic environment, and the second time with investment restrictions but the same economic environment. We could then see whether in the second period the market price of risk reduction fell as a result of the restriction. But as we all know it is never possible to run history twice, and for this reason a direct confrontation of the theory with the evidence does not seem possible. It is possible, however, to get some indirect evidence on the diversification benefits of foreign investment and at the same time shed some empirical light on two other important questions raised in the finance and economics literature. Each will now be discussed in turn.

Corporate Versus Individual Diversification in the International Capital Market

One of these questions centers around the so-called homemade diversification theorem that was discussed in a somewhat different context in Chapter 4. This theorem states that firms need not engage in diversification in the form of domestic merger or international acquisition in order to widen the opportunity set of households, for in a perfect capital market households themselves can obtain the diversification directly by appropriate portfolio policies. This is particularly obvious in the context of the CAPM where all investors hold a share of the market portfolio which contains all the individual risky production processes. In that world the merging of two or more individual risky firms would do nothing to the opportunity set confronting households, since the individual risky production processes would still remain in the common market portfolio. Moreover, it would not alter matters if a new production process was created by an existing firm or emerged as a separate firm, for in either case it would be held by all investors in the new market portfolio.

The same principle would apply when we move into the area of international diversification, provided all markets are perfect. In this case there is no reason to think that U.S.-based firms can achieve international diversification on any different terms than U.S. portfolio investors holding the securities of foreign firms. This is particularly true when U.S. firms obtain their foreign affiliates by merely purchasing the securities of existing foreign firms. Within the CAPM framework of constant returns to scale and homogeneous inputs across countries,[10] the proposition is also true for any project newly created by an existing U.S. firm, for if the project is economically profitable and worth undertaking, it could have been undertaken either by local residents or the residents of some third country. Consequently, in a perfect market of the type assumed in CAPM, U.S. direct investments abroad should not, in principle, provide any new diversification benefits that were not already available or could alternatively be created by some entity other than an existing U.S. firm. The empirical question, then, is whether real world markets are perfect enough, which we will test by seeing if different portfolios of American companies—that differ in their ownership of foreign affiliates—have different market prices of risk reduction over a given time period.[11] In other words, does a portfolio made up predominantly of U.S.-based multinational firms have a different (perhaps higher) market price of risk reduction than a similar portfolio[12] comprised primarily of companies owning domestic production processes? If there are differences observed across these two portfolios and it turns out that the portfolio containing the U.S.-based multinational companies has a higher price of risk reduction than the portfolio containing the domestic firms, then this observation would be consistent with the view that firm diversification abroad provides portfolio benefits for domestic investors. Such a result, if observed across a large sample of portfolios, would be consistent with the twin views of market imperfection in the sense discussed above, and the fact that foreign investment per se provides domestic investors with diversification benefits.[13] On the other hand, suppose we would only observe such results during periods when there were restrictions against portfolio investment or homemade diversification but none against business investment or firm diversification. This empirical result would be consistent with the view that foreign investment per se is beneficial to domestic investors, but not with the view that capital markets are imperfect in and of themselves; in other words, government restrictions on portfolio investment are the cause of the imperfection. Suppose, finally, that we sampled portfolio returns and risk measures only over those periods of time when there were no government restrictions on portfolio or direct investments abroad, or when there were equivalent restrictions on both types of investment. In these cases, if we found no differences in the price of risk reduction between the portfolios that differ in terms of their foreign business investments, this result would be consistent with market perfection but would yield no information on the question of whether foreign diversification was any better than any other kind of diversification that might exist between the various portfolios compared.

Fortunately, the type and time pattern of U.S. foreign investment restrictions in the 1960s and 1970s will enable us to shed some light on both the question pertaining to capital market perfection and that of whether international diversification is observably different from other dimensions of diversification. The period of actual government restrictions on foreign investment extended from September 1964 to January 1974. The first type of restriction imposed was aimed primarily at portfolio investment in that it taxed the income earned on foreign securities. The purpose of the tax was to reduce the yield differential between U.S. and foreign securities and thereby dampen U.S. investors' demand for foreign securities, which in turn was contributing to the balance of payments deficit experienced at that time. This tax was the previously mentioned IET, and it was in effect from September 1964 to January 1974. However, what is important for our purposes is the fact that from September 1964 to January 1968, IET was the only explicit restriction against foreign investment, and this restriction was primarily aimed at portfolio investment or homemade international diversification.[14] The second explicit restriction enacted in January 1968 came in the form of the previously mentioned FDIP and was aimed at direct investment or corporate international diversification, particularly investment in Europe. FDIP remained in effect until January 1974 when both it and IET were allowed to lapse.

This type and time pattern of U.S. foreign investment restrictions will enable us to perform an empirical experiment that allows us to shed some light on the joint hypotheses that capital markets are relatively perfect and that foreign diversification is valued in terms of risk reduction by portfolio investors. This empirical experiment will be carried out within the framework of CAPM but will not constitute a test of that description of general equilibrium. In this connection recall the definition of equilibrium in the capital market for the market portfolio; namely:

$$E(\tilde{R}_M) = R_F + S_M \sigma(\tilde{R}_M)$$

where

$E(\tilde{R}_M)$ = the expected return on the market portfolio containing all the risky projects in society;
R_F = the return on riskless projects;

S_M = the market price of risk reduction or $[E(\tilde{R}_M) - R_F]/\sigma(\tilde{R}_M)$;
$\sigma(\tilde{R}_M)$ = the standard deviation of the rate of return on the market portfolio.

As we have emphasized throughout this discussion, the term S_M is a
very important macroeconomic parameter, for it represents the rate at which
society can trade excess return $E(\tilde{R}_M) - R_F$ for risk $\sigma(\tilde{R}_M)$. In the formation
of the market portfolio within the CAPM, it is assumed that households
weight the constituent parts (i.e., the j individual firms making up the market portfolio) so as to maximize S_M. In this context it is obvious that any
government restriction on foreign investment would lower S_M, the market
price of risk. What we want to know is whether government restrictions on
foreign investment are measurably different from any other type of restriction they might impose on diversification, such as a restriction on the size of
firms or type of business activity. In addition we would like to know whether
the capital market approaches perfection in the sense that firm diversification is preferred to homemade diversification.

Our strategy for shedding some empirical light on these important
questions will proceed as follows. We will pick a sample of U.S. companies,
form a "market" portfolio, and then selectively remove certain subsamples
of companies (based upon the extent of their foreign operations and other
distinguishing characteristics), noting any change in the "market" or portfolio price of risk reduction S_M on the reconstructed portfolio. We will then
perform this experiment over a number of different time periods when there
were restrictions on U.S. foreign investment of various forms as well as some
periods when there were no restrictions. As we will see below, this kind of test
can help shed some light on the question of whether the firm, through foreign acquisition policy, can do something for individual investors that in
principle they can do for themselves with appropriate portfolio diversification.

Specifically, our empirical experiment will be as follows. First, we will
choose a sample of companies and form a value-weighted "market" portfolio. The sample we have chosen, with some exceptions, are the 175 companies in the Moody Composite Stock Index.[15] We then chose four time periods in which to analyze this proxy market portfolio: (1) January 1959 to
September 1964, a period beginning with Europe's return to currency con-
vertibility and ending with IET, a period with few restrictions on the export
of U.S. capital; (2) September 1964 to January 1968, a period in which there
were restrictions against portfolio investment (IET) but no mandatory restrictions on direct or business investments overseas; (3) January 1968 to
January 1974, a period in which there were restrictions against both portfolio (IET) and direct (FDIP) investments; and finally, (4) January 1974 to
January 1977, a period in which there were no restrictions on portfolio or

direct investments. Returning to our market portfolio, as measured by the Moody Composite Stock Index, we then formed three separate portfolios: (1) the market portfolio without a subset of 21 multinational firms[16]; (2) the market portfolio without a subset of 21 domestic firms industry matched with the above-mentioned 21 multinationals[17]; and (3) the market portfolio without a subset of 21 domestic firms size matched with the multinationals.[18] On each of these reconstructed portfolios (the original Moody portfolio minus 21 companies picked in the above-described way) we computed an S_M or portfolio price of risk reduction. This provides us with three S_Ms: $S_M(1)$ on the original portfolio minus 21 multinational firms, $S_M(2)$ on the original portfolio minus 21 domestic firms (with some foreign operations) industry-matched with the multinationals, and $S_M(3)$ on the original portfolio minus 21 domestic firms (with virtually no foreign involvement) size matched with the multinationals.

The reason we are comparing reconstructed portfolios to each other is that capital market theory tells us that to take any 21 companies out of the market will lower the market price of risk as the opportunity set facing investors' shifts to the lower right of Figure 6.1. As far as foreign investment restrictions are concerned, the issue is whether international diversification is in some sense different from other aspects of diversification. One procedure might be to randomly pick portfolios of 21 companies and remove them from the market and then compute an S_M for the reconstructed portfolio. If we did this a number of times we could compare our reconstructed $S_M(1)$ (the S_M on the original portfolio minus 21 multinational firms) to the average S_M on the randomly reconstructed portfolios in order to assess the value of international diversification. Computation limitations forced us to proceed in a different direction. That direction was to form the reconstructed portfolios in a limited number of ways that would allow us to compare various aspects of diversification such as the "foreignness" of a portfolio, the industry composition of a portfolio, and the size of the productive processes within a portfolio. Thus industry composition and size were other aspects of diversification we wished to compare to the foreign composition of portfolios.

We are now in a position to state the test procedure. We will compare the three S_Ms with each other over the four different time periods described above. If there are significant imperfections in the international capital market, we would expect to observe $S_M(1) < S_M(2) < S_M(3)$ for all four periods. In other words, the reconstructed portfolio without the 21 multinationals (i.e., the portfolio with the smallest amount of firm investments overseas) would have the least favorable trade-off (lowest S_M) between risk and return, compared to the other two reconstructed portfolios that have a heavier concentration of overseas investments at the firm level.[19] Results of this kind would be consistent with the view that diversification at the firm level provides individual investors with investment opportunities that they could not obtain on their own account and that these benefits are not contingent upon whether there are restrictions on the international mobility of portfolio investment. If this turns out to be the case, and foreign direct investment is the only means by which individual households can obtain international diversification, then government restrictions on direct investment would result in a less favorable trade-off between risk and return in the capital market, and this in turn could reduce the supply of risky capital advanced by the household sector. This would be one disadvantage of foreign investment restrictions that would have to be offset by its other alleged advantages.

On the other hand, if the international capital market approaches the idealization of a perfect market then we would expect firm diversification to be important only during those periods when governments impose restrictions on portfolio investment, thus precluding or at least impeding investors from achieving international diversification on their own account. Consequently we would expect to observe $S_M(1) < S_M(2) < S_M(3)$ for the period September 1964 to January 1968 in the United States when the IET, to some extent, prevented investors from achieving international diversification. For the other three time periods we would expect $S_M(1) \approx S_M(2) \approx S_M(3)$. For these time periods it should not matter which group of 21 firms are withdrawn from the original sample, since the opportunities for foreign diversification are available to the investors themselves in the securities markets overseas. Moreover, this case, too, provides indirect evidence that the opportunity for access to foreign-generated returns enhances the risk-return trade-off confronting domestic investors in the United States. This indirect evidence would be contained in the above-described inequalities between the three S_Ms for the period in which IET was in effect, for in this period we would be able to observe in the U.S. capital market the alleged advantages of international diversification.

The results of this empirical experiment are presented in Table 6.1. The column headings describe the four time periods, which differed in terms of the type of foreign investment restrictions. The row headings present the S_Ms for the three reconstructed portfolios. In column 2 we can see that the removal of 21 multinational firms from the Moody Composite Stock Index is associated with a lower trade-off between risk and return, S_M, on the reconstructed portfolio than removing either the industry-matched or size-matched sample of 21 domestic firms.[20] This was precisely the period when government restrictions were primarily directed against homemade diversification. Moreover, the differences are quite large with $S_M(3)$ (the portfolio containing the largest amount of foreign investment at the firm level) being roughly four times the size of $S_M(1)$, the portfolio containing the smallest amount of foreign investment at the firm level. In this period transnational firms were providing investors with nonreplicable diversification opportunities, and these opportunities were clearly observable in the risk-return trade-

Table 6.1. The Risk-Return Trade-Off for Selected Portfolios and Time Periods

	January 1959 to September 1964 — No restrictions on foreign investment	September 1964 to January 1968 — IET	January 1968 to January 1974 — IET and FDIP	January 1974 to January 1977 — No restrictions on foreign investment
$S_M(1)$	0.2680	0.0321	0.0498	0.1481
$S_M(2)$	0.2742	0.0602	0.0482	0.1330
$S_M(3)$	0.2672	0.1177	0.0651	0.1107

$S_M = (\bar{R}_M - R_F)/S(R_M)$ where:

$\bar{R}_M = $ the average return earned on a reconstructed portfolio for the period in question;

$R_F = $ the average interest rate on U.S. Treasury Bills for the period in question;

$S(R_M) = $ the standard deviations of the reconstructed portfolio for the period in question.

off in the U.S. stock market. Furthermore, it is interesting to observe from Table 6.1 that removing the 21 industry-matched firms from the Moody Composite Stock Index produced the second lowest risk-return trade-off on the reconstructed portfolio, thus reminding us that this reconstructed portfolio also has a substantial foreign involvement at the firm level. Column 2 is certainly consistent with the view that international diversification is desirable from the point of view of domestic investors and that this aspect of diversification seems to be more important than industry classification or size at least in terms of the risk-return trade-off.

On the other hand, the results for the other time periods listed in the column headings tell a somewhat different story. For example, when both FDIP and IET were in effect (see column 3) the differences in the S_Ms on the three reconstructed portfolios are very much reduced, although $S_M(3)$ (the S_M on the portfolio containing the greatest amount of foreign investment at the firm level) is still somewhat greater than $S_M(1)$ (the S_M on the portfolio containing the smallest amount of foreign investment at the firm level). The differences between the S_Ms tend to evaporate for those periods with relatively few restrictions on foreign investments. During these periods the S_Ms are virtually identical (column 1 for 1959–1964) or, if anything, favor the portfolio containing the least amount of foreign corporate investments (column 4 for 1974–1977). There is little evidence in the U.S. stock market, at any rate, that indicates investors have a preference for portfolios containing firms with substantial foreign operations during those periods which are relatively free of restrictions on capital export.

Our reading of Table 6.1 suggests that the advantages of corporate international diversification become more apparent when individual investors are constrained in forming optimal portfolios. This was most noticeable during the period 1964–1968 when IET was in effect and impeded individual investors from obtaining international diversification on their own account. During this period, investors bid up the prices of U.S.–based multinational firms in their attempt to obtain international diversification at the firm level, and thereby increased the returns to be earned on portfolios containing substantial foreign investments at the firm level. This is reflected in the differences in the three S_Ms on the reconstructed portfolios over the period 1964–1968 with the largest S_M, $S_M(3)$, associated with the portfolio containing the largest amount of firm investments overseas, while the smallest S_M, $S_M(1)$, was associated with the portfolio containing the smallest amount of foreign investments at the firm level.[21] This indirect evidence is consistent with the view that the foreign dimension of diversification is relatively more important than the industry or size dimension, and this should be taken into account when contemplating foreign investment restrictions. In those periods in which there were relatively few restrictions or restrictions against both firm and individual investments overseas, the inclusion or exclusion of

firms with large foreign investments did not have much of a differential effect on the risk-return trade-off for the three portfolios analyzed. These results are consistent with the view that firms can only provide diversification
opportunities for portfolio investors when portfolio investors are constrained in some way from obtaining the diversification on their own account, as they were during 1964–1968, the period of IET. This is what we
would expect to observe if the capital market was relatively perfect, and
therefore the results of our experiment across time periods differing in terms
of the types of foreign investment restrictions is certainly consistent with the
perfect market hypothesis.

The Effectiveness of the Federal Direct Investment Program

A hotly debated issue following the passage of FDIP in January 1968
centered around the impact, if any, it would have on the activities of U.S.
multinational firms. First, it is important to remember that the stated objective of FDIP was to reduce the U.S. financing of U.S. investments overseas
(principally, European investments) and thereby alleviate the balance of payments deficit that was being incurred at that time. Two views have emerged
on this subject. On the one hand, Stevens (1972) maintains that this restriction did not reduce the volume of capital expenditures of U.S. affiliates, but
instead forced the parent company to finance these expenditures with funds
obtained abroad, principally Europe.[22] On the other hand, Herring and Wil-
let (1972) suggest that FDIP raised the cost of capital to multinational firms
and thereby reduced the volume of foreign capital expenditures.

An alternative interpretation suggested by the Herring-Willet line of
reasoning would be that FDIP caused a misallocation of resources within
U.S.–based multinational firms and that investors reacted by bidding down
the prices on their securities so that the risk-return trade-off on portfolios
that contained these companies would fall. With a lower risk-return trade-
off on these portfolios, investors would then supply less risk capital to these
firms. This line of reasoning would suggest that we compare the S_Ms on our
three reconstructed portfolios between the period January 1968 to January
1974 (when FDIP and IET were in effect) to the preceding period, September
1964 to January 1968 (when only IET was in effect). If the misallocation of
resources was recognized by portfolio investors then we would expect to observe the largest decline (or smallest rise) in $S_M(3)$, the portfolio containing
the largest amount of foreign investment, and the smallest decline (or largest
rise) in $S_M(1)$, the portfolio containing the smallest amount of foreign investment at the firm level between these two time periods.

Returning to Table 6.1 we see that the portfolio S_Ms behaved in exactly
this way. Comparing $S_M(3)$ between columns 2 and 3 we see that during the
period of FDIP and IET this portfolio trade-off between risk and return fell

to a mere 55 percent of its value in the preceding period when IET was the only restriction facing investors. Moreover, $S_M(1)$ did not, in fact, fall between these two periods but instead rose to 155 percent of its earlier value. Finally, $S_M(2)$ is in between, as it should be, and fell to 80 percent of its value when only IET was in effect. The evidence between these two periods suggests that the portfolio with the largest volume of foreign investments at the firm level suffered the greatest decline in its risk-return trade-off, thus implying that FDIP had a differential effect on U.S. multinational firms. However, it should also be noted that the removal of FDIP in January of 1974 did not give rise to a larger increase in $S_M(3)$ than $S_M(1)$, as our argument suggests. In fact, the relative changes between columns 3 and 4 are the opposite from what we would expect, although there were some fundamental changes in the world economy ranging from the oil embargo to a more sharply fluctuating exchange rate system in the latter period that may perhaps have made foreign operations riskier. For these reasons we are less inclined to draw any strong inferences regarding the effect of removing all forms of investment restrictions in January 1974.

Summary and Conclusions

To sum up, then, foreign investment restrictions have been advocated for a number of different reasons. At the theoretical level, a number of economists have shown that in a perfectly certain world characterized by diminishing returns to the capital input, a restricting country can earn the equivalent of a monopoly profit by imposing an "optimal tariff" on foreign investment. At the public policy level, a number of groups have advocated restrictions on U.S. foreign investments (e.g., the Burke-Hartke Proposals) on the grounds that a given reduction in foreign investment will be accompanied by a given expansion of domestic investment, employment, and output. In this chapter we have presented theoretical and empirical arguments suggesting that the benefits from restricting foreign investment are less than were previously supposed when risk and uncertainty are explicitly incorporated in the analysis. In the uncertain world we analyzed, investment restrictions were shown to be detrimental to households in the restricting country in that it forces them to hold a greater amount of risk per unit of expected return than was the case in the prerestriction equilibrium. This decline in the market price of risk reduction, in turn, could set in motion wealth and substitution effects that cause investors to reallocate their initial endowments toward riskless investments and away from risky investments. It is far from clear that this kind of reallocation would be in the national interest.

In a certain sense these conclusions regarding the undesirable effects of foreign investment restrictions are obvious. All they mean is that constrained equilibriums are not, in general, as desirable as unconstrained equilibriums. What is not so obvious is how to devise an empirical experiment to test this proposition, and that is probably why we do not have a rich empirical literature on foreign investment restrictions.

In this paper we have tried to make a start in this direction using the CAPM as a loose theoretical framework. The CAPM makes a prediction that when starting from an unconstrained equilibrium and then removing certain investment opportunities from the opportunity set, we could confidently expect a reduction in the so-called market price of risk reduction. The CAPM does not tell us whether one type of restriction aimed at one type of investment opportunity is relatively more or less harmful than some other type of restriction in terms of the reduction in the risk-return trade-off. It was our hypothesis that restrictions against foreign diversification were important enough to be detected in the data, at least relative to restrictions on the size and industry aspects of diversification.

Yet in order to test our hypothesis regarding the relative importance of foreign diversification, it was necessary to differentiate between restrictions aimed at portfolio or homemade diversification and those aimed at direct investment or corporate diversification. In a perfect capital market it would not matter whether investors achieved international diversification on their own account or via the investment activities of firms, and thus it is apparent that any empirical work in this area will shed light on the joint hypotheses of capital market efficiency as well as the diversification benefits of foreign investment. In testing these propositions we analyzed the risk-return trade-off for three reconstructed portfolios that differed from one another on the basis of how heavily the firms in each portfolio were involved in production overseas. In order to test for market efficiency we analyzed the risk-return trade-off on these three portfolios over four different time periods that differed in terms of the type of restrictions imposed against foreign investment. Our results indicate that when barriers to portfolio or homemade diversification like IET exist, firms with substantial foreign operations provide investors with opportunities that they are unable to obtain on their own account. During this period the capital market was imperfect, but the imperfection was the obvious result of the man-made barrier to homemade diversification. Moreover, it was during this period that we could observe, in the U.S. capital market, investor preference for international diversification (at least when compared to the product line and size dimensions of diversification) in that the risk-return trade-off was more favorable for the portfolio containing the largest amount of foreign investment at the firm level and the least favorable for the portfolio containing the smallest amount of foreign investment at the firm level.[23] For those time periods when there were either no restrictions on foreign investment or restrictions on both portfolio and direct investments it was difficult to observe any systematic differences in the trade-off between risk and return among the three reconstructed portfolios we analyzed. This conclusion is consistent with the implication of a relatively perfect international capital market, but provides no evidence on the relative desirability of international diversification.

Finally, we did attempt to assess the effect of the FDIP on capital market prices and, in particular, how it might have affected U.S.-based multinational firms. We did find some evidence that the enactment of FDIP was associated with a greater reduction in the risk-return trade-off for those portfolios containing the largest amount of foreign investments at the firm level. Nevertheless, the inability to account for other factors that might have affected the risk-return trade-off for the period immediately following the removal of foreign investment restrictions suggests a cautious interpretation of the results. We personally feel that the evidence is mildly supportive of the view that the FDIP did have an effect on the risk-return trade-off in the U.S. capital market and that the effect was focused on U.S.-based multinational firms. Yet we would be less than sanguine in concluding that more work cannot profitably be done before we close the book on this important question.

Notes

1. The stringent assumption of riskless lending and borrowing can be replaced with the equally stringent assumption of unlimited short-selling with little change in the structure of the model. This has been shown by Black (1972) and has come to be called the zero-beta portfolio (a portfolio whose returns are uncorrelated with the market portfolio—hence, zero-beta—and a minimum variance) model of asset prices. The zero-beta portfolio replaces riskless borrowing and lending, and much subsequent research on CAPM proceeds on this assumption rather than the original riskless borrowing and lending assumption of Sharpe (1964) and Lintner (1965). Our own empirical work, to be presented below, will proceed on the basis of the original development of the CAPM, since for our purpose there is a natural interpretation to the difference between the expected return on the market portfolio and the risk-free rate of interest.

2. For a selective survey of this literature see the articles by Fama (1970), Jensen (1972), and Miller and Scholes (1972), as well as the criticism of this literature by Roll (1977).

3. In a sense it is somewhat strange to use CAPM in this way since efficient markets (assumption (4) above) are assumed in developing CAPM in the first place. It is often said in reply to this seeming contradiction that any empirical test of market efficiency based on CAPM is a joint test of CAPM and market efficiency, so that the strongest conclusion that might be drawn is that the absence of departures from the model predictions are merely consistent with the theory of efficient markets. This is an acknowledged weakness of the model, but it still does not prevent us from obtaining a better understanding of our financial system than in the absence of the model.

4. Many of these tests are based on what has come to be known as residual analysis. Tests of this type take the form of the following regression:

(i) $\tilde{R}_{j,t} = \gamma_{0,t} + \gamma_{1,t}\hat{\beta}_j + \tilde{\epsilon}_{j,t}$

where

$\tilde{R}_{j,t}$ = asset j's random return at time t;
$\gamma_{0,t}$ = a constant which in CAPM is the riskless rate of return at t;
$\gamma_{1,t}$ = a constant parameter which in CAPM should be equal to excess return on the market or $R_M - R_F$ at time t;
$\hat{\beta}_j$ = the beta for asset j generally estimated by relating asset j's return to the market return;
$\tilde{\epsilon}_{j,t}$ = a random disturbance term which incorporates the "news" which is particularly relevant to asset j at time t.

The residual actually computed is:

(ii) $\hat{\epsilon}_{j,t} = R_{j,t} - \hat{\gamma}_{0,t} - \hat{\gamma}_{1,t}\hat{\beta}_j$

Taking an average across companies that experience the same event but at different points in time (such as stock dividends and stock splits), it is possible to observe the extent to which the "news" incorporated in the residual affects the return on asset j as well as the length of time that "news" influences the return.

5. One anomaly that reappears with some degree of regularity in empirical work on the capital market is the so-called small-firm effect; namely, small firms yield higher returns to investors than large firms with comparable risk. This has been empirically documented in a wide variety of capital market studies including those of Gordon (1962), Miller and Modigliani (1966), and the papers appearing in the June 1983 Symposium on Size and Stock Returns in the *Journal of Financial Economics*. Whether this result is a true departure from market efficiency or merely the outcome of a series of measurement errors has still not been decided in the finance literature.

6. Including nonmarketable assets like an individual's human capital and objects of art.

7. The profit-maximizing level of foreign investment is one where capitalists in the creditor country equate at the margin the returns per unit of capital earned on domestic and foreign investments.

8. It is well known that lump-sum bribes between debtor and creditor could restore the competitive equilibrium and thereby restore world output to its prerestriction level. This preferred solution, however, is generally thought to be unsatisfactory from the point of view of the creditor country since the collection and distribution of the bribe may prove to be difficult in actual practice.

9. One possible indirect test would be to correlate the foreign earnings generated on U.S. direct investment enterprises to U.S. domestic earnings (profit before interest payments but after taxes). The correlation between these two aggregate earnings streams is 0.92 for the period 1966–1975. The correlation on the first differences of the two earnings series drops to 0.50. Since these correlations are less than unity they provide some evidence that foreign business investments are providing some diversification benefits to U.S. portfolio investors. Yet we cannot rely too heav-

ily on this evidence since earnings reported in financial statements are often subject to wide margins of error, particularly during periods of inflation. We will try to blend this type of evidence with evidence from the capital market in order to get a more complete picture of the diversification benefits of U.S. foreign business investments.

10. It used to be thought, in the 1950s and early 1960s, that U.S. inputs were in some sense superior to foreign inputs in that U.S. managers could do a better job than their foreign counterparts (see Dunning 1969). This thesis was also advanced as an explanation of the so-called Leontief (1953) paradox that U.S. exports contained a higher labor content than U.S. imports and vice versa for the capital content. This was disturbing to the factor proportion explanation of the pattern of trade between countries since it was generally believed that the United States at that time was a capital-rich, labor-poor country. In the 1970s and 1980s this thesis of the superiority of American inputs has tended to fade.

11. Actually the term "portfolio price of risk reduction" would be more suitable here since we are no longer speaking of the market portfolio. In what follows we will use the terms interchangeably.

12. Similar in the sense that the production processes in both portfolios are in the same line of business and of the same size in terms of sales, profits, and assets.

13. This latter point would not be denied by MacDougall and Kemp, for their restriction reduces the income of investors while increasing the income of laborers. The point at issue is whether a reduction in income to the capitalist class resulting from a restriction in a certain environment, and the reduction in the market price of risk resulting from a restriction in an uncertain environment, will both affect the supply of capital advanced by investors to the production process. If it does, this is a side effect of restriction that must partially or totally offset the gain in income resulting from the restriction à la the argument of MacDougall and Kemp.

14. To be sure, there was an attempt on the part of the government to talk firms out of making new investments abroad during this period, and this type of moral suasion was loosely formalized into the Voluntary Restraint Program in 1965. There is no evidence, however, that this program had much of an effect on direct investment; indeed, the evidence seems to be that direct investment rose and thereby led to the mandatory program initiated in 1968. For more on this see Krainer (1967).

15. In particular we excluded New York banks and all insurance companies because it was difficult to get information about the extent of their foreign operations. In addition, we substituted Standard Oil of Indiana for Standard Oil of Ohio because the Indiana company satisfied a size criterion better than Ohio in one of the tests. Our reason for choosing a portfolio like the Moody Composite Stock Index is that it is manageable in the sense that we could analyze the financial reports of each individual company in order to gain an insight into certain operating characteristics of the firm. In principle we would want a larger portfolio, in fact, the market portfolio. Yet it would be impossible, given the resources at our disposal, to thoroughly analyze the operations of individual companies for very large portfolios such as the New York Stock Exchange Composite Index or the market portfolio. The compromise is then one between size of portfolio and the feasibility of analyzing its constituent parts. Our decision was that for purposes of a first inspection of the data, the 175 firms in the Moody Composite Stock Index was a reasonable compromise and hence an appropriate place to start. At present Moody's no longer computes the index.

16. Foreign involvement was measured by averaging overseas sales and profits for 1975, 1974, and 1973 (when available) from the annual reports of the various companies in our sample portfolio. What we did was to go through all the annual reports for the firms in the sample and pick the 21 with the greatest percentage of sales and profits generated overseas. On average, 60 percent of the total profits of these companies was generated abroad. We might add that it was assumed that if a particular company was one of the top 21 multinational firms in 1973–1975, it was assumed it was also in the top 21 in 1959 and all intervening years.

17. The industry matching was achieved in terms of product lines. Thus, in our original sample we had three international oil companies that were matched with three domestic oil companies, four electronic firms with a substantial foreign involvement matched with four domestic electronic firms, two international mining companies matched with two domestic mining companies, and so on. It should be noted that these 21 industry-matched companies were involved in foreign investments and trade, but that their involvement was not as great as our top 21 multinational firms.

18. The size-matched companies were picked on the criteria of having the smallest foreign involvement but having profits of comparable size to the 21 multinational firms. As a result, this sample of companies was drawn primarily from the utility, railroad, and retailing industries.

19. An alternative way of stating the same proposition is that the reconstructed portfolio without the 21 size-matched firms (the portfolio containing the largest amount of foreign investments at the firm level) would have the most favorable trade-off between risk and return, as measured by S_M, than the other two reconstructed portfolios.

20. Unfortunately it is not possible to carry out a statistical analysis of the differences between $S_M(1)$, $S_M(2)$, and $S_M(3)$ for this particular time period. The reason is that while we might basically assume that the individual S_Ms are approximately normally distributed, they clearly are not independent within a time period, due to the domestic business cycle. Moreover the nature of the correlations between the S_Ms is unknown.

21. In this connection it should be noted that the differences between $S_M(1)$ and $S_M(3)$ were primarily attributable to the *ex-post* computed standard deviation, suggesting that the opportunity set implied by the two portfolios shifted downward for the portfolio containing the least amount of firm foreign investments. Thus the computed standard deviation for the two portfolios were virtually identical (0.034 versus 0.033), but the excess returns on the portfolio containing the largest amount of firm foreign investments were approximately two-thirds higher than the excess returns earned on the portfolio containing the smallest amount of firm foreign investment (0.0076 versus 0.0046).

22. Under FDIP all countries were scheduled into three categories. Schedule A countries were primarily the less-developed countries, and they were accorded the most favorable treatment in that they could receive direct investments from the United States, equivalent to 110 percent of the 1965/1966 average. Schedule B countries included the United Kingdom, Japan, Australia, New Zealand, and Middle East oil countries. Their quota for U.S. direct investment was 65 percent of the 1965/1966 level. Finally, Schedule C countries were primarily the developed Western European

countries where the restrictions were the most severe. These countries could only receive direct investments from the United States in an amount equivalent to 35 percent of the level prevailing in 1965/1966.

23. Actually this study is measuring the extreme impact effect of a restriction on foreign investment. It is extreme in the sense that our test assumes the restriction eliminates the top 21 U.S.-based multinational firms, including their domestic operations. It is an impact effect in that it examines the reconstructed portfolio's risk-return trade-off before investors revalue the remaining securities in that portfolio. Over a period of time, of course, investors would readjust the weights on the constituent securities in all three reconstructed portfolios, and hence the postadjustment risk-return trade-off could be different from the preadjustment trade-off we attempted to measure in our experiment. Unfortunately, this is the strategy we must follow when we are unable to run history twice. The other point we would like to make in this connection pertains to our proxy market portfolio, namely, the Moody Composite Stock Index of approximately 175 firms. No doubt it would have been preferable to analyze a larger portfolio, other things remaining equal, just as we would prefer the universe to any finite sample from that universe. Other things, however, never remain equal, and there are often heavy costs involved in enumerating the universe. The time-honored tradition in statistical decision making would be to draw a larger sample of firms, say the Standard and Poor Composite Stock Index of 500 firms, and repeat the experiment. If the results of our experiment with this larger sample were qualitatively the same as the results reported in this chapter, we might then go ahead and repeat the experiment with a still larger sample of firms, say all the firms in the New York Composite Stock Index. If all three experiments with successively larger samples yielded the same qualitative result—that reconstructed portfolios containing large amounts of foreign investments at the firm level had a more favorable risk-return trade-off than portfolios containing small amounts of foreign investments at the firm level for the period 1964-1968—then reasonable men and women might come to believe with some confidence that investors value international diversification. It is in this spirit that our experiment with the sample of firms drawn from the Moody Composite Stock Index has been conducted, and we can only hope that our results will encourage others to analyze large samples.

Part III

The Financial Economics Of Aggregate Demand And Supply

——7——

Keynesian and Monetarist Analysis of Aggregate Demand

Introduction

In Parts I and II we explored a number of finance-related issues within the general framework of conventional microeconomics. Chapter 2 launched this study with a presentation of the Fisher theory of intertemporal consumption in a perfectly certain environment and perfect exchange markets. One of the important insights of this model centered around the social role of a perfect capital market in facilitating the utility-maximizing distribution of consumption between the present and the future for a representative household. Stated somewhat differently, this optimal distribution of consumption over time would imply a socially optimal level of investment. Setting aside some important but perhaps unanswerable ethical questions about the ownership of initial endowments, this classical model described a rational and efficient allocation of scarce resources in the economy. From these insights financial economists would come to propose a number of decision rules for the practical management of an individual enterprise, and these rules were, by and large, based on the principle of maximizing the present value of scarce resources. Equally important, the Fisher analysis with perfect capital markets also indicated why certain financial decisions were not particularly relevant insofar as determining the present value of the enterprise, and much of financial economics to this day remains preoccupied with these issues.

In Chapter 3 we extended the Fisher analysis in a different direction, that of describing a general equilibrium for a partnership economy comprised of workers and capitalists. When output in this partnership economy is generated by a CES production function and preferences of the two groups of agents can be described by the usual convex indifference curves—along with our previous assumptions of perfect certainty and perfect markets—the model generated utility-maximizing levels of employment, leisure, investment, consumption, future output, and the distribution of that output among capitalists and workers. In this classical set-up the time laborers do not spend in work merely reflects their demand for leisure. Only when markets are imperfect (which in Chapter 3 took the form of a government- or union-mandated minimum wage) will the resulting allocations be suboptimal.

In Chapter 4 we continued our study of the coordinating role of a capital market by exploring a model of wealth allocation and capital asset price formation in an uncertain environment. The analytical framework within which we studied these problems was the familiar two-parameter capital asset pricing model, a model based on constant returns to scale production and the maximization of expected utility. Within the framework of this model we observed that when it was possible to separate every investor's portfolio into two subportfolios (one comprising riskless investments, the other risky investments) the structure of security prices in the capital market was such that every investor faced the same economy-wide trade-off between risk and return.[1] Moreover, in maximizing this trade-off between risk and return, households optimally allocate the scarce investment input between the riskless and risky productive sectors in the economy, a subject we explored in Chapter 5. However, this will not be the case if investors are in any way precluded from obtaining efficient diversification, and in Chapter 6 we empirically observed the deterioration in the return/risk trade-off that accompanied the U.S. government restrictions on foreign investments by U.S. residents during the 1960s and early 1970s.

One of the striking features of the artificial economies considered in Parts I and II is that they are all driven by utility maximization within the framework of perfect markets. They are, in other words, engines for maximizing the utility of individual agents. For this reason the practical social problems of involuntary unemployment and unanticipated inflation that occur in actual economies with imperfect markets are generally difficult to motivate within these models of general equilibrium except in very *ad hoc* ways such as assuming any number of ways in which markets might be imperfect. One example of an *ad hoc* procedure that described unemployment was presented in Chapter 3 in the form of a government- or union-determined wage rate that was set independently of the preferences of all workers. How and why such a pegged wage rate was set in the first place was not, nor could not, be discussed in any economically rational way in the context of these utility-maximizing models. Similarly, unanticipated inflation posed no particular social problem in our CAPM economy simply because all agents in this economy held pro-rata shares to the output produced in both the riskless and risky sectors of production in the economy. Since the harmful effects of unemployment and inflation are not the natural outcomes of model economies based on utility maximization in perfect markets with constant returns to scale technologies, it is not surprising that some economists less sympathetic to the wandering "invisible hand" would turn their attention towards other types of artificial economies. In these types of model economies utility maximization, perfect markets, perfect certainty, and constant returns to scale technologies are either not assumed or operate beneath the surface in an unobtrusive way so that a Pareto efficient level and structure of production is not the natural and inevitable outcome for the economy.

Accordingly, in this chapter we will continue our discussion of certain economy-wide issues, although within a different framework than the microeconomic structure used up to this point. In particular our discussion will center around such issues as the determination of the level and composition of national income, the price level, and the yield on capital assets. As can be seen, some of the questions asked will be those we have been asking at several points in our inquiry; others will be different. These questions and the model economies used to address them constitute the subject matter of macroeconomics. Much of the history of macroeconomics can be described in terms of controversy centering around theoretical, empirical, and public policy issues. Like other branches of economics part of this controversy arises out of differences in assumptions that evidently cannot be resolved by empirical research alone. But also, like other branches in economics, controversy continues because some economists tend to ask slightly different questions of the contending models, thereby creating the illusion of controversy where none really exists.

For almost a half century much of this controversy has swirled around the ideas promulgated by the Cambridge University economist John Maynard Keynes.[2] What were the ideas of Keynes in the field of macroeconomics, and how might they best be described? It is a great tribute to the intellectual force of the man that his work is evidently subject to a wide variety of interpretations by highly competent scholars ranging from the so-called IS-LM explanation first introduced by Hicks (1937) and more recently discussed in Friedman (1974) and Blinder and Solow (1974), to the so-called disequilibrium and rationing interpretations provided by Clower (1965), Leijonhufvud (1968), Barro and Grossman (1971), Malinvaud (1977), and recently reviewed by Drazen (1980).

In what follows we will present the interpretation originally proposed by Hicks. We follow this strategy for a number of reasons. To begin with, the IS-LM apparatus—while certainly not a complete statement of all that Keynes had to say about macroeconomics, particularly those aspects dealing with aggregate supply—does capture in a clear and simple way many of the unique features that rightly or wrongly have come to be associated with Keynesian economics. The second and related reason is that as Friedman

(1974) has demonstrated, the IS-LM framework is general enough to incorporate certain strands of monetarist thought, and hence it is possible to make rough comparisons between monetarist and income-expenditure models. Finally, the IS-LM schemata, more than the other interpretations of the Keynesian system, highlights the financial dimension of macroeconomic theory; and it is this financial dimension of economic activity that constitutes the principal subject matter of this work.[3] It must therefore be understood that our review of the Keynesian macroeconomic system will be both brief and highly selective. The fact that it will be brief is not particularly bothersome since most financial economists are well acquainted with the model. The selective nature of this review is of course more difficult to justify. In this connection we have been guided by our desire to compare and contrast certain aspects of the Keynesian financial system to the Fisher model and CAPM, which have already been presented in Chapters 2–6. In addition the IS-LM framework is a convenient way to introduce one of the most important and unresolved issues in macroeconomics, namely, the determination of prices and real output in static equilibrium as well as their fluctuations over the business cycle.

Accordingly, this chapter will proceed in the following way. The next section presents the IS-LM description of macroeconomic equilibrium. The original and rudimentary specification of that model by Keynes will be described in the first part of that section. We will also compare and contrast the financial theory underlying the rudimentary model to the Fisher model and CAPM. Of course, as a general rule, rudimentary models are easy to criticize, and this model proved to be no exception. The criticisms generally centered around the fact that the model provided no internally generated description of the formation of output prices, and professional opinion increasingly came to the conclusion that even a rudimentary model should not ignore such an important economic and politically sensitive variable.[4] In the second part of the following section we incorporate prices in the model and find that this does not necessarily mean incorporating them to everyone's satisfaction. As we mentioned above, this area of inquiry is one of the last great frontiers in macroeconomic analysis where professional opinion can either be characterized as divided or nonexistent. The question is simply this: If nominal GNP changes in response to a change in aggregate demand, how much of the change will take the form of a change in real output and how much of the change will be in prices? This problem, and several first generation solutions, will be presented. As we will see, none of these first generation solutions are particularly attractive, and as a result we continue the discussion in Chapter 8 to second generation explanations. Finally, we conclude this chapter by summarizing the discussion, but more importantly pointing the way in which we personally feel the analysis must proceed if we are to obtain a more satisfactory explanation of the price and output composition of a change in nominal GNP.

A Simple Model of Macroeconomic Activity

The Rudimentary Income-Expenditure Model

Introduction and Some Assumptions

The pre-Keynesian macroeconomics, or the quantity theory of money, tended to emphasize the role of money in economic life: first its role as a medium of exchange and then its role as a temporary store of value. This relationship between money and transactions, and then money and income, was emphasized almost to the exclusion of other possible relationships. Keynes changed this in part by drawing attention to the composition of total output between consumption goods (expenditures he felt were conditional on income) and investment goods (expenditures he felt were relatively independent of income).[5] In fact it was only insofar as money had some bearing on the demand for consumption and investment goods that he incorporated it into his system. This interest in the components of aggregate demand led him to wonder whether there were any circumstances in which total spending by households and firms would ever be so low as to preclude the full utilization of productive resources offered for sale in the economy. This of course was a question that simply could not arise in the classical general equilibrium described in Chapter 3 where it was assumed that the mere act of creating an output strongly implied an equivalent demand.[6] By the same token Keynes is often viewed as having devoted much less attention to the determinants of aggregate supply than his classical predecessors. Before presenting his rudimentary model it will be useful to first describe certain aspects of the economic environment.

The economy we will study consists of households and firms. All production is carried out by firms and is subject to some measure of risk.[7] Intertemporal variations in this unexplained risk alters the perceived profitability of investment and thereby alters the demand for investment goods by firms. While the cost of capital in the financial market is presumed to be a market-determined price, wage rates and product prices will be assumed fixed. Here it should again be noted that nonrudimentary income-expenditure models attempt to incorporate wages and prices into the analysis, but critics often contend that they are usually incorporated in *ad hoc* ways. Consequently, any change in national expenditure in this economy will be reflected solely in a change in real output and employment.[8]

What kinds of decisions must households make in this model economy? One important decision centers around the formulation of a plan for intertemporal consumption. This plan will define a desired level of current consumption and current savings for every household in the economy, and it is this savings that is made available to firms for purposes of adding to their stocks of productive capital. Of course, in an uncertain environment the intended savings of households may not equal the intended additions to the capital stock by firms for any given time period, nor the savings and investment that actually occurs in the equilibrium. When this is the case national income and the yield on financial assets will continually change until there is equality between intended savings and investment, at which point there will be an intertemporal consumption equilibrium for households and level of investment by firms.

This naturally brings up the question as to the forms which the accumulated savings or deferred consumption of households might take in this simple artificial economy. It will be assumed here that there are only two forms in which this wealth might be held by households. One form is a riskless monetary-type asset that serves both as a medium of exchange and a store of value. Why this asset exists and how it actually comes to be created will for now remain outside the scope of our discussion. The other financial asset in the system is the security used to finance the productive activity of firms. Since the purpose of our discussion here is not to compare one firm to another—one of the tasks of the capital asset pricing model presented in Chapter 4—we can simplify the job before us by assuming that all firms in the risky sector of the economy are identical in the sense of Modigliani and Miller and produce the same product.[9] Accordingly, the net income of these risky firms is capitalized in the financial markets to form market prices, and fluctuations in this capitalization rate constitute one of the risks of holding accumulated wealth in the form of risky securities. To sum up, then, households have two forms in which they can hold their current and previously accumulated wealth: a safe monetary asset yielding a relatively small return and a risky security yielding a relatively high expected return.

At this point we might ask: What role, if any, do household wealth and firm capital play in this economic system? Any answer to this question would presumably depend upon the length of the time framework of the model. In this connection we will interpret Keynes' analysis as describing the very short run, and for this reason we will ignore all wealth and capital stock effects on households' demand for new savings and the demand by firms for new investment goods. This obviously is a shortcoming, particularly when it comes to appraising the wisdom and effectiveness of certain government demand management policies in nonartificial economies. Moreover it is precisely in this area that the monetarist critique of the income-expenditure approach has been most effective in highlighting the important role played by the price level in a longer-run analysis, for the command over currently produced output that is embedded in wealth is very much influenced by the commodity price level at any given point in time. We have chosen to ignore wealth effects on the demand for and supply of new output at this juncture since we will not be concerned with the wisdom or effectiveness of government financial policy in actual economies, but instead the concern in this chapter will be focused on the unique features of Keynes' artificial economy. In our opinion the unique aspect of his model economy is how he structured the macroeconomic process in terms of a product market equilibrium condition and a financial market equilibrium condition and not the particular arguments that may or may not be contained in the consumption and investment demand functions of households and firms in actual economies.

The Model

With the above description of the environment we can now discuss in somewhat greater detail how firms and households make spending decisions in this economy where prices and wage rates are assumed to be fixed.[10] Consider first the problem of the household. Over any given interval of time a representative household generates an income from the sale of labor and capital services to the firms in the economy. This income or endowment can either be spent on consumption goods in the present or saved and invested in financial assets for a future consumption. The division of an income between current consumption and saving, was, according to Keynes, determined primarily by the income of the household and secondarily by the market yield on risky securities. Note the similarity to the Fisher model discussed in Chapter 2. While Fisher incorporated household preferences and opportunities directly into his analytical framework, both he and Keynes ascribed a role to income and the yield on capital assets in determining the level of current consumption spending. The important feature of this consumption-income relationship for Keynes, however, was its presumed stability.

What happens to the amount of household income that is currently saved in this system? This savings is available to finance the new capital expenditures of firms, which represents the second and relatively unstable source of aggregate demand, or it can be hoarded in the form of the riskless monetary asset. To complete our discussion of the IS part of the IS-LM framework, we must now discuss the determinants of the demand for new investments by firms. Actually, Keynes' theory of the demand for investments by firms was very similar to Fisher's in that it was argued to depend upon a comparison between the yield or internal rate of return on new investments and the current yield on the entire stock of capital as reflected in the yield on risky securities in the capital market. In other words, if businesses can expect to earn a higher return on new investments than their shareholders are currently earning on the embedded capital stock of the firms in the economy, then these investments will be undertaken today and become part of the capital stock tomorrow. New investments should then be carried to the point where the internal rate of return on these investments just equals the cost of capital or the expected rate of return on risky securities in the capital market.[11]

We can then see that four variables are uniquely related to one another in the IS part of the IS-LM system; namely, aggregate household savings (or consumption), national income, aggregate investment by firms, and the cost of capital or yield on risky securities in the financial market. These four variables will continually adjust until households are satisfied with their intertemporal consumption plans and firms with their new investment plans. Therefore, in order to complete our verbal discussion of the income-expenditure theory, we must consider in somewhat greater detail the financial system within which the yield on risky securities is determined.

Toward this end observe that after households make a consumption-saving plan, a decision must be made regarding the form in which they will hold their total accumulated wealth. Nonhuman wealth in this model economy can only be held in two forms: a safe asset like money that yields a relatively small return, and the risky securities used to finance the productive activity of firms, which in turn yields a relatively high expected return. Before Keynes, there was a tendency to compartmentalize the financial system. The money-type asset was presumed to be held exclusively for the purpose of consummating monetary transactions, and as such its demand was viewed as being determined by both the level of transactions and certain institutional characteristics of the economy centering around the synchronization of cash receipts and disbursements. All other nonhuman wealth in the classical system was assumed to be held in the form of securities issued by firms, since these securities yielded a higher return than the money-type asset. This bifurcation of the classical financial system was partly the result of the tendency of classical economists to ignore uncertainty, or at least not to incorporate it formally into their analyses. Keynes modified this view in a very fundamental way by suggesting that in an uncertain environment there were additional reasons to hold money besides consummating transactions. In particular, he suggested that households might want to hold money in their portfolios as a store of value when they expected securities to fall in value by an amount greater than the interest revenue received over some time interval. He called this motive for holding money in an investment portfolio liquidity preference, and he related it to the difference between future expected market valuations and current market valuations on risky securities. In fact Keynes carried this idea to the extreme; all accumulated wealth for any and every individual investor was either held in the form of money or risky securities, but not both, as suggested by the portfolio theory developed in Chapter 4.[12] In other words, he assumed in this theory of speculation that each individual investor held a fixed opinion or expectation regarding the future value of risky securities, which was continually compared to the current market valuation. Changes in this current valuation or yield—which in turn are observable to all investors in the market—would then change the perceived profitability of holding money versus the risky securities. Moreover, if opinions or expectations varied widely across investors, such a change would result in some households switching from money to securities while others switch from securities to money. In this way the aggregate demand for money was influenced by security yields—rising when yields were low (i.e., when valuations were high) and falling when yields were high (i.e., when valuations were low). To sum up, then, the demand for money or the safe asset was divided into two parts: a transaction part positively related to the level of transactions or national income and a speculative part negatively related to the current yield on risky securities.[13]

Having discussed the determinants of the demand for money or the safe asset, we can now turn our attention to the supply of money. In this rudimentary economy it will be sufficient to assume that the supply of money is determined outside of the model in some way; although we could with equal ease relate it to the yield on risky securities on the grounds that banks, like other businesses, vary the supply of their product (the rental of money) with the yield on risky securities.[14]

Having described both the supply and demand for money we can now state the required condition for equilibrium in this simple Keynesian financial system. This required condition is the equality between the demand and supply of money. Equilibrium in the money market along with equilibrium in the product market (i.e., the equality between household savings and the investments of firms) would then imply equilibrium in the market for risky securities, the only other market in this economy in which agents can transact.

To summarize, then, the rudimentary Keynesian system presents a macroeconomic equilibrium in terms of three markets: (1) a market for new output or, what is the same thing, the market for consumption and investment goods; (2) a market for a risk-free asset or money; and (3) a market for the risky securities of firms. Equilibrium in any two markets automatically implies an equilibrium in the third market. These market equilibriums, in turn, evolve in this artificial economy as firms solve their optimal capital budgeting problem, and households solve their intertemporal consumption problem simultaneously with their portfolio allocation problem. What is somewhat interesting is that the problems faced by agents in the Keynesian system are the same problems discussed in the Fisher and CAPM economies in Chapters 2, 3, and 4.

Before presenting an arithmetical description of the economy we have just discussed verbally, it would be useful to compare and contrast varying aspects of the solutions to the portfolio allocation problem offered by the Keynesian theory of liquidity preference and the portfolio theory underlying the capital asset pricing model discussed in Chapter 4. First consider the similarities. Both models basically have only two broad categories of assets which investors can hold; a riskless asset and a risky asset. The CAPM does allow for a number of different risky assets in contrast to the single risky asset in the Keynesian system, but the fact that all investors in the CAPM hold various shares in the market portfolio renders this distinction somewhat irrelevant. Another similarity between the two approaches to portfolio selection is their attempt to explain the social risk premium; that is, the difference in yields on risky and risk-free financial assets. Again, it would appear that CAPM generates many risk premiums on the individual risky securities that make up the market portfolio, but the fact that these risky securities can only be held in the market portfolio makes the distinction between individual assets and the portfolio of assets somewhat meaningless.

The differences between these two theories are in a sense even more interesting since they reflect very different views of investor behavior under uncertainty. Recall that in the single-period CAPM with separation, households were assumed to hold identical or homogeneous expectations on the return distributions of the different risky securities. The implication of this assumption was that all investors group the different risky securities in exactly the same way and thereby form and hold a common mutual fund called the market portfolio. The extent to which this market portfolio is combined with riskless borrowing or lending by individual households depends upon their wealth endowments and aversion to risk, which are allowed to differ among investors in this analysis. The end result is that all households hold well-diversified portfolios in terms of the different individual risky securities. Properly interpreted, this is a sensible conclusion but is obtained at the cost of an extreme assumption; namely, all investors have the same information set and process this information in exactly the same way when forming the market portfolio and establishing relative valuations in the capital market. The Keynesian theory of liquidity preference is very different even though it also attempts to explain the social risk premium and the composition of individual investor portfolios. According to this theory of portfolio selection, all investors are viewed as speculators shifting between the risky and riskless asset depending upon their individual expectations regarding the future yield on the risky security. Thus, one of the differences between the Keynesian theory and the CAPM is that investors in the former hold the riskless asset or the risky asset but not both; the latter theory, on the other hand, allows investors to hold both types of assets. The second difference between the two theories is that individual portfolio composition depends upon the wealth endowments and risk aversion of investors in the CAPM, but depends upon investor expectations in the theory of liquidity preference. This plunging into the safe asset or risky asset but not both would seem to be an unattractive implication of the Keynesian analysis, since we do not ordinarily think of all investors as rank speculators. Be that as it may, what does seem attractive about the Keynesian hypothesis is that a smooth aggregate functional relationship between money demand and the current yield on risky securities requires individual opinion regarding the future course of yields to differ across investors, something that could not happen in the CAPM set-up. Which assumption is better depends upon the question posed by the researcher. For purposes of analyzing risk aversion—that dimension in which investors can differ in the CAPM—homogeneous expectations is probably the more useful hypothesis. On the other hand, when trying to account for slow adjustments in the economy or for costly bankruptcy, the heterogeneous expectations of liquidity preference theory is probably the more useful hypothesis. Unfortunately no single set of assumptions is rich enough to derive all the empirically relevant hypotheses in financial economics.

The financial theory of income determination we have just described can be formalized in the following equation system.[15,16]

$$S = F(Y,r) \qquad 0 < F_Y < 1, \ F_r > 0 \tag{7.1}$$
$$I = G(r) \qquad G_r < 0 \tag{7.2}$$
$$S = I \tag{7.3}$$
$$M_D = L(Y,r) \qquad L_Y > 0, \ L_r < 0 \tag{7.4}$$
$$M_S = M_0 \tag{7.5}$$
$$M_D = M_S \tag{7.6}$$

where

S = aggregate savings in the economy;
I = aggregate investment in the economy;
Y = national income;
r = the yield on risky securities in the capital market;
M_D = aggregate demand for money balances;
M_S = aggregate supply of money.

Equation (7.1) states that savings is a function of income and the yield on capital assets and captures the intertemporal consumption decision of households. Equation (7.2) pertains to the productive use of those savings where it is hypothesized that investment by firms is a negative function of the cost of capital, given managers' expectations of the marginal efficiency of investment schedule.[17] A necessary condition for macroeconomic equilibrium is that planned savings by households must equal planned investment expenditures by firms, and this condition is presented in equation (7.3). Taken together, equations (7.1), (7.2), and (7.3) describe the intertemporal consumption pattern chosen by this society; namely, how much of an equilibrium income will be spent on current consumption and how much will be saved and invested in new capital goods for the purpose of providing a future consumption. Note, also, that these three equations describe the flow variables (or income statement items) in the Keynesian system; in other words, income and spending per unit of time.

Contemporaneous with the solution to this intertemporal consumption problem, households are confronted with the second problem of deciding the type of asset to hold in their portfolios. The choice here is between riskless money and risky securities currently yielding r in the capital market. Our strategy will be to explicitly analyze the market for money, since as we argued earlier, equilibrium in the markets for money and new output will also imply an equilibrium in the market for risky securities. The market for money in this economy is described in equations (7.4) through (7.6). Equation (7.4) presents the demand for money, and as we observed above, money is demanded for transactional purposes and for speculation. The transaction component of demand is some function of transactions—the purchase and sale of goods and services—and is proxied with national income. The speculative component of the demand for money is some function of the current yield on risky securities in the capital market. For a given distribution of future expected yields on risky securities, a decline (rise) in the current observable yield will increase (reduce) the speculative demand for money. The supply of money is given in equation (7.5) where, for simplicity, it is assumed to be determined by factors outside the system. Finally, the equilibrium condition for the money market is given in equation (7.6) when the demand for money equals the exogenous supply of money. Note that unlike the equilibrium in the market for new output described in equation (7.3)—which equilibrates flows of savings and investments—the equilibrium in equation (7.6) equilibrates stocks of financial assets at a given point in time.

The Keynesian system can be further interpreted by substituting the behavioral relationships into the equilibrium conditions and then totally differentiating the system.[18] For equation (7.3), which describes the intertemporal consumption equilibrium, we obtain:

$$\frac{dr}{dY} = \frac{F_Y}{G_r - F_r} < 0 \qquad\qquad (7.3a)$$

This equation represents the slope of the IS curve of Hick's (1937) IS-LM analysis. The IS curve relates the combinations of national income and yields on financial assets that equilibrates the desired flow of household savings to the desired flow of new investment expenditures by firms. In Figure 7.1 a linearized version of the system is presented, and there it can be seen that the IS curve slopes downward since a reduction in the cost of capital r stimulates investment via equation (7.2), thereby driving up both national income and savings.

Consider next the money market equilibrium in (7.6), which describes the solution to the household portfolio problem. Putting (7.4) and (7.5) into (7.6) and then totally differentiating the system for a given supply of money provides an arithmetical expression for the slope of the LM curve.

$$\frac{dr}{dY} = -\frac{L_Y}{L_r} > 0 \qquad\qquad (7.6a)$$

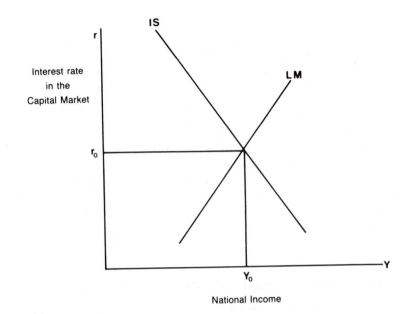

Figure 7.1. Income and Wealth Allocation in a Simple Model of Macroeconomic Activity

The LM curve presents the various combinations of national income and yield on securities that equilibrates the money market; that is, where the supply and demand for the safe asset, money, are equal. The linear LM curve in Figure 7.1 is upward sloping since a rise in national income will increase the transaction component of the demand for money and, with a fixed supply of money, necessitates the sale of risky securities, thereby driving up the yield on risky securities.

In this model economy the equilibrium (which is characterized by the simultaneous solution to the current intertemporal consumption problem and the portfolio allocation problem) is represented by the point of intersection between the IS and LM schedules. This equilibrium defines the level of national income, the yield on risky securities, the levels of savings and investments, and the composition of portfolios between riskless and risky assets. With such a model economists have asked a number of interesting questions concerning the nature of a macroeconomic equilibrium. One question is whether the demand for output in the equilibrium is sufficient to provide work for all those who want to work at the institutionally fixed wage assumed in the model. A second question is: To what extent will variations in the supply of money influence the equilibrium? While these and a host of other questions usually asked by economists are of doubtless importance, they can only be answered, if at all, by introducing a number of additional complications to this avowedly "square one" model. Moreover, our interest in this kind of model will lie in a different direction. Accordingly, we will not pursue these important policy questions here, but instead return to the basic model for a further consideration of certain variables that have been omitted from the analysis. In particular we must explicitly incorporate the price level into the model if for no other reason than the fact that changes in the price level have historically been a matter of great political concern in market economies. Furthermore, the introduction of prices will be shown below to have some important implications for financial relationships and the coordination of private production. Our first attempt to incorporate prices into the discussion will be within the framework of aggregate demand that we have been discussing up to this point. As we will see, however, a different framework will be required to successfully incorporate prices into the system, and this framework will be the subject of much of our discussion in the next several chapters.

Macroeconomic Equilibrium and the Price Level

Up to this point we have set aside any consideration of prices in our model economy, and thus any change in aggregate demand is fully reflected in a change in real output and employment. Common everyday experience suggests, however, that changes in the level of economic activity typically have both an output and price level dimension. If this is true then prices should be formally incorporated into the model. Following Bailey (1962) and Friedman (1974) this can be accomplished at the most basic level by recasting the system in equations (7.1) through (7.6) in real terms. With such a system we could begin to raise the question of the decomposition of nominal GNP between prices and real output. Accordingly the new system becomes:

$$s = f(y,r) \qquad 0 < f_y < 1, \ f_r > 0 \tag{7.1i}$$
$$i = g(r) \qquad g_r < 0 \tag{7.2i}$$
$$s = i \tag{7.3i}$$
$$M_D = Pl(y,r) \qquad l_y > 0, \ l_r < 0 \tag{7.4i}$$
$$M_S = M_0 \tag{7.5i}$$
$$M_D = M_S \tag{7.6i}$$

where

$s = S/P$ = real savings in the economy;
$i = I/P$ = real investment in the economy;
$y = Y/P$ = real output;
P = a suitable measure of prices.

As can be seen, there are seven variables (s, i, y, r, M_D, M_S, and P) to be determined by only six equations. The system as it stands is indeterminate.

This can be remedied by adding one more equation to the model contained in equations (7.1i) through (7.6i). According to Friedman, how that missing equation is formulated divides the economics profession into those primarily oriented toward the relationship between money and economic activity and those primarily interested in the composition of aggregate demand as between demand conditional on income (e.g., consumption) and demand independent of income (e.g., investment).

Within the context of this interpretation, the rudimentary income-expenditure system considered above adds the missing equation in the following way:

$$P = P_0 \tag{7.7a}$$

In other words, the price level is not endogenous to this particular system, but is determined by institutional and historical factors.[19] Inserting this price level equation into the equilibrium conditions given in (7.3i) and (7.6i) yields:

$$f(y,r) = g(r) \tag{7.3ia}$$

$$M_0 = P_0 l(y,r) \tag{7.6ia}$$

or two equations in the two unknowns of y and r. These equations are nothing more than the familiar IS-LM scheme, and their simultaneous solution yields the equilibrium level of real output $y = Y/P = y^*$ and rate of return on risky securities r^* in the capital market.

A classical or monetarist solution proposed by Friedman (1974) is to take real output as given.

$$Y/P = y = y_0 \tag{7.7b}$$

If real income is determined exogenously, then the equilibrium condition in (7.3i) can be written as:

$$f(y_0, r) = g(r) \tag{7.3ib}$$

a single equation determining r. Let the solution value of this required rate of return on securities be r^*, which means the demand for investment goods by firms determines the risky rate of return in the capital market. Next, insert this solution value for the required rate of return on risky securities into the portfolio equilibrium condition given in (7.6i) to get:

$$M_0 = Pl(y_0, r^*) \tag{7.6ib}$$

Multiplying both sides by y_0, and recognizing that $y_0/l(y_0, r^*) = v_0$ represents the real income velocity of money, gives us the ancient equation of exchange:

$$M_0 v_0 = P^* y_0 \qquad\qquad (7.6ib1)$$

or an equation determining the equilibrium level of prices in the economy. According to Friedman this solution to the missing equation problem assumes that real output evolves from a general equilibrium model that describes quantities supplied and demanded in the different sectors along with relative prices, and that equation (7.6ib1) determines the equilibrium level of prices.[20]

As mentioned above, these two solutions to the missing equation problem delineate the major schools of macroeconomic thought in a simple way. Moreover, it is also clear that the two proposed solutions describe the conditions of supply in the economy. In the connection the rudimentary income-expenditure model assumes the economy is operating under conditions in which the aggregate supply schedule is infinitely elastic. This is the segment of the supply schedule associated with unemployment, and the social problem of unemployment would seem to have strongly influenced Keynes' development of the income-expenditure theory. On the other hand, the classical quantity theory assumes the economy is operating at a point where the aggregate supply schedule is infinitely inelastic. Within the context of this long-run model the economy is presumed to be operating at the utility-maximizing level of full employment, and any change in nominal demand will be solely reflected in price level changes.

These two descriptions regarding the conditions of supply in the economy are presented in Figure 7.2. On the vertical axis we measure the price level, while on the horizontal axis we measure real output and employment.[21] The rudimentary income-expenditure solution fixes the price level at P_0, and all changes in aggregate demand and nominal GNP are reflected in output and employment. The classical monetarist solution, in turn, fixes the level of employment and output at (y_0, N_0). Any change in demand here is reflected by changes in the price level, since by assumption the economy is operating at full employment.[22] Nonetheless, economists were to become increasingly critical of this description of the supply schedule even as a gross first approximation. This growing criticism was the result of brute empirical facts; namely, in nearly all periods for which we have data, prices and output are observed to change together.

As we mentioned on a previous occasion, demand (in the form of an unresolved problem) can generally be expected to call forth a supply of potential solutions. This area of inquiry has proven to be no exception. In this connection, what would be more natural than to draw the aggregate supply schedule as sloping upward in contrast to the sharp right angle presented in

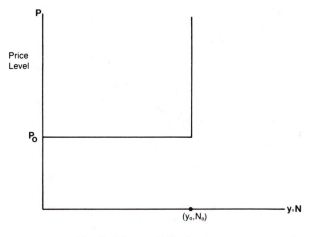

Real Output and Employment

Figure 7.2.   Aggregate Supply in a Rudimentary Keynesian and Classical Model

Figure 7.2? This is done in Figure 7.3. Moreover, this type of supply schedule provides yet a third solution to the missing equation problem.[23] The missing seventh equation here simply becomes:

$$P = P(y) \qquad P_y > 0 \tag{7.7c}$$

The intertemporal consumption and portfolio equilibrium conditions can then be written as:

$$f(y,r) = g(r) \tag{7.3ic}$$

$$M_0 = P(y)l(y,r) \tag{7.6ic}$$

or two equations in the two variables y and r.

And yet even this solution does not inspire much enthusiasm. One unfortunate feature underlying this supply schedule is that it assumes: " . . . money wages to be sticky, so that employment can be raised by an inflation that lowers real wages" (Blinder and Solow, 1974, p. 30). Some economists are inclined to criticize this solution to the missing equation problem on the grounds that an upward-sloping supply schedule for output implies a negative relationship between labor supply and the real wage rate, since money wages are assumed to be constant. It is then concluded that workers must be subject to a form of money illusion, and the question is whether money illusion can ever characterize an economically correct solu-

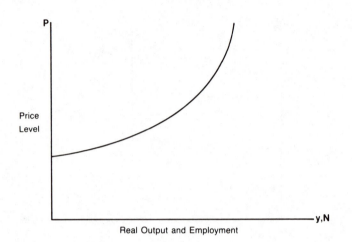

Figure 7.3.   Aggregate Supply in an Eclectic Macroeconomic Model

tion to the missing equation problem and the shape of the aggregate supply schedule.

   In our opinion a negative relationship between labor supply and real wage rates is not necessarily evidence of irrational behavior on the part of workers, particularly in an uncertain environment. In Chapter 10 we will construct an argument suggesting that currently employed workers will accept a reduction in real wages so that currently unemployed workers might find work. Of course these workers must be compensated for any reduction in real wages, and one form this compensation might take in an uncertain world is to reduce their risk of becoming unemployed sometime in the future. This idea of risk and return sharing among different types of workers will be seen in Chapter 9 to evolve from certain ideas in financial contracting. However, before presenting these ideas it will be useful to now summarize the model economies we have discussed in this chapter.

Summary and Conclusions

   The objective of this chapter has been to present a financial description of macroeconomic activity that in a number of ways parallels the various household allocation problems developed and discussed throughout this work. The similarities to previous discussions are striking. For example, in Chapter 2 we discussed Fisher's theory of household allocation under conditions of certainty, and observed that consumption and investment decisions were separated for the individual thanks to the existence of a perfect capital market. Yet in Chapter 3 for all households taken together we observed that consumption and investment were jointly determined with interest rates by tastes, technology, and initial income endowments. In Fisher's perfectly certain and frictionless world, there was no risky asset nor was there a need for money; hence income and portfolio allocation were one and the same. The discussion then switched to an uncertain environment in Chapter 4 where we presented the capital asset pricing model. In the CAPM we encountered a second separation; namely, one between distributing capital among the different risky firms in the market portfolio (the so-called security analysis problem) and then distributing capital between the risky and riskless sectors of production in the economy (the so-called investment management problem). This analysis, however, did not provide a solution to the income allocation or intertemporal consumption problems, but instead took total savings as given.

In a sense these two ideas—income allocation between current consumption and investment, and portfolio allocation between riskless and risky securities—are combined in the Keynesian description of a macroeconomic equilibrium, or at least the IS-LM version of that analysis. In the IS part we observed the varying combinations of national income and yields in Figure 7.1 that solve the intertemporal consumption problem. In the LM part of the analysis we observed the varying combinations of national income and yields on financial assets that solve the wealth or portfolio allocation problem. The end result was that the simultaneous solution to both the income and wealth allocation problems yields a macroeconomic equilibrium; that is, equilibrium levels of national income, consumption, investment, and the rate of return on securities in the capital market.[24]

These results were achieved within the framework of a rudimentary income-expenditure model when the price level was assumed to be determined by outside forces. When we incorporated prices directly into the analysis, difficulties immediately arose. The entire system then became indeterminate in that there were more economic variables to be explained than equations available for explanation. Accordingly there followed several attempts to close the system with some long lost supply equation, but by and large these attempts have proven to be a disappointment. We therefore still do not have an adequate economic explanation—one that incorporates rational behavior on the part of all participants to the productive process—of how aggregate supply adjusts, in terms of prices and real output, to changes in aggregate demand.

We believe the problems associated with a heretofore inadequate specification of aggregate supply stem primarily from the failure of the analysis to provide firms (and the different input contributors that compose the firm) with objectives, the attainment of which involves some optimal way of varying real output and prices during the period of supply adjustment.[25] In other words, up to this point the goals and objectives of firms—along with their fulfillment via price and output adjustments—have not been adequately incorporated into our discussions of macroeconomic activity. What are the objectives of firms in the income-expenditure or monetarist descriptions of macroeconomic activity? Presumably the objective would be profit or stock market value maximization. This of course is a somewhat narrow objective, since a rational supply adjustment must also accommodate other rational contributors to the production process such as creditors and workers. Yet even profit or wealth maximization would only seem to be explicitly incorporated in equation (7.2) where businesses are presumed to carry new capital expenditures to the point where the marginal efficiency on new investments equals the cost of capital prevailing in the financial market. But this kind of profit or stock market value maximization does not address the problem of short-run supply adjustment, since by assumption new investment has no effect on short-run supply. Since it would seem that demand-oriented models such as the quantity theory and the income-expenditure theory have little or nothing to say about supply, at least as demand theories, we will be free to construct our own theory of supply adjustment.

Our theory of supply adjustment will be presented in Chapter 9. A key feature of this theory will be to link the supply adjustment to the welfare of the various participants in the production process. In order to do this we will have to provide a more detailed description of the financial claims that define the interests of these participants (as well as the interrelationships of interests among participants) than was considered in the classical and income-expenditure theories. Since modern productive activity usually requires a number of different types of input contributors, and each type of contributor tends to have a unique financial interest defined by a unique financial contract, we will see that the goals and objectives of an enterprise will be multidimensional. This must necessarily be the case, for otherwise the gains and losses associated with a particular supply adjustment will benefit some contributors while harming others. These considerations will lead us to a careful study of financial contracts and the role these contracts play in guiding the price and output decisions of firms when demand conditions change. But this is getting somewhat ahead of our story. Economists have not ignored the supply response of a market economy subject to changes in aggregate demand, and in Chapter 8 we will review several strands of that insightful work.

Notes

1. Recall again that the structure of the risky subportfolio was assumed to be identical among individual investors (the result of homogeneous expectations among investors regarding the pattern of returns on risky assets), but that the magnitude of

both subportfolios could differ among investors (due to differences in risk aversion and wealth endowments). We mention these characterizations of portfolio behavior in the *CAPM* again, since there will be similarities and differences in the characterization of portfolio behavior set forth later in this chapter.

2. For the original statement of these ideas see Keynes (1936).

3. Emphasizing the financial aspects of the Keynesian system is certainly in keeping with Keynes himself since he was first and foremost a student of finance. In this connection see Harrod (1951) for a clarification of the fact and fiction regarding his financial acumen, which evidently surfaced in his early days at Eton. Keynes would appear to have been one of the few and random exceptions to the efficient market hypothesis. For an attempt to document this see Chua and Woodward (1983).

4. Nonrudimentary Keynesian models have attempted to fill this void. For an example of this kind of model see Sargent (1979).

5. In this connection it should be noted that national income and product accounts were just emerging in the United Kingdom and the United States, and therefore it can be presumed that this breakdown of national expenditures was not unknown to him.

6. In a world of perfect certainty and perfect markets, specialization in production based on comparative advantage was not considered to be a barrier to utility maximization subject to the endowment constraint by the classical school of economic thought. Thus, even if clothing workers were paid in cloth, they could exchange their cloth for whatever market basket of goods and services they desired in a world of perfect certainty and perfect markets. In a world of uncertainty and imperfect markets these same clothing workers may be constrained in what they demand by what they think they can sell their cloth for in the market. This is one of the main lines of argument in the disequilibrium account of the Keynesian system.

7. The most explicit reference to risk concerns the marginal efficiency of investment which, along with the cost of capital in the capital market, determines the level of aggregate investment. This marginal efficiency of investment was deemed by Keynes to fluctuate a great deal from time to time in actual economies. Finally, new investment is assumed to have no effect on aggregate supply in the period in which it is undertaken.

8. This must assume that there is some unemployment in the system in the first place, for otherwise output could never rise within the time framework of the model.

9. This one good assumption rules out any importance of income redistribution effects associated with changes in tastes and technology.

10. What, in effect, we are doing is assuming that employment is the only variable determined in the labor market, and that it is determined on the demand side by firms. The alternative interpretation is that the aggregate supply schedule in the economy is horizontal at the fixed price, and variations in aggregate demand determine aggregate output.

11. Thus, at any given moment, businesses are contemplating a number of capital projects each with their own internal rate of return. These capital projects with their associated internal rates of return form what Keynes called the marginal efficiency of investment schedule; that is, a schedule of subjective expected internal rates of return on the different projects. This subjective distribution of internal rates of return is assumed to be fixed by firms for the time period of the model.

12. Keynes' theory of liquidity preference was modified by Tobin (1958) when the latter showed that portfolio diversification (each investor holding both cash and risky securities) based on homogeneous expectations could also produce a negative relationship between money demand and the yield on risky securities in the capital market.

13. We ignore the other motives Keynes attributed to the desire to hold money such as precautionary and financial motives. These are strictly subsidiary motives in the context of the rudimentary model we are describing and can be safely set aside.

There are several other comments that might be made at this point regarding liquidity preference. To begin with, it should be noted that in Keynes' view, different households will generally have different expectations regarding the future yield on risky securities. These expectations in turn are distributed among different investors, and this distribution is assumed to be fixed. Changes in the current and observable yield on financial securities will then change the relative desirability of holding money balances or securities in a portfolio, and this is why Keynes argued that the speculative demand for money was negatively related to the current and observable yield on risky securities. A reduction in the current yield on risky securities will induce some investors at the margin to sell their securities and hold cash because their expectation is that on balance security yields will rise in the future. The negative relationship between money demand for speculators and the current yield on risky securities can be described by a smooth curve if there are a sufficient number of portfolio investors holding diverse expectations regarding the future yields or valuations on risky securities. The second point worth noting is that some financial economists (e.g., Baumol 1952 and Tobin 1956) have suggested that the transaction motive for holding money is negatively related to the yield on securities. The arguments here parallel those developed in inventory theory and point out that interest revenues and possible capital gains are benefits associated in holding transaction balances in securities, and that transaction costs of moving into and out of securities must be deducted from these benefits in order to evaluate the holding of transaction requirements in securities. Thus, when yields are high, agents will find it relatively more profitable to hold transaction requirements in the form of securities and incur the costs of cashing in those securities when cash payments are to be made. One advantage of incorporating the yield sensitivity into a transaction motive for holding money is that there is no easy empirical way to differentiate money balances held for transaction purposes and money balances held for speculative purposes. For an empirical test of Keynes' liquidity preference that tries to make this differentiation, see Krainer (1969) where customer-free credit balances held at brokerage firms are used to proxy speculative money balances. The results of these empirical tests are consistent with the Keynesian hypothesis of liquidity preference.

14. Similarly we will set aside the issue of causality (does a change in money cause a change in GNP, or does a change in GNP cause a change in the supply of money, or is the causation in both directions?) between money and national income since we are interested in describing the Keynesian system and do not intend to use the model to simulate the effects of monetary policy. For a discussion of the causality issue see Sims (1972) and the several papers in the Carnegie-Rochester Conference Series on Public Affairs, a supplement to the *Journal of Monetary Economics*, Vol. 10, 1979.

15. Remember that in this part of our discussion the price level is assumed to be fixed. Hence, changes in nominal GNP and other nominal variables (represented below by capital letters) will also reflect changes in real variables.

16. Subscripts on a variable will indicate differentiation; e.g., $F_Y = \partial S/\partial Y$.

17. We are aware of the problems associated with the discounted cash flow or marginal efficiency of investment approach to capital expenditure decisions at the individual firm level as originally pointed out by Lorie and Savage (1955) and Hirschleifer (1958). If the reader chooses, he or she can give a present value interpretation to equation (7.2) which overcomes many, but not all, of these problems.

18. At this point our model economy contains six variables ($S, I, Y, r, M_D,$ and M_S) and six equations and is therefore mathematically determinant.

19. Some economists in the income-expenditure tradition have suggested that the so-called Phillips curve closes the system described in equations (7.1i) through (7.6i). The Phillips curve—a subject we will discuss in Chapter 8—postulates that the rate of change of money wages or prices is negatively related to unemployment, which is taken to be a proxy for excess demand in the labor and goods markets. Thus it might be argued that if we knew the rate of change of prices and some initial starting price level, then we would know the entire time sequence of prices, including the particular price level associated with any given macroeconomic equilibrium. Nevertheless we must still have some historically given initial price level, and this is what is meant when it is said that prices are determined by outside factors.

20. This has come to be called the classical dichotomy; that is, the separation of nominal from real magnitudes in the economy. In this kind of model economy, employment (and real output generated by some production function) is determined at the intersection point of supply and demand schedules in the labor market. Thus, firms demand labor up to the point where the marginal product of labor equals the real wage, and workers supply labor up to the point where the real wage rate equals the marginal rate of substitution between real income and leisure. According to this theory any change in nominal magnitudes (e.g., changes in the stock of money or level of expenditures independent of real income) will be reflected in offsetting shifts in the supply and demand schedules in the labor market, leaving the total volume of employment and output unchanged. For a more complete description of the classical model see Sargent (1979, chap. 1).

21. In this simple artificial economy there will be no attempt to distinguish between output and employment since we are mainly concerned with comparing classical and income-expenditure theories of macroeconomics equilibrium. We do not mean to suggest, however, that a one-to-one correspondence between output and employment always exists in actual economies.

22. For a given stock of money the slope of the aggregate demand curve for the economy described in equations (7.1i) through (7.6i) can be shown to be:

$$\frac{dy}{dP} = \frac{(-M/P^2)l_r}{f_y/(g_r - f_r) + l_y/l_r} < 0$$

23. For a description of this solution see Blinder and Solow (1974).

24. Since the risky securities are assumed to be perfect substitutes for each

other in the Keynesian system, the risk premium $[E(R_M) - R_F]$ of Chapter 4 is what is actually determined in the IS-LM analysis.

25. As we mentioned above, money illusion on the part of workers or institutional factors that make wage rates rigid on the down side are the usual means by which it is possible to justify an upward-sloping aggregate supply schedule. With these kinds of assumptions an upward-sloping supply schedule is consistent with profit maximization but not with utility maximization on the part of all workers.

—8—

The Phillips Curve and
Rational Expectations Models
of Aggregate Supply

Introduction

In Chapter 7 we described a conventional short-run model of aggregate demand for an entire society. The model was kept simple for the express purpose of highlighting the differences in professional opinion regarding strategy toward the modelling of aggregate economic activity. It was then noted— following Friedman (1974) and Blinder and Solow (1974)—that this "square one" model of income determination fell one equation short of a price level and output description of the macroeconomic process. Moreover, it soon became apparent that what was missing was an adequate description of the supply side of the economy. There then followed a first generation discussion of how the various schools of macroeconomic thought modelled the supply side of the economy and thereby provided the so-called missing equation. In this connection we also discussed the financial arrangements of the firms in the conventional models with a view toward determining whether or not these arrangements shed some light on the supply adjustment of an economy. Unfortunately the financial arrangements were not rich enough to provide any insight into the pricing and output decisions of firms. By and large this same implication surfaced in our discussions in Chapter 4 concerning capital market equilibrium, for there, too, we observed an independence between financing and operating decisions. In this regard the two contending macro models analyzed in Chapter 7 were not unlike the capital asset pricing model discussed in Chapter 4 in that all three are one-security models of the production process and are driven by equity value maximization.

In this chapter we will continue the analysis by considering second and higher generation attempts to supply the missing equation. Over time, according to Tobin (1974), the price level variable of interest has slipped several derivatives so that the relationship to be studied now is one between inflation and the acceleration of inflation, and the level of output and unemployment.[1] One of the first economists to analyze this relationship was A. W. Phillips (1958) and his empirically derived curve, which related the rate of change of money wages to the percentage of the work force unemployed, initiated one of the most important and controversial research areas in macroeconomics in the post-World War II period.[2] What the Phillips curve seemed to suggest was that there was a relatively stable negative relationship between wage inflation (or price inflation, assuming a constant percentage markup over wage costs) and unemployment. Consequently society seemed to be faced with a choice between two evils: it could, through its government, choose less unemployment and higher output by accepting a higher rate of inflation, or it could choose less inflation, but only at the cost of higher unemployment and a lower level of output. Regardless of the choice, government financial policy would play a key role in the actual amount of unemployment and inflation a society would experience in actual fact.

The success of the Phillips curve was almost instantaneous, and understandably so. Look at what it delivered. First and foremost, it preserved the deeply ingrained Renaissance ideal that Western men and women, at any rate, are indeed masters of their collective economic fate. More important, it tempered the unabashedly optimistic Keynesian expression of that ideal by pointing out that just because we are masters of our fate does not necessarily mean we can alleviate all economic problems at the same time. This provided balance and a sense of proportion along with the opportunity for exhibiting political judgment. Just what combination of unemployment and inflation a society should work toward could be left to the political process, and political parties in the United States attempted, to a certain extent, to differentiate their styles of administration by picking different points on the Phillips trade-off curve. When an idea in economics has that much to offer it is indeed hard to refuse.

In the remainder of this chapter, we will review the birth and development of this economic idea. Since a great deal of professional economic research has been carried out in this area, our review of developments must be selective as well as brief.[3]

Macroeconomic Adjustment and the Labor Market: An Overview

Toward this end it will first be useful to briefly say a word about the determinants of employment in the market for labor services, since an analysis of the labor market underlies much of the research in this area. Consider then Figure 8.1, which presents the typical partial equilibrium description of the labor market where the supply and demand for labor services are oppo-

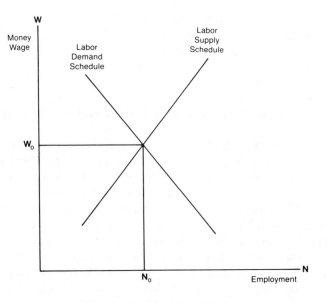

Figure 8.1.   The Labor Market

site functions of the money wage rate, when output prices and labor productivity are assumed to be constant. The intersection of the supply and demand schedules determine the equilibrium money wage rate, W_0, and the level of employment, N_0. Moreover, once the level of employment is determined in the labor market, the level of real output is then determined by the aggregate production function. The somewhat delicate if not difficult problem is to explain just how a change in government financial policy will work its way through an economic system with rational agents to effect the supply and demand schedules for labor services, output prices, money wage rates, employment, and the level of output. In this connection it must be remembered that money wage rates and product prices are determined in separate but related markets, and hence workers and capitalists must form estimates of what they will in fact be after the output is produced and priced and the income distributed to both factor input contributors. When workers and capitalists are blessed with perfect foresight this poses no problem. On the other hand, when agents cannot accurately predict what effects government policy will have on the system—in particular, the effect on product prices— then it becomes more difficult to assess the effects such policies might have on the levels of employment and output. Thus the description of the labor market presented in Figure 8.1 is not rich enough to adequately describe the employment and output effects resulting from a change in policy. In order to

assess these effects we must first understand how government financial policy changes money wage rates and prices, and then how agents perceive and
react to changes in wage rates and prices.

The Phillips Analysis of the Labor Market and Supply Adjustments

One of the first attempts to shed some light on the dynamic nature of
adjustments in the labor market was provided by Phillips. There are several
different ways to present the Phillips analysis, and we will choose one that
assumes the supply of labor services by workers depends only on the money
wage rate. With this assumption in hand, consider panel A of Figure 8.2
where we present three states of excess supply (i.e., the negative of excess
demand) in the labor market: (1) zero excess supply at wage rate W_0, (2) negative excess supply at W_1, and (3) positive excess supply at W_2. Conventional
economic analysis suggests that whenever a market is in disequilibrium and
experiences negative excess supply, there will be a tendency for prices (or
wage rates, in this case) to rise. Similarly, prices will tend to fall when excess
supply is positive. In the context of the labor market this suggests a relationship between the rate of change in money wages and the excess supply of
labor; namely, when excess supply is negative, money wage rates tend to rise,
and when excess supply is positive, wage rates will tend to fall. Phillips, however, wanted a more tractible measure of excess supply than the one implied
in the directly unobservable supply-and-demand framework presented in
Figures 8.1 and 8.2. He obtained one by the simple expedient of defining the
excess supply of labor in terms of the percentage of the workforce unemployed.[4] Consequently the dynamic adjustments that take place in the labor
market as a result of shifts in the unobservable supply-and-demand schedules could be summarized by a negative (and convex) relationship between
the unemployment rate, U, and the percentage rate of change in money
wages, $\dot{W}/W$, as pictured in panel B of Figure 8.2. Phillips then proceeded
to measure this relationship for the United Kingdom over the period
1861–1957, and empirically obtained the curve that now bears his name.[5]
Subsequent interest, however, shifted from the Phillips curve, or the relationship between unemployment rates and wage inflation, to one between
unemployment rates and price inflation, $\dot{P}/P$, on the grounds that firms apply a roughly constant markup over prime labor costs when setting the selling
prices for their goods and services. In this way the Phillips relationship—
which was originally directed toward a dynamic analysis of the labor market—was transformed to one between price inflation and output (the other
side of the unemployment coin) and thereby thought to provide a superior
second generation solution to the missing equation problem. This new relationship is pictured in panel C of Figure 8.2. Yet we cannot repeat too often
that Phillips himself did not make this transformation in his original article,

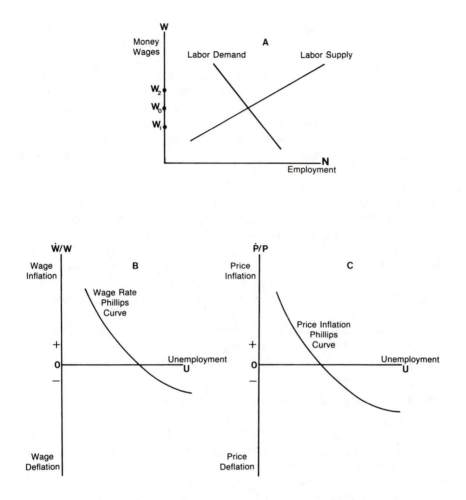

Figure 8.2.   The Labor Market and the Phillips Curve

and as we indicated in note 5 he was well aware of the potential dangers. Thus, while we will follow the convention of referring to the relationship between the unemployment rate and price inflation as the Phillips curve, we must remember that in writing, at any rate, Phillips had certain reservations.

And the reservations soon began to surface. On the empirical front new evidence from the late 1960s and 1970s proved to be inconsistent with a stable relationship between the unemployment rate and price inflation for a number of countries. While politicians may have professed that they could, if elected, push the Phillips curve toward the origin, economists were reporting that the relationship was apparently shifting outward over time. This was not good news. Moreover some economists even suggested that the relationship just might be positive, not as a long-run equilibrium proposition, but as a transitory phenomenon that could last for decades as society adjusted its institutions to changing rates of inflation induced by the supply shocks most market economies were experiencing during that time.[6] These empirical observations were accompanied by a number of theoretical objections. Phillips was not alone in understanding that his relationship between wage inflation and the unemployment rate (as a proxy for excess supply in the labor market) had more empirical and common sense support when price level changes could be safely ignored. It all goes back to Figure 8.2 where it was assumed that the supply of labor services is a function of the nominal wage rate, provided output prices can be taken as given. However, if businesses are constantly marking output prices up when wage rates rise, it would only seem reasonable that workers would eventually learn to take that fact into account when offering their labor services on the market. Not to do so would be evidence of either an inordinately long learning process or, worse yet, irrational behavior. Most economists are inclined to reject this latter explanation out of hand. The former explanation of why workers may not take inflation into account immediately when bargaining for money wages is still being debated among professional economists. In any event, while economists will continue to disagree about how long it might take workers (or capitalists for that matter) to realize that prices are changing, when in fact they are changing, hardly anyone now believes that it will take forever.

The Natural Rate of Unemployment Hypothesis

Abraham Lincoln once said: "You can fool all the people some of the time, and some of the people all of the time, but you cannot fool all the people all of the time." The Lincoln distinction between the short run and long run became the foundation for the third generation analysis of the adjustment process and eventually became known as the natural rate of unemployment hypothesis. The natural rate hypothesis suggests that in the short run, workers and capitalists can indeed misread the price system, particularly when there is an unexpected monetary shock. The reason they misread it is that a monetary shock that unexpectedly alters the rate of change of the general price level blurs changes in relative prices upon which firms make employment and output decisions and workers or their organizations make labor supply decisions. Nevertheless any short-run change in the supply and demand for labor and output that arises from misperceiving movements in relative prices will tend to be corrected in a longer run when all the participants in the economy come to better understand the nature and implications of the unexpected short-run monetary shock. What this hypothesis implies, in other words, is that setting aside short-run disturbances, there will be a natural rate of unemployment in the economy determined by a host of more basic considerations such as unemployment insurance schemes, availability of information concerning job opportunities, occupational barriers to entry, and other factors bearing on labor mobility. This unemployment is more frictional in nature than the involuntary type envisioned by Keynes. More importantly this natural rate of unemployment is impervious to government financial policy within a longer time framework unless the government is prepared to increasingly surprise the private sector with successively larger doses of policy action.[7] Obviously the government can only go so far in this direction. An excellent description of this distinction between the short run and long run is contained in Friedman (1977, pp. 456–457) and is worth repeating here.

> Start from some initial stable position and let there be, for example, an unanticipated acceleration of aggregate nominal demand. This will come to each producer as an unexpectedly favorable demand for his product. In an environment in which changes are always occurring in the relative demand for different goods, he will not know whether this change is special to him or pervasive. It will be rational for him to interpret it as at least partly special and to react to it, by seeking to produce more to sell at what he now perceives to be a higher-than-expected market price for future output. He will be willing to pay higher nominal wages than he had been willing to pay before in order to attract additional workers. The real wage that matters to him is the wage in terms of the price of his product, and he perceives that price as higher than before. A higher nominal wage can therefore mean a lower *real* wage as perceived by him.
>
> To workers, the situation is different: what matters to them is the purchasing power of wages not over the particular good they produce, but over all goods in general. Both they and their employers are likely to adjust more slowly their perception of prices in general—because it is more costly to acquire information about that—than their perceptions of the price of the particular good they produce. As a result, a rise in nominal wages may be perceived by workers as a rise in real wages and hence call forth an increased supply, at the time that it is perceived by employers as a fall in real wages and hence calls forth an increased offer of jobs. Expressed in terms of the average of perceived future prices, real wages are lower; in terms of the perceived future average price, real wages are higher.
>
> But this situation is temporary: let the higher rate of growth of aggregate nominal demand and of prices continue, and perceptions will adjust to reality. When they do, the initial effect will disappear, and then even be reversed for a time as workers and employers find themselves locked into inappropriate contracts. Ultimately, employment will be back at the level that prevailed before the assumed unanticipated acceleration in aggregate nominal demand.

The natural rate hypothesis can be described quite succinctly in graphical form as in Figure 8.3. There we observe a series of negatively sloped short-run Phillips curves, each one associated with a given expectation of future inflation on the part of workers and capitalists. These curves have come to be called the "expectation adjusted" Phillips curves, since successively higher curves are associated with higher rates of expected inflation. Consider, then, an initial situation in which there is an expectation of zero inflation and unemployment is at its natural rate U^*. The short-run expectations adjusted Phillips curve describing this situation is labelled A. Now let there be a monetary expansion that in the end raises the inflation rate to B percent in the figure. According to this theory unemployment will now move to its unnatural short-run disequilibrium rate of U_{ST} as frictionally unemployed workers and capitalists misperceive the relative price relationships associated with the hitherto unanticipated change in the price level occasioned by the expansionary monetary policy. Eventually, so the argument goes, both capitalists and laborers will come to realize that barring any new unexpected monetary shock, the price level will now be changing at the rate of B percent per period. When this realization occurs (and the theory does not tell us when it will occur) the economy will find itself on a new short-run Phillips curve associated with B percent expected inflation.[8]

What level of unemployment and output characterizes the new long-run equilibrium when all participants come to expect B percent inflation? Many economists would argue that if the initial equilibrium was a true long-run equilibrium where laborers and capitalists have solved their intertemporal consumption and labor-leisure problems as described in Chapter 3, then there would seem to be little reason not to believe that unemployment would return to its former level of U^*. From a pedagogical point of view, this argument is perhaps most easily understood when we assume that all unemployment in the initial equilibrium is of a voluntary nature and shared among all laborers—e.g., all laborers work 40 hours per week when in fact they would voluntarily work more or less depending upon whether the real wage was higher or lower. When this is the case the unanticipated rise in money wages may fool these workers into thinking that their real wage in terms of general consumption goods has risen and therefore lead them to supply more labor services to capitalists—who in turn think real wages (in terms of their product price) are falling compared to the initial equilibrium wage—thereby reducing unemployment *qua* leisure and raising real output. Sooner or later these workers will come to realize that their higher money wages are not turning out to be the higher real wage they anticipated, and consequently they are no longer in equilibrium with respect to their labor-leisure allocation of time. The remedy is then to simply cut back the number of hours they are now working to that prevailing in the initial equilibrium. If capitalists and laborers were satisfied with the level and distribution of in-

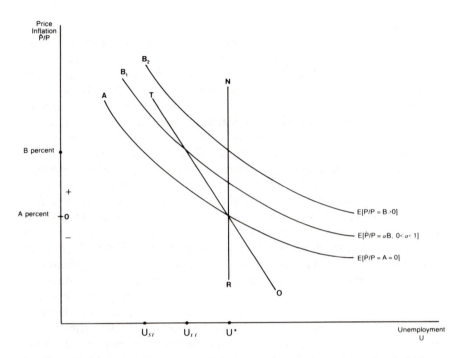

Figure 8.3. Long-Run and Short-Run Inflation-Unemployment Trade-Off

come in the initial equilibrium (and that is the definition of a long-run natural rate equilibrium), then there is no reason why they should not return to it, for there is an appropriate wage agreement, when the economy is experiencing a *B* percent inflation rate, that will enable both parties to return to the initial position. In this sense the rate of unemployment described by *U** is a natural rate and is unaffected by government financial policy.

In one sense the trade-off between inflation and unemployment in the natural rate hypothesis centers around the distribution of income. When the economy is in some initial long-run equilibrium such as *U**, the level of output and distribution of income among capitalists and laborers is fixed, setting aside population growth and technical progress. Of course both parties would prefer to obtain a larger share of the output pie in the market place if it were possible. When there is an unexpected increase in the price level, stemming from an expansionary monetary policy, both parties come to believe that they can obtain a larger share of the pie, and therefore both join together to bake it. This is the short-run output response of the expansionary monetary policy. Why then doesn't the economy continue producing this higher level of output? The answer must be that after the uncertainty created by the change in the inflation rate of general prices is diminished (due to a better understanding of the monetary environment acquired by agents over time), either capitalists or laborers come to be dissatisfied with both their level and share of total output. For the disgruntled party the extra income earned in going from U^* to U_{ST} does not merit the expenditure of additional labor or capital services required to produce the larger output. The disgruntled party therefore votes with its factor service to return to U^* where both parties grudgingly agreed to produce and distribute the social output in a certain way. If they could not agree—as they did not at U_{ST}—then U^* by definition could not constitute a natural rate of unemployment.

The natural rate hypothesis distinction between the short run and long run is pictured in Figure 8.3. There we can see that when the inflation rate in the economy (described on the vertical axis) moves from A percent to B percent, the short-run Phillips curve shifts from A to B_2. How do we know that over time the curve will shift to B_2, no more, no less? We know the curve must shift to B_2, for this is the only short-run Phillips curve that is consistent with B percent expected inflation and the natural rate of unemployment U^*. Any other curve would relate the natural rate of unemployment to a different expected inflation rate than that given by B percent per period. Furthermore, according to this hypothesis all subsequent changes in the anticipated inflation rate of a given percent will shift the short-run Phillips curve by an equivalent amount so that in long-run equilibrium all unemployment is exactly at the natural rate U^* and therefore independent of the inflation rate in the economy. Thus, in equilibrium there is no trade-off between inflation and unemployment, and the long-run Phillips curve is nothing more than the vertical line NR passing through the natural rate of unemployment U^* in Figure 8.3.

Others disagree with the practical significance of this view regarding the effectiveness of government financial policy. Their disagreement is partly based on empirics and partly on their prior views of agent behavior. In terms of Figure 8.3 they might argue that an unanticipated change in the inflation rate of B percent may not always shift the short-run Phillips curve by a proportionate amount in what might be considered a very long period of time, but instead shift the short-run curve a fraction of the distance, say to B_1, rather than the shift to B_2 required by the natural rate hypothesis. The end result is that in some long run (in terms of calendar time) there does exist a negative relationship between unemployment and the inflation rate, although this relationship is less sensitive (i.e., more steeply sloped) than the short-run relationship. Such a long-run relationship is presented in Figure 8.3 by the line TO where a B percent inflation eventually becomes associated with an unemployment rate of U_{LT}; a rate somewhere between the short-run rate of U_{ST}—where participants in the economy were initially fooled by the impact of the expansionary monetary policy—and the unemployment rate of

U^*. Practical explanations of this generally take the form of arguments to the effect that it could take laborers or capitalists an inordinate length of time to learn the implications of the monetary expansion or contraction, whichever the case might be. Those critical of this explanation label it irrational or demeaning to the intelligence of agents, while those who defend it speak of costs associated with adjusting the labor force and the acquisition of information. To an outsider, theoretical purity (or simplicity, depending on your prejudices) seems to reside on one side of the argument while the intellectually stifling barrier of reality resides on the other.

The Keynes-Phillips model, along with the natural rate hypothesis, has done much to clarify our thinking about the conditions under which money is neutral in a long-run classical analysis. We suspect the classical economists learned this important truth with a set of ideas that drew from their own actual economic experiences, and future generations will learn it again from their own actual economic experiences. Yet the debate over the efficacy of government financial policy continues and will continue to be debated as long as economists differentiate their insights along the dimension of time. The classical tradition has been to explore economic issues within the context of "economic slow time;" that is, the length of time it takes to remove uncertainty from the system and all participants learn the true model that drives the economy. In this time framework government financial policy is irrelevant, just like private financial policy discussed in Chapter 4. Those economists who follow the income-expenditure tradition choose to study the system in short-run disequilibrium when participants have not yet discovered the model that drives the economy. Within the disequilibrium—just as in the Modigliani-Miller disequilibrium of $V_L \neq V_u$—there is the prospect of obtaining an arbitrage profit or a "free lunch," something which is unthinkable within the context of a long-run equilibrium. The implication is that, for better or worse, government financial policy is more likely to impact on the level of output and unemployment when it creates a disequilibrium characterized by uncertainty than when that disequilibrium and uncertainty are dissipated by time and the learning of economic agents. Thus the adherents to both schools of thought argue at cross-purposes with one another in the sense that they tend to impose the time dimension and degree of uncertainty that is unique to their own framework of analysis when discussing economic policy. The old argument concerning the relative importance of income and wealth effects now evolves into a new argument between rational expectations and the presumed ignorance of agents during short-run disequilibrium.[9] One would suppose that empirical analysis could resolve the question of the time dimension and the effectiveness of policy, but it soon became apparent, when testing the natural rate hypothesis, that reconciliation would not be coming from that direction.

Empirical Tests of the Natural Rate Hypothesis and the Theory of Rational Expectations

Empirical tests of the natural rate hypothesis generally begin with a statement regarding the behavior of money and real wages, which can be described as follows:

$$\dot{W}/W = \alpha(\dot{P}/P)^* + \beta(U) + \gamma(LP) \tag{8.1}$$

$$(\dot{W}/W - \dot{P}/P) = (LP) \tag{8.2}$$

Equation (8.1) says that the rate of growth of money wages, $(\dot{W}/W)$, is some positive function α of the expected inflation rate, $(\dot{P}/P)^*$, a negative function β of unemployment, U, and a positive function γ of the rate of growth of labor productivity, (LP). In equation (8.2) the rate of growth of real wages is determined by the rate of growth of labor productivity. By inserting (8.1) into a rearranged (8.2) we obtain the relationship between price inflation and labor productivity, unemployment, and expected price inflation; namely:

$$(\dot{P}/P) = \alpha(\dot{P}/P)^* + \beta(U) - (1 - \gamma)(LP) \tag{8.3}$$

In (8.3) we can see that a change in the expected inflation rate, other things remaining equal, shifts the relationship between inflation and unemployment just as it did in Figure 8.3 when agents came to expect a B percent inflation rate when previously they expected an A percent inflation. Similarly, an increase in the rate of growth of labor productivity shifts the short-run Phillips curve toward the origin by the factor $(1 - \gamma)$. This is one reason why economists and public policymakers are so concerned about labor productivity, for if one accepts the notion of a Phillips trade-off, then an increase in the growth rate of labor productivity will reduce the cost of any given unemployment policy the government may want to follow in terms of inflation. A rise in the growth rate of labor productivity is one way we can "have our cake and eat it too."

The actual empirical tests of the natural rate hypothesis generally proceed by analyzing (8.1) or (8.3). In order to statistically analyze either, it is necessary to, among other things, describe the process by which price inflation expectations are formed. In the early empirical work it was often assumed that inflation expectations were generated by the adaptive mechanism:

$$(\dot{P}/P)^*_t = \sum_{1}^{N}{}_i \theta_i(\dot{P}/P)_{t-i} \qquad \theta_i \geqslant 0 \tag{8.1a}$$

with the identifying constraint

$$\sum_{1}^{N} {}_{i} \, \theta_i \, = \, 1.0 \tag{8.1b}$$

Incorporating (8.1a) and (8.1b) into (8.1) or (8.3), an estimating equation is obtained in terms of observable variables. The equation is then estimated to see whether $\alpha = 1.0$, a result which is consistent with the natural rate hypothesis; or $\alpha < 1.0$, a result that indicates a long-run expectations adjusted trade-off between unemployment and inflation.[10]

By and large the early studies found $\alpha < 1.$[11] Almost immediately, however, those who were skeptical on theoretical grounds discounted these results, pointing out that the tests actually conducted in these experiments were joint tests; tests of the sought-after unemployment-inflation trade-off, and tests of the ancillary expectations generating mechanism described in (8.1a) and (8.1b). As such these empirical tests were subject to various interpretations, and therefore could not be regarded as being definitive, just as we noted in Chapter 6 that certain empirical tests conducted with the CAPM concerning capital market efficiency could not be regarded as being definitive.

Over time these criticisms crystallized around the ideas promulgated by those economists following the rational expectations tradition, a tradition started by John Muth (1961).[12] One early criticism in this tradition was offered by Sargent (1971) and centered around the possible bias against the natural rate hypothesis when the empirical test incorporated the adaptive expectations mechanism described in (8.1a) and (8.1b). In this connection suppose the actual inflation rate is generated by the following autoregressive process:

$$(\dot{P}/P)_t = \sum_{1}^{N} {}_{i} \, \theta_i \, (\dot{P}/P)_{t-i} + \epsilon_t \tag{8.1c}$$

where ϵ_t is an independent identically distributed random variable with mean zero and constant variance. Sargent's point is that equation (8.1a) with constraint (8.1b) will not, in general, be a rational expectations generator unless the actual inflation rate is described by (8.1c). Yet (8.1c) combined with the constraint in (8.1b) implies high intertemporal serial correlation of the inflation rate, and such serial correlation was not observed in the U.S. data, at least prior to 1971. The implication then is that the θ_i coefficients should sum to a number less than unity. By constraining these coefficients to sum to unity—as the adaptive expectations model does—an upward bias is imparted to the estimates of θ_i and a corresponding downward bias to the estimate of α in equation (8.1), and hence we mistakenly reject the natural rate hypothesis.

In a later paper Sargent (1973) proposed an alternative test of the natural rate hypothesis; a test that does not directly rely on expectations being generated by the adaptive mechanism described in (8.1a) and (8.1b). The empirical strategy was to decompose the actual inflation rate into a systematic and unsystematic component. According to the natural rate hypothesis the systematic component of the inflation rate should have no effect on unemployment since all contracts in the labor market should reflect this component of the inflation rate. On the other hand the unsystematic or random component of the inflation rate could have an effect on unemployment via the surprise effect discussed above. In his statistical experiments Sargent finds that the coefficient on the unsystematic component of the inflation rate is larger (although not significantly different from zero) than the coefficient on the systematic component, a result that is in accord with the natural rate hypothesis. Yet in two of his tests the numerically smaller coefficient estimated on the systematic component of the inflation rate is actually statistically significant, while, as we mentioned above, the numerically larger coefficient on the unsystematic component is insignificantly different from zero. This result is not consistent with the natural rate hypothesis. Thus, while Sargent raises a relevant question with respect to those tests of the natural rate hypothesis that incorporate adaptive expectations, his own tests of this hypothesis are somewhat inconclusive.

An alternative strategy to test the natural rate hypothesis was developed by Lucas (1973). According to Lucas the short-run Phillips curve would be steeper when there is considerable variability in the inflation rate (i.e., the variance of the inflation rate) compared to a situation where the inflation rate as well as expectations regarding the inflation rate are relatively stable. The argument is that business and labor in any particular sector of the economy will perceive wildly fluctuating prices to be more likely the result of aggregate monetary disturbances and less likely the result of changes in relative prices about which they are presumably more knowledgeable and which, in turn, will influence the supply and demand for labor in that sector. On the other hand, when changes in the inflation rate are small, business and labor will have more difficulty in distinguishing between monetary disturbances and relative price changes, and therefore are more likely to be fooled by a change in the inflation rate. Computing variances for the price level and output level for 18 different countries over the period 1952–1967, Lucas finds that the two do not move together, as would be implied by a stable short-run Phillips relationship. This evidence is argued to be consistent with the natural rate hypothesis in the sense that the hypothesis suggests that any negative relationship between inflation and unemployment (or positive relationship with output) is the result of misperceptions on the part of laborers and capitalists, and these misperceptions are less likely to arise when the inflation rate itself is highly unstable. Yet this support for the natural rate hypothesis is somewhat weakened by the fact that unemployment and inflation are not completely contemporaneous, and therefore Lucas was forced to impose a specific lag structure on the data. For this reason the results, while suggestive, certainly cannot be taken to be the last econometric word on the natural rate hypothesis.[13]

Finally, Barro (1977) (1978) and Barro and Rush (1980) have carried out a series of econometric experiments which they have interpreted as supporting both the natural rate hypothesis discussed above and the closely related theory of rational expectations to be discussed below. While both of these theories attribute economy-wide fluctuations to the inability of private agents to accurately forecast changes in relative prices in an uncertain environment (say in response to changes in monetary growth rates), these authors go one step behind the price changes in their experiments to measure the output and unemployment response to actual and unexpected changes in monetary growth rates. This strategy was followed partly in response to the rather poor econometric performance of various price surprise terms in the empirical work of Sargent (1976) and Fair (1979) in their tests of the natural rate hypothesis. In any event, the Barro-Rush research indicated that unanticipated changes in the M1 measure of money[14] have a powerful effect on unemployment rates and real output, while raw changes in money growth rates have minimal effects, a finding that accords with the policy implications of the natural rate hypothesis and the theory of rational expectations. Additional tests were carried out that related unemployment to both unanticipated and actual changes in M1 growth rates, and it was found that only the unanticipated component had any effect on unemployment.

These results were somewhat disappointing to those who felt the government should try to stabilize the economy with discretionary monetary policy, since the only way it would seem that the monetary authority can influence real activity is to fool the private sector. Of course controversial results like these were immediately criticized on theoretical and empirical grounds.[15] Consider, in this connection, the following two theoretical objections. First, Barro (1981, p. 71) himself admits his work sheds no light on the mechanisms by which unexpected changes in monetary growth rates alter unemployment and real output. The mechanism in the natural rate and rational expectations theories centers around private agents confusing price level changes for changes in relative prices in their sectors and as a result making erroneous production adjustments. Since the mechanisms by which monetary growth rates affect the real economy are the essence of both the natural rate and rational expectations theories, the Barro-Rush empirical results will not contribute much to our understanding or acceptance of these theories themselves. There is, in other words, a black box in this work that stands between monetary policy and real output, and this black box contains the relevant theory. Whether it is the price confusion of the natural rate or rational expectations theories, or some other theory, is not addressed in the Barro-Rush work. A second theoretical objection has to do with the logical consistency in which the monetary authority conducts policy. In their theoretical framework the predictions of private agents are supposedly equivalent to the equilibrium values of the variables the agents are trying to predict. One variable agents are trying to predict in this model is the growth rate of M1. According to the Barro-Rush econometric model the monetary growth rate is partly determined by the monetary authorities' attempt to reduce unemployment that is currently being reported for the previous year. Thus, when unemployment rises in period $t - 1$, the Federal Reserve is presumed to react by increasing the growth rate of M1 in period t. However, the underlying theory suggests the Federal Reserve should know that only unanticipated changes in the growth rate of M1 will affect unemployment and real output. Furthermore, the theory also requires that the authorities know that private agents accept this view regarding monetary influences on the economy. And yet when this is the case they cannot hope to reduce unemployment by predictably raising the monetary growth rate, since private agents will take their predictable policy into account when forming their own expectations of the monetary growth rate. In this way a change in the monetary growth rate in response to unemployment of the previous period becomes fully anticipated and hence cannot, according to the theory, influence unemployment in the current period, something the monetary authority should have known in the first place. One possible interpretation is that the Barro-Rush econometric set-up is inconsistent with the theory they are trying to validate. Besides these theoretical objections, a number of statistical and methodological issues have surfaced. To begin with, their estimating equations for unemployment and real output are reduced-form equations, whereas to evaluate the underlying theories we would need the structural representation from which these estimating equations were derived. In other words we have no information on the theoretical structure from which these estimating equations are the reduced form. A second and common criticism, when expectations or anticipations play a role in the analysis, revolves around the robustness of the results. Will the Barro-Rush findings— that only the unanticipated portion of the monetary growth rate have real effects on output and employment—stand up if a different model of the monetary growth process were used? The question is important, particularly in light of the criticism that in their work the monetary authority is behaving in an irrational manner. In turn this would seem to raise a more fundamental question in this line of research; namely, what model or models do agents use in forecasting variables that are important when it comes to making supply adjustments? It is doubtful that we will ever reach consensus on this matter. Consequently, as things stand now (in 1984), it is for theoretical rather than empirical reasons that many economists have come to accept the natural rate hypothesis. For this reason we return to the theoretical work in this area, which now takes the name of "rational expectations" or the "new classical economics."

Rational Expectations, Supply Adjustment, and Business Fluctuations

As we have observed in the last several sections, the twin assumptions of rational expectations and market equilibrium played key roles in the theory and econometrics of the natural rate of unemployment hypothesis. These same assumptions were to be used by a new generation of monetary economists, such as Barro (1981), Lucas (1972) (1975) (1977) (1980), Sargent (1976), and Sargent and Wallace (1975), to discuss essentially the same theoretical and policy issues but from a somewhat different perspective. That perspective centered around the supply response of rational agents to unanticipated changes in the purchasing power in the system, and the translation of this supply response into a theory of the business cycle. An associated issue centered around the extent to which government stabilization policy might smooth out these fluctuations in employment and output besides the obvious way of not causing them in the first place.

The central question posed in this literature was how to construct a model economy based on maximizing behavior of individual agents with rational expectations and market clearing in which changes in aggregate money supply would induce positively correlated price and output (employment) adjustments that seemed to be observed in the time series of real economies. Before discussing the models proffered by these new classical economists, let us first see how the old fixed-price Keynesian model described in Chapter 7 would go about answering this question. Toward this end consider an increase in the supply of money initiated by the Central Bank. This expansion in money will work its way through the system and reduce the rate of interest, provided, as Keynes pointed out, the schedule of liquidity preference remains fixed. The reduction in the rate of interest would then be expected to induce businesses to expand the level of investment, provided, of course, that the marginal efficiency of capital (investment) schedule remained fixed. An increase in investment, in turn, would then raise the level of output and employment via the multiplier process, provided that the consumption function remains fixed. In this way a monetary disturbance would eventually lead to a change in output and employment, although, as we have noted, there are some possible slips along the way. The key link between money and output was seen to be the rate of interest or cost of capital that in turn triggered a change in investment demand. Put somewhat differently, monetary disturbances worked their way through the economy via the financial market by influencing the cost of capital and then the level of investment demand.

Since prices were assumed to be fixed in the rudimentary model presented in Chapter 7, these monetary disturbances translated into changes in real output and employment.

The approach taken by the new classical school of economics was to be different.[16] They chose not to emphasize financial markets and the cost of financing investment, but instead focused their attention on the profitability of investment or what Keynes called the marginal efficiency of capital (investment) schedule. In taking this approach the perceptions and expectations of economic agents with regard to the present and future state of the markets they operate in turns out to play a crucial role in the analysis. To see this, consider an expansion in the stock of money, just as we did in the previous paragraph. According to this school of thought, an expansion in the money supply will lead to higher prices, although the analysis is silent as to who or what is the cause of these higher prices. In any event prices are rising in most sectors, although not necessarily at the same rate. The question then becomes how agents will respond to the higher prices, particularly in terms of adjustments in output, man-hours worked, and the composition of output as between consumption and investment spending.

Consider first the response of managers as agents for the owners of individual firms. Their output and investment decisions will depend on how they view the increase in prices that are occurring in their particular sector.[17] If they view the price increase as part of a general inflationary process then they will do nothing, since the real rate of return in the sector remains unchanged. On the other hand, if for some reason they view the price increase as unique to their sector, there will be a real response, although what that real response will be depends upon whether the relative price increase is perceived to be transitory or permanent. If it is perceived to be transitory the response will be to temporarily increase the work time of existing employed workers through overtime and to satisfy some of the temporarily higher-priced demand from existing inventories. What they will not do, however, is to permanently expand the capacity of the enterprise by accumulating capital and acquiring a larger permanent workforce. This they will do only if they perceive the relative price change to be one that is permanently in their favor, for then it will be profitable to gear the enterprise up to produce a permanently higher level of output.

Managers, however, are not the only agents in the economy. Workers, too, are agents and their decisions on whether to work or not have an important bearing on whether the level of output produced in the sector is increased or not. Suppose then that the managers here view the price rise following the expansionary monetary policy to be a permanent relative price increase for their sector, and therefore wish to hire more workers and accordingly offer a higher wage. If the higher money wage is a higher real wage, and if the higher real wage is viewed as a permanently higher real wage, then evidently more labor services will not be forthcoming. Instead the worker will tend to demand more leisure. This outcome is not defended on theoretical grounds, but instead rests on empirical observation. Over very long periods of time higher real wages do not call forth a larger supply of labor services for the average individual worker. This outcome also rests on the empirical observation that there seems to be no significant correlation between real wages and cyclical variations in real output and employment. So what then will call forth a larger supply of labor services, for clearly such is needed if output is to expand to a higher level? Again empirical observations (e.g., Ghez and Becker 1975, and Lucas and Rapping 1969) seem to suggest that workers will, in the short run, substitute work for leisure when the higher wages are perceived to be transitory. Thus, in order to obtain an output and investment response to higher prices, managers must view the price increase as being permanent, for in this case they will want to expand the productive capacity of their firm because it is possible to earn higher returns; and yet workers must view any resulting wage increases as being transitory, for otherwise they will not supply the requisite labor services that will help create the higher level of output that characterizes cyclical expansions in economic activity.

As we observed in the previous section this is the same form of argument used to rationalize a short-run trade-off between unemployment and inflation. Monetary disturbances, then, are viewed as a major cause of business fluctuations but only insofar as these disturbances are not recognized for what they really are; and also to the extent they set in motion a combination of price perceptions that induce businesses to expand the level of output and the share of output going to investment, while at the same time inducing workers to supply a greater quantity of labor services. Of course, eventually managers and/or workers come to realize that their price perceptions were wrong and that their induced demand and supply of output and employment turned out to be nonoptimal compared to what they were in the equilibrium immediately preceding the monetary disturbance. Their attempt to return to their initial output, employment, and investment position then sets in motion the cyclical downturn which will echo for some time across certain sectors, like the capital goods sector, until eventually they return to the former natural rate equilibrium of employment and output.

Thus, in order to induce fluctuations in real output and employment, agents must be fooled by the change in the price level caused by the monetary disturbance, and this fooling seems to occur roughly twice a decade. Of course, eventually they do learn and return to their former and more natural positions, and perhaps this is the rational part of business fluctuations. Nevertheless, why rational agents who evidently learn the probability laws that routinely govern returns in their own sector cannot incorporate macroeconomic disturbances into their output and employment plans is not, in the opinion of some economists, given adequate attention in the new classical macroeconomics. In answer to this criticism it is sometimes suggested that the agents' knowledge is sector specific for a host of institutional reasons, and as a result they can misread the price system during an inflationary or deflationary period. Why a credible information gathering business would not evolve and help eliminate these fluctuations in output and employment from the system is not made convincingly clear to certain skeptics, particularly since the new classical economists argue that the business cycle is a recurrent event. Yet it is easy to lose sight of what they have accomplished. They have constructed a model of business fluctuations where agents make decisions in their own self-interest and within an equilibrium framework. Certain features of these models—particularly the information structures assumed—have evoked criticisms, but criticisms we are sure the originators of these models welcome, for on the whole, they have raised the dialogue to a higher level. Other features—particularly the effect of monetary disturbances on the profitability of production and investment—complement the older Keynesian view with its emphasis on financial markets and the cost of capital. In Chapter 9 we hope to build on both of these paradigms to derive some additional insights into the nature of supply adjustments and fluctuations in economic activity.

Summary and Conclusions

This completes our small sample review of the supply adjustment literature as the economy moves from one price-output (unemployment) combination to another in response to a change in aggregate demand initiated by government policy. The existing literature, as we have seen, is built around a detailed analysis of the labor and product markets. In the labor market, capitalists (or their agents, firm managers) enter into an agreement with workers (or their agents, labor unions) over the amount of money wages to be paid and the amount of labor services to be supplied to the production process. The labor market, like the wheat market, was then studied in terms of the classical supply-and-demand paradigm of partial equilibrium analysis. According to this model labor supply *intended* for the production process by workers is a positive function of the real wage rate, while labor demand *intended* by capitalists was argued to be a negative function of the real wage rate. Typically, however, workers and capitalists do not negotiate a labor contract in terms of real wages, but instead strike a bargain in terms of money wages. This is not to say that real wages are an unimportant factor underlying the supply of and demand for labor services, for when bargaining over money wages, both parties form an estimate of the future course of product prices. However, these estimates in an uncertain environment can go wrong, and consequently at least one party to the labor contract will be disappointed when the uncertainty regarding the future movement of the price level is eliminated through the passage of time. According to the natural rate hypothesis this uncertainty over the future course of real wages is the means by which government financial policy will have an effect on employment and real output in the economy, although how long this effect can last is subject to a great deal of empirical debate. Thus it is possible that an expansionary monetary policy that creates inflation can actually result in capitalists and laborers temporarily supplying a greater quantity of factor inputs and thereby creating a larger output. The increased employment and output is the result of one or both parties wrongly estimating their real income. Yet the theory would argue that this forecasting error cannot last forever. When in fact the forecasts are adjusted and the agents are able to see through the inflation to the level and distribution of income, they will in turn adjust their respective supplies of factor inputs insofar as their present supplies are inconsistent with their intertemporal consumption and labor-leisure preferences. If the initial situation before the monetary expansion was a natural rate equilibrium (in that both laborers and capitalists concurred in producing and distributing a particular level of output), then it is quite likely that both participants will return to that natural level and distribution of real income once they come to realize that the inflation itself need not redistribute income if it is fully incorporated into their contracts with one another.

In concluding this review of the traditional literature we have observed that the questions and issues surrounding the supply adjustment of an economy during a business cycle are intertwined with the level and distribution of income between workers and capitalists. The natural rate and rational expectations models are modern-day descriptions of the classical full-employment theory under certainty. They are long-run equilibrium models where only real factors such as changes in tastes, population growth, technological progress, and the institutional framework of the society can change the characteristics of the natural rate equilibrium. The Keynesian tradition, on the other hand, chooses to explore these issues within a disequilibrium framework. Moreover, that tradition survives not so much because it provides an internally generated description of how and why the system happens to be in disequilibrium (it does not), but rather because economists have found the problems associated with disequilibrium to be of interest and for which they can be expected to provide a solution. In any event, subsequent developments in both classical and Keynesian models have looked for a solution to the supply adjustment problem in the labor and product market. It is somewhat curious that capital markets and financial instruments have, by and large, been ignored.[18] Yet, as we have indicated on a number of occasions in this work, financial securities are themselves claims to future output; and when they are traded on well-developed and efficient capital markets their observable prices can be expected to reflect all relevant information, including information on the future course of money wages, product prices, and the level of production. But even more importantly, the many different types of securities issued by a single firm remind us that production is a cooperative effort carried out by many different input contributors. On the other hand we have seen that conventional theory is intensely individualistic in that it attempts to describe fluctuations in aggregate output and employment by analyzing the optimal supply decisions of individual agents. Our approach in Chapter 9 will be quite different. We will group these individual agents together in a firm. Within this firm these agents will create an output and contract with one another as to how they will share that output or the money proceeds of that output. In our set-up these output-sharing contracts will be financial securities. The business cycle will then be analyzed from the point of view of how the firm (or collection of individual agents) should adjust inputs, outputs, and output prices in response to a monetary shock when individual input contributors hold different types of financial contracts. As we will see, this approach will produce a somewhat different view of business activity and fluctuations than the more conventional approaches.

Notes

1. Inflation itself is the process by which all prices in the economy rise at the same rate. In this connection we must remember—in line with our discussion in note 19 in Chapter 7—that in a certain sense inflation and the rate of change of the inflation rate cannot provide an internally generated solution to the so-called missing equation problem, since the exact price level that would emerge in a macroeconomic equilibrium would depend on both the inflation rate and some historically given initial price level. While the inflation rate might be developed within the model, the historically given initial level of prices comes from outside the model. In this sense the Phillips curve to be discussed below cannot be taken literally as the Keynesian solution to the missing equation problem, since the equilibrium price would then be partly determined by the historically given initial price. Having said this, it in no way can diminish our interest in seeking a relationship between output (or unemployment) and the inflation rate as a means for understanding the process of supply adjustment over time. Any such relationship, if stable, would be of considerable importance and interest for a host of reasons in a market economy.

2. While Phillips is generally credited with initiating this line of economic inquiry, Lipsey (1960) clarified and refined a number of the more basic ideas, and much of what today passes for Phillips curve analysis was developed by Lipsey. Furthermore, Irving Fisher (1973) apparently was aware of a statistical relationship between unemployment and price level changes as early as 1926. He analyzed the problem in terms of the employment effects that could arise from unanticipated inflation. The distinction between anticipated and unanticipated inflation was important in his

analysis, and in this sense he was a precursor of the "natural rate" school of thought to be discussed below.

3. For a more complete review of the main developments in this literature see the surveys by Santomero and Seater (1978) and Gordon (1981). Research continues to be done in this area, although the emphasis has changed from a theoretical and empirical focus centering on the unemployment-inflation trade-off to the more general question concerning the effectiveness of discretionary monetary and fiscal policy.

4. Thus, when the excess supply of labor is negative the unemployment rate is low, and when excess supply is positive the unemployment rate tends to be high. It should also be pointed out that while for theoretical purposes unemployment is taken to be an unambiguous variable, there are a host of conceptual as well as practical problems associated with its measurement. In this connection see Darby (1976), Feldstein (1976), Hall (1970), and Lucas (1978).

5. Actually, Phillips (1958) measured this relationship over three separate periods: 1861-1913, 1913-1948, and 1948-1957. While no test statistics were reported, the scatter diagrams provide support for the hypothesized negative relationship. In reading Phillips' article one cannot help but feel that those who came after him ascribed more importance to this relationship than Phillips himself did. This is nowhere expressed more clearly than in his concluding sentences: "The statistical evidence . . . seems in general to support the hypothesis . . . that the rate of change of money wage rates can be explained by the level of unemployment and the rate of change of unemployment, *except in or immediately after those years in which there is a sufficiently rapid rise in import prices to offset the tendency for increasing productivity to reduce the cost of living.*" Phillips, it would seem from the above quotation, clearly understood that his hypothesis required relative stability of product prices, and that when product prices were rising sharply, the negative relationship between unemployment and the rate of change in money wage rates would not hold. He ends his article with a clear warning: "There is need for much more detailed research into the relationship between unemployment, wage rates, prices, and productivity."

6. For some discussion on this point see Friedman (1977).

7. Of course government policies dealing with the regulation of job opportunities (e.g., minimum wages, licensing, etc.), unemployment compensation, and the distribution of income could be expected to have an important affect on the natural rate of unemployment.

8. See Friedman (1968) and Phelps (1967) (1970). Above we gave the Friedman version of the dynamics surrounding the adjustment, wherein essentially both capitalists and laborers misunderstand the expansion of aggregate demand and both think reducing unemployment to U_{ST} is consistent with their individual welfare. Obviously there are other versions wherein one group—generally capitalists—perceives the monetary expansion correctly due to superior information and then locks the other group into what turns out to be an inappropriate employment contract.

9. What is even more interesting is that the same economists tend to be on the same side of the debate in terms of the relevant dimension of time. Those who in the earlier campaign championed income effects over wealth effects now argue for the relevance of uncertainty and and disequilibrium in assessing the impact of monetary and fiscal policy, while those who were on the side of wealth effects now assess

the effectiveness of policy in the long run of rational expectations. Opinion on economic policy issues does not seem to change, although the arguments by which those opinions are reached do change in response to both innovations in theory and the economic experiences of the society.

   10. Alternatively, ignore the productivity term and assume in the long run that the expected inflation rate comes to equal the actual inflation rate. Then equation (8.3) can be rewritten as:

$$(\dot{P}/P) = [\beta/(1 - \alpha)] \, (U)$$

When $\alpha = 1.0$ we obtain the long-run vertical Phillips curve predicted by the natural rate hypothesis. On the other hand, if $\alpha < 1.0$, then a long-run trade-off between unemployment and inflation exists, and the government is then presented with a choice between alternative combinations of unemployment and inflation.

   11. In this connection see the study by Solow (1969), the review of a number of studies by Tobin (1975, Vol. II, pp. 20–32), and the aforementioned article by Santomero and Seater (1978).

   12. The theory of rational expectations has been used to analyze a wide variety of macroeconomic issues, most of which cannot be discussed in our short review of traditional treatments of aggregate supply. The term itself is worth discussing since it resembles the notion of homogeneous expectations used to develop the capital asset pricing model in Chapter 4. According to the theory of rational expectations in a stochastic environment, economic agents use all relevant information in an optimal way when forming expectations on some future variable in the economic system. What exactly does this mean? By and large this statement is taken to mean (see Lucas 1977, p. 27) that economic agents become so well attuned to their economic environment that the subjective probability distribution they use in forecasting a particular economic variable is equivalent to the objective probability distribution that is implied by the true model that actually generates the outcome of the economic variable in question. Moreover, all agents come to use this same "true" distribution when forecasting the variable, hence the resemblance with homogeneous expectations. Since agents learn the true distribution generating the economic variables in the system, their predictions on average will be correct. Finally, even when their predictions are wrong in a particular period, the forecast error is just as likely to be positive as negative. Yet, a number of economists (e.g., B. Friedman 1979) wonder whether in a world where information is costly to obtain we can ever approach the idealization of decision making under uncertainty that is described in the theory of rational expectations, at least within the time framework considered relevant for analyzing short-run fluctuations in the economy.

   13. Research in this area is ongoing and results are being revised about as fast as they are being produced. For example some of Lucas' intranational results bearing on the natural rate hypothesis (which are not reported here) were subsequently found by Lucas (1976) to be invalid and uninteresting. Moreover, his cross-country study was expanded in sample size by Alberro (1981) who observed the same phenomenon; namely, the reaction of real output and employment to nominal shocks is positive but becomes weaker the higher the variance of the nominal shock. The testing procedure used by Lucas and Alberro has been criticized by Barro (1981) in that he reproduces the empirical results (i.e., real output is positively related to nominal shocks, but the

response diminishes with the variance of the nominal shock) with non-Phillips curve mechanical models.

14. Anticipated monetary growth rates in the Barro and Rush study were obtained from a regression of actual current monetary growth rates on: one- and two-period lagged values of monetary growth rates, the current deviation of actual real federal government expenditures from their exponentially computed trend values, and a measure of the unemployment rate lagged one period. The lagged unemployment rate is included on the grounds that the monetary authority varies the money supply in response to changes in the unemployment rate, thereby attempting to stabilize the economy. Unanticipated monetary growth rates are then taken to be the residuals from this regression equation. These residuals (which proxy for monetary surprises) are then used as arguments in regressions explaining unemployment rates and real GNP. An additional explanatory variable used in these regressions is a measure of military conscription on the grounds that it proxies for variations in the labor force participation rate and government expenditures, and therefore may affect both unemployment rates and real GNP.

15. For a sample of these criticisms see Small (1979), Blinder (1980), Gordon (1980), and Weintraub (1980).

16. For a lucid description of this class of business cycle models see the review by Lucas (1977).

17. According to Lucas (1973) the output or supply response of an individual firm (and hence all firms) to a monetary shock depends critically on the information structure in each individual market. If suppliers knew at all points in time their own local price and all other prices in the system, then a change in the supply of money would have no effect on real output, provided all input contributors were initially in both a production and consumption equilibrium. When this is the case a change in the money supply will only give rise to a proportional change in the price level. Suppose, however, that firms only know their own current local price but not the *current* price level. Suppose, also, that these firms know the past history of both their own local price and the price level, which in turn implies they know the historical distribution of the deviation of their local price relative to the price level. Given this kind of information structure, consider now an expansion in the money supply that initially raises the firm's local price. Is the rise in the local price a rise in relative price in favor of this particular sector or industry, or is it merely part of a general inflation? The firm has no way of knowing for sure, given its presumed ignorance regarding the current price level. The problem facing the firm is therefore to ascertain whether the rise in its local price represents a change in relative prices—which in turn will induce a change in supply of real output to this market—or is merely part of a general inflationary process; and it will attempt to solve this problem using the past history of the price level, the historical distribution of the local price relative to the general price level, and the current local price.

To formalize this argument consider the following supply function (in logs) for market m.

(i) $\quad (q - q^*)m = \gamma[P(m) - E\{P \,|\, I(m) \}] \qquad \gamma > 0$

where
q = the log of output supplied to market m;
q^* = the log of the natural level of output supplied to market m;

$P(m)$ = the log of local price in market m;
P = some suitable measure of the log of the general price level;
$I(m)$ = the relevant information set in market m to be used in predicting P; and
E = the expectation operator.

What is needed is a theory telling us how agents in market m form $E\{P \mid I(m)\}$. In developing one, recall that firms know the past history of P, and from this history form the normal prior distribution for the current unknown P. The mean and variance of this prior distribution are taken to be $\bar{P}$ and σ^2. Recall, also, that firms were presumed to know the historical relationship between the local price $P(m)$ and the general price level P. Suppose the percentage deviation Z of $P(m)$ from P is normally distributed with expected value $E(Z) = 0$ and $\mathrm{Var}(Z) = \tau^2$. The forecasting problem then becomes one of deriving the posterior mean of P using the prior estimate of $\bar{P}$ and the current observable local price $P(m)$, which is presumed to be the mean of a sample drawn from the distribution of P. What weights should be attached to these two means—$\bar{P}$ and $P(m)$—to form the optimal revised estimate of the expected value of the current price level? There is a well-known theorem in statistical decision theory (see for example Jedamus and Frame 1969, p. 206) that states that these two means from normal distributions should be weighted, respectively, by $\theta = \tau^2/(\tau^2 + \sigma^2)$ and $(1 - \theta)$; that is,

(ii) $E\{P \mid I(m)\} = \theta\bar{P} + (1 - \theta)\,P(m)$.

Putting (ii) into (i) then yields the supply schedule in market m.

(iii) $(q - q^*)m = \gamma\theta\{P(m) - \bar{P}\}$.

When τ^2 is relatively small (as it will be for those sectors whose prices are highly correlated with the general price level), the change in $P(m)$ will tend to be interpreted as part of a change in the general inflation rate and the supply schedule will be vertical, thus indicating an absence of any output response to a change in aggregate demand. On the other hand, when σ^2 is small (that is, the economy experiences very little general inflation), variations in $P(m)$ will quite naturally be interpreted as reflecting changes in relative prices, and the slope of the supply schedule will approach the limiting value of γ. Averaging over all markets in the economy then yields the aggregate supply function

(iv) $(Q - Q^*) = \gamma\theta(P - \bar{P})$

Here, then, we have a model economy where agents behave as rational Bayesian decision makers, and yet output supplied to the market can exceed or fall short of the natural rate of production as a result of forecasting errors. It is this kind of micro behavior that induces business cycles in the Lucas variant of the rational expectations model.

18. For some discussion concerning the role of capital markets see Barro (1981) and Grossman and Weiss (1982).

Part IV

The Financial Economics of a Partnership Economy

——9——

A Financial Contracting Theory
of the Firm

Introduction

In Chapter 8 we presented a brief and selective historical review of the conventional theory of supply adjustment for an economy experiencing a cyclical change in aggregate demand.[1] This supply response was primarily developed within the framework of the labor market and the product market. There we observed that when starting from some long-run natural rate equilibrium, an unexpected expansion in the money supply that raises prices and money wage rates in the first instance would only call forth a greater quantity of employment and output when suppliers and demanders of labor services misperceive their own individual incomes or their relative share in the increased income. According to this approach money-induced business cycles are the result of forecasting errors by rational Bayesian decision makers in their attempt to predict changes in consumer tastes. With the passage of time these misperceptions or forecasting errors will be recognized for what they are, and when they are, agents will adjust supply downward toward the long-run natural level of employment and output. In this way employment and production of goods and services in an economy sometimes goes above or below the long-run trend in response to changes in the general inflation rate, and this would seem to be one of the key relationships that empirically characterizes business cycles in market economies.

There can be no doubt that this approach to the modelling of supply decisions by rational producers provides us with many valuable insights into the nature and causes of business fluctuations in capitalistic economies. Furthermore, this modelling strategy, more so than most others, extends to macroeconomics one of the most fundamental and cherished propositions in value theory; namely, the proposition that optimizing agents adjust quantities supplied to the marketplace in response to changes in relative prices. The business cycle, then, arises from the fact that agents operate in an uncertain environment, and hence the actual supply adjustments made will reflect their inability to forecast accurately. If the environment were certain, the business cycle would then presumably disappear.

While it is true that these models based on Bayesian decision making have taken us a long way toward a better understanding of certain aspects of business cycles, it is also true that they have not been able to explain everything that seems to occur in an economy subject to business fluctuations. In this connection the equilibrium approach cannot explain the existence of a number of fundamental characteristics that are observed in all capitalistic economies, such as the many different kinds of contracts we observe in real market economies.[2] In particular, the theory is silent on the role of financial securities (a specific type of contract) and markets in both the transmission or causes of cyclical fluctuations. Perhaps finance is irrelevant at the micro and macro levels of economic activity, but at least these kinds of propositions should be demonstrated within the context of an economy where financial securities are presumed to exist. Unfortunately, the auction market framework of the new classical macroeconomics is not well suited to address this issue. For these reasons and others we think it appropriate to begin looking elsewhere for additional insights into an understanding of supply adjustments and the business cycle.

That elsewhere, in our opinion, is the capital market. The capital market valuation of a firm reflects all the relevant information in all markets in which the firm operates, including the labor market. Thus a new wage agreement or change in consumer tastes for the firms' products are both reflected in the market price of the firms' securities. These securities, in turn, take two basic forms: debt or priority claims and equity or residual claims. Both represent the marketable claims to capital's share in the produced output.[3] It is therefore clear that anything in the product or factor market that in some way alters the quantity and quality of the income accruing to capital can be expected to influence the market valuations of the bonds and stocks of the firm in question. Moreover, the marketplace in which bonds and stocks are traded has the enviable reputation of being a relatively efficient market, which, among other things, implies that it processes information swiftly and in an unbiased manner, insofar as that information has an effect on the material well-being of the firm.[4] Thus today's market prices on bonds and stocks reflect prices and quantities that are expected by investors to emerge in product and factor markets tomorrow.

To sum up, then, the valuations placed on private bonds and stocks represent an assessment of the relevant future supply-and-demand relationships in input and output markets, and by definition this assessment must represent the best collective judgment of all those investors who hold their accumulated wealth in the form of securities. Any exogenous shock—including any that arise from government financial policy—that effects these markets will first have an effect on bond and stock prices. In this way the securities market—which is the market for future claims to consumption—is a good indicator as well as predictor of the implications stemming from a change in the firm's environment.

Yet the matter does not end here. It is equally important to remember that the private firm is managed in the interests of its input contributors. Traditionally it has been assumed that the firm is managed (in the sense that it makes short-run price and output decisions) for the benefit of those individuals who provide the capital inputs; more particularly, those who hold the equity or residual claim to the end-of-period output. More recently it has been recognized that stockholder welfare cannot be the only consideration guiding corporate behavior, since productive inputs are contributed by a diverse group of individuals. In this connection special significance has been attributed to the fact that managerial inputs in most large corporations are contributed by different individuals than those who provide the capital input. Accordingly there have been attempts to modify the theory of the firm to accommodate this fact of separation of ownership and control, and these accommodations have given rise to managerial or behavioral theories of the firm, including a renewed interest in the principal-agent relationship between capital contributors and managers.[5] The primary thrust of all these amendments to the classical theory of the firm is to blunt the goal of profit or stock market value maximization as the sole criterion governing firm behavior by admitting other possible goals such as sales maximization or growth maximization. These other goals, according to this approach, are in many cases partly intended to diversify the firms' operations; not so much to protect the stockholders—since we have seen in Chapter 4 they can achieve this diversification themselves—but to protect the human capital of the top managers where the costs of individual diversification are presumably much higher. Furthermore it is often said that these other goals provide some psychological satisfaction to managers, and no doubt there are occasions when this satisfaction does motivate corporate behavior.

In this chapter and in Chapter 10 we will not emphasize these characterizations of managerial motivation primarily because they have been discussed elsewhere. Rather the approach to be taken here will be to study the role of the manager in reconciling the conflicting interests of different input contributors particularly within the context of business fluctuations. In taking this approach our analysis will represent a return to the classical view of the manager as a hired input who is disciplined by the market for managers.

Where we differ from the classical view is that one of the goals of our managers will be to make product market and financial market decisions that purposefully influence the return and risk absorbed by the different input contributors or partners in the firm in such a way that these contributors will initiate and sustain productive activity. In their attempt to implement these decisions they will vary the price and quantity of the produced output, and these variations in turn will provide the basis for a rational and equitable supply adjustment for the economy over the business cycle.[6]

The development of this theory will be the objective of this chapter and Chapters 10 and 11. We begin here by first describing the financing of productive activity. Since the financing of production will play a key role in our theory of the supply adjustment, we will also describe the conditions required for capital market equilibrium. This discussion of capital market equilibrium will provide the basis for our contract theory of firm management offered at the end of this chapter. In this theory of firm management managers will vary output (employment), prices, and methods of financing output expansion or contraction in response to changes in aggregate demand in such a way as to coalesce the economic interests of the various suppliers of inputs to the production process. In the process of coalescing the economic interests of the cooperating factors of production or partners in the enterprise, a supply adjustment will emerge in the economy; and this supply adjustment will be the topic of discussion of the second and third sections of Chapter 10. Moreover, in those sections the supply adjustment will be discussed both in terms of a single-firm economy and a multifirm economy with complete and incomplete investor diversification. The fourth section of Chapter 10 describes the welfare of various groups (e.g., the young and old) in the workforce, and how their interests are coalesced within the firm over the business cycle. The analysis then continues in the fifth section of Chapter 10 with a discussion of the policy implications that would seem to follow from the model. The specific policy issues studied will center around the effectiveness of government financial policy and the ancient question reviewed in Chapter 4 concerning the debt-equity decisions of private firms. Contrary to our earlier analysis, we will see that financing decisions are interrelated with operating decisions (e.g., employment and pricing decisions) as firms adjust supply to meet demand over the business cycle. Chapter 10 ends with a summary that draws the material together from Chapters 9 and 10. Finally, Chapter 11 presents a discussion of: (1) the evolution of debt and equity contract forms in our artificial economy, and (2) a detailed (but stylized) numerical example of a contract economy adjusting supply in response to a change in aggregate demand induced by an expansion in the money supply. Together Chapters 9, 10, and 11 form the core of our theory of supply adjustments over the business cycle. While the hypotheses advanced in these chapters are relatively simple, certain definitions and concepts used in their construction may appear somewhat unusual. Whether these hypotheses are relevant, however, bears no necessary relationship to their simplicity or the unusual definitions and concepts used in their development, but rather, how well their implications accord with reality. In Chapter 12 we will present some evidence concerning these questions.

Production, Financing, and Capital Market Equilibrium

Some Preliminary Assumptions

At the outset it will be useful to set forth a number of simplifying assumptions concerning private production. Toward this end it will be convenient, at least initially, to view all firms in the economy as one composite firm producing single good under conditions of technological uncertainty. The one-good assumption will both ease the exposition and by and large conform with the IS-LM macroeconomic models described in Chapter 7. Thus the object of interest here will be the general level of output and prices and not the structure of prices and outputs between the different sectors in the economy. Later on in Chapter 10 we will indicate how the one-good assumption might be relaxed and still preserve the general flavor of the supply adjustment presented in this chapter.

Moving on we must consider the different ways in which it is possible to classify the factor inputs in the production process. In the economics literature factor inputs are typically classified according to their physical characteristics and grouped around land, labor, and capital. These factor inputs are collected by firms and then transformed by a production function into an output or income which in turn is distributed to those individuals who provided the inputs. Thus, wages represent the claim of laborers, rent the claim of landowners, and profit the claim of capitalists. When assuming an uncertain environment, the finance literature further subdivides the claim of capitalists into interest on priority claims like bonds and the residual profit that goes to stockholders.

Output-Sharing Agreements

The input classification scheme we will use below borrows from both the economics and finance classification schemes. For purposes of analyzing short-run aggregate supply the physical attributes of factor inputs are not their only distinguishing characteristic. On the contrary, we believe that one of the more important ingredients binding the different partners in the production process together are the terms on which they mutually agree to share the output they jointly create, an ingredient that has generally been ignored in other descriptions of the cyclical adjustment of supply. There are, of course, a variety of possible sharing rules that can bring the diverse factor inputs to join forces in the firm for purposes of producing an output. In our study of supply adjustment for the entire economy, we will draw a distinction between two simple forms of output-sharing agreements: a fixed priority claim like bond interest and principal repayment and a residual equity claim like stockholder income.

Of the two the simplest and most straightforward sharing rule is an equity or pro-rata claim to the residual end-of-period output. Under this compensation scheme, individual households supply factor services in exchange for a percentage claim to the produced output, whatever that output might be, in an uncertain environment. In effect all input contributors are stockholders under this type of sharing rule, and the individual incomes of the contributors will be directly proportional to the aggregate income of the productive enterprise. While individual input contributors may disagree on the original assignment or endowment of their pro-rata claim to the future output—such claims presumably based on marginal productivity considerations and the degree of competition in the factor market—once these claims are established all contributors will share in the fortunes or misfortunes actually experienced by the productive enterprise.

Since the interests of individual households providing factor services to the firm are more or less coalesced under equity-sharing agreements, why then do we not observe this type of compensation scheme exclusively? One reason is risk aversion. Some individuals loathe planning their consumption around a fluctuating income stream, and for this reason would prefer to exchange their factor service for a fixed priority claim to the end-of-period output.[7] Of course, if this group is to receive a fixed claim, others must be found to take the variable residual claim to output. A second reason centers around preference orderings for income and consumption that are not independent of the state of the economy. Thus one group of contributors may prefer to receive a relatively large share of the produced output when the economy is operating below its expected long-run trend, while some other group may have a relative preference for income when output is above its long-run trend. These reasons suggest that a mutually advantageous agreement or contract might be arranged between these two different groups of individual input contributors.

One of the most important and distinguishing features of a capitalist economic system is the freedom to make these output-sharing agreements.[8] Yet invariably these agreements will have to be monitored. In addition, if there is a subsequent conflict over the meaning of the agreement, then the disagreement must be adjudicated by some outside party. In fact, these disagreements occur frequently and have given rise to an entire industry (e.g., legal and accounting services) devoted to the monitoring and adjudication of contract disagreements. Since adjudication is not an end in itself—in the sense that it appears in the utility function of very few individuals—it is a social cost that is only justified if the agreements themselves enable the remaining factor inputs to create a larger output than would be created without these contracts between the cooperating factors of production and the adjudication industry.

The next question that might be asked is how our classification scheme based on output-sharing agreements relates to the more traditional classification scheme based on the physical attributes of the factor inputs. In an uncertain environment the relationship is not very exact. There are some laborers who contribute labor services in exchange for a fixed priority claim to the end-of-period output. These claims are called wages. On the other hand, other laborers (e.g., piece workers and commission salespersons) exchange their labor services for a pro-rata share of the end-of-period output. Their income pattern over time is very much like that of a stockholder. Moreover the same dichotomy exists for the factor of production capital. Some capitalists provide their capital input service in exchange for a priority claim to the produced output. These capitalists are called creditors or bondholders. Stockholders, on the other hand, provide their capital input in exchange for the variable residual claim to the end-of-period output. The same could be said for the landlord. It would, therefore, seem that compensation schemes are not necessarily linked uniquely to a specific type of factor input.[9] For this reason we will discuss the firm's supply adjustment from the point of view of both bondholders and stockholders, and for the moment neglect the welfare of workers and landlords. Our reason for focusing the analysis of supply adjustment around these two claimants to capital's share in the produced output is that these claims, unlike the claims held by laborers, are traded in a capital market where it is possible to directly observe the effects of the supply adjustment on bond and stock prices. Moreover, by observing the capital market price of bonds we can infer the general well-being of those laborers who hold the nonmarketable fixed wage claims to the produced output; claims that in our model turn out to be very much affected by the future supply adjustment of the firm.

Some Assumptions Regarding Labor, Capital, and Time

Our analysis of supply adjustment, then, will focus on the two output-sharing agreements embodied in bondlike and stocklike contracts. Before beginning, however, there are several details pertaining to the labor market and the supply of capital services that must first be clarified. To begin with, nonmanagerial labor participates in production by providing labor services in exchange for a fixed priority claim that is precisely defined in a labor contract. In a money economy this labor contract will specify, among other things, the money wage rate for a given amount of labor services (e.g., one hour) and that money wage rate will remain fixed for the life of the contract.[10] The length of time fixed by the labor contract (say, three years) will then constitute the time horizon for the analysis. Consequently, the money wage rate will be assumed to be fixed throughout the supply adjustment, and the only labor market decision open to managers is to determine the level of employment. Furthermore, how this money wage rate and any other feature of the labor contract is actually agreed upon among the contracting parties is outside the scope of this study.

Consider next the physical capital input. The main assumption to be invoked here is the typical one of holding constant the stock of productive capital. Thus the only way the firm might increase the level of real output is to hire more workers if they are available for the hiring. In a longer-run analysis the managers of the firm could vary the level of output as well as the capital/labor ratio by varying both capital and labor. This assumption regarding the fixity of capital is typical in the macroeconomic literature where it serves the purpose of separating short-run demand theory from long-run growth theory.

Our reason for differentiating a short run from a long run by fixing the money wage rate and the stock of physical capital will be to emphasize a somewhat different distinction from that envisioned by the conventional macroeconomic theory. By fixing the money wage rate and the stock of capital we also limit managerial choice over the time horizon for which this model is assumed to apply to one of varying the price and level of output and the financial requirement associated with any change in the level of employment and output. The end result is that the short-run choice variables of price and output (employment) are precisely the objects of interest in the so-called "missing equation" problem, and the manager's job of coordinating the factor inputs in the production process will be to vary price and output and the financing of output over the business cycle in such a way as to apportion the adjustment benefits and costs to both bondholder- and stockholder-type claimants. The question then arises as to how managers should vary these decision variables under their control in the short run in order to accommodate a change in aggregate demand. Our hypothesis will be that managers should vary the level of output (employment), the price of output, and the financing of changes in output and employment in such a way as to preserve the initial input-sharing and output-sharing arrangements that initiated the production process. In this way the supply adjustment will not be used to unilaterally alter the existing contracts that coordinate production in the first place. Accordingly, we will now turn our attention to these contracts, and, in particular, those embodied in bonds and stocks. When this is completed, we will return to the question of short-run decision making in the firm.

Stocks, Bonds, and Investor Welfare Over the Business Cycle

Up to this point in our discussion, financial arrangements have been broadly defined to include marketable and nonmarketable claims to the future output-income streams produced by the firm. We would now like to focus attention on the two capitalist claims to output, namely, conventional bonds and common stock. At several points in this work we have noted that different types of capitalists tend to have different interests in the firm by virtue of the fact that they hold different claims to the net income of the enterprise. For example, in Chapter 4 we indicated that once both bondholders and stockholders contribute the initial capital to start the firm, there will be a temptation for stockholders to adapt a riskier technology than the one advertised to bondholders before they made their initial investment. Such a policy will tend to redistribute wealth from the bondholders to the stockholders in the firm, because in a certain sense the stock can be thought of as a call option on the firm, as suggested by Black and Scholes (1973). Moreover, Galai and Masulis (1977) demonstrate that the value of this option grows as the risk of the underlying assets of the firm increases. These wealth redistributions between bondholders and stockholders associated with a change in technology would be of no importance if bondholders and stockholders were one and the same, as they were in the simple CAPM with separation. Yet in actual fact bondholders and stockholders are not generally the same, and in the second section of Chapter 11 we discuss some of the reasons (e.g., differences in risk aversion, costs of diversification, and differing expectations among investors concerning the firm's future income) why this tends to be the case. When bondholders and stockholders are not the same individuals it is necessary to formulate a different set of objectives for managers to follow than the conventional objective of managing the firm solely in the interest of the stockholders, since we have just seen that this objective will in all probability abrogate the implied risk-and-return-sharing agreement that launches productive activity in the first place. Toward this end it will be useful to discuss in somewhat greater detail certain contractual aspects of bonds and stocks, particularly those aspects that affect bond and stock valuations in the capital market. When we have a better understanding of the factors that effect market valuations—which in turn indirectly reflect bondholder and stockholder welfare—we will return to the question of the short-run objectives of a bondholder/stockholder-managed firm.

We begin with common stock. In exchange for their capital contribution shareholders receive a residual claim to the future net income of the firm. The claim is residual in the sense that other contributors to the productive enterprise have a prior claim to the future income. In an uncertain environment, stockholders come to absorb a greater amount of the risks associated with private production than bondholders, since a favorable state of nature will tend to result in a sizeable surplus income over and above the fixed claim of creditors, but an unfavorable state may leave nothing. Consequently, the consumption possibilities for stockholders will exhibit greater variability than for bondholders.

Next consider bonds. The unique feature of a bond contract is its attempt to stipulate in advance the precise time pattern of money payments to be made to the bondholder. These payments are fixed by the contract and enjoy a legal priority over the nominal residual claim of the stockholders. For this reason bonds in the same firm are relatively safer than stock. However, there are certain disadvantages. When production has been completed and nature has been either very stingy or munificent, bonds may turn out *ex-post* to be a relatively poor investment in that they might help absorb the loss in the former case but only receive their contractual claim in the latter case. Moreover, in a monetary economy even if the firm honors the monetary income claim in the bond contract in all states of the world, the fixed monetary income received by the bondholders will buy a varying quantity of real output depending upon the movement of the price level. Of course all of these possibilities, to the extent recognized, will be reflected in the capital market prices of bonds. What is clear, nonetheless, is that the output sharing that actually takes place between bondholders and stockholders will generally bear no precise relationship to their relative contributions of capital.

For this reason bondholders and stockholders will be differentially affected by many firm decisions, as noted by Smith and Warner (1979). As we mentioned above, one source of disagreement concerns the riskiness of the firm's production technology in that bondholders, by the very nature of their risk aversion, would prefer the firm to implement a less risky technology than stockholders would. A second area of potential disagreement would revolve around the short-run supply response to a cyclical change in aggregate demand. It is clear that stockholders would prefer an unanticipated expansion in supply to take the form of higher product prices and any output expansion to be financed with bonds, whereas bondholders would prefer a reduction in product prices and an expansion in output financed with stock. On the other hand, if the supply adjustment involves a contraction, bondholders would prefer a reduction in output prices whereas stockholders would prefer that output and employment be reduced and stock repurchased with the freed-up resources. In other words, stockholders would always prefer unanticipated supply adjustments to be managed in such a way that their share in financing the inputs goes down while at the same time their share in the expected output goes up. Bondholders, in turn, would want the same result but only from their perspective. If both groups behave rationally they will be unable to achieve their own individual objectives at all points in time, but there is nothing to preclude them from negotiating with one another over how they might share the expected output and the financing of the inputs during various stages in the business cycle, particularly if they are unwilling to attempt to predict the business cycle in the first place.

Input Sharing, Output Sharing, and Capital Market Equilibrium

Given bondholder and stockholder preferences for cyclical adjustments in terms of input and output sharing—even though they are subject to negotiation in the end—it is now possible to analyze certain aspects of capital market equilibrium. To arrive at the basic idea involved we will begin by assuming a given stock of labor and capital inputs financed with bonds and stocks, along with a given production plan or technology. By fixing the inputs and the production plan we also fix the *ex-ante* distribution of the end-of-period output, as well as the share of expected output going to bondholders and stockholders.

With these assumptions it is possible to describe the input- and output-sharing arrangements of a bondholder/stockholder-financed firm in terms of a simple box diagram as displayed in Figure 9.1. On the two horizontal axes we present the amount of the fixed inputs I invested in the economy by bondholder- and stockholder-type claimants. The bondholders' share in the financing of these inputs, $I(B)$, is presented along the lower horizontal axis and the stockholders' share, $I(S)$, on the upper horizontal axis. As we move from left to right on the horizontal axis, bondholders provide a larger share of the total inputs, while a right-to-left movement along the horizontal axis implies that stockholders are providing a larger share of the inputs. The two vertical axes, in turn, measure the total expected output, $E(X)$, generated by the firm and to be divided between bondholders and stockholders. The left vertical axis measures the expected income going to bondholders, $E(X_b)$, while the right vertical axis moving from top to bottom measures the expected income going to stockholders, $E(X_s)$. Every point within the box represents an allocation of inputs and expected output and hence an expected

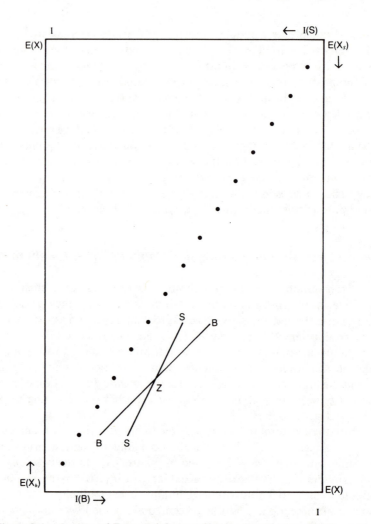

Figure 9.1. Input and Expected Output Sharing in a Partnership Economy

rate of return on the investment of the two different contributors to productive activity. Thus the line *BB* describes the constant terms on which bondholders can exchange their input for a share of the expected output of the
economy in and around the solution allocation located at point *Z*, while *SS*
describes this same relationship from the point of view of stockholder-type
claimants.

Consider the allocation of inputs and expected outputs represented by the point Z.[11] This particular allocation is located to the lower right of the imaginary diagonal line running from the lower left-hand corner to the upper right-hand corner of the box, and is positioned in such a way that the rate of return on bondlike claims is less than the rate of return on stocklike claims. The result, of course, is consistent with the relative priorities of the two types of claims to the expected income of the firm, but the exact location will depend on the relative risk aversions and input endowment of bondholders and stockholders. Note that from such an initial allocation that initiates productive activity, a movement upward or to the left from Z would represent a clear improvement for bondholders and a clear loss for stockholders in that for the same input contribution bondholders would come to receive an ever-increasing share of the fixed expected output, and alternatively for a given expected output they would be providing a decreasing quantity of inputs to the production process. Similar benefits would accrue to stockholders if the departure from Z was downward or to the right, and these benefits would come at the expense of the bondholder. The end result, then, is that if Z represents the input- and expected-output-sharing agreement between bondholders and stockholders that launches the productive enterprise, then any subsequent supply adjustment that moves the allocation upward, downward, to the right, or to the left of the old equilibrium allocation at Z will in effect abrogate the original agreement by making one claimant better off but only at the expense of the other. The possibility of departing from the initial allocation at point Z in this way would not be consistent with rational behavior on the part of input contributors.

The description of input and expected output sharing presented in Figure 9.1 can be illustrated in a slightly different geometrical form that will prove to be useful in Chapter 10 when we discuss the pricing, output (employment), and financing decisions of firms over the business cycle. In this connection consider Figure 9.2 which describes the various combinations of input and expected output sharing that give rise to a given and sustainable valuation of a bondlike and stocklike claim.[12] On the vertical axis we plot the ratio of expected output going to bondholders to the expected output going to stockholders; that is, the ratio $E(X_b)/E(X_s)$. As we move up the vertical axis, more of a given expected operating income goes to bondholders and less to stockholders, with the reverse being true as we move down the axis. On the horizontal axis we measure the ratio of inputs supplied by bondholders to the inputs supplied by stockholders, namely, B/S. A movement from left to right implies that more of a given quantity of inputs are being supplied by bondholders and less by stockholders, with the result that bondholders are absorbing a larger amount of the total financing and risk of the productive enterprise. On the other hand, as we move from right to left, stockholders in turn provide a larger share of the fixed inputs and hence take on a larger share of the risk.

Consider next the line *BB* in panel A of Figure 9.2.[13] The line *BB* represents those combinations of capital input and expected output sharing between bondholders and stockholders that equate the supply and demand for bondlike claims in the bond market at some long-run sustainable valuation for one unit of a bond. In other words every point on *BB* represents those

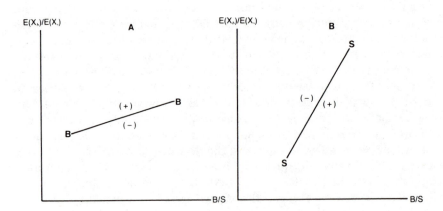

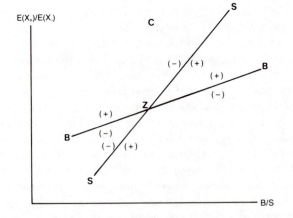

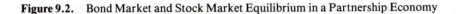

Figure 9.2. Bond Market and Stock Market Equilibrium in a Partnership Economy

combinations of input and expected output sharing that results in a constant capital market price for bonds. The *BB* schedule slopes upward, since if we start from some point on the schedule, a reduction in the share of expected income going to bondholders can only be offset by a reduction in the share of inputs financed by bondholders if the bond market is to remain in equilibrium at the initial equilibrium bond price.[14] Similarly a rise in the share of inputs provided by bondholders can only be offset by bondholders receiving a larger share of the expected output if the initial equilibrium price of bonds is to be maintained. Thus points above *BB* represent higher but nonsustainable disequilibrium market valuations on bonds, while points below represent lower disequilibrium market prices on bonds.

A similar exercise can be performed for the stocklike claim and is presented in panel B of Figure 9.2. The axes in B are the same as those in A, and hence the interpretation of stock market equilibrium in the fixed input and fixed expected output case will be the mirror image of bond market equilibrium. Accordingly, the upward-sloping schedule *SS* (in and around the solution allocation at point *Z* in Figure 9.1) defines those combinations of capital input and expected output sharing between bondholders and stockholders that produce a sustainable long-run valuation for common stock given the state of nature. The schedule slopes upward because a reduction in the share of inputs provided by stockholders (a movement to the right from some initial position on *SS*) can only be offset by a reduction in the share of expected income to be received by stockholders if the initial equilibrium stock market price is to prevail.[15] Likewise an increase in the share of expected income going to stockholders requires an increase in the share of the total capital inputs provided by stockholders in order to preserve the initial equilibrium valuation on stocks. Thus points below *SS* represent higher than sustainable valuations on common stocks, while points below represent lower stock prices.

Up to this point we have been considering the bond market and stock market equilibrium in isolation from one another. When the firm is formed and bondholders and stockholders agree on a specific sharing of the input as well as the expected output, there will only be one point in the body of Figure 9.2. Nonetheless it will be instructive to superimpose the linear *BB* and *SS* schedules in and around the initial input- and output-sharing agreement at point *Z*. This is done in panel C. Note from panels A and B that both *BB* and *SS* slope upward, and the question of which one is the steeper naturally arises. In panel C we have drawn the *SS* schedule steeper than the *BB* schedule because debt represents a prior legal claim on the income and resources of the firm and is therefore less affected by technological risk in general than common stock.[16] Risk, therefore, has two dimensions in this analysis. One dimension is in terms of financial support, that is to say, the level of input sharing as measured by B/S. The greater the financial support provided by one type of security, the greater the risk that class of security bears in the production process, other things remaining equal. The "other things remaining equal" pertains to the second dimension of risk, namely, the relative priority of the two claims to the income and resources of the firm. The first dimension of risk is measured by B/S and is measured along the horizontal axis, while the second dimension is measured in terms of the relative steepness of the BB and SS schedules.

Panel C also enables us to illustrate the potential conflict that might arise in a bondholder/stockholder-financed firm. In this connection consider the input- and output-sharing agreement that initiates productive activity and is represented by the point Z in Figure 9.2. Suppose, in some subsequent supply adjustment, the firm followed certain policies that allowed stockholders to receive a larger share of the expected income without providing any additional financial support. Such an adjustment would be described by a movement downward from point Z and constitute a renegotiation of the original agreement between bondholders and stockholders to the detriment of the bondholders. The same would be true if the subsequent supply adjustment resulted in a movement upward from Z, although here the benefits would be conferred to bondholders, and stockholders would end up in a less desirable position than in the initial equilibrium. Moreover, any supply adjustment that altered the input-sharing agreement without altering the output-sharing agreement—such as a movement to the right from Z, which favors stockholders, or to the left, which favors bondholders—will also represent a unilateral renegotiation of the original contract that provided the basis for commencing productive activity. These subsequent departures from Z remind us that bondholders and stockholders have an incentive to preclude any supply adjustment decisions that unilaterally alter the initial input- and output-sharing agreement. Not to preclude such decisions would only confirm the famous dictums of P. T. Barnum, "There is a sucker born every minute," and Nicholas Murray Butler, "Often but three generations from shirt-sleeves to shirt-sleeves."

It is clear that capitalists are not suckers, although with some bad luck particular stockholders or bondholders could end up in shirt-sleeves in an uncertain world. The job before us, then, will be to work out a set of management rules that eliminate the potential contract renegotiation that could accompany future supply adjustments over the business cycle. In a more complete model of the firm, these rules would also cover long-run decisions like the optimal size of the firm and the factor input mix in production. Our focus in this work will be on the short-run decisions. Accordingly, we will now suggest a combination of managerial decision rules that take input- and output-sharing agreements into account as the firm and the economy adjusts its short-run supply to a change in aggregate demand. These decisions in turn will result in pricing, output (employment), and financing adjustments that are rational in the important sense that no single group of capitalists, like bondholders or stockholders, receive all the benefits or incur all the costs associated with the supply adjustment.

Management Objectives in a Bondholder/Stockholder Financial Firm

Introduction

With the above description of certain aspects of production, financing, and capital market equilibrium, we now consider one possible strategy that might guide firm decisions when capital inputs are provided by both bondholders and stockholders. Of course the question of the motivation of firm activity is not particularly new. In fact the objectives of a private firm in a capitalist system have long been debated to the point where many economists simply do not care any longer just so long as they can predict reasonably well the firm's reaction to a change in its environment.[17] Just such a position has been cogently advanced by Solow (1971, p. 319) when he reminds us that: "It is perhaps more important to know how firms respond to changes in data like tax rates, interest rates, wages, investment subsidies and the like." He then goes on to compare a traditional stock market value maximization model to a growth-in-assets model and finds that the response to a change in data (e.g., factor prices and taxes) is qualitatively the same. One possible conclusion to draw from this study is that the question of managerial objectives should perhaps be set aside and more attention devoted to the task of empirically measuring the firm's response to changes in the data, a task that is and has long been in process across a wide range of environmental changes.

At any rate, given our discussion on capital input sharing, output sharing, and capital market equilibrium in the previous section, it is not possible for us to ignore the managerial objectives governing the firm's supply response to a change in its environment, for the simple reason that those decisions that maximize stockholder welfare cannot always be expected to maximize the welfare of other contributors. In other words, the short-run supply response to a change in the environment will be qualitatively different for a stock market value maximization model than for a model that maximizes the present value of all claims to the end-of-period output. Consequently, instead of singling out a particular contributor to the production process (such as the stockholder) and developing a rationalization of firm management around that contributor's welfare, we will emphasize the multicontributor or partnership aspect of firm production and outline a theory of firm management based on the coalescing of the divergent interests of these different input contributors. Toward this end we will develop the theory in terms of just two contributors: bondholders and stockholders. Yet as we have noted on a number of occasions, bondholders and stockholders stand in proxy for all those input contributors that exchange factor services for a fixed priority claim and residual claim to the end-of-period output produced by the firm.

Supply Adjustment and Investor Welfare

Introduction

In this connection recall our earlier discussion where, among other things, it was assumed that over the time period to be analyzed by this model, the only product market decisions under managerial control were the pricing and production (employment) decisions. In addition it was observed that any expansion in employment and output would require additional financial support from bondholders and/or stockholders in that workers typically require a compensation for their input service before the output is produced. Likewise a contraction will release funds from production which can then be returned to these two claimants. Consequently, when developing our theory of firm management over the business cycle, it will be incumbent upon us to consider how the pricing, output (employment), and financing decisions affect the welfare of bondholders and stockholders.

Pricing Decisions and Investor Welfare

Toward this end consider the relationship between pricing, output (employment), and financing decisions of the firm, and the input and expected output sharing between bondholders and stockholders discussed in the previous section. We will start with the firm's pricing decision. In the one-good economy we are currently analyzing it must be the case that any unanticipated change in the price of output will redistribute the relative shares of the output among bondholders and stockholders. The result is simply due to the fact that bondholders are promised a fixed monetary income, but what that monetary income will buy in terms of real output depends on the movement of the price of output. Thus an unanticipated decline in the price of output—with the level of output held constant—will redistribute the share of real income in favor of bondholders and away from stockholders. Likewise an unanticipated rise in the price of output will redistribute real income from bondholders to stockholders. This redistribution of real income stemming from an unexpected change in the price of output will be reflected in the capital market valuations of bonds and stocks as described in Figure 9.2. These changes in capital market prices in turn merely reflect the changes in bondholder and stockholder welfare that must arise when the price of output is unexpectedly altered after these two claimants create the firm and initiate production. It would therefore seem that the pricing decision of the firm represents a means by which the implied income-sharing rule between bondholders and stockholders that brought forth the financial contribution required to launch the productive enterprise is nullified.

Employment, Output, and Financing Decisions: Effects on Investor Welfare

In a similar manner the financing associated with the decision to change the level of employment and production will have the effect of renegotiating the implied input- or risk-sharing agreement between creditors and stockholders from what it was when the firm commenced operations. For example, if equity (whether of the internal or external variety is irrelevant) is used to finance a future expansion in employment and output, then stockholders will come to absorb a larger share in the total financing of the enterprise, while the bondholders' share will be diminished. The protection for the bondholder arises from the fact that they now have a priority claim on a larger collection of resources than they did in the initial equilibrium, thereby enabling them to more easily weather the next (and inevitable) contraction. Contractions in employment and output will release financial resources, which if returned to stockholders will reduce their financial stake and hence risk in the enterprise, while at the same time increasing the share of inputs financed by bondholders. Thus future supply adjustments that take the form of changes in employment and output alter the financial requirements of the firm. These changes in financial requirements, in turn, carry the potential of redistributing the financial support and risk between bondholders and stockholders from what it might have been when the business enterprise was first brought into existence. The capital market prices of bonds and stocks will reflect these changes in input sharing that accompany the supply adjustment. In this connection it is important to point out that it is the welfare of the investors who *initially* provided the financial support to launch productive activity that is in jeopardy, for to them the subsequent redistribution of input sharing will be unanticipated. Those investors who buy the securities during the subsequent supply adjustment will confront capital market prices that fairly reflect the new implied input- and output-sharing arrangement, although they must be aware of the fact that with the passage of time they, too, will be old bondholders and stockholders facing the problem of how the firm will adjust supply in the future.

It is therefore easy to see that bondholders would, if given the opportunity, establish different management objectives than stockholders when the firm is required to adjust supply in response to an exogenous change in demand. Thus when demand expands, bondholders would prefer a supply adjustment less in terms of a rise in the price of output (or preferably a price reduction) and more in terms of an expansion in output financed with equity. This type of supply adjustment would reduce the risk on bonds (particularly in the next contraction), since bonds would be providing a smaller share of the total financial needs of the firm, while at the same time leaving unchanged or increasing the bondholders share of the expected output per unit of input. The bondholders' gain in this particular adjustment would come at the expense of the old stockholders, since new stockholders would price the stock to reflect the new implied input- and output-sharing agreement. Stockholders, on the other hand, would prefer a supply adjustment more in terms of a higher price of output and less in expanded output unless the expansion were financed with debt. This adjustment would be advantageous for old stockholders in that they would now receive a higher share of the total output for the same or possibly smaller relative contribution to the total required capital inputs. The stockholders' gain in this particular supply adjustment would come at the expense of the old bondholders, since new bondholders would confront bond prices that reflect the new implied input- and output-sharing agreement.

The same reasoning would apply to a contraction. In this case bondholders would prefer a reduction in the price of output and the level of output, provided the financial resources released were used to retire bonds. If the stockholders could control the adjustment they would opt for a reduction in the level of output and use the proceeds to retire stock, and either hold constant or raise the price of output. Here, again, whatever the old bondholders (stockholders) gain, the old stockholders (bondholders) lose. How then is the firm to be managed when its two principal suppliers of financial resources propose objectives that on the surface, at least, seem irreconcilable? As we mentioned before the conventional macroeconomic theory assumes stock market value maximization, and hence supply adjustments are presumably managed with this end in mind. Yet as we have seen the result of this objective is that bondholders will experience a deterioration in the capital input- and output-sharing agreement over time. Moreover, if this view is accepted it is hard to see why private risky debt claims would exist as a viable compensation instrument, since bondholders would help absorb the losses associated with unexpectedly depressed business conditions but yet be denied the benefits commensurate with their capital resource contribution when the state of nature is unexpectedly generous. As a contract form per se, debt has many unattractive features when anticipations go astray.

"Equitable" Supply Adjustments: The Pricing, Production, and Financing Decisions of a Coalescing Management

We have seen that when the firm is managed in the interests of a single input contributor there is the possibility, if not inevitability, that future supply adjustments will be used to unilaterally abrogate an existing input- and expected-output-sharing agreement among the several contributors or partners in the enterprise. Such a possibility cannot be conducive for the attainment of efficient production in an uncertain world, since it imposes an additional and unnecessary risk on the economic system; namely, the risk of renegotiating the original input- and output-sharing agreement, which in turn redistributes wealth among the two claimants. In this sense a firm can be compared to a football team, and maximum output per unit of input, like team victory, is best achieved when all input contributors are united in the common endeavor rather than seeking an advantage over one another. For this reason it would seem sensible to propose firm objectives and rules of management that balance, in some meaningful sense, the conflicting interests and welfare of the various contributors to private production. In an uncertain environment bondholder and stockholder welfare in our short-run model are influenced by input and expected output sharing.[18] One possible solution to the supply adjustment problem, then, is that managers should be instructed to use pricing, production, and financing decisions in such a way as to either maintain the initial trade-off between input and expected output sharing between bondholders and stockholders, or adjust risk and return together during the business cycle. For example, if a particular pricing decision redistributes income from one type of claimant to the other, the firm manager should compensate the aggrieved party with an output and financing decision that redistributes risk toward the party that benefited from the pricing decision. This type of decision making within the firm could arise when suppliers of financial resources come together when forming the enterprise and work out what might be called an "assignment rule" as to how *future* unexpected supply adjustments are to be managed. The principal feature of this assignment rule or agreement is that the firm cannot be managed so that the process of adjustment confers both risk and return advantages to one group of financial contributors at the expense of the other group. Thus, if during an expansion in supply the firm in the first instance expands employment and output and finances this growth with equity, thereby shifting the risks of financing production towards stockholders, then firm managers will be instructed to compensate the stockholders in the second instance by raising the price of output which in turn shifts income from bondholders to stockholders. Thus a unilateral redistribution of firm risk initiated by a stage-one production and financing decision will be offset, according to our assignment rule, with a stage-two pricing decision that redistributes firm income. In this way risk and return are adjusted together by the firm's pricing, production, and financing decisions so that neither bondholders nor stockholders receive all the benefits nor absorb all the costs associated with the expansion in supply. In this case bondholders end up providing a smaller share of the financial needs of the firm and as a result their risk in terms of surviving the next contraction is reduced, while stockholders receive a larger share of the expected output.

A contraction in demand could be managed in just the opposite way. Here the firm would reduce the level of employment and output and use the financial proceeds to retire stock (or pay out high dividends relative to earnings) and thereby shift the burden of financing the enterprise at the margin to bondholders who are now better able to bear it because of the financing decision in the previous expansion. This stage-one decision affecting the output and financing of the firm should then be followed with a stage-two decision that lowers the price of output and thereby redistributes income toward bondholders who now have a relatively larger financial stake in the firm. In this case, too, both claimants share in the contraction, with bondholders ending up with more risk but also relatively more real return, while the stockholders' return falls along with their financial commitment to the firm. In any event the purpose of our managerial assignment rule is to prevent both bondholders and stockholders from using the adjustment process per se to exploit one another by renegotiating the implied contract between debt and equity that provided the basis for collecting the financial resources and initiating productive activity in the first place.[19]

At this point we might ask, by what mechanism do bondholders prevent stockholders from using the supply adjustment to expropriate their wealth? One possibility here would be creditor representation on the board of directors, which in the United States is the ultimate repository of corporate decision-making authority. For many small and medium-sized firms in the United States that for one reason or another obtain external financing exclusively from banks, this is often the mechanism by which creditors monitor and defend their financial interest in the enterprise. Moreover, in many large European and Japanese firms, creditors as well as workers are represented on their equivalent to the board of directors and are thus in a position to express their views regarding the supply adjustment. On the other hand, creditor representation on the board of directors tends to be minimal for large U.S. corporations. Yet this does not necessarily imply that bondholders have no means at their disposal to influence the supply adjustment of firms. The mechanism relied upon here is the actual bond contract itself. The bond contract is a series of covenants or agreements that generally place restrictions on the debt-equity mix in financing assets, dividend policy, and the composition of assets as between liquid (cash and marketable securities) and nonliquid capital. Some of these covenants can be combined together, as we will see in Chapter 10. For example the debt-equity restriction could be related to a liquidity requirement such as the ratio of cash to total assets. Thus, as the debt-equity ratio rises the bond contract might call for the cash-asset ratio to rise also, and conversely when leverage declines. Most of these restrictive covenants tend to be financial in nature, but as we will see in Chapter 10 they will have an indirect bearing on the pricing, employment, and output decisions of firms. With this description of how management could, in principle, coalesce the interests of bondholders and stockholders during the supply adjustment, we can now move on to consider these adjustments within the context of the business cycle.

Notes

1. Selective in the sense that we did not review the many interesting developments that have taken place in the so-called quantity-constrained and implicit contracts models of macroeconomic activity. For a review of these important developments see, respectively, Drazen (1980) and the Supplement to the *Quarterly Journal of Economics* (1983).

2. Long-term labor contracts have been incorporated into rational expectations models by Fischer (1977), Phelps and Taylor (1977), and Taylor (1980), among others. One of the objectives of this second generation of rational expectations models is to revive the case for countercyclical stabilization policy. By and large these models do not have as their primary purpose the accounting for additional stylized facts concerning the movement of economic variables over the business cycle, which will be our purpose in Chapters 10–12.

3. There are no corresponding marketable claims to an individual worker's share in the produced output since human beings cannot be forced to work in a free

society. This is a fundamental distinction that separates human and nonhuman capital. This, of course, does not mean that human beings have no present value (i.e., a discounted value of a future labor income stream) nor that at any particular point in time they are unable to realize this present value in certain limited ways in the capital market by borrowing against future labor income. Yet, while the laborer's claim to the income stream of firms is not represented by a marketable financial security as in the case of bonds, this claim is very much like a callable bond. Consequently the factors in the adjustment process, such as variations in both the quantity and price of output, will also influence the implied capitalized value of the worker's claim to future output in much the same way they affect the market price of debt securities.

4. It is for this reason that Lucas (1975, pp. 1120–1121), in his theory of the business cycle, does not have an efficient economy-wide market for securities since such a market places too much information in the hands of economic agents to obtain the kinds of price and output adjustments we seem to observe in actual business cycles. We agree that security markets convey a great deal of information to managers and other decision makers but will argue below that this does not necessarily preclude a rational explanation of cyclical variations in the price and level of output produced in the economy.

5. For a sample of this literature see Alchian and Demsetz (1972), Ross (1973), Jensen and Meckling (1976), Fama (1980), and the various papers appearing in the June issue of the *Journal of Law and Economics* (1983) devoted to the topic "Corporations and Private Property."

6. Rational and equitable in the sense that our partners (e.g., bondholders and stockholders), when initiating productive activity, could agree to adjust supply in terms of price and output in a particular way, given a change in aggregate demand.

7. In the case of workers this risk aversion is reinforced by the immediacy of their consumption needs vis-à-vis the length of time of the production process. Thus, after the production process commences but before it is concluded, capitalists advance laborers the present value of their priority claim against the end-of-period output. In principle and fact there could be n such sequences of wage payments before the particular product was finished and sold.

8. These output-sharing agreements give rise to a potential additional source of uncertainty; namely, the possibility that one party to the contract may be able to slip out of the agreement. The objective of covenants in bond contracts is to reduce the probability of this possibility from occurring and thus eliminate or reduce this socially unnecessary risk.

9. In this connection it is interesting to observe that managers—who in our theory are charged with coalescing the interests of different input contributors—tend to receive both a fixed priority claim (salary) and a variable residual claim (bonus), making them in some sense both a bondholder and a stockholder. This would seem to be a sensible compensation scheme for those in the firm whose product market decisions influence the welfare of both bondholders and stockholders.

10. The main purpose of a labor contract for a given period is to reduce the transaction costs of combining labor and capital services in the production process.

These transaction costs can be quite large, and in some instances capitalists have granted purchasing-power guarantees in the labor contract in order to avoid the shortening of the contract period in the face of accelerating inflation. This is because the current money wage rate is not the only negotiable item in establishing the basis for labor's participation in the production process in nonartificial economies. These other items, such as working conditions and procedures regarding the laying off or the dismissing of workers, will also have an important effect on determining the effective cost of labor services. Here the cost to the firm often takes the form of a reduced output. Some of these issues have been rigorously analyzed in the implicit contract literature developed by Baily (1974), Gordon (1974), and Azariadis (1975). One of the objectives of this literature has been to provide a micro theoretical foundation for the rigid wage assumption that pervades much of Keynesian economics. Roughly the argument is that in a world of incomplete markets, risk-averse workers attempt to reduce the variation in their wage income, due to cyclical variations in the marginal productivity of labor, by entering into an employment contract with risk-neutral firms that fixes the wage rate over the contract period, thereby making wages independent of the state of the economy and the marginal productivity of labor at all points in time over the life of the labor contract. Among other things the contract calls for wages to be less (more) than the marginal revenue product of labor when the economy experiences favorable (unfavorable) states. In other words, the employment contract contains an implicit insurance policy which workers can evidently only buy from their employers. A great deal of research has and is being conducted in this area, and some of the results presented in Chapters 10 and 11 will depend on assumptions that implicit contract theory attempts to justify.

   Another technical detail set aside is whether money need exist in the type of economy we are currently exploring. We will merely assume it does exist and leave it at that.

   11. It is assumed throughout this discussion that both types of input contributors participate in productive activity, thus ruling out corner solutions. For a further discussion see the second section of Chapter 11.

   12. There are, of course, many valuations in the body of Figure 9.2, but only one is presumed to constitute a long-run sustainable valuation given the state of nature. Questions concerning the exact pricing equation for bondlike and stocklike securities or where these sustainable equilibrium schedules are located in Figure 9.2 remain outside the scope of this analysis.

   13. We are again assuming that BB is linear in the neighborhood of the equilibrium given by Z.

   14. Bond market equilibrium can be described by:

(i) $P_b = f[E(X_b)/E(X_s), B/S] = C_b$

where P_b = the capital market price of a bond; C_b = a constant. Linearizing the model and taking the total differential and setting it equal to zero yields:

(ii) $\dfrac{d[E(X_b)/E(X_s)]}{d(B/S)} = -\dfrac{\partial P_b/\partial(B/S)}{\partial P_b/\partial[E(X_b)/E(X_s)]} > 0$

Since the numerator is presumed to be negative while the denominator is positive, the right-hand side of (ii) is positive, thus indicating BB is upward sloping.

15. This can be established in exactly the same manner as the bond market equilibrium described in note 14. Thus, we can write:

(i) $P_s = g\,[E(X_b)/E(X_s), B/S] = C_s$

(ii) $dP_s = \dfrac{\partial P_s}{\partial[E(X_b)/E(X_s)]}\, d[E(X_b)/E(X_s)] + \dfrac{\partial P_s}{\partial(B/S)}\, d(B/S) = 0$

where the first partial derivative on the right-hand side is negative while the second is positive. Rearranging (ii) yields the desired result, namely,

(iii) $\dfrac{d[E(X_b)/E(X_s)]}{d(B/S)} = -\,\dfrac{\partial P_s/\partial(B/S)}{\partial P_s/\partial[E(X_b)/E(X_s)]} > 0$

16. The BB and SS schedules in Figure 9.2 are derivable from the BB and SS schedules in Figure 9.1. To see this, suppose bonds and stocks were identical securities. Then the slopes of BB and SS in both Figures 9.1 and 9.2 would be identical in the neighborhood of Z and one schedule would be superimposed on the other. Now give the bond-type security priority. This will have the effect of making bonds less sensitive to changes in B/S in Figure 9.2 in and around Z, which in turn implies that bonds have a relatively lower expected return in and around Z in Figure 9.1 compared to stock. Thus, if we start from Z in Figure 9.2 and move equidistant to the right (increasing the share of inputs provided by bondholders) and left (increasing the share of inputs provided by stockholders), the compensation in terms of income sharing by bondholders will be smaller than that required by stockholders. As a stylized example, consider the following assumed sharing rules for bondholders and stockholders in the neighborhood of Z in Figure 9.1.

$E(X_b) = B$
$E(X_s) = 2S$

Here we see that bondholders only demand half the expected output per unit of input than stockholders, and thus $E(X_b)/E(X_s) = 1/3$ and $B/S = 2/3$ at point Z in Figure 9.2. An alternative way of saying the same thing is that for providing 40 percent of the inputs, bondholders demand, on a priority basis, 25 percent of the expected output, while stockholders put up 60 percent of the inputs but lay claim to 75 percent of the expected output. Finally we remind the reader that in Figures 9.1 and 9.2 and the stylized example, we do not claim to have located point Z or derived the equilibrium input/output-sharing rules for this economy. Point Z and the sharing rules evolve from the preferences, risk aversion, and endowments of the two claimants, along with the technology in the economy. Our purpose is rather to show that if Z is an initial equilibrium sharing rule then departures from Z upward, downward, to the right, and to the left will involve redistributions that make one party unambiguously better off but only at the expense of the other input contributor.

17. Alternative objectives include sales maximization and growth rate of asset maximization subject to a profit constraint that supposedly is just sufficient to keep

stockholders from discharging the managers. These alternative objectives stem in large measure from the observation that for most large corporations there is a separation of ownership and control, and that the welfare of those who own and those who control the firm's resources are not identical. As we observed in Chapter 4 this is in considerable measure due to the fact that stockholders have an opportunity to diversify their wealth across different projects or firms in the economy, whereas managers are typically forced to invest their human capital in a single project or firm for various reasons, including the fact that managerial efficiency is directly related to experience gained in specialization.

In the past several years there has been a renewed interest in a number of these issues, and this renewed interest has taken the form of a new literature concerned with incentive compatibility and executive compensation. For a sample of some of the theoretical and empirical work in this area that builds upon the assumption that the welfare and information set of managers and owners are not necessarily the same across a wide variety of business decisions, see Mirrlees (1976), Harris and Raviv (1979), Holmstrom (1979), and Amihud and Lev (1981).

18. In this connection we cannot overstress the distinction between current and future stockholders and bondholders, and that management decisions must be oriented toward the current input contributors. Clearly, in this sense it is appropriate to say that the future will take care of itself, but the past needs some assistance, or at least assurance that the firm will not be managed in a manner detrimental to their interests.

19. To maintain the initial input and expected output agreement in the presence of an unexpected change in demand, the firm would respond by leaving output prices unchanged and financing the expansion or contraction in output in exactly the same way as economic activity was originally financed. Even though this adjustment would be rational from our point of view, there seems to be no empirical support for it, as we will see in Chapter 12.

—10—

A Financial Contracting Theory
of the Business Cycle

Introduction

In Chapter 9 we presented a theory of firm management that attempted to rationalize cooperative production in a market economy. This rationalization in turn implied certain combinations of price, output (employment), and financing adjustments as the firm and the economy moved through various phases of the business cycle. In one sense this theory shares certain fundamental ideas that have also been developed in the implicit contract literature where risk-averse workers join together with risk-neutral (or less-risk-averse) capitalists in a labor agreement that governs labor's participation in the production process. One important feature in some of these models (e.g., Grossman and Hart 1983) is that for moral hazard reasons a fixed wage rate and variable employment contract is often the only feasible labor agreement attainable when capitalists enjoy an information advantage over workers regarding the true state of the economy. Our labor agreement and bond contract have the same property. On the other hand, in our set-up an efficient economy-wide bond and stock market precludes this type of informational asymmetry among factor input contributors, and this will constitute one of the differences between our own model and implicit contract theory.

What we will do in this chapter is describe in somewhat greater detail the interaction between the pricing, production, and financing decisions of rationally managed firms, and the effects of these decisions on the capital market valuations of bonds and stocks over the business cycle. We will see that when firm managers are required by some sort of contract to apportion risk with return in the course of adjusting supply upward or downward from its long-run natural rate level, the resulting pricing and production decisions will give rise to an upward-sloping supply schedule of the kind often observed in empirical studies of the business cycle. For the most part these discussions will be carried out in terms of a single representative firm producing a single product, since this would seem to be the easiest way to describe our risk-and-return-sharing theory of cyclical supply adjustments in the economy. Later we will relax this assumption and consider supply adjustments in the more realistic and complicated n-firms and n-goods economy. Finally we will conclude this chapter with a summary of the materials presented here and in Chapter 9, since together they form the core of our description of what occurs in a contract economy during business cycles.

Pricing, Production, and Financing Adjustments
Over the Business Cycle

Expansion

Before beginning this discussion it is important to note that there is considerable disagreement as to whether monetary factors or real factors (e.g., oil shocks, crop failures, and changes in tastes and technology) initiate changes in aggregate output. We do not wish to take sides in this debate since it is not necessary to do so for our purpose which is to describe how an economy will adjust its supply in response to a change in demand. Nevertheless it is true that there is a tradition in the business cycle literature for discussing these issues within the context of a money-induced change in aggregate demand, and in order to compare and contrast our own approach to the other approaches, it will be useful to make the same assumption regarding the origins of the change in demand.[1] A second maintained hypothesis in these kinds of discussions is, if anything, even more controversial than the origins of the demand shift; namely, the question of whether there are any *involuntarily* unemployed resources in the economy at the time of the demand shift. Some discussions assume there are (why else is the monetary authority increasing aggregate demand?), while others assume that any existing unemployment is of a purely voluntary or frictional nature, reflecting the current tastes and income expectations of input contributors. Here the choice of assumptions is much more difficult in that there are strong traditions for both. And yet from our perspective the choice is not particularly critical, although it will change certain implications and interpretations of our analysis of supply adjustment. With some hesitation in this connection we will move forward by assuming that there are involuntarily unemployed resources (at the prevailing nominal prices for factor services) in the economy, and that this is the reason why the monetary authority attempts to expand money demand.[2]

With these working assumptions, then, consider an economy that for some reason is currently experiencing a level of unemployment that the gov-

ernment would like to remove. Furthermore suppose that the government
responds to this state of affairs in the factor input market by expanding the
supply of money in order to stimulate aggregate demand and hopefully reduce the level of unemployment. According to some macroeconomic models
the increase in the money supply will, in the short run, raise the value of all
assets in the economy. This reduction in the interest rate and the higher valuation placed on assets is then argued to stimulate both investment and consumption spending on new output, which in turn the government hopes will
reduce the involuntary unemployment in the system. How much of this increased spending or expansion in money GNP takes the form of a higher
price level or a higher volume of real output? Economists of nearly all per-
suasions and ordinary laymen, for that matter, would probably say both
prices and real output would change, provided the economy was not already
experiencing a "high" rate of inflation or a "severe" depression. Where
there is sharp disagreement—at least among economists—is over the microeconomic processes by which prices and real output change in response to a
change in aggregate demand.

   The framework of analysis developed in Chapter 9 provides another
microeconomic description of the price-output composition of the change in
nominal GNP over the business cycle. The key idea in this description centered around the contractual agreements between bondholder- and stockholder-type claimants concerning input and output sharing in different states
of the economy. In our set-up, different input contributors—for reasons of
differential risk aversion and state-dependent preferences over relative income and risk—come together within the institutional framework of the
firm and contract with one another for shares of inputs and outputs in different stages of the business cycle. These agents, who put together the firm,
know that the economy will fluctuate around some long-run growth path,
and rather than try to anticipate these fluctuations (as they do in rational
expectations accounts of the business cycle) and engage in some form of intertemporal speculation with regard to the supply of their input, they contract in advance for shares in the supply of inputs and receipt of output in
different states of the economy. In a monetary economy, where prices and
the level of production are free to vary in response to changes in demand,
nominally denominated fixed income claims and variable residual income
claims are contract forms that can potentially achieve a variety of cyclical
sharing of capital inputs and net income within the firm. For example,
within this framework it is possible that cyclical expansions (contractions)
could be characterized by falling (rising) prices and higher (lower) levels of
production and financial leverage. In other words the economy could experience a positively sloped Phillips curve within the context of our theory of
input and output sharing, provided the firms in the economy financed the
expansion on balance with debt. As we will see later in this chapter this particular cyclical sharing of capital inputs and net income that gives rise to a
positively sloped Phillips curve would occur when firms pursue a relatively

safe production strategy during periods of expansion and a risky strategy during contractions. Alternatively, in our theory a negatively sloped Phillips curve or upward-sloping supply schedule would require firms to finance expansions with equity. Again, later we will see that this positive correlation between prices and output (employment) would occur if the firms in the economy followed risky production strategies during expansions and safe strategies during contractions. Since the empirical evidence reported in Chapter 12 seems to support the latter type of supply adjustment, we will focus our attention on that case: namely, (1) stockholders contract for a relatively large share of the social income during periods of cyclical expansion, but also agree to put up a relatively large share of the capital inputs; while (2) bondholders contract for relatively large shares of capital inputs and income during periods of cyclical contraction. Nevertheless we must not lose sight of the fact that the opposite kind of Phillips relationship and input/output-sharing agreement can also be rationalized within this theory of a partnership economy.

We are now in a position to verbally describe the dynamics of these cyclical sharing rules and their associated pricing, production, and financing adjustments over the course of the business cycle. First consider the case of cyclical expansion. One of the first effects of an expansion in aggregate demand triggered by an expansion in the stock of money will be experienced in the capital market where portfolio investors attempt to predict the consequences of a change in purchasing power in the system in terms of risk and return sharing. Our discussion suggests that one possible capital market response to this expansion in demand will be a rise in stock prices as investors become more optimistic and perceive a less risky environment, which in turn allows firms to pursue relatively more risky production strategies. For convenience only, we will assume that bond prices remain unchanged for the moment. What then will be the supply response of the firm to these conditions in the capital market, or more particularly, how should the firm vary output prices, production (including employment), and the financing of production in response to this change in the firm's environment? The answer provided by our theory of a bondholder/stockholder-managed firm is that pricing, production, and financing decisions should be made so that current bondholders and stockholders in some way share the benefits and burdens associated with the supply adjustment in both input and output markets. Consequently, in response to this signal of rising stock prices our coalescing managers should expand employment and production, and finance the expansion with equity. The financing of this expansion in productive activity with equity will reduce the financial leverage of the firm and thereby provide the bondholders with a thicker equity cushion with which to confront any subsequent contraction. The first-stage adjustment of expanding employment and output financed with equity will eventually bring to an end the rise in stock prices for at least two interrelated reasons. To begin with, the expansion in equity financing will tend to satisfy the increased demand for stock by optimistic stock investors initially triggered by the expansionary monetary policy. The second reason is that stockholders are now coming to absorb a larger share of the risks associated with production by virtue of their larger investment in the firm without, for the moment, receiving a relatively larger return. As the disequilibrium of rising stock prices is removed by the firm's employment, production, and financing decisions, a disequilibrium of rising bond prices is created by these very same decisions. The reason bond prices are now rising is that the first stage in the supply adjustment confers all the benefits to bondholders in that they are now providing a relatively smaller share of the total financial requirement but still receiving the same real expected income per unit of input. According to our theory of the firm, the contract between bondholders and stockholders that first gave birth to the enterprise would now require a reconciling management to compensate stockholders for their increased risky investment in the firm. This the managers can do in the second stage of the supply adjustment by raising output prices. By raising the price of output—holding employment and output temporarily constant—the disequilibrium of rising bond prices will eventually be brought to an end, since the real expected income of the firm is now being redistributed from bondholders to stockholders to compensate for the redistribution of risk occasioned by the stage-one employment, output, and financing adjustment. Of course those policies that tend to bring the bond market back into equilibrium will, by their very nature, create a disequilibrium of rising stock prices, and so the process will continue to repeat itself.

What we observe, then, in the expansion phase of the business cycle is a step-up in the level of employment and output financed with equity along with increasing output prices, that is, an upward-sloping supply schedule. This will continue until eventually the long-run risk contingent equilibrium prices are attained in the bond and stock market, at which point the nominal supply of firm output is adjusted—at least in the opinion of bond and stock investors—to the new demand in the economy occasioned by the expansionary monetary policy. In this way signals from the capital market are translated—with some noise of course—by firm managers into pricing, employment, output, and financing decisions, and these decisions determine the price-output composition of a change in nominal GNP. What is more important, however, is that this price-output composition of a change in nominal GNP is the result of a rational supply adjustment in that both bondholders and stockholders who jointly create the firm could agree in principle, if not detail, to expand supply in this way, given an unexpected expansion in aggregate demand. After the new capital market and product market equilibrium is attained, stockholders will earn a larger expected real return but also absorb a larger share of the risks in the production process over the business cycle, while bondholders will earn a relatively smaller real return but also accept a smaller risk in financing production over the business cycle.

The final point worth noting here is that the exact price-output composition of the change in nominal GNP will depend upon how responsive the equilibrium valuations of bonds and stocks are to both changes in the price level (the allocator of real income between bondholders and stockholders) and the level of employment, output, and the financing mix which allocates risk in this model.[3]

Contraction and Supply Adjustment

A similar exercise can be carried out for the opposite case; namely, one where for some unknown reason the economy is experiencing overemployment and a price level rising at a rate considered undesirable by the government. The textbook description of the monetary authority's response to this situation would discuss the means by which the money supply is reduced and how this in turn would affect interest rates and asset valuations, which in turn would reduce aggregate demand in the system. This reduction in aggregate demand would be partly reflected in lower output prices and a lower level of employment and output, thereby partially achieving the objective of the monetary authority. Our interest is in how a management coalescing the interests of bondholders and stockholders will accommodate the reduction in aggregate demand in terms of output prices, production, and the financing of production.

As before, the first market to experience the impact of the reduction in the money supply will be the capital market where portfolio investors attempt to assess the product market consequences of the contractionary monetary policy. Again let us assume for the sake of convenience that only the bond market remains in equilibrium but that the stock market is thrown into a disequilibrium of falling stock prices as stock investors come to expect that the preferred supply of nominal output by the firm must be reduced in order to efficiently accommodate the reduction in aggregate demand occasioned by the contractionary monetary policy. Alternatively stock prices start falling because investors become more pessimistic as they begin to perceive that a riskier environment will prevail in the near future, thereby suggesting that the firm will pursue a safer production strategy.

The question then becomes: How should firms respond to this signal from the stock market? In the end we know that output, employment, and prices must fall, or at least not rise at as high a rate as they were rising before the reduction in aggregate demand. One possible stage-one reaction would be for the firm to reduce the current level of output and employment. These decisions would reduce the financial requirements of the firm. Suppose the managers returned the released funds to shareholders either directly by purchasing stock in the market or more subtly by not reducing the dividends paid on stock commensurate with the reduction in the firm's earnings. The effect of this output and financing decision would be to raise the financial leverage of the firm and thereby shift the burden of financing production from stockholders to bondholders. One reason this financing strategy is possible is that in the preceding expansion the financial leverage of the firm was reduced as a matter of policy and with the next contraction squarely in mind. In any event this shift in financial burden will reduce the risk exposure of stockholders since they now have a smaller investment in the firm, and will eventually bring to an end the disequilibrium of falling stock prices.

Nevertheless eliminating the disequilibrium of falling stock prices by reducing output and employment and returning capital to stockholders will invariably create a disequilibrium of falling bond prices. Bond prices will fall because the financial decision to return the excess funds on balance to stockholders will have the effect of shifting financial risk at the margin to bondholders who are now providing a larger share of the total financing than they were in the initial equilibrium before the contraction in demand. In stage two of the adjustment process something must be done for bondholders, since up to now they have borne a disproportionate share of the burden associated with the supply adjustment. The remedy would be a reduction in the price of output, or at least a reduction in the rate of increase from that previously expected by bondholders and stockholders. The decision to reduce output prices or their rate of increase in stage two would have the effect of redistributing the falling expected real output from stockholders to bondholders, and thereby provide the latter with some compensation for the risk transfer that occurred in stage one of the supply contraction.[4] This stage-two price reduction would eventually eliminate the disequilibrium of falling bond prices, but of course in the process create a new disequilibrium of falling stock prices. The whole process will then be repeated until eventually the capital market and product market will be in equilibrium, at which point the actual supply of nominal output by firms is equal to the lower preferred supply or capital market equilibrium supply in the economy. Moreover this particular reduction in supply allocates the burdens to both stockholders and bondholders. In the new equilibrium shareholders will earn a relatively low income but also have a relatively small investment in the firm, while bondholders will find their real expected return higher along with their share in financing production.

A Geometric Illustration of Supply Adjustment
Over the Business Cycle

Our analysis of supply adjustment over the business cycle can be *illustrated* geometrically along somewhat the same lines as our discussion of input and expected output sharing presented in Figure 9.2. In this connection consider Figure 10.1. On the vertical axis we measure the real wage, $\bar{W}/P$. For the short run the money wage rate $\bar{W}$ is taken to be fixed by the labor contract and thus output price is the only variable on the axis. The role

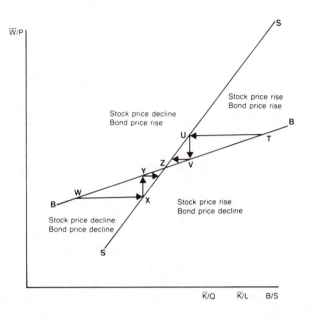

Figure 10.1.   Cyclical Supply Adjustment in a Contract Economy

played by the price of output in our system is one of allocating the real social income between bondholders and stockholders, although here, unlike the fixed-input/fixed-expected-output case considered in Chapter 9, the levels of inputs and outputs are free to vary.[5] For this reason the vertical axis in Figure 10.1 is not strictly comparable to that in Figure 9.2.

On the horizontal axis we measure the capital-output ratio $\bar{K}/Q$ (where Q = the expected end-of-period real output produced by the firm), or what is the same thing in our short-run analysis, the capital-labor ratio $\bar{K}/L$. Again we differentiate the long run from the short run by holding the stock of productive capital inputs constant, and consequently the only variable on the horizontal axis is the level of expected real output and employment. As we have mentioned on a number of occasions, employment and production require financial support which can be raised either by new bond or stock issues on the capital market or by retaining the earnings of stockholders. A useful measure of the financial decisions of firms is embodied in financial leverage, which in turn can be written in a number of different ways, including the ratio of debt financing to equity financing, or B/S. The leverage measure B/S represents an important decision variable in the hands of firm managers, for it is the means by which the risks of production are allocated between bondholders and stockholders.

In our model financial risks are to be jointly allocated with real income during the supply adjustment process. For this reason any pricing decision by the firm that redistributes return should, according to our theory, be accompanied by a financing decision that redistributes risk in a corresponding manner. The end result is that in our model economy an agreement is reached between bondholders and stockholders whereby future unexpected expansions in employment and output (a movement toward the origin for $\bar{K}/Q$ and $\bar{K}/L$ in Figure 10.1) are financed with stock, whereas contractions are financed with debt. This hypothesized agreement which coordinates production thus implies that the financial leverage variables, B/S, can also be displayed on the horizontal axis in Figure 10.1.

In the body of Figure 10.1 we present the conditions required for capital market equilibrium; that is to say, the combinations of price, output (employment), and financing adjustments that for a given state of the economy produces an equilibrium valuation for bonds and stocks. These conditions reflect in a rough (although inexact) way the theory of bond and stock valuations presented in Chapter 9, except that the price of output and financial leverage are the agreed-upon means by which real expected return and financial risk are to be redistributed among bondholders and stockholders during the supply adjustment. Thus the schedule BB slopes upward since an unexpected rise in the price of output reduces the real returns earned by bondholders and thereby drives down the capital market valuation of bonds. This decline in bond prices can only be offset, according to our analysis, by an expansion in employment and output financed with equity, which in turn reduces the financial leverage and risks associated with bond ownership. The implication, then, is that points above BB represent disequilibriums of high bond prices, while points below represent low bond prices.

The schedule SS also slopes upward but for the opposite reasons. In this case an unexpected rise in the price of output will increase the real return of current stockholders and thereby be reflected in higher capital market valuations on stock. The sustainable long-run equilibrium stock price can be restored by increasing the share of financial risk absorbed by current stockholders, and this is accomplished when the firm finances an expansion with equity. For this reason points above SS represent disequilibriums of lower stock prices, while points below characterize higher stock prices. As in Figure 9.2, we have drawn the SS schedule steeper than the BB schedule on the grounds that bonds represent priority claims to the output and resources of the firm and hence are less affected by output fluctuations than stock.

With Figure 10.1 it is possible to put the cyclical variation in pricing, employment, production, and financing decisions of firms into a framework that bears a resemblance to the Tinbergen (1952) and Mundell (1962) "principle of effective market classification." In this connection consider the first case of cyclical supply adjustment discussed above, namely, an expansion in aggregate demand initiated by government financial policy. Point T describes this economy immediately after the expansion in the money supply when stock prices are high in anticipation of an improvement in business conditions. If firms "assigned" employment, production, and financing decisions as a stage-one correction to stock market disequilibrium and pricing decisions as a stage-two correction to bond market disequilibrium, the economy would approach full equilibrium (i.e., product market and capital market equilibrium) at point Z via the intermediate points U (stage one) and V (stage two). The reverse assignment would lead to instability.[6]

The second case considered above was that of monetary contraction and can be illustrated with reference to point W where the market value of stock is low in anticipation of a deterioration in future business prospects. Using the same assignment rule (only reversing the employment, production, financing, and pricing decisions of firms) our idealized coalescing managers would guide the firm and economy toward full equilibrium at point Z via points X (the stage-one output, employment, and financing adjustment) and Y (the stage-two price level adjustment). Again the reverse assignment would lead the economy further from the equilibrium described by Z. In this way the capital market and a management pledged to the welfare of all input contributors would provide rational guidance to the pricing, output (employment), and financing decisions of bondholder/stockholder-managed firms as supply adjusts to changes in nominal demand. Finally the equilibration of supply to demand is accomplished in such a way that the advantages and disadvantages of the adjustment in terms of input and expected output sharing are in some sense fairly apportioned between bondholders and stockholders, as required in the contract that coordinates cooperation in production between these two claimants. When firms adjust supply in this way there is a rationale in financing production with both bondlike and stocklike claims to the end-of-period output.

Many Firms and Many Goods

Introduction

Up to this point our discussion has been based on the assumption that a single good is being produced in the economy by a single firm financed with bonds and stocks. These assumptions have enabled us to highlight, in as clear a manner as possible, the conflict that invariably arises among those who supply factor services to the firm in exchange for a bondlike or stocklike claim to the end-of-period output. When this conflict is highlighted, as it has been up to this point, it is easy to see that certain supply adjustments in the economy make more sense than others in terms of rationalizing factor cooperation in productive activity. Our theory of aggregate supply is nothing more than an attempt to explain away factor cooperation in an uncertain environment, and as such it places great weight on the effect of pricing, production, and financing decisions on risk and return sharing among the input contributors over the business cycle.[7]

The assumption of a single good is very useful in that it facilitates a separation of macroeconomic phenomena, like a change in aggregate demand, from relativistic microeconomic phenomena, such as changes in tastes and technology, that bear upon supply-and-demand relationships between separate markets. To the extent that macro events can be separated from micro phenomena, this distinction is fruitful in that it might enable us to gain some fundamental insights into the workings of an entire economy without becoming entrapped in structural detail.

In our capital market analysis of the cyclical adjustment of supply for an entire economy, this separation between macroeconomics and microeconomics would seem to be crucial. This is because the price of our single good is, simultaneously, a price that (1) allocates real expected income among bondholders and stockholders and thereby affects the capital market valuation of these securities, and (2) represents, in the sense discussed in note 4, a decision variable set by coalescing managers with the view of influencing bondholder and stockholder welfare in some purposeful manner. It might therefore seem that when we move from a one-good to an *n*-good framework of analysis, this dual use of the price of output would be difficult to justify in principle. Thus it might be argued that the capital market price, say, of Quaker Oats bonds, is influenced by prices in general and only very remotely by the price of a box of Quaker Oats. If this is the case it would seem to call into question our risk/return-sharing principle initiated by a coalescing management as a rational way in which to manage a supply adjustment. To see this, recall that our stage-two adjustment of changing output prices was designed to correct bond market disequilibrium by redistributing the real income of the firm between bondholders and stockholders; but unless oatmeal looms large in the consumption basket of investors, the change in the price of a box of Quaker Oats will have very little effect on the market price of Quaker Oats bonds in terms of the real income redistribution effect.

Many Goods and Investor Diversification

It is not impossible to obtain essentially the same kinds of results we obtained above for an *n*-good economy where the *n*-goods were not perfectly correlated over time. The assumption we would then need is that bondholders and stockholders hold diversified portfolios comprised of the companies that produce the products they consume. The purpose of the diversification would be to contribute inputs and hold claims on output to perfectly reflect the consumption preferences of the investor. When this is the case every individual bondholder would own a pro-rata share of the total priority claim to future output generated by private firms. The same would be true for the individual stockholder who held a market portfolio of stocks, for that investor would then hold a pro-rata share of the aggregate residual claim to the end-of-period output. If this were the case, how could bondholder- and stockholder-type claimants protect themselves from each other during the supply adjustment process? The answer, of course, is that they would protect themselves in exactly the same way as in the one-good world discussed above. When jointly forming the n different enterprises, bondholders and stockholders would write into every bond contract the same supply adjustment agreement they did when holding the bondlike claim in the single-firm economy. Every individual firm would then be required to adjust its own supply to its individual cyclical demand by financing expansion with equity and contractions with debt, as well as varying its individual output price in a procyclical manner. By holding all bonds or all stocks—including those in Quaker Oats—each individual investor could achieve the cyclical pattern of relative income and risk that presumably gives rise to the creation of bondlike and stocklike contracts in the first place.

Supply Adjustments in the Absence of Investor Diversification

At this point it would be tempting to move forward and attempt no further justification for the one-good assumption that guided our thinking earlier in this chapter. This strategy would be partly in keeping with the methodology of the new classical macroeconomics, for as Lucas (1980, p. 696) reminds us: "One of the functions of theoretical economics is to provide fully articulated, artificial economic systems that can serve as laboratories . . ." and that: "To serve this function well, it is essential that the artificial 'model' economy be distinguished as sharply as possible in discussions from actual economies." On the other hand we do not think this methodological observation necessarily precludes the economist from exploring or perhaps explaining away any apparent discrepancy between artificial and actual economies, and in this spirit we will continue our discussion of contracting in an n-good world, and any resemblance it might bear to the kind of contracting discussed above for the one-good world.

In pursuing this issue further, it is clear that input contributors in actual economies do not generally hold market portfolios of bondlike and stocklike claims that match up with their consumption preferences as was assumed in the previous subsection. Moreover this particular attempt to justify our approach is somewhat embarrassing, given our general reluctance to use the capital asset pricing model as the basis for analyzing this and other issues related to the general question of wealth redistribution. Nevertheless the idea of a contract between bondholder- and stockholder-type claimants having a bearing on the shape of future supply adjustments has considerable appeal, and does not in itself imply any particular degree of investor diversification nor any precise form the bond contract provisions might take. The question we must now try to answer, then, is the following: In a world where an individual investor holds only a limited number of different bonds or stocks but consumes a wide variety of products, and where the bond contract does not explicitly prescribe the individual firm's pricing and production decisions, is the cyclical supply adjustment that evolves in the economy indistinguishably different from that implied by our single artificial firm explicitly managed in the joint interests of its bondholders and stockholders?

There is much—including the empirical evidence offered in Chapter 12—to suggest that the answer to this question is "no." To begin with, just because an individual does not own a market portfolio of bonds or stocks does not necessarily mean that the interests and welfare of individual bondholders or stockholders in a particular firm are identical. Whenever inputs are advanced by different individuals possessing different types of claims to the end-of-period output of the firm, future production and financing decisions will always have a differential effect on the welfare of the initial claimants, independent of their specific consumption plan. Here it is important to remember that what is at issue is the welfare of initial bondholders and stockholders. New bondholders and stockholders will always have the benefit of obtaining claims at prices that reflect the current risk-and-return-sharing agreement, but as we observed earlier, today's agreement could be different from yesterday's or tomorrow's, for that matter. Thus an expansion in output financed with new bonds issued today will invariably infringe on the safety of the debt outstanding yesterday to the extent the new issue is unanticipated by the old bondholders.[8] Bondholders would prefer not to be surprised in this manner, and for this reason they tend to insert restrictive covenants in the bond contract that limit the amount of debt relative to equity the firm may issue over the life of the bond contract. This restriction on financial policy is one way old bondholders can protect their initial position in the firm from new rapacious stockholders.

The investment and production decisions of the firm are another source of conflict between present bondholders and future stockholders. To begin with, bondholders who initially contribute capital to an enterprise whose announced intention is to operate in a relatively safe sector—say the construction and maintenance of a domestic telephone service—would have good reason to be dismayed if the company subsequently branched out in a relatively risky sector, say the telecommunication business in politically unstable countries. While this particular example is not really within the spirit of the assumptions set forth in the second section of Chapter 9, it does indicate that asset decisions have a material effect on the welfare of bondholders. More in keeping with our assumptions, the distinction between liquid and nonliquid (the tying up of funds in working capital in our short-run model) assets would be particularly relevant here. Risk-averse bondholders would prefer, other things remaining equal, an asset structure tilted in favor of safe liquid assets. Moreover, these preferences often take the form of a restrictive covenant in the bond contract that constrains the firm to hold a certain proportion of its debt (e.g., compensating balances on bank loans) or total assets in safe liquid form such as cash or marketable securities. In this connection it used to be said of bankers in more opportune times that they only want to lend to those who lend to them. This is the natural instinct of creditors, and when they lose this instinct, as on occasions they do, they are more apt to end up an owner rather than a creditor, at which point the instinct tends to be regained. In any event, it is significant to observe that these liquidity requirements are also financial in nature.[9]

It is our contention that these kinds of financial constraints, written into the bond contract to protect the bondholder's financial position in the firm, act in such a way, although not perfectly, as to direct the firm to adjust supply in a manner not distinguishably different from that implied in our one-good/one-firm world where managers directly and explicitly coalesced the interests of bondholders and stockholders during the adjustment process. Let us consider this matter further. In the one-good/one-firm world analyzed above, the supply adjustment was characterized by a purposeful combination of firm-specific pricing, production, and financing decisions that redistributed returns (the pricing decision) commensurate with any redistribution of risk (the financing of production decision) between the different types of claimants to the end-of-period output. In this world, bondholders and stockholders were not only protected from one another in the micro sense of financial constraints discussed in the two previous paragraphs, but they were also protected from one another in the macro sense for the case when the price level unexpectedly changed as a result of an expansion in aggregate demand. In this case the redistributive effects of unexpected inflation or deflation were offset by a financing decision that redistributed risk, and our assignment rule for managing the firm was specifically designed with this end in mind. Yet the micro restrictions that take the form of constraints on various aspects of financial policy designed to protect creditors from firm-specific decisions (which otherwise would be made in the interests of owners) also tend to provide some protection against the economy-wide redistribution of income associated with unanticipated changes in the price level during various stages in the business cycle.

In developing this view further, suppose the agreement that unites bondholders and stockholders to carry out productive activity within the institutional framework of the firm contains only two provisions that are financial in nature: one relating to the debt-equity ratio, and the other to some measure of liquidity and safety of the underlying assets, such as the ratio of safe assets to risky assets appropriately defined. As we observed in note 9 it is rational for both types of input contributors to write the agreement so that these two financial provisions or constraints are directly linked to one another. What this means is that if the managers of the firm should for some business reason raise the debt-equity ratio, they would be under some contractual obligation to raise the ratio of safe assets (e.g., cash) to risky assets (e.g., inventories), thereby making the firm a safer investment for bondholders who are now providing a larger share of the inputs.

Within this contractual or balance-sheet-matching framework, consider now an economy where for some reason actual employment and output are below their potential levels (at least in the eyes of the monetary authority), and to rectify this situation the monetary authority initiates an expansion in the money supply. The question then becomes one of how an individual firm in an n-firm economy will adjust its supply in response to an expansion in aggregate demand, given that the contract between bondholders and stockholders in this firm contains these two financial provisions. When the money supply expands, our representative firm experiences an expansion in the demand for its products. What might be the reaction of the firm's managers (elected by the stockholders but constrained by the bondholders) to this expansion in demand? Suppose these optimistic managers think that this is precisely the moment to take what they and the stockholders would consider a prudent businessman's risk. What form might such a prudent risky business strategy take in this stylized example? One risky strategy would have our representative firm raise both output prices and the level of production. This would be a risky strategy because the firm's now optimistic managers would not know for sure whether they could immediately sell the higher level of output at the higher price. In fact they could expect their inventories or risky assets to temporarily rise as a result of this pricing and production strategy. Safety-minded bondholders, on the other hand, would tend to oppose any business strategy that increased the risk of the firm. Can this particular firm move forward when bondholders oppose the asset implications of the supply adjustment proposed by managers acting on behalf of the stockholders? The answer of course is "yes," and the two financial provisions in the bond contract were designed with this type of conflict in mind. The bondholders in effect tell the stockholders they can adjust supply (via the risky strategy of raising prices and the level of production) in a way that makes the firm riskier by restructuring the assets, provided they also restructure the financing by reducing the debt-equity ratio. This the stockholders do—since they were a party to the initial agreement containing these two balance-sheet provisions—by financing their higher level of inventories with equity. The end result in this hypothetical model economy is that during expansions in business activity the managers coalesce the interests of bondholders and stockholders by raising product prices and the level of production and financing the expansion with equity. In terms of risk and return sharing, our bondholders end up with a smaller share of real income (to the extent the price inflation was unanticipated), but with a greater margin of safety due to the fact that on balance stockholders have financed the expansion in production. Stockholders, in turn, end up with a greater share of the net income of the firm, but in turn are required to reinvest their inflationary gain in the firm. In this way two balance-sheet constraints designed to protect bondholders from the potential exploitative management policies of stockholders work in such a way that risk and return are shared together.

Consider next the case of a contraction in aggregate demand. With the prospect of reduced business activity stockholders become more safety minded and pessimistic, and propose to bondholders a supply adjustment that contracts the level of employment and production and reduces prices. But what is to be done with the financial resources released from the firm when it reduces its work force and the level of its output? At this point the firm is under no pressure from the debt-equity constraint in the bond contract since equity was used to finance the previous expansion. Stockholders quite naturally propose that these financial resources be returned to them. This, they point out, could be achieved if the firm would maintain the level of dividend payments that were made in the previous expansion even though current earnings are now falling. Bondholders of course would be inclined to oppose this particular supply contraction, since, with other things remaining equal, it would have the effect of raising the debt-equity ratio. Yet, as we have seen, the contract between bondholders and stockholders will not permit other things to remain equal. In effect stockholders are told that they can go ahead and contract supply and use a portion of the released financial resources to pay dividends, which in light of current earnings seem high, but that they must now pursue a safe business strategy by building up the liquidity and safety of the firm's assets which deteriorated in the course of the previous expansion. In attempting to meet this liquidity and safety requirement, the firm reduces the price of its products in order to reduce inventories and increase the ratio of cash-type assets to risky assets, and in this way makes the firm a safer investment for the bondholders who now are providing a larger proportion of the total financial support. Contractions in supply are then characterized by a reduction in employment, output, and output prices compared to what economic agents expected before the recession was set in motion with a reduction in aggregate demand. Moreover, in the process of contracting its supply the firm increased its debt-equity ratio and the liquidity and safety of its total assets in accordance with the two financial provisions contained in the bond contract. In this way the shape of the supply adjustment was partly determined by the agreement between bondholders and stockholders that coordinated productive activity in the first place.

We would like to close this part of our discussion by reminding the reader of an old saying on Wall Street that best sums up the idea we are trying to express; namely, "Bulls get a little, bears get a little, but pigs get nothing."

Bulls and bears look very much like stockholders and bondholders in a world where the firm is managed in the interests of both. Pigs, however, look like stockholders (bondholders) who are determined to exploit bondholders (stockholders) in all subsequent supply adjustments, and they will get nothing—or at least nothing in the way of capital inputs—from rational investors. Our analysis of a one-good/one-firm economy points to the kind of supply adjustments that would rationalize initial cooperation between bondholders and stockholders. In this world an assignment rule on subsequent supply adjustments can protect both contributors from one group gaining an advantage over the other during the process of adjustment itself. Yet the world we actually observe is not that of a single firm nor a single good. In this context, it is somewhat surprising—at least to us—that the balance-sheet-matching covenants we tend to observe in the bond contract of a single firm, specifically designed to prevent stockholders from expropriating the wealth of bondholders at the micro financial risk level, can go so far towards providing both claimants with some protection from each other when there is an unexpected change in the price level resulting from a change in government financial policy. What is "far," of course, is an empirical question, and one we will address in Chapter 12.

Labor and the Supply Adjustment Process

Introduction

Up to now we have discussed the supply adjustment of firms solely from the point of view of those contributors who provide the capital inputs. The welfare of workers was ignored not because we think their welfare unimportant, but because the idea of input and output sharing can be more clearly articulated when studying the relationship between bondholders and stockholders. With the insights gained in studying supply adjustments from the perspective of capitalists, we can now consider in a general way the effects on workers.

In this connection it is important to immediately note the similarities and differences between employed workers and bond investors insofar as their participation in the production process is concerned. Both provide a factor service to the firm in exchange for a fixed priority claim to the end-of-period money income and as a result the real income of both relative to stockholder-type claimants will tend to follow the same path over the business cycle, rising in recessions and falling during expansions. However, there are also important differences. To begin with, there are institutional limitations that tend to preclude market transfers of an individual laborer's claim to future output, whereas there are no such restrictions on bonds. The reason why labor's claim to output is nonmarketable is that human beings cannot be forced to work against their will. A second difference pertains to their respective alternatives to participating in the production process of any given enterprise. There are, evidently, significant imperfections or codes of behavior in the labor market that tend to make the forced consumption of leisure the alternative to employment during the contraction phase of the business cycle. Bonds, on the other hand, are traded in centralized and relatively perfect markets so that the retirement or laying off of bonds in one non-bankrupt company can be easily remedied by the "unemployed" bondholder investing in some other company with minimal differences in the rate of return. For these reasons we must be somewhat cautious when comparing the welfare of workers to bondholders during the supply adjustment process.

Expansion, Contraction, and the Welfare of Workers

With this caveat in mind consider, then, the situation confronting different individual workers during the expansion phase of the business cycle. As we observed above, the supply adjustment during this phase of the cycle was characterized by a rise in output prices, and an expansion in employment and output financed with equity. We also observed that during the expansion the real returns on bonds declined, but so did bondholders' financial stake in the firm. Similarly, the real purchasing power of the fixed money wage rate will also decline. The question is whether workers will be worse off as a result of the decline in real wages.

In providing an answer to this question we must make a distinction between at least two different types of workers. There is first the unemployed worker who now becomes employed as a result of the expansion in supply. This worker is clearly better off since he or she would never join the work force if the utility of income obtained by working did not exceed the disutility associated with the work itself. The second type of worker that must be considered is the one already employed before the unexpected expansion in aggregate demand. This worker will experience a reduction in real income as the price inflation that accompanies the expansion partially erodes the purchasing power of the fixed money wage rate. The interesting question, however, is whether the risk (in terms of future unemployment) of the currently employed worker is in any way diminished during the expansion in supply, as was the case for existing bondholders. The answer to this question would appear to be "yes" for two interrelated reasons. The first reason is the seniority system of "last in, first out" that characterizes most labor agreements. The workers newly hired during the expansion will be the first to be laid off in the next contraction. Here, too, the analogy with bondholders is striking in that the newly hired workers provide a protective cushion for older workers just as equity provides the cushion for bondholders. Thus the seniority system for workers is what priority is for bondholders; namely, a mechanism by which an existing employed factor input contributor protects its economic position in the enterprise from subsequent intrusions from other and similar factor inputs. The seniority principle, in turn, is generally reinforced by a second consideration; that is, the fact that more experienced workers are preferred, if not more productive, than less experienced workers. This might be reflected in relative wage rates between the two groups of workers, but the risk aversion of workers tends to reward experience with relative job security rather than the relative wage differential that would exist in a riskless environment. Consequently, the mere passage of time between the various phases of the business cycle increases the experience and perhaps the productivity of the initially employed worker vis-à-vis the newly hired worker. The end result is that the gain in experience and productivity along with the priority agreement of seniority both operate to reduce the redundancy risk of the initially employed workers, and this reduction in risk can be viewed as compensation for the reduction in real wages that is associated with an expansion in aggregate supply.

In the contraction phase the risk and real wages of the employed worker are just the reverse of those experienced during the expansion. During this phase of the business cycle the newly hired workers of the previous expansion are the first to be laid off, and the protective cushion sheltering those who have been employed will fall. Of course these loyal workers who see their seniority slowly eroding in the contraction will be partly compensated by the reduction in output prices during stage two of the supply adjustment process, which in turn raises their real income.

The conclusion that seems to emerge from this discussion is that the real return and risk confronting both an initial bondholder and an employed worker follow the same path, and that path is countercyclical in this model, for both real return and risk fall during expansions and rise during contractions in business conditions. Moreover, in their respective contracts, both tend to impose a particular supply adjustment on the enterprise that uses the expansion phase of the cycle to prepare for the next contraction. Their instincts tell them that survival in the winter and spring of contraction requires a form of fattening up of the firm in the summer and autumn of expansion.

While the similarities between workers and bondholders are interesting their differences suggest that the analogy cannot be pushed too far, particularly when it comes to issues concerning public policy. Even in our world bond investors can diversify their capital among the bonds of a number of different companies. Workers, on the other hand, cannot by assumption diversify their human capital in any direct way. Furthermore, indirect attempts to diversify with unemployment insurance schemes are typically more costly to operate than investment mutual funds because of the moral hazard problem. For this reason and others, unemployment in the labor market is considered a more serious social problem than the equivalent of unemployment in the capital market, since the latter kind of unemployment would appear to be entirely voluntary. Yet, insofar as risk and return sharing are concerned, it would seem that organized workers would subscribe to our assignment rule in adjusting supply for much the same reasons as bondholders.

Supply Adjustment and Financial Policy

Introduction

What are the financial policy lessons to be learned in a contract economy where firms adjust supply in the short run according to an assignment rule that redistributes risk with return among bondlike and stocklike claimants? In this section we will briefly discuss this question in terms of two important policy issues in financial economics; namely, can the government with aggregate demand management policies achieve some optimal pattern of price, output, and employment over the business cycle, and second, is there an optimal way to finance private production over the adjustment period? It is curious that, broadly speaking, many financial economists would agree that there is scope for an active and purposeful monetary and fiscal policy that could, in principle, reduce the amplitude of economic fluctuations, and yet these same economists would by and large deny that private financial policy can do anything to improve the financial opportunities available to investors in the marketplace. The theory of firm behavior presented in this chapter implies a somewhat different conclusion.

Government Policy

Stabilization Policy

Before beginning our discussion of the effectiveness of government intervention in the financial or product market, we should put these questions and issues in perspective by asking about the specific objectives of monetary and fiscal policy, and more importantly, asking why they are needed in the first place. According to one line of argument the problem arises because of the human proclivity to exaggerate, on occasions, what is unknown in the future. Thus the private sector, in its pursuit of self-interest in an uncertain environment, will every so often expand or contract production from its normal level to a level which on subsequent reflection can only be considered excessive. These short-run excessive fluctuations in employment, output, and prices are inherently detrimental in that they impose an additional element of risk—over and above the objective risks generated by nature—on the system. Moreover fluctuations in employment and prices will redistribute the social income in what may be a capricious manner. For these reasons the government is presumed to have some obligation or even a duty to use the tools at its disposal (control over the supply of money, government expenditure, and taxation) to counter these private excesses and stabilize the economy. When the expansion in the private sector is excessive and inflation is proceeding more rapidly than normal, then government should counteract this expansion with an appropriate monetary and fiscal policy designed to reduce the temporarily high rate of inflation. On the other hand, when the private sector is unduly pessimistic about the future and firms cut back employment below its normal level, then government should step in with an expansionary monetary and fiscal policy which, hopefully, will reduce the temporarily high unemployment. By this account the private sector is generally on the correct course, but there are the occasional swings in expectations that give rise to the infrequent and unhealthy departures from the normal state of economic affairs, and these departures are what government is under some obligation to counteract.[10]

The underlying assumptions of activist stabilization policies are that government can recognize the points in time when the private sector is off its normal course, and the tools at its disposal such as monetary and fiscal policy are capable of nudging the private sector back toward the natural or normal rate of employment and output. Both assumptions have, quite naturally, been challenged in the literature; and while the analysis of this chapter has nothing to say about the former, it does have something to say about the price-employment-output combinations government can attain with a given monetary and fiscal policy. To begin with, in our framework the equilibrium capital market schedules BB and SS determine the final resting place for the economy in terms of employment, output, and prices. Thus, a change in monetary policy must change portfolio investor's expectations and shift the BB and SS schedules by just the right amount in order for the private sector to grope back to the normal or natural rate of unemployment and price inflation deemed appropriate by the monetary authority.

Skeptics may doubt whether the monetary authority could ever devise an appropriate policy to achieve a targeted unemployment or inflation rate when that policy must be diffused through a risk-and-return-sharing private sector. This, of course, is the problem; namely, the variables of interest to the monetary authority—such as employment (or unemployment) and prices—are the same variables the private sector adjusts in response to the change in monetary policy in the first place. Among other things this suggests that the monetary authority is unable to affect the price level without affecting the levels of employment and output over those ranges actually observed in the historical data. Our theory tells us that prices, employment, and output are adjusted together in the product market. It would be an unusual combination of BB and SS schedules that would produce a Keynesian adjustment solely in employment and output or a monetarist adjustment in prices. Of course this property is not exactly unique to our analysis in that it is shared with all those second generation Keynes-Phillips and monetarist-rational expectations models discussed in Chapter 8. Our objective in the capital market approach followed in this chapter was to show that such a price-output relationship need not rest solely on some presumed imperfection in the labor market or forecasting error in the product market, but instead evolves from a rational and orderly way of conducting business in a contract economy where input contributors have different preferences for relative income and risk in different states of the economy. Thus while the government can inject or remove purchasing power from the system, it will be the private sector that translates the change in purchasing power into pricing, employment, and output decisions, and these decisions, according to our theory, will be made in a way that redistributes risk with return among input contributors.

The analysis presented here suggests that there is not much scope for an active stabilization policy since any such policy must first be filtered through the contracts of the private sector. And yet it is also true that at least in a cyclical context our agents fully realize that changing rates of inflation redistribute the social income during various stages in the business cycle. Consequently one of the criticisms that points to the inflationary side effects of a monetary policy designed to reduce unemployment is somewhat muted in the sense that in our theory agents design bondlike and stocklike contracts with cyclical variations in the inflation rate in mind. In other words the contracts themselves are a product of the cyclical variation in the inflation rate, and to the extent that government policy accommodates this variation it is doing nothing more than was expected. Thus our analysis suggests that a cyclical expansion in the inflation rate should not necessarily preclude the monetary authority from attacking unemployment whenever and for whatever reasons it exceeds the politically perceived natural rate.

Government Regulation and the Financial System

Before leaving this discussion on government financial policy, it is useful to again reiterate why the monetary authority is unable to alter employment without altering prices in the economy. In other words, why is it that we hardly ever experience an extreme Keynesian or monetarist supply adjustment? The reason is—as we have stressed throughout the discussion in this chapter—that some input contributors hold priority claims on the end-of-period output while others hold a residual claim. When this is the case an unexpected change in aggregate demand and supply will have a differential effect on the two types of input contributors, and in order to rationalize factor cooperation, both risk and return must be adjusted together. This generally means that prices and output, along with the financing of output, will change during the supply adjustment process. There would probably be less of a redistribution and hence less of a stabilization problem if all input contributors held stocklike claims to the output generated in the private sector. For example, if all laborers, bondholders, and stockholders could contribute their factor services to some gigantic firm containing the production processes of the entire private sector in exchange for a pro-rata share (determined in some way) of the end-of-period output, then the income redistribution associated with any given change in aggregate demand would simply not occur, as it did not occur in our capital asset pricing model discussed in Chapter 4. In such a world (and Japan may be an example of that world) all contributors would share in the benefits of expansion and all would bear their proportionate share of the losses associated with contraction, and a coalescing management (either human or contractual) need not balance risk with return by altering prices, employment, output, and financing in some judicious way.

Of course, the CAPM idealization of perfect diversification is evidently impossible within our current institutional framework, particularly insofar as the labor input is concerned. Nevertheless a number of government rules and regulations, which in principle are reversible, have had the effect of encouraging debt financing of private production. Many financial intermediaries are either precluded or severely restricted by government from buying equity securities. In addition, the tax deductibility of interest payments has undoubtedly, to a certain extent, encouraged firms to issue debt rather than equity securities. From the point of view of an optimal system of taxation, this particular exemption seems to make little sense. Why should the burden of taxation between capitalists and laborers be determined in part by the nature of capital's claim to the end-of-period output? Both the tax deductibility of interest payments and the restrictions against stock purchases by certain financial intermediaries encourage the use of debt financing, and thereby create a conflict between the different types of investors, which in turn shapes the type of supply adjustment the economy experiences in response to a change in demand. On these and other grounds one might therefore advocate that the tax deductibility of interest payments be eliminated and that nonbank financial institutions, at any rate, be allowed to hold common stock. Since commercial banks are the guardians of the money supply, it may be desirable to restrict their asset acquisitions to the holding of government debt. By removing these restrictions on investors and eliminating the subsidy on debt financing, the volume of debt flotations relative to equity would decline (but not necessarily disappear) over time and thereby mitigate some of the inherent conflicts between capital input contributors. The advantage that might be expected from these kinds of reforms is that future supply adjustments would be less encumbered by the contractual constraints that at present tend to shape the price-output fluctuations experienced over the business cycle. The battle with nature is difficult enough, and any reform which reduces the conflict among ourselves as input contributors would improve the financial system, particularly if that conflict is partly the result of government regulation.

Private Financial Policy

The final policy issue we will briefly discuss in this section centers around the financing of production over the business cycle within our present institutional framework. This issue is a favorite among financial specialists where, for some time, much to the disappointment of practicing financial managers, the academic wisdom has been that financial leverage and dividend policy do not matter, or at least do not matter very much. As we mentioned in Chapter 4 this view was originally associated with Miller and Modigliani (the latter also being a forceful advocate of an active and discretionary government financial policy), and was thought to apply to a single firm at a given point in time when capital markets were assumed to be relatively perfect. It was never made clear whether the result extended across time, although Modigliani and Miller (1959, pp. 661–662) were aware that some financial decisions turn out to be better than others in retrospect. The trick, as they point out, is to know at the time of the decision which of the alternatives will produce the better results.

It would seem that over time, at any rate, the private financial policy implications of our analysis are somewhat different from those of Miller and Modigliani. Moreover, these differences arise precisely for the reasons they themselves have long recognized; namely, the interrelationship between financing and operating decisions of the firm. Their entire analysis is designed to separate financing and operating decisions, and if such a separation is possible, their irrelevance propositions follow as a matter of course. The reason we obtain an optimal pattern of financing over time (i.e., a negative relationship between financial leverage and dividend policy, on the one hand, and business activity) is because our analysis constructs this dependence as a requisite condition for the financing of production with debtlike and equitylike claims to the produced output. In other words, it is precisely because debt and equity securities represent competing claims to the future income of the firm that management policies in the product market must be directly linked to financing decisions if there is to be a rationalization of a bond-and-stock-financed enterprise. When debt securities are riskless (the MM assumption) or investors buy shares in a mutual fund containing all the debt and equity securities of risky firms in the system (the CAPM assumption), financial policy will be irrelevant. When neither of these assumptions hold, financial and operating decisions cannot be separated, and consequently there will be a systematic pattern to the debt-equity and dividend payout policy over the period of the supply adjustment.

This systematic pattern of financing production is the result of the risk-sharing arrangements embedded in the bond contract. In this connection recall that during periods of expansion in business activity the firm financed the higher level of employment and output with equity and thereby reduced financial leverage and the risks absorbed by bondholders. This reduction in risk to bondholders was accomplished with a financing decision and represents a form of compensation that offsets, in whole or in part, the loss in real income earned on bonds as a result of the decision to raise output prices during this phase of the business cycle. Moreover, this improvement in the financial health of the firm provides the safety cushion for bondholders in the next contraction. Thus our theory of supply adjustment would predict a decline in financial leverage and dividend payout during periods of economic expansion.

In the contraction we observe a different set of financial decisions which again happen to be systematically related to operating decisions. During this phase of the cycle the dividend payout ratio rises as earnings fall and dividend payments remain constant or fall by a smaller amount. In addition, any new financial requirement will be obtained by issuing some form of debt. Both decisions will raise financial leverage as the firm uses up the protective cushion created during more prosperous times. Moreover this shift in risk from stockholders to bondholders happily coincides with a corresponding redistribution of real income within the firm as output prices are reduced and the economy slips further into recession. Financial leverage and the dividend payout ratio would therefore be expected to rise during recessions. The end result is that financial decisions are systematically related to product market decisions over the trade cycle, and this relationship provides the rationale for using both debt and equity when financing production.

Summary and Conclusions

One of the great debates in macroeconomics centers around the price-output composition of a change in the aggregate money income of a society. As we observed in Chapter 7 the monetarist and income-expenditure versions of the IS-LM model of aggregate economic activity originally posed the problem, but their respective solutions took the form of an assumption which neither group considered satisfactory. In this spirit an extreme version of the monetarist model of aggregate demand assumed that the supply schedule for the economy was infinitely inelastic at the level of full employment, or viewed differently, the unemployment in the system was in some sense a "natural" or normal level of unemployment. In this paradigm all changes in money national income are represented by changes in the price level. The competing income-expenditure model of demand came to be associated with the opposite assumption; namely, the aggregate supply schedule was assumed to be infinitely elastic, and all changes in national income are reflected in a higher level of real output. The former became known as the inflation model, while the latter was known as the depression model. Reasonable men and women began to wonder whether there was some truth in both models.

The great debate spilled over into Chapter 8 where it began to take on certain dynamic overtones. The variables of interest now became the rate of change of the price level and the rate of unemployment. Here again those following the monetarist and income-expenditure traditions separated themselves over the relevant time period in which a change in aggregate demand initiated by government financial policy would be reflected in a change in unemployment and real output. At one end of the spectrum there were those models based on an extreme form of the theory of rational expectations that implied that there was no meaningful time dimension in which a government-induced change in aggregate demand would be reflected in a change in unemployment and real output. For this class of economic models there is no long-run or short-run trade-off between unemployment and inflation; the so-called Phillips curve and aggregate supply schedule are vertical at the natural rate of unemployment and output. Monetary policy in this framework only determines the inflation rate. At the other end of the spectrum are those who believe that no matter what the time framework, there is some trade-off between unemployment and inflation, which also implies an upward-sloping supply schedule. To be sure these economists were prepared to draw a distinction between a short-run and a long-run trade-off, and by and large recognized that the relationship was more sensitive in the short-run. Nevertheless these economists proposed models in which there was some scope for an active government financial policy in determining the actual combinations of unemployment and inflation that the economy would experience, while the former group proposed models in which monetary policy determined only the inflation rate, and the policy issue for them quite naturally centered around the optimal inflation rate.

Those following the eclectic Keynes-Phillips tradition were faced with what some unsympathetic observers would call a monumental problem, and that problem was the economic rationalization of an upward-sloping supply schedule, or in its alternative form, a negatively sloped Phillips curve. Everyone interested in this question, starting with Phillips, felt that the solution would eventually be found in the labor or factor input market. Unfortunately, their efforts to date have not reduced the range of professional opinion on this question partly because: "This (upward sloping) aggregate supply curve comes from assuming some stickiness or money illusion in the labor market;"[11] or a combination of coincidental forecasting errors by laborers and capitalists. Traditionally economists have been wary of wage stickiness and money illusion and erroneous forecasting rationalizations of the supply curve, and these instances were not to be exceptions.

It is against this background of differing professional opinions that we offered our own description of the price-output composition of a change in nominal GNP based on financial contracting. In a sense this explanation can be viewed as complementing the wage stickiness or money illusion or fore-casting error rationalizations of an upward-sloping supply schedule that have come to represent such an important part of the eclectic Keynesian tra-dition and the new classical macroeconomics. Contrary to the strategy pur-sued by the new Keynesians and monetarists, our analysis did not seek a di-rect solution to the problem of aggregate supply solely in the market for labor, but instead focused attention on the input/output-sharing agreements embodied in bondlike and stocklike contracts that were made by factor con-tributors when initiating productive activity. Agents in our world were ob-served to have different aversions to risk. They know in a general way that demand will change from time to time in the future, but unlike agents in the rational expectations world they are unwilling to make forecasts of demand shifts at all future points in time, much less speculate on the basis of these forecasts. Instead they contract with one another over shares of inputs to be provided in production and shares of output to be received when demand in the system departs from its long-run trend. Bond-like contracts implicitly stipulate that the holders are to receive a fixed but relatively small share of the output when demand is above its long-run trend, although in return it is also stipulated that they will provide a relatively smaller share of the required inputs. On the other hand, during periods of contraction bondholders will still receive a fixed but now relatively large share of the produced output, although now the contract requires them to put up a relatively larger share of the required inputs. The stocklike contract is then merely the cyclical com-plement to the bondlike contract. This focus led quite naturally to a study of bond and stock markets where input and output sharing in factor markets are reflected in bond and stock prices. Moreover changes in aggregate de-mand that are either initiated or facilitated by government financial policy will be quickly reflected in changes in equilibrium valuations placed on bonds and stocks as investors assess any subsequent supply adjustment in terms of the input/output-sharing agreements implied in these contracts. Consequently, when security prices are high (low), optimistic (pessimistic) portfolio investors foresee a favorable (unfavorable) business climate con-ducive to expansion (contraction) in aggregate supply. This is the sense in which the capital market performs an important signalling function that pro-vides a general direction to the supply response of firms when there is a change in aggregate demand.

Providing a general direction to the supply response of firms is one of the social roles of a capital market. The capital market instruments themselves, however, were argued to have a direct effect on the shape of the supply adjustment. The general theme of this chapter and Chapter 9 has been that the input/output-sharing agreements contained in bondlike and stocklike contracts will have an important bearing on the actual price-output composition associated with a cyclical change in nominal GNP. This result stems from the fact that these two types of contracts represent the claims to the produced output that are held by the different input contributors, and thus embody the risks and returns associated with production in an uncertain world. Pricing and output decisions were seen to have a material bearing on the risk and returns earned on bonds and stocks, and our investors were assumed to hold these claims through the business cycle. The problem confronting the manager of the firm, then, is that these input contributors— who in turn have different preference orderings over relative shares of income and risk in different states of the economy—would, if unrestrained, follow pricing, output, and financing policies over the business cycle that would confer income and risk benefits to their class of contract at the expense of the class of contract held by their coproducers. Given that bondholder and stockholder welfare is differentially affected by pricing, production, and financing decisions when firms adjust supply over the business cycle, it is only natural that some form of agreement be worked out between these two groups of claimants as to how these adjustments will in fact be made, if there is to be an economic rationalization of a bond-and-stock-financed enterprise. The objective of this agreement is to reconcile or coalesce the otherwise conflicting interests of bondholders and stockholders during the adjustment process. We suggested that the specific means by which this reconciliation might be achieved is that any cyclical pricing decision that redistributes the real income of the firm among the two claimants should be accompanied by a cyclical employment, output, and financing decision that redistributes the financial burden and risks among the claimants in the same direction. Thus the original agreement regarding input and output sharing, upon which initial factor input cooperation is based, constrains managers to a certain extent to make pricing, output (employment), and financing decisions so that returns accompany risk for both forms of contracts over the business cycle.

In Figure 10.1 we provided a graphic illustration of this type of supply adjustment. The advantage of this illustration is that it captures in graphical form the dynamic characteristics of one possible rational supply adjustment; and this one, as we will see in Chapter 12, is not inconsistent with the data. A change in aggregate demand thus shifts the equilibrium valuation schedules for stocks and bonds as the capital market anticipates the supply adjustment that will eventually take place in the product market. The implied contract in the two different types of securities themselves will then shape the actual supply responses (through reconciling managers) in terms of price level, employment, output, and financing adjustments as the economy moves toward the new product and capital market equilibrium. A numerical example of this type of supply adjustment will be presented in Chapter 11.

In developing our explanation of the supply adjustment process we assumed, for a large part of the discussion, that our artificial model economy was comprised of a single good which, in turn, was produced by a single firm. As we pointed out, this was an assumption of convenience designed to get immediately to the heart of the problem of input and output sharing, and how pricing, production, and financing decisions would affect the welfare of bondholders and stockholders over the business cycle. When moving to an n-good/n-firm economy with imperfect investor diversification, we were mildly surprised to see that much the same supply adjustment seemed to evolve for the entire economy, even though bondholder and stockholder conflicts were localized to firm-specific decisions. These localized and firm-specific conflicts were seen to be partly resolved by a host of covenants—primarily of a financial nature—in the bond contract specifically designed to prevent stockholders from expropriating the wealth of bondholders in subsequent supply adjustments. Thus restrictions pertaining to financial leverage, dividend policy, and the liquidity and safety of assets are the means by which bondholders attempt to protect themselves from future stockholders in a given firm. Yet it is as if some "invisible hand" guides individual bondholders and stockholders to draw up the bond contract for an individual firm in such a way that not only are both protected from each other in the micro sense of firm-specific decisions, particularly financial decisions, but also the protection tends to extend to the macro risk of an unexpected change in the price level.

The strategy followed in this chapter has been to study aggregate supply adjustments from the perspective of those who supply the capital resources to firm production. The reason we chose this strategy is that the capitalist's claims to the income generated by the firm are not only marketable, but also traded in relatively efficient markets. For this reason the capital market prices of different types of securities will reflect both the fortunes of the firm in general as well as the output-sharing agreements of the particular type of security in question. We are thus provided with some outside information—that is, market information—regarding the effect of supply adjustment on the welfare of different types of capital input contributors. Our description of supply adjustment, however, was not solely intended to reflect the fortunes and misfortunes of bondholders and stockholders over the business cycle, but rather the welfare of all input contributors. To our way of thinking, one of the distinguishing characteristics of cooperative production is the nature of the different claims input contributors obtain to the produced output, and in this study these claims took the relatively simple form of a fixed priority claim and a variable residual claim. In this context bonds were taken to proxy for the former while stocks proxied for the latter claim to output.

Since the labor market provided the focal point of traditional analysis in this area, we did discuss the supply adjustment from the perspective of workers. To begin with, the worker's claim to output, although not marketable, does resemble the claim held by the bondholder in that it is typically fixed in monetary terms. This suggests that the cyclical pattern of risk and return of old and experienced workers may not be too different from that of bondholders. In fact, we observed that in some respects the labor contract was strikingly similar to the bond contract. Both contracts emphasize the priority of some initial group of input contributors. Clearly the old come before the young in these arrangements. It is also curious that both types of contracts work in their own individual ways to push the firm in the direction of following those kinds of employment and financing policies during the expansion phase of the trade cycle that better enable existing workers and bondholders to survive the next contraction. These contractual arrangements are the result of both pessimistic and risk-averse workers and bondholders who value more highly a relatively large share of the social output during periods of contraction compared to expansion. Their main fear is unemployment and bankruptcy rather than the loss of real income that comes during periods of expansion when the actual inflation rate exceeds the expected rate. Many of the covenants in both types of contracts reflect this fear. Perhaps they are wise, for there is a certain sense of finality associated with unemployment and bankruptcy, whereas inflation seems to be a temporary evil that can be remedied to a certain extent during the next round of contract negotiations. In a former day it may well have been that unemployment and bankruptcies were the principal economic disorders experienced by workers and bondholders, and the contracts we observe today merely reflect these disorders. If new disorders should develop, such as a highly erratic inflation rate, then in the future we could expect to see new forms of labor and bond contracts that attempt to shelter workers and bond investors from these economic disorders.

Two important policy issues were discussed in the fifth section of this chapter. Both concern the effectiveness of a discretionary financial policy; in particular whether a government with demand management policies can systematically influence the price-output (employment) composition of a change in nominal GNP, and whether there is an optimal way to finance private production. With regard to the first issue, both the Phillips approach and the competing rational expectations hypothesis suggest that the price-output composition of a change in money national income was uniquely determined by government financial policy. At one point the early Phillips analysis seemed to offer the policymakers a stable trade-off between unemployment (output) and inflation in some meaningful short run. The extreme version of rational expectations, on the other hand, offered an adjustment solely in terms of price level variation. The conventional wisdom on the second issue of financing private production was quite different in that here conscious dividend and leverage policies were considered useless.

Our description of the adjustment process suggested different conclusions. In the case of the price-output composition of a change in nominal GNP, it was observed that while government financial policy may affect the aggregate demand in the system, the private sector with their risk-and-return-sharing agreements will determine the actual price-output combinations that are experienced over the business cycle. In terms of Figure 10.1, if the government knew the location of the *BB* and *SS* schedules, it would have the basis on which to formulate a discretionary policy. Here, as in the Phillips curve approach, the alternatives open to the policymaker may not be particularly attractive. Our own personal opinion is that knowledge regarding the location of the *BB* and *SS* schedules would be difficult to obtain in a dynamic market economy subject to supply-and-demand shocks, since it would put the government in the security market forecasting business. There is ample evidence to suggest that this would indeed be a most difficult business.

With regard to private financial policy the arguments presented in this chapter and in Chapter 9 suggest that there is an optimal and systematic pattern of financing production over the business cycle. It is important to note, however, that this optimal pattern of financing is not due to any comparative advantage the firm might enjoy over individual portfolio investors in terms of market opportunities and forecasting ability, as was suggested by the pre-MM literature in financial economics. Rather our result is the direct consequence of the agreements that coordinate production in an uncertain world where the firm is required to adjust supply at future points in time. Financial policy in this agreement is directly linked to operating policies of the firm, since both were found to influence the risk and return of bondholders and stockholders.

In conclusion we would remind the reader never to lose sight of the fact that these particular implications regarding public and private financial policy are the result of our attempt to find an economic rationale for a bond-and-stock-financed firm when both capital market instruments are subject to risk and both are held by different input contributors. Financial economic theory, by and large, precludes these possibilities, and as a result derives the usual irrelevance propositions for the financing of the private firm, while at the same time much in macroeconomics implies an optimal government financial policy for the entire economy. Yet our goal will be accomplished if we have at least shown that a number of interesting issues in macro and micro financial economics have different interpretations and implications when we depart from the conventional framework, and in this spirit we hope that our departures in this chapter and in Chapter 9 will stimulate further explorations into these important areas.

Notes

1. There is nothing, of course, to preclude both real and monetary factors from initiating a change in aggregate demand. For example, the development of a new product (e.g., the home computer) or an improvement in an old product (e.g., an attractive, fuel-efficient automobile) can temporarily change the tastes and spending patterns of consumers. Therefore the expansionary policy of the central bank better enables consumers to bring forward their purchases of these products, which in turn leads to more "bunching" in aggregate demand. It is in this sense that we will speak of monetary factors initiating changes in aggregate demand.

2. Perhaps for the reasons discussed in implicit contract theory. Alternatively the unemployment could be the result of an insufficient number of wage rates in the economy due to the fact that labor markets are costly to maintain.

3. At this point it might be useful to consider one limiting case in terms of the economic conditions prevailing at the point in time when the government expands the money supply. Suppose the economy was in an initial inflationary state and all resources were fully employed. An increased expansion in the money supply would only be reflected in still higher rates of inflation. To the extent the high inflation was unanticipated by both bondholders and stockholders, income would be redistributed from the former to the latter. In our contractual world, managers would use the inflationary gain to completely retire debt and thereby compensate bondholders for their reduction in relative income by reducing their relative share in the financing of the inputs.

4. For pedagogical purposes we are pretending that our reconciling managers change the price of output in order to redistribute real income (in a monetary economy) between bondholders and stockholders, but conventional economic analysis tells us that output prices change when there is positive or negative excess demand in product markets. This difference in interpretation of the source of the change in product prices is more apparent than real and is not independent of the claim structure in the economy. In our artificial economy investors not only know there will be cyclical fluctuations around the long-run growth path, they also know there will be positive excess demand during expansions and negative excess demand during contractions. Moreover they took this knowledge into account when developing their bondlike and stocklike contracts. The bond contract is a fixed money income priority claim and is tailored to redistribute income in favor of bondholders in periods of cyclical contraction when excess demand in product markets is expected to be negative. The stock contract is a variable residual income claim and is tailored to redistribute income in favor of stockholders in periods of cyclical expansion when excess demand in product markets is expected to be positive. This is the sense in which we speak of managers changing output prices in order to redistribute income between

bondholders and stockholders. What we do not mean is that managers can set product prices independently of product market conditions.

5. The price variable P in Figure 10.1 can be interpreted as an inflation rate or a deviation from some expected inflation rate.

6. The reverse assignment would in effect liquidate the firm by reducing output prices and contracting the level of production using the released funds to buy back the equity, all in the face of an expansion in aggregate demand. The rise in stock prices would be the result of the firm's stock repurchase decision plus the fact that an ever-growing number of shareholders would come to recognize the fact that the discrepancy between the actual and optimal supply (given the demand in the system) in this economy was becoming wider. Bond prices would be rising because the real returns on bonds would be increasing as a result of the pricing decisions of the firm that redistributes real income from stockholders to bondholders. If managers persisted in these decisions they would surely be fired by rational input contributors.

7. It is interesting to compare the approach taken here to that of the "new classical macroeconomics" of Friedman, Lucas, Sargent, Barro, Wallace, and others. The primary differences seem to be twofold. To begin with, the new classical approach focuses attention on the individual agent, be he or she a worker or capitalist. Our approach, like implicit contract theory, emphasizes the team or cooperative element in productive activity. As a result, it leads quite naturally to the notion of an agreement or contract between the different input contributors. The second primary difference is related to the first and centers around the agent's approach to decision making under uncertainty. The new classical approach views agents as optimal individual Bayesian decision makers who make supply decisions at all points in time on the basis of their expectations regarding the movement of relative prices in their individual sectors. In the model described here, agents choose a sector to invest their factor input for reasons outside the scope of this analysis. Once in a given sector these investors or partners (who differ in terms of risk aversion and income preferences over states of the economy) come to an agreement regarding the accommodation of future changes in demand in terms of input and output sharing. In other words our agents contract in advance for different shares in total output and input when the sector in which they operate deviates from its long-run growth path. Both descriptions of business fluctuations accord an important role to changes in aggregate demand. Where they differ is that the new classical approach views aggregate supply responses within business cycles as the result of an accumulation of forecasting errors. In other words the business cycle is the result of mistakes. The approach taken here, on the other hand, suggests that business cycles are the natural outcome of a market economy in which individuals are free to vary their expenditures over time, and are facilitated more or less to this end by expansions or contractions in government financial policy. This suggests to us that one of the questions to be asked in a study of the business cycle is how different types of agents fare in terms of risk and return sharing. We studied this question in the context of contracts between the different input contributors; contracts that defined shares of inputs to be supplied by agents and shares of outputs to be received by agents in different stages of the business cycle. We then studied the kinds of pricing, output, and financing decisions that would fulfill these contracts and thereby rationalize cooperation between bond-

holder-type and stockholder-type claimants in initiating productive activity within the institutional framework of the firm.

8. Differential priority between the old and new bonds will not necessarily overcome this problem. For more on this see Krainer (1977).

9. In principle the two types of restrictions or constraints should be linked together so that as the firm comes to be more highly levered, it should also be required to invest in safer and more liquid assets. On the other hand, when leverage declines the constraint should be relaxed and noncash or riskier assets should be permitted to assume a relatively more important position in the firm's balance sheet.

10. Historical examples of the private sector deviating from its long-run growth path (without some initial prodding from government financial policy) in such a way that monetary and fiscal policies can set the economy back on the right course are somewhat difficult to describe or document. Perhaps the tulip and South Sea bubbles are cases in point. But what about crop failures or oil boycotts? Can a recession induced by oil boycotts and crop failures be eliminated with an expansionary monetary policy? How can money substitute for oil or food in the short run? Can it help in some longer run by making the adjustment to a more foodless and oil-less economy easier? These are not particularly easy questions to answer, and disagreement still prevails among professional economists as to whether any instability in the private sector can be corrected by stabilization policies, or whether in fact government is the source of cyclical instability in the first place. Moreover, even if the latter assessment is in fact correct, it is not entirely clear that some random monetary shocks might not be beneficial, particularly if they serve the purpose of preparing agents to better accommodate the more serious nonmonetary shocks that periodically bombard the economy.

11. See Blinder and Solow (1974, fn. 140, p. 72).

—11—

A Further Analysis
of a Partnership Economy

Introduction

In Chapter 10 we set forth in outline form a theory of how the business sector ought to adjust supply when aggregate demand deviates from some expected long-run trend. This is the problem of the business cycle. One of the key assumptions of this theory was that when agents come together to form the business enterprise they exchange their factor service for a fixed priority or a variable residual claim to the nominal income of the firm, but not both. By participating in production in this way, input contributors differentiate their interests or welfare relative to one another insofar as supply must be adjusted to future changes in aggregate demand. In order to reconcile or coalesce these differentiated interests our theory of the firm suggests that an agreement or contract is made among the different input contributors, broadly defining how supply adjustments are to be managed in the future. The agreement we discussed directed the managers of the firm to adjust risk with return during the supply adjustment process. Thus, if stocklike claimants experience higher returns during the expansion phase of the business cycle as a result of the pricing decisions of firms, then stockholders should be required to finance the associated increased level in real activity, thereby reducing the risks of bondholders. In this way bondholders and stockholders share the benefits and costs associated with the business cycle. The end result of such an agreement is that both claimants contract with one another in advance for risk and return in the different states of the economic environment, and the pricing, output (employment), and the associated financing decisions are the means by which the enterprise implements the agreement.[1] The key factor that shapes the composition of nominal income is then seen to

240

be these agreements or contracts between factor input contributors that attempt to define the cyclical distribution of risk and return in the economy.

In this chapter we wish to extend and amplify several of the ideas introduced in previous chapters. Since these extensions and amplifications are not necessarily interrelated, they will follow no particular order in their development in this chapter. Accordingly we will begin by discussing some of the factors that motivate the creation of debt and equity instruments as contract forms when the economic environment is uncertain. In this part of our discussion it will be assumed that there is no governmental taxing authority, and hence debt and equity claims will be seen to evolve from investor preferences for risk and return. Our selective extensions and amplifications continue in the third section of this chapter where we present a rather detailed stylized example of a dynamic supply adjustment for an economy experiencing a demand shock along the lines described in Figure 10.1. This is done in order to provide the reader with a better understanding of how a contract economy responds in our model when the monetary authority alters the level of aggregate demand from its expected long-run trend. Finally, we conclude the chapter with a short summary and prepare the way for Chapter 12.

Contract Forms in an Uncertain Economic Environment

Our macroeconomic analysis assumed that input contributors in an economy tend to separate themselves into two groups: those who hold a bondlike claim and those who hold a stocklike claim to the nominal income of the firm. It is of course true that these two types of contract forms have long been observed in market economies, and this fact of common observation is perhaps sufficient justification for analyzing an equilibrium in which all producing agents are either bondholders or stockholders. The question, however, is whether these contractual arrangements can be motivated by more fundamental economic principles. In this section our objective will be to illustrate how these contract forms might evolve in a private ownership economy and their implications for the cyclical distribution of the social income.

Toward this end we first consider the question of the cyclical distribution of income. Recall from our discussion in Chapter 9 that the firm's present resources or factor inputs generate a probability distribution of future possible outputs, and this distribution is quite independent of the particular claim structure used to finance the inputs. While the claim structure has no bearing on the distribution describing tomorrow's produced output, it does uniquely define the class distribution of income between bondholders and stockholders for every state of the economy. Thus, in exchange for their factor input, bondholders receive a fixed priority claim to a given nominal income. Once the price level is given, this nominal income represents a fixed priority claim to a given amount of output, and this claim is independent of the state of the economy that actually materializes tomorrow. Stockholders, in turn, receive what is left after bondholders are paid their fixed nominal claim; and what is left can turn out to be a great income if nature is generous, or possibly a personal obligation to bondholders if the state of the economy is in deep depression. Consequently bond and stock contracts in effect represent an agreement for determining the class distribution of income over all possible states of the economy. In recessions (all those outcomes in the left tail of the output distribution) bondholders implicitly contract for a relatively large share of the total social income, while stockholders contract for a small share. In expansions (all those outcomes in the right tail of the output distribution) the distribution of income between bondholders and stockholders is reversed. When by chance the actual output produced equals the level expected, then bondholders and stockholders will share output in the way they originally expected when initiating productive activity.

Having seen that the claim structure of an enterprise or an economy determines the cyclical distribution of income between input contributors, we must now ask why this claim structure generally takes the form of debt and equity securities. The reason would seem to be that risk-averse input contributors derive utility from splitting the return stream of a firm in this particular way. To illustrate this point consider a world in which there are restrictions on short sales, no risk-free assets, and differences in risk aversion among investors. This economic setting is graphically displayed in Figure 11.1 where we observe two input contributors, B and S, who by virtue of their equal input contributions are presently copartners in some enterprise M generating an expected rate of return $E(R_M)$ and risk $\sigma(R_M)$ measured in some relevant way.[2] The output of risk and return (measured in terms of rate of return) in this two-person model economy is represented by the point M in the body of the figure, and since investors B and S are copartners we can also draw their individual convex indifference curves at this point M when both are holding equity-type claims. As can be seen in the figure, B's indifference curve intersects S's indifference curve from below at point M, thus indicating that at that point B-type investors are relatively more risk averse than S-type investors. It would therefore seem that B and S have an incentive to restructure the contract presently underlying the securities they received in exchange for their factor services. From the point of view of individual B, any security offering a combination of risk and return lying between their own and S's indifference curve would represent an improvement in their welfare as measured by expected utility. These welfare-improving combinations of risk and return for B-type investors are displayed in the dotted area of Figure 11.1. A similar potential improvement exists for the relatively less risk-averse

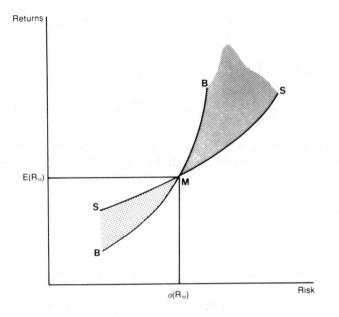

Figure 11.1. Risk and Return Sharing in a Partnership Economy

S-type investor, in that any contract giving them a combination of risk and return lying between their own and *B*'s indifference curve to the upper right of *M* would raise their expected utility. These combinations of risk and return are represented by the dashed (shaded) area in the figure. If a bond contract can be created which places *B* investors in the dotted area while at the same time the associated levered stock contract places *S* investors in the dashed area of the figure, then bonds and levered stock will evolve from what was formerly an all unlevered equity claim structure.[3] In this way a point like *Z* in Figure 9.1 would come to represent an equilibrium input/ output-sharing agreement between bondholders and stockholders when input contributors accept debt or equity claims in exchange for their factor service.

This argument can also be illustrated in terms of a stylized numerical example. Toward this end consider an enterprise or economy that at the moment is jointly owned by two separate individuals or groups of individuals, *B* and *S*. These investors, in turn, are assumed to have inherited the enterprise or economy from their parents. Let *X* represent the real returns of this firm/ economy and assume they are uniformly distributed with a probability density function described by:

$$f(X) = \begin{cases} 0.01 \le X \le 100 \\ 0, \text{ otherwise} \end{cases} \tag{11.1}$$

Since B and S are presently copartners in the enterprise the first two raw moments of X for both investors are, respectively:

$$E(X_B) = E(X_S) = \frac{1}{2} E(X) = \frac{1}{2} \int_0^{100} 0.01XdX = 25.0 \tag{11.2}$$

$$E(X_B^2) = E(X_S^2) = E\left[\left(\frac{1}{2} X\right)^2\right] = 0.25 \int_0^{100} 0.01X^2dX = 833.33 \tag{11.3}$$

Furthermore suppose the preferences in terms of real returns for these two individuals can be described by the following specific quadratic utility functions:

$$U_B(X) = X_B - 0.025X_B^2 + 15 \tag{11.4a}$$

$$U_S(X) = X_S - 0.005X_S^2 \tag{11.4b}$$

The expected utility for these two copartners will then be given by:

$$E(U_B) = E(X_B) - 0.025E(X_B^2) + 15 = 25.0 - 20.833 + 15.0 = 19.67 \tag{11.5a}$$

$$E(U_S) = E(X_S) - 0.005E(X_S^2) = 25.0 - 4.167 = 20.833 \tag{11.5b}$$

The question now is whether both of these individuals can be made better off in the expected utility sense if this all-equity firm can be financially converted into a debt and levered equity firm. Suppose that in this connection the relatively more risk-averse individual B exchanges his or her equity claim for a newly created debt security with a promised payment of 20 units of output per period. The expected return and expectation of return squared for B then becomes:

$$E(X_B) = \int_0^{20} 0.01XdX + 20 \int_{20}^{100} 0.01dX = 18.0 \tag{11.6a}$$

$$E(X_B^2) = \int_0^{20} 0.01X^2dX + (20)^2 \int_{20}^{100} 0.01dX = 346.67 \tag{11.6b}$$

When these values for $E(X)$ and $E(X^2)$ are substituted into the expected utility function for B we get:

$$E(U_B) = E(X_B) - 0.25E(X_B^2) + 15 = 18.0 - 8.67 + 15.0 = 24.33 \tag{11.7}$$

which is greater than the expected utility of 19.67 B obtained when holding the equity claim on the economy. In other words, given these two alternatives, investor B is clearly better off holding the debt claim with a promised payment of 20 than the unlevered equity which offers a pro-rata share in the real returns generated by the factors of production.[4] A similar calculation can be made for S when he or she exchanges unlevered equity in the enterprise for the newly created levered equity. The first two raw moments of X for the levered equity claim then become:

$$E(X_S) = (0) \int_0^{20} 0.01 dX + \int_{20}^{100} 0.01(X-20)dX = 32.0 \tag{11.8a}$$

$$E(X_S^2) = (0)^2 \int_0^{20} 0.01 dX + \int_{20}^{100} 0.01(X-20)^2 dX = 1706.67 \tag{11.8b}$$

Substituting (11.8a) and (11.8b) into (11.5b) yields the following value of expected utility for investor S:

$$E(U_S) = E(X_S) - 0.005E(X_S^2) = 32.0 - 8.533 = 23.467 \tag{11.9}$$

Comparing equations (11.9) and (11.5b) we see that investor S is better off in the expected utility sense after exchanging the old unlevered equity for the new levered equity in the firm.[5]

In concluding this section it is important to remember that stylized numerical examples prove nothing, but they are sometimes useful in illustrating an economic point. With this caveat we have tried to illustrate how an all-equity economy might evolve into a debt and equity economy for a world in which investors have quadratic utility functions with different degrees of risk aversion and the distribution generating real returns is uniform. We feel obliged to demonstrate this point because in Chapters 9 and 10 it was assumed that B-type individuals will only hold the bondlike claim in exchange for their factor service, and S-type individuals the stocklike claim. This, of course, is only an assumption of convenience invoked to highlight the fact that bondholders will have a different interest in the firm than stockholders by virtue of their differences in risk aversion. Actually, even within the context of our specific numerical example and abstracting from transaction costs, it is easy to show that both types of investors would obtain an even greater amount of expected utility if they held some amounts of both securities in the firm.[6] Nevertheless it will always be the case in the above-described numerical example that investor B will hold a relatively larger share of the bonds and a relatively smaller share of the stock than investor S; and in this sense the two investors will have a different perspective regarding the present and future management decisions of the firm.

Supply Adjustment and the Business Cycle: A Stylized Example

Introduction

At this point it might be useful to present a detailed numerical example suggesting how firms in the artificial economy we have created would adjust supply in response to a money-induced expansion in aggregate demand. Of course it is clear that a stylized example can never establish the correctness of the hypotheses advanced here and in Chapters 9 and 10, or whether these hypotheses are of interest in addressing any real-world economic issues. Rather the numerical example presented in this section is intended to illustrate how an economy—where input contributors hold bondlike and stocklike claims to the produced output—might adjust the level of production, the price of goods and services, and the financing of production during various phases of the business cycle so as to coalesce or fairly balance the interests and welfare of all those input contributors that initiated productive activity.

The Economy: Agents and Input/Output-Sharing Arrangements

Toward this end consider an economy with a money supply of $500 that currently is in long-run static equilibrium. Production in this economy started some time in the past when bondholders and stockholders financed a stock of capital currently valued at $1,000 consisting of $500 of finished goods inventory and $500 of infinitely lived capital equipment. This stock of capital along with 50 good experienced workers produce 1,000 units of expected output, and each unit of output carries a price tag of $1. These workers bargain for a money wage of $10 per worker for a single production run, and this wage is fixed by contract for three time periods or production runs, which in this example happens to correspond to the half-life of a business cycle. The total wage bill is then currently $500, which in turn leaves $500 to be split between bondholders and stockholders.

In setting up the firm on the production side of the economy it will be assumed that the initial contract called for bondholders to finance 40 percent of the capital stock, with stockholders financing the remaining 60 percent. It is also assumed that in the present economic environment the required rate of return for bondholders on their investment in the firm is 25 percent, while for stockholders it is 67 percent. Accordingly bondholders have a priority claim to $100 of the firm's net income available for distribution to capitalists, while stockholders have a residual claim for the remainder or $400.

The sharing of financial inputs and net income between bondholders and stockholders can also be displayed graphically for this hypothetical economy. In this connection first consider Figure 11.2. The total value of the

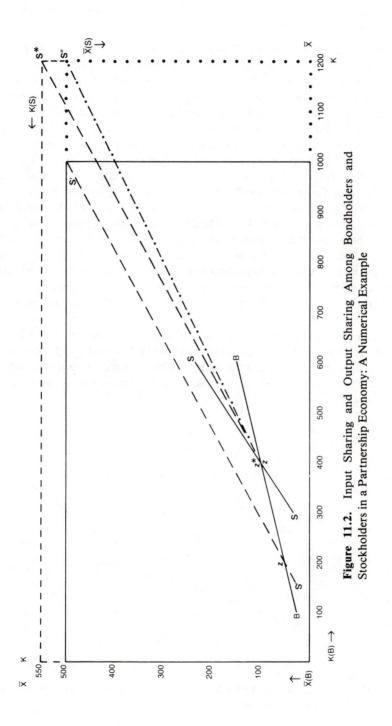

Figure 11.2. Input Sharing and Output Sharing Among Bondholders and Stockholders in a Partnership Economy: A Numerical Example

247

economy's nonhuman capital, K, is measured along the horizontal axis, with the amount financed by bondholders, $K(B)$, presented on the lower horizontal axis and the amount financed by stockholders, $K(S)$, measured along the upper horizontal axis. The left- and right-hand vertical axes measure the expected net income, $\bar{X}$, available for distribution to bondholders, $\bar{X}(B)$, and stockholders, $\bar{X}(S)$. Points within the box measure both rates of return (e.g., $\bar{X}(B)/K(B)$ and $\bar{X}(S)/K(S)$) and input/output sharing between bondholders and stockholders (e.g., $K(B)/K(S)$ and $\bar{X}(B)/\bar{X}(S)$). In the current equilibrium—represented by the contract point z in the inner solid-lined box—bondholders provide $400 of the total financing and have a claim of $100 to the net income of the firm, while stockholders provide the remaining $600 of financing and claim the residual income of $400. Thus, for providing 40 percent of the total required financial support, bondholders obtain 20 percent of the firm's net income. Stockholders provide 60 percent of the investment and lay claim to 80 percent of the expected net income. As we have discussed earlier this nonproportional sharing of financial inputs and net income is a result of the priority and residual nature of the bond and stock contract.

The sharing of financial inputs and expected income between bondholders and stockholders is displayed somewhat differently in Figure 11.3. The horizontal axis measures the ratio of debt to equity financing, that is, $K(B)/K(S)$; the vertical axis in turn measures the ratio of bond to stock in-

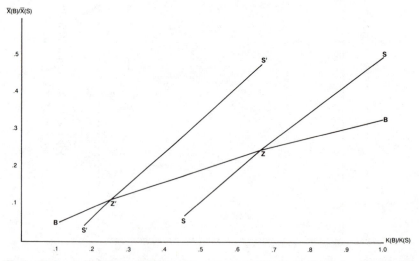

Figure 11.3. Initial Capital Market Response to a Monetary Shock in a Partnership Economy: A Numerical Example

come, that is, $\bar{X}(B)/\bar{X}(S)$. In the body of the figure the line BB represents those combinations of $K(B)/K(S)$ and $\bar{X}(B)/\bar{X}(S)$ yielding bondholders their required rate of return on their financial investment in the firm, which in this stylized example is 25 percent. Similarly the line SS represents those combinations of $K(B)/K(S)$ and $\bar{X}(B)/\bar{X}(S)$ yielding stockholders their required rate of return of 67 percent on their investment in the firm. The contract point z for this diagram then represents the pair of points $K(B)/K(S)$ and $\bar{X}(B)/\bar{X}(S)$ for which bondholders and stockholders both earn their required rates of return on their investments in the firm. In this example the initial equilibrium Z is $(K(B)/K(S) = 0.67, \bar{X}(B)/\bar{X}(S) = 0.25)$.[7]

Having described the initial equilibrium for this model economy (i.e., initial values for $K(B)$, $K(S)$, $\bar{X}(B)$, and $\bar{X}(S)$), we now want to study the impact of a positive monetary shock on the employment, output, pricing, and financing decisions of firms when the objective of managers is to maintain the contractual agreements in terms of future contract points between bondholders and stockholders. These firm decisions characterize business cycles. The key idea in our theory of supply adjustment is that bondholders and stockholders implicitly contract with one another for future shares of income, $\bar{X}(B)/\bar{X}(S)$, and financing, $K(B)/K(S)$, of the firm at various points in the business cycle. We can think of this agreement to share the net income and financial requirements of the firm as a series of future contract points which managers are instructed to attain with cyclical pricing, production, and financing decisions whenever the firm/economy deviates from its long-run growth path. What the actual contract point for any particular expansion or contraction might be will depend upon the risk aversions and endowments of both bondholder- and stockholder-type investors. In the numerical example presented below, we will merely assume the existence of a particular contract point for a given monetary expansion in the economy, and then discuss the implications of this contract point for pricing, employment, output, and financing decisions. Toward this end we will introduce an expansion in the supply of money and then trace the adjustment process in two discrete (and highly artificial) steps: one step describing the decision to expand employment and output and financing the expansion with equity (the financial input sharing or risk-absorption adjustment); the other step describing the decision to raise output prices (the net income sharing or return adjustment). Table 11.1 will present an overview of each step, including the state of the economy in the initial equilibrium. During each step of the supply adjustment—including the initial equilibrium—we will present the financial statements for the firm, and the workers, bondholders, and stockholders who provide the firm with labor and capital services. Finally, each step in the adjustment process will be portrayed graphically in Figures 11.2, 11.3, and 11.4.

Table 11.1. The Economic History of a Partnership Economy: A Numerical Example

Item	$t = 0$	$0 < t < 1$	$t = 1$	$t = 2$
M	$500	$700	$700	$700
P	$1		$1	$1.04167
Q	1,000		1,200	1,200
W	$10		$10	$10
L	50		70	70
$R(B,MV)$	0.25	0.25	0.25	0.25
$R(S,MV)$	0.66	0.5625	0.5625	0.5625
PQ	$1,000		$1,200	$1,250
WL	$500		$700	$700
$\bar{X}$	$500		$500	$550
$\bar{X}(B)$	$100		$100	$100
$\bar{X}(S)$	$400		$400	$450
I	$500	$700	$700	$700
FC	$500	$500	$500	$500
$K(B)$	$400	$400	$400	$400
$K(S)$	$600	$800	$800	$800
$R(B,BV)$	0.25		0.25	0.25
$R(S,BV)$	0.66		0.50	0.5625
$P(B)$	$100		$110	$100
$N(B)$	4		4	4
$P(S)$	$10	$11.85	$8.89	$10
$N(S)$	60		80	80
Z	(0.66, 0.25)		(0.50, 0.25)	(0.50, 0.22)

At this point it will be helpful to introduce the following notation.

Balance Sheet Items

Assets

M = Government created fiat money;
I = Inventories of finished goods;
FC = Infinitely lived fixed capital;
K = Total nonhuman capital;
WLR = Wage bill receivable;
$\bar{X}(B)R$ = Bond income receivable;
$\bar{X}(S)R$ = Stock income receivable;

Liabilities and Equities

$K(B)$ = Total debt at economic book value;
$K(S)$ = Total equity at economic book value;
$P(B)$ = Market price of one bond;
$N(B)$ = Number of bonds outstanding;
$P(S)$ = Market price of one share of common stock;
$N(S)$ = Number of shares of stock outstanding;
WLP = Wage bill payable;
$\bar{X}(B)P$ = Bond income payable;
$\bar{X}(S)P$ = Stock income payable;
NW = Net worth.

Income Statement Items

P = Price of one unit of output;
Q = Total units of output produced during the period;
PQ = Total revenues for the period;
W = Wage rate per unit of labor input;
L = Units of labor input worked during the period;
WL = Total wage bill for the period;
$\bar{X}$ = Expected net income for bondholders and stockholders;
$\bar{X}(B)$ = Expected income of bondholders;
$\bar{X}(S)$ = Expected income of stockholders.

Other Items

C = Consumption of goods;
$R(B,BV)$ = Rate of return earned on book value of bonds;
$R(B,MV)$ = Required rate of return of bondholders;
$R(S,BV)$ = Rate of return earned on book value of stocks;
$R(S,MV)$ = Required rate of return for stockholders;
$z = [K(B), \bar{X}(B); K(S), \bar{X}(S)]$;
$Z = [K(B)/K(S), \bar{X}(B)/\bar{X}(S)]$.

The Initial Equilibrium: $t = 0$

We now have before us a numerical example of an artificial economy similar in spirit to the one created in Chapters 9 and 10. We have also presented a geometric description of the initial equilibrium for this economy in Figures 11.2 and 11.3. Now we can begin our journey through the expansion phase of the business cycle. Toward this end Table 11.1 presents a tabular overview of the supply adjustment for this economy beginning with period $t = 0$ and ending with the new supply equilibrium in $t = 2$. Since Table 11.1

is intended to provide the reader with a sense of the general direction in which this economy is moving, we will not provide a detailed commentary on the table itself. What we will do first is present and discuss the financial statement of the firm as it passes through period $t = 0$.[8] We will also present (but without commentary) the financial statements for workers, bondholders, and stockholders. As we will see, these statements reflect the transactions the factor input contributors have with the firm. Finally, we conclude this subsection with a description of the monetary shock that initiates this particular business cycle, including the capital market response to that shock. In the following two sections we will follow this model economy through periods $t = 1$ and $t = 2$.

The financial statements for the firm and the three input contributors in the initial equilibrium are presented in Table 11.2. Each transaction throughout the period will be numbered to facilitate the discussion and comparisons between financial statements.

1. The firm begins the period with a total capital of $K = \$1000$ comprised of finished goods inventory of $I = \$500$ and fixed capital $FC = \$500$. The initial financing of this capital stock was provided by bondholders and stockholders in the amounts $K(B) = \$400$ and $K(S) = \$600$. It is further assumed that there are four bonds priced in the market at $100 per bond and 60 shares of stock priced at $10 per share of stock.

2. The second transaction of the firm in this period records the cash sale of $500 of finished goods inventories to the 50 experienced workers who accumulated the cash balances in the previous period for labor services rendered.

3. The next transaction involves production in which the firm combines the 50 experienced workers with the fixed capital to produce $Q = 1000$ units of output with each unit of output priced at $1. This output when produced and priced is then put into the firm's finished goods inventory where it is valued at $PQ = \$1000$. In producing this output the firm incurs the following obligations to the factor input contributors: (i) wages payable to workers, $WLP = \$500$; (ii) interest payable to bondholders, $\bar{X}(B)P = \$100$; and (iii) earnings available for dividends to stockholders, $\bar{X}(S)P = \$400$.

4. In the fourth set of transactions the firm pays cash to bondholders of $100 and to stockholders of $400, thereby discharging the obligations to capitalists incurred in transaction 3.

5. Bondholders with their cash income of $100 buy finished goods from the firm and subsequently consume these goods. Stockholders use their cash income of $400 to buy goods from the firm, but they only consume $200, holding back the remaining $200 for possible future investment in the firm should the business climate improve in some way.

6. The sixth transaction records the firm paying cash to its 50 workers in the amount of $500 for labor services rendered in transaction 3.

**Table 11.2. Financial Statements for a Partnership Economy:
Initial Equilibrium ($t = 0$)**

Firm

1	I	+ $500	$K(B)$	+ $400	1
1	FC	+ $500	$K(S)$	+ $600	1
1	K	+ $1,000			
2	I	− $500			
2	M	+ $500			
3	I	+ $1000	WLP	+ $500	3
			$\bar{X}(B)P$	+ $100	3
			$\bar{X}(S)P$	+ $400	3
4	M	− $500	$\bar{X}(B)P$	− $100	4
			$\bar{X}(S)P$	− $400	4
5	M	+ $500			
5	I	− $500			
6	M	− $500	WLP	− $500	6
7	I	+ $500	$K(B)$	+ $400	7
7	FC	+ $500	$K(S)$	+ $600	7
7	K	+ $1,000			

Workers

2	M	− $500			
2	I	+ $500			
3	WLR	+ $500	NW	+ $500	3
6	WLR	− $500			
6	M	+ $500			
	I	− $500	NW	− $500	

Bondholders

1	$K(B)$	+ $400	NW	+ $400	1
3	$\bar{X}(B)R$	+ $100	NW	+ $100	3
4	$\bar{X}(B)R$	− $100			
4	M	+ $100			
5	M	− $100			
5	I	+ $100			
	I	− $100	NW	− $100	
7	$K(B)$	+ $400	NW	+ $400	7

Stockholders

1	$K(S)$	+ $600	NW	+ $600	1
3	$\bar{X}(S)R$	+ $400	NW	+ $400	3
4	$\bar{X}(S)R$	− $400			
4	M	+ $400			
5	M	− $400			
5	I	+ $400			
	I	− $200	NW	− $200	
7	$K(S)$	+ $600	NW	+ $800	7
7	I	+ $200			

7. The firm ends the period as it began with I = \$500, FC = \$500, K = \$1000, $K(B)$ = \$400, and $K(S)$ = \$600.

At the beginning and end of t = 0 the economic book value of bonds and stocks are equal to the market value of these securities. At the end of the period the capital market closes and remains closed until the beginning of period t = 1.

These transactions are also recorded in the financial statements of workers, bondholders, and stockholders and are displayed separately in Table 11.2. Since these financial statements reflect the sequence of transactions each input contributor has with the firm, there will be no need to comment further on the economic events that occur in t = 0.

Between periods t = 0 and t = 1 the environment of this economy changes in a very fundamental way when 20 young and less productive workers announce they are available for employment at the immutably fixed contract wage of W = \$10 per worker per period. Since these workers have no money they are unable to communicate their potential demand to the firm. They are, however, able to communicate their discontent at being unemployed to the monetary authority in this economy, and in response to this discontent the monetary authority gives each unemployed worker a \$10 cash grant, thus increasing the money supply to M = \$700.

Bondholders and stockholders observe these new events with great interest and then consult their agreements with one another as to where this particular expansion contract point might be for the firm/economy. Suppose the contract point for this particular monetary expansion requires input/output sharing of Z^* = $[K(B)/K(S)$ = 0.50, $\bar{X}(B)/\bar{X}(S)$ = 0.22] with $R(B,MV)$ = $R(B,BV)$ = 0.25 and $R(S,MV)$ = $R(S,BV)$ = 0.5625. Compared to the initial contract point in t = 0 of Z = $[K(B)/K(S)$ = 0.67, $\bar{X}(B)/\bar{X}(S)$ = 0.25] subject to $R(B,MV)$= $R(B,BV)$ = 0.25 and $R(S,MV)$ = $R(S,BV)$ = 0.67, the new equilibrium has stockholders financing a relatively larger share of production and receiving a relatively larger share of the net income of the firm/economy. Note that in this particular example the stockholders contracted to increase their share in the financing of production by a relatively greater amount than their share in the net income of the firm. While this is only an example, it suggests a greater willingness on the part of stockholders to finance production during periods of expected expansion than during periods like those characterizing the initial equilibrium of t = 0. This is reflected in the reduction of the stockholders' required raste of return from 67 percent in the old equilibrium to 56.25 percent in the new expansion equilibrium. One possible reason for this reduction in the required rate of return is that perhaps stock investors perceive a safer environment now that the monetary authority has taken steps to incorporate the unemployed workers into the economic life of the society. In any event, as we mentioned above, this example assumes the existence of a new postexpansion contract point, this contract point has the property that whenever stockholders provide a larger share of the capital inputs they will also obtain a larger share of the net income of the firm. As we will see below, this new contract point will set in motion movements in stock and bond valuations which in turn will induce managers to vary employment, output, and output prices so as to direct the firm/economy toward the new expansion equilibrium in a manner consistent with the agreement between bondholders and stockholders that initiated productive activity in the first place.[9]

These significant developments can also be described geometrically in terms of Figures 11.2 and 11.3. In this connection the reduction in the rate of return required on common stock that accompanied the monetary expansion is pictured initially in Figure 11.2 as a shift in the SS schedule to the less steep $S'S'$ schedule. The new SS schedule (the slope of which is the new required rate of return of 56.25 percent) now intersects the BB schedule at z'; and while markets are closed, the implied market valuation of stock is now $400/0.5625 = \$711/60 = \$11.85$ per share. The lower required rate of return on stock is also displayed in Figure 11.3. There we can see that the SS curve shifts to $S'S'$ and intersects the BB curve at a $Z' = (0.25, 0.11)$, whereas in the initial $t = 0$ equilibrium $Z = (0.67, 0.25)$. It should be clear that neither z' nor Z' will be the postexpansion contract point for bondholders and stockholders, since up to this point in time there has been no change in supply in the economy. Nevertheless it will still be useful to analyze the Z' contract point in Figure 11.3, since it provides information on stock and bond prices in the initial stages of the supply adjustment.

We can now summarize the events that have taken place during this interperiod unit of time. It all began when new (and what will turn out to be less) productive workers arrived on the scene (in a world with only one wage rate) and created a perceived unemployment problem in this contract economy. The monetary authority responded to this unemployment problem by expanding the supply of money, which took the form of cash grants to the unemployed workers. This expansion in the supply of money in turn shifted the input/output-sharing contract point for the firm and resulted in a reduction in the rate of return required by stockholders. In other words the change in monetary policy coupled with the state of the real economy changed the required return for stockholders and the sharing of net income and financial support. That such a change might occur after the enterprise was initially created by bondholders and stockholders was fully anticipated by both types of investors, and in their contract with one another they jointly agreed upon how they would share the net income as well as the financial requirements of

the firm in this particular environment. The firm's first product market response—designed ultimately to take the economy to the new contract
point—now takes place when all markets open for business in period $t = 1$.

The Production Response: $t = 1$

The production response of the firm/economy to the new environment
will first be analyzed from the point of view of its transactions with the input
contributors, just as was done in period $t = 0$. These transactions are presented in Table 11.3 and will be numbered in the same way as in Table 11.2.
After having discussed the production response in terms of the financial accounts, we will then consider the effect in the capital market; in particular,
the effect on input/output sharing between bondholders and stockholders as
displayed in Figures 11.2 and 11.4. In this way we hope to illustrate the nature of the interrelationship between capital and product markets, which
provided the foundation for our theory of supply adjustment in Chapters 9
and 10.

The firm's financial statement is presented in Table 11.3 and records
the transactions for $t = 1$.

1. The firm begins period $t = 1$ with $I = \$700$, $FC = \$500$, and $K = \$1200$.
   These assets are financed with $K(B) = \$400$ and $K(S) = \$800$. Notice that
   the additional \$200 of stock associated with the inventory investment made
   between periods $t = 0$ and $t = 1$ is carried in the financial statement at
   their economic book values. Yet as we will see below, the capital market
   values of both bonds and stocks will depart from their economic book
   values during this period.
2. The next transaction to take place has workers purchasing the entire inventory of goods and services held by the firm. The old experienced workers
   use the cash they earned in $t = 0$, and their purchases amount to \$500. The
   less productive young workers use the \$200 cash grant from the monetary
   authority to purchase their goods. Both groups of workers consume their
   goods within the period.
3. The firm then hires the 50 experienced workers and the 20 previously unemployed young workers, and with the fixed capital produces an output of
   $Q = 1200$ with a selling price $P = \$1$ per unit of output. Notice here that
   the output did not expand in the same proportion as the number of workers
   between $t = 0$ and $t = 1$. The old workers in $t = 0$ with the same amount
   of fixed capital produced on average 20 units of output per worker, whereas
   the old and new workers together in $t = 1$ produce on average slightly more
   than 17 units of output per worker. Thus production is subject to diminishing returns. In any event, in producing an output valued by the accountants
   at $PQ = \$1200$—which is immediately placed in finished goods inven-
   tory—the firm incurs obligations to workers of $WLP = \$700$, to bond-
   holders of $\bar{X}(B)P = \$100$, and to stockholders of $\bar{X}(S)P = \$400$. The new

Table 11.3. Financial Statements for a Partnership Economy: The Quantity Adjustment ($t = 1$)

		Firm			
1	I	+ $700	$K(B)$	+ $400	1
1	FC	+ $500	$K(S)$	+ $800	1
1	K	+ $1,200			
2	I	− $700			
2	M	+ $700			
3	I	+ $1,200	WLP	+ $700	3
			$\overline{X}(B)P$	+ $100	3
			$\overline{X}(S)P$	+ $400	3
4	M	− $500	$\overline{X}(B)P$	− $100	4
			$\overline{X}(S)P$	− $400	4
5	M	+ $500			
5	I	− $500			
6	M	− $700	WLP	− $700	6
7	I	+ $700	$K(B)$	+ $400	7
7	FC	+ $500	$K(S)$	+ $800	7
7	K	+ $1,200			

		Workers			
2	M	− $700			
2	I	+ $700			
3	WLR	+ $700	NW	+ $700	3
6	WLR	− $700			
6	M	+ $700			
	I	− $700	NW	− $700	

		Bondholders			
1	$K(B)$	+ $400	NW	+ $400	1
3	$\overline{X}(B)R$	+ $100	NW	+ $100	3
4	$\overline{X}(B)R$	− $100			
4	M	+ $100			
5	M	− $100			
5	I	+ $100			
	I	− $100	NW	− $100	
7	$K(B)$	+ $400	NW	+ $400	7

		Stockholders			
1	$K(S)$	+ $800	NW	+ $800	1
3	$\overline{X}(S)R$	+ $400	NW	+ $400	3
4	$\overline{X}(S)R$	− $400			
4	M	+ $400			
5	M	− $400			
5	I	+ $400			
	I	− $400	NW	− $400	
7	$K(S)$	+ $800	NW	+ $800	7

workers are now incorporated into the economy, and monetary policy in this contract economy has presumably accomplished its objective.

4. The firm then pays cash of $100 to bondholders and $400 to stockholders, thereby extinguishing the obligations incurred to capitalists in transaction 3.
5. Bondholders and stockholders then use their cash of $500 to buy $500 of product from the firm. This product is consumed within the period.
6. Next the firm pays $700 in cash to its 70 workers, which discharges the wage obligation in transaction 3. Since workers have already consumed product in this period (transaction 2) the cash balances will be held until the next period.
7. Finally, the firm ends the period with $I = \$700$ and $FC = \$500$ financed with $K(B) = \$400$ and $K(S) = \$800$. The financial condition of the firm—at least in terms of economic book values—is the same as it was at the beginning of the period.

The production response of the firm in $t = 1$ can also be transcribed to Figure 11.2. Recall that in the initial equilibrium of $t = 0$ the firm had $500 invested in inventories and $500 invested in fixed capital, and thus the horizontal length of the box was $1000 or the total capital in the economy. Now we observe that in $t = 1$ the total capital in terms of book value has increased to $K = \$1200$, with bondholders still providing $K(B) = \$400$ and stockholders providing $K(S) = \$800$. Therefore our box in $t = 1$ must be extended another $200 to accommodate the higher level of inventories the firm is now holding. This horizontal extension is pictured in Figure 11.2 with dotted lines. The vertical width of the box, which represents the expected net income of the firm going to capitalists, does not change from the $\bar{X} = \$500$ in the initial equilibrium. This must be the case, for as we observed in transactions 3 and 4 of the firm's financial statement, bondholders are still earning $\bar{X}(B) = \$100$ and stockholders $\bar{X}(S) = \$400$. This implies that the SS schedule for $t = 1$ is given by the dotted/dashed line S'' which intersects the BB schedule at point z.

It is of course clear that S'' cannot represent an equilibrium sharing of financial inputs and expected net income. This is because the rate of return or slope of the S'' schedule is less than the required rate of return implied by the slope of the $S'S'$ schedule, which as we saw above represents the new equilibrium sharing of inputs and net income between bondholders and stockholders. In other words the rate of return associated with S'' is $\bar{X}(S)/K(S) = \$400/\$800 = 0.50$, whereas the equilibrium required rate of return implied by $S'S'$ is 56.25 percent. Clearly stockholders have invested too much in the firm in $t = 1$ for the income they are currently receiving, and one of the jobs of a coalescing management in the next period will be to raise output prices in order to increase the income of stockholders, thereby justifying their higher investment of $200 in the firm.[10]

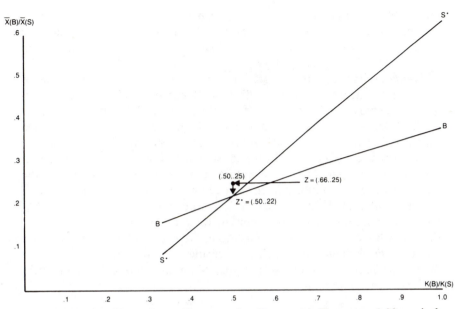

Figure 11.4. Capital Market Adjustments in a Partnership Economy: A Numerical Example of a Cyclical Expansion

Figure 11.4 provides still another useful description of the interrelationship between production and financing decisions as they impact on the capital market valuations of bonds and stocks in this economy. Figure 11.4 has the same set of axes as Figure 11.3. As we saw in Figure 11.3 the initial equilibrium in $t = 0$ was given by $Z = (0.66, 0.25)$, and this point is displayed in Figure 11.4. The new equilibrium turns out to be the intersection of the (as yet undiscussed) S^*S^* and BB curves at Z^*, and this new equilibrium at Z^* will come to represent the new contract point or equilibrium sharing of financial inputs and net expected income between bondholders and stockholders in the next period, $t = 2$. The S^*S^* and BB curves are obtained by taking the combinations of $K(B)/K(S)$ and $\bar{X}(B)/\bar{X}(S)$ that yield bondholders and stockholders their respective required rates of return of 25 percent and 56.25 percent. Now, from the financial statement for the firm in $t = 1$ (see Table 11.3), we observe that $K(B)/K(S) = \$400/\$800 = 0.50$ and $\bar{X}(B)/\bar{X}(S) = \$100/\$400 = 0.25$. This combination of $(0.50, 0.25)$ is seen in Figure 11.4 to lie above the equilibrium combination given by $Z^* = (0.50, 0.22)$. In Chapters 9 and 10 we suggested that this region is characterized by high but disequilibrium market valuations for bonds, and low but disequilibrium market valuations for stock. In other words, stock valuations in $t = 1$

are low. In this numerical example they turn out to be $400/0.5625 = $711/80 shares or $8.89 per share, whereas in $t = 0$ and $t = 2$ they are in fact $10 per share. Likewise, in $t = 1$, bond valuations are above their equilibrium levels. This is the case because the point (0.50, 0.25) in $K(B)/K(S)$ and $\bar{X}(B)/\bar{X}(S)$ space is on a BB curve for which the required rate of return turns out to be 27.5 percent, whereas the equilibrium BB curve is one for which the required rate of return for bondholders is 25 percent. A $400 investment yielding 27.5 percent provides bondholders with an $\bar{X}(B) = $110, which when capitalized at the required rate of return of 25 percent results in a capital market price on bonds of $110/0.25 = $440/4 bonds = $110 per bond. This is to be compared to a bond valuation of $100 in $t = 0$ and $t = 2$, the initial and ending equilibriums for this economy. The total market value of the firm is then $1151 at the end of $t = 1$, while the economic book value as represented in the financial statement in Table 11.3 is $1200. In the next period we will see what managers must do in order to equilibrate market with economic book values for the firm's securities, and what this will imply for the equilibrium sharing of risk and return among bondholders and stockholders in this economy.

The Pricing Response: $t = 2$

Having developed in some detail the characteristics of our model economy in the initial equilibrium and the output-expanding phase of the business cycle, we will proceed somewhat more rapidly in describing the inflation phase of an expansion in economic activity. As before we will first go through the firm's financial statement for $t = 2$ and then consider the capital market response to the inflation in Figures 11.2 and 11.4.

The financial statements for the firm, workers, bondholders, and stockholders in $t = 2$ are presented in Table 11.4.

1. The firm begins $t = 2$ as it ended $t = 1$ with the following assets, liabilities, and equities: $I = $700, $FC = $500, $K = $1,200, $K(B) = $400, and $K(S) = $800 all in terms of economic book value.
2. Workers use the $700 in cash earned in $t = 1$ to buy goods from the firm.
3. The firm then hires the 70 workers and with the fixed capital produces $Q = 1200$. Managers price this output at $1.04167 per unit of output and then transfer it to finished goods inventory at a value of $PQ = $1250. In producing this output the firm incurs liabilities to workers of $WLP = $700 and bondholders of $\bar{X}(B)P = $100. This leaves $450 for the stockholders, which represents an increase of $50 from $\bar{X}(S)$ in $t = 1$. In fact it was the managers' objective to raise output prices to this level in order to increase stockholder income to $450, for then the market value of stock becomes

Table 11.4. Financial Statements for a Partnership Economy: The Price Adjustment ($t = 2$)

Firm

1	I	+ $700	$K(B)$	+ $400	1
1	FC	+ $500	$K(S)$	+ $800	1
1	K	+ $1,200			
2	I	− $700			
2	M	+ $700			
3	I	+ $1,250	WLP	+ $700	3
			$\bar{X}(B)P$	+ $100	3
			$\bar{X}(S)P$	+ $450	3
4	M	− $550	$\bar{X}(B)P$	− $100	4
			$\bar{X}(S)P$	− $450	4
5	M	+ $550			
5	I	− $550			
6	M	− $700	WLP	− $700	6
7	I	+ $700	$K(B)$	+ $400	7
7	FC	+ $500	$K(S)$	+ $800	7
7	K	+ $1,200			

Workers

2	M	− $700			
2	I	+ $700			
3	WLR	+ $700	NW	+ $700	3
6	WLR	− $700			
6	M	+ $700			
	I	− $700	NW	− $700	

Bondholders

1	$K(B)$	+ $400	NW	+ $400	1
3	$\bar{X}(B)R$	+ $100	NW	+ $100	3
4	$\bar{X}(B)R$	− $100			
4	M	+ $100			
5	M	− $100			
5	I	+ $100			
	I	− $100	NW	− $100	
7	$K(B)$	+ $400	NW	+ $400	7

Stockholders

1	$K(S)$	+ $800	NW	+ $800	1
3	$\bar{X}(S)R$	+ $450	NW	+ $450	3
4	$\bar{X}(S)R$	− $450			
4	M	+ $450			
5	M	− $450			
5	I	+ $450			
	I	− $450	NW	− $450	
7	$K(S)$	+ $800	NW	+ $800	7

$450/0.5625 = $800/80 shares = $10 per share. Now the book value and capital market value of the stock are one and the same.

4. The firm then pays $550 in cash to bondholders ($100) and stockholders ($450), eliminating the obligation to capitalists incurred in transaction 3.
5. Capitalists buy $550 of goods from the firm (528 units priced at $1.04 per unit) and consume these goods during the period.
6. The firm pays $700 in cash to workers for the work performed in transaction 3. These money wages of $700 will now only buy roughly 672 units of output in the next period, whereas at the beginning of this period they bought 700 units of output.
7. At the end of the period the firm has an inventory of 672 units of product priced at $1.04167 per unit for a value of $I = 700. Fixed capital is still $500. This $1200 of capital is financed with debt of $K(B) = 400 and equity of $K(S) = 800.

The pricing decision of the firm in this, the second and final, stage of the supply adjustment is next discussed in Figure 11.2. The managers' decision to raise the price of output—with no change in the level of output—will have the effect of enlarging the vertical width of the box in the figure, as the expected net income of capitalists rises from $\bar{X} = 500 to $\bar{X} = 550. This is indicated by a new upper horizontal axis $50 higher than the old axis and represented by the dashed line. The SS schedule then shifts from S'' to S^*, intersecting the BB schedule at point $z^* = z$. Notice that S^* has a steeper slope than S'' (but the same slope as $S'S'$), indicating that the rate of return rose from 50 percent in $t = 1$ to 56.25 percent in $t = 2$ as a result of the pricing decision, and thus stockholders are now earning their required rate of return. In the new equilibrium bondholders are providing 1/3 of the total financing in exchange for slightly more than 18 percent of the firm's expected net income. Stockholders in turn put up 2/3 of the total financing and claim roughly 82 percent of the new expected income.

Finally this new equilibrium is portrayed in Figure 11.4 where we show the firm/economy moving from a $[K(B)/K(S), \bar{X}(B)/\bar{X}(S)]$ combination of $(0.50, 0.25)$ in $t = 1$ to the new equilibrium of $Z^* = (0.50, 0.22)$ in $t = 2$. In moving from the old position to the new equilibrium contract point, the economy is now on a BB and SS curve where bondholders and stockholders both earn their required rates of return of $R(B, MV) = 0.25$ and $R(S, MV) = 0.5625$, which in our model is determined by the current monetary policy and general economic environment. As a result, stock values $P(S)$ rise from $8.89 at the end of $t = 1$ to $\bar{X}(S)/R(S,MV) = $450/0.5625 = $800/80 shares = $10 per share. Moreover, bond valuations $P(B)$ fall from $110 per bond at the end of $t = 1$ (the result of being on a BB curve associated with a rate of return of 27.5 percent when in fact the required rate of return of bondholders in the current state of the economy is only 25 percent) to $\bar{X}(B)/R(B,MV) = \$100/0.25 = \$400/4$ bonds $= \$100$ per bond in the new equilibrium in $t = 2$.

The economy has now at last completed its supply adjustment, and both the capital market and the product market are in a new and different contract equilibrium than the one that prevailed in $t = 0$. In this equilibrium stockholders receive a larger share of the net income of the firm than they did in the old equilibrium, but they are also providing a larger share of the financial requirement. We have seen in this model economy, then, that risk in the form of a production and financing decision has been adjusted with return in the form of a pricing decision as the firm coalesces the welfare of bondholders and stockholders during the expansion phase of this hypothetical business cycle.

Summary

In this section we have presented a detailed numerical example of how the artificial economy created in Chapters 9 and 10 would adjust supply in terms of employment, output, prices, and financing when there is a change in aggregate demand. The key elements in our theory of supply and the business cycle were seen to be twofold: (1) supply decisions by firms over the business cycle must be made to conform to the joint interests of the different input contributors (which in this model takes the form of a series of contract points) when they hold different types of claims to the produced output, if there is to be a rationalization of initial factor cooperation in production; and (2) the capital market prices of bonds and stocks anticipate the new contract point, which in turn implies a new product market equilibrium, and in this way provides direction to the pricing and production decisions of firms in this economy. It is no wonder, then, that the numerical example presented here has been somewhat tedious since there is so much going on in the capital and product markets of this society.

The business cycle in our numerical example began with a perceived unemployment problem due in large measure to the fact that there are an insufficient number of wage rates in the economy. The monetary authority was then assumed to respond to this problem by expanding the supply of money, which took the form of cash grants to the unemployed workers in the system. With the prospects of a higher level of economic activity, stockholders were required by contract to increase their investment in the firm, which took the form of financing a higher level of finished goods inventory.

Moreover, associated with the improved business climate was a lower required rate of return on common stocks, which in turn raised the implied value of shares in $0 < t < 1$.

The expansion phase of the business cycle was then in full swing. The first product market response of the firm in this example was to expand the level of employment and output in period $t = 1$. In this stage of the business cycle the principal beneficiaries of the production response were the bondholders who ended the period with a safer financial investment by virtue of the fact that stockholders increased their investment in the firm. In the next period, $t = 2$, the firm compensated their stockholders for the increased risk they were bearing by raising output prices and thereby redistributing real income from bondholders to stockholders. The end result of the new expansion equilibrium or contract point in $t = 2$ was that bondholders ended up with both a lower level and share of the real expected net income in the economy, but with a safer investment in which to confront any subsequent recession; the stockholders, on the other hand, ended up with a larger level and share of the real net income of the firm, but at the cost of providing a larger financial investment in the production process.

The supply adjustment affected workers in much the same way it did capitalists. In the new equilibrium in $t = 2$ old experienced workers claimed a lower level and share of the total real labor income, but their seniority will provide relative protection from layoffs in subsequent recessions. Young workers, on the other hand, ended up with a larger level and share of the real labor income than they had in the initial equilibrium of $t = 0$, but they will be the first to go when the economy slips into a recession.

Finally, the capital market valuations on bonds and stocks provided the direction for these price and output adjustments of the firm. In the period between $t = 0$ and $t = 1$—when the required rate of return on stock fell from 67 percent to 56.25 percent—the implied market price on stock was $400/0.5625 = $711/60$ shares $= 11.85 per share, whereas in $t = 0$ it was $10 per share. The firm responded to this price signal in the stock market by expanding employment and production, financing this expansion with equity. In fact, in our example the firm went too far in this direction during $t = 1$, and as a result the market value of stock at the end of the period was seen to be $400/0.5625 = $711/80$ shares $= 8.89 per share. Moreover, bond valuations rose from $100 per bond in $t = 0$ to $110 at the end of $t = 1$. Again the firm followed the capital market signal by raising output prices in $t = 2$, driving both stock market and bond market valuations to their new equilibrium book value levels of $10 per share and $100 per bond. Consequently our bondholders and stockholders, old experienced workers and young workers, fairly share—in the risk and return sense—the benefits and costs associated with business fluctuations. Moreover, if they did not, new contract forms would emerge in the economy.

Summary and Conclusion

In this chapter we have attempted to clarify several ideas set forth in Chapters 9 and 10 pertaining to rational supply adjustments in a contract economy where input contributors hold different types of claims to the end-of-period output. We began by suggesting that risk aversion could account for the existence of bondlike and stocklike claims to the produced output, and that the problems of moral hazard and transactions costs probably limit the variety of these two basic contract forms, which we actually observe in input markets. It was also observed that debt and equity contracts imply different positions in the distribution of income for those who hold them through the ups and downs of the business cycle. The fixed priority claim in bonds provides the holder with a large share of real income in recessions and a relatively smaller share in expansions. The reverse is true for the variable residual claim of common stocks. Finally we provided a detailed numerical example of an economy passing through the expansion phase of the business cycle. Our purpose in presenting this example was to again illustrate how risk and return sharing can be achieved with product market and financial decisions in a contract economy, and how they not only produce Phillips-type relationships, but also how they rationalize factor cooperation in productive activity. Throughout our discussion in Chapters 9–11 we have asserted that these production, pricing, and financial adjustments are equitable and hence optimal. Let us now see whether there is any evidence that market economies actually adjust supply in this manner.

Notes

1. The reaction of our agents to uncertainty is to use contracts to implement contingency plans in the event of unforeseen occurrences. These contingency plans force or constrain the firm to adjust supply in such a way that no single claimant receives all of the benefits nor absorbs all of the costs associated with the adjustment. The approach taken by the rational expectations school of thought discussed in Chapter 8 was seen to be different, in that during various phases of the business cycle, agents made decisions in their own interests independent of how they related to one another in the productive process. The business cycle itself is then seen to be the result of a series of forecasting errors on the part of these agents regarding the nature of price changes. In our set-up interdependent agents recognize the reality of unforeseen

changes in aggregate demand, but instead contract with one another for shares of risk and return during various stages of the supply adjustment process.

2. One relevant measure might be the standard deviation of the rate of return generated on the factor inputs, although our discussion would not necessarily preclude other measures.

3. It is clear that individuals B and S would reject a departure from M in Figure 11.1 if the new combination of risk and return would lie below either of their indifference curves, since at least one party would suffer a reduction in expected utility. By the same token it is impossible to restructure unlevered equity into debt and levered equity and obtain returns higher than $E(R_M)$ and risk lower than $\sigma(R_M)$ for both B-type and S-type investors. The ambiguous zones would appear to be those combinations of risk and return lying above S's indifference curve but below $E(R_M)$ for B investors, and above B's indifference curve but to the right of $\sigma(R_M)$ for S investors. The difficulty with these combinations of risk and return is that both B-type and S-type investors are unambiguously better off with both bonds and levered stock, and the question then becomes whether they are relatively better off with one type of security or the other. Thus, if a debt instrument is so attractive in terms of risk and return that no one wants to hold the associated levered equity, then clearly this debt instrument cannot be created. The same would apply for levered equity. Thus, in order to successfully restructure the claims of what was initially an unlevered equity firm we must simultaneously create: (1) debt securities that raise the expected utility of some subset of the initial investors, and (2) associated levered equity securities that raise the expected utility of the remaining investors.

4. On the other hand it can be shown that giving investor B the levered equity claim reduces his or her expected utility to only 4.33.

5. If investor S was given the debt claim, his or her expected utility would fall to 16.267, which is lower than the expected utility provided by levered or unlevered stock.

6. For example, giving investor B 80 percent of the bonds and 20 percent of the stock yields expected utility of roughly 30.147, which is greater than the expected utility obtained from owning just bonds. Similarly, giving investor S 20 percent of the bonds and 80 percent of the levered stock yields expected utility of approximately 31.351, which is greater than the 23.467 given in equation (11.9) when S only holds stock.

7. The BB and SS schedules in Figure 11.3 are numerically computed by taking all possible combinations of financial leverage (e.g., $0 \leq K(B)/K(S) \leq \infty$ where $0 \leq [K(B), K(S)] \leq \$1000$ in units of 100) and net income sharing as measured by $\overline{X}(B)/\overline{X}(S)$. For the BB schedule, $\overline{X}(B)$ is obtained by multiplying each $K(B)$ by the 25 percent return required by bondholders, and $\overline{X}(S)$ is then determined residually as the difference between net income $\overline{X} = \$500$ and the required $\overline{X}(B)$. For the SS schedule, $\overline{X}(S)$ is computed by multiplying each $K(S)$ by the stockholders' required rate of return of 67 percent, and $\overline{X}(B)$ is then determined residually as the difference between $\overline{X} = \$500$ and the required $\overline{X}(S)$. The firm is created and production takes place when the sharing rules of the two claimants are consistent with one another and the requisite capital inputs valued at 1000 are supplied by bondholders and stockholders.

In this particular numerical example the equations for *BB* and *SS* are, respectively:

(i) $\dfrac{\bar{X}(B)}{\bar{X}(S)} = \dfrac{1}{K(B)/K(S) + 2} [K(B)/K(S)]$

(ii) $\dfrac{\bar{X}(B)}{\bar{X}(S)} = -0.250 + 0.750 \dfrac{K(B)}{K(S)}$

To solve for the equilibrium *Z* we first equate (i) and (ii) to obtain the equilibrium $K(B)/K(S)$, which after rearranging is:

(iii) $0 = 0.75 \left[\dfrac{K(B)}{K(S)}\right]^2 + 0.25 \dfrac{K(B)}{K(S)} - 0.5$

The positive root of this equation turns out to be $K(B)/K(S) = 0.67$. Inserting 0.67 into (ii) then provides the equilibrium $\bar{X}(B)/\bar{X}(S)$ or 0.25. Thus, *Z* in the initial equilibrium of $t = 0$ is (0.67, 0.25), as stated in the text.

8. In these statements balance sheets and income transactions will be combined in a single financial statement.

9. Recall from Chapter 10 that in an *n*-good and *n*-firm environment with incomplete investor diversification these agreements are contained in the bond contract. There we observed that two relatively simple balance-sheet constraints linked together could produce supply adjustments that are qualitatively similar to those we have been analyzing in a one-good and one-firm economy. The balance sheet constraints would directly link the debt-equity ratio to the ratio of safe assets to risky assets. Thus, when the firm increases (decreases) its safe to risky asset ratio, the contract between bondholders and stockholders calls on managers to increase (decrease) the debt-equity ratio. In this connection the risky business strategy of raising output prices and the level of production will eventually reduce the safe-to-risky-asset ratio as more of the higher priced output ends up in speculative inventories. This speculative business strategy will tend to redistribute income and wealth from bondholders to stockholders as the option value of the stock increases. On the other hand, if the debt-equity ratio is directly related to the safe-to-risky-asset ratio then this wealth transfer could be undone by financing the expansion in speculative inventories with equity. The new contract point would have stockholders claiming a larger share of the riskier net income (the result of the pricing and production decision) of the firm, but in turn financing a larger share of the riskier assets. Risk and return are proportionally shared in this supply adjustment. Finally, the exact functional form of the positive relationship between the debt-equity ratio and the safe-to-risky-asset ratio will depend upon the demand elasticities for the firm's products and the risk aversions of its stockholders and bondholders.

10. The production and financing adjustments presented in $t = 1$ are for illustrative purposes only, and one of the things they illustrate is that disequilibrium valuations are created in the capital market when production and financing adjustments taken together are nonoptimal. The equilibrium product market adjustment in $t = 1$ would involve the hiring of 61.1 workers for a wage of $10 per worker to produce

1,111 units of output priced at $1 per unit. Under these conditions the firm's balance sheet would show: I = \$611, FC = \$500, K = \$1,111, $K(B)$ = \$400, and $K(S)$ = \$711. The income statement in turn would appear as follows: PQ = \$1,111, WL = \$611, $\bar{X}$ = \$500, $\bar{X}(B)$ = \$100, and $\bar{X}(S)$ = \$400, which would provide stockholders with their required rate of return of 56.25 percent. This equilibrium t = 1 production and financing adjustment can be observed in Figure 11.2 where the S^* line crosses the upper dotted horizontal axis (for $\bar{X}$ = \$500) of the box in and around K = \$1,111.

—12—

Financial Contracting:
Some Empirical Evidence

Introduction

In Chapters 9–11 we presented a theory of aggregate supply adjustment for a market economy in which the individual suppliers of factor services to firms hold either a bondlike or stocklike claim to the produced output. In this theory price and output adjustments were linked to financing adjustments so that over time the risk-adjusted returns on debt instruments were proportionally maintained to the return on equity instruments. When pricing, production, and financing decisions are made in this way no single input contributor receives all the benefits nor incurs all the costs associated with the adjustment process itself.

There are several important differences between the artificial world we have created and that assumed in the more conventional macroeconomic models. To begin with, conventional theory—to the extent it incorporates a micro description of firm behavior—emphasizes those decisions in the supply adjustment that are directly linked to the welfare of the stockholders of the different firms in the economy. For example, in the new classical macroeconomics the focus of attention is on the individual firm's quantity response to a perceived change in relative prices. Stockholder profits in these models directly govern the quantity response of firms. Moreover, in conventional theories it is either assumed that prices are determined outside the model (e.g., the fixed-price Keynesian system) or that they evolve out of the auction markets of competitive general equilibrium, as, for example, in the full-employment monetarist and rational expectations models. Our own description of supply adjustments, on the other hand, focused attention on the partnership aspects of production; that is to say, on the combination of product market and financing decisions that coalesce the welfare of *all* input contributors to the firm. Prices in this model economy do not just evolve from an auction market, but are part of an overall coordinated business strategy designed to shift returns with risk among the different groups of input contributors over the business cycle. One strong implication of this theory is that production and financing decisions cannot be separated in a study of the business cycle. And yet we have observed, on a number of different occasions in this book, that separation is a key maintained hypothesis in the analysis of static equilibrium models in finance. In fact it was only by linking financing decisions to operating decisions over time that we were able to rationalize factor input cooperation within the institutional structure of the firm, and this rationalization provided the basis for our description of the price and output composition of a change in money national income. The general question we will address in this chapter is whether this view of the firm and aggregate supply has any empirical validity.

Before presenting and discussing the empirical results, several words of caution would seem to be in order, particularly concerning the possible achievements of empirical experiments in this area.[1] To begin with, it should be noted that historically, at least, there have been very few examples of important contending theoretical views that have been reconciled at the empirical level. This is particularly true in the areas of economics and finance that touch most closely to our theory of the business cycle. Certainly the econometric work centered around the Keynesian, monetarist, and new classical models has done little to unify professional opinion regarding most aspects of the macroeconomic process. Divergent policy prescriptions to the same perceived economic problems have been advocated and continue to be advocated by adherents to all three schools of thought. Moreover this indictment applies with equal force to a number of propositions advanced in the finance literature where, among other things, econometric work has failed to resolve the long-standing question regarding the relevance of company financial policy. Scholars in the traditional school of thought (both new and old) still contend with the Miller-Modigliani school of thought as to whether there is an optimal dividend and debt-equity decision for the firm, even though a great number of statistical experiments have purported to answer these questions. In this connection one might for good reasons suspect that it is the failure of the financial economist *qua* econometrician to properly specify the functional form and the appropriate empirical proxies for the relevant variables within the theoretical models that accounts for the fact that econometric evidence fails to decisively reject more of the contending economic theories. By and large the null hypothesis fares badly in this area of finance and economics. And yet this failure to reject the host of theories outstanding in these areas might actually be evidence supporting the methodological observation of Friedman (1974, pp. 145–146) that: ". . . there is no such thing as 'the' theory, there are theories for different problems or purposes." Therefore, in approaching our task in this chapter we will for the most part be guided by two principles: (1) "All models are wrong but some are useful" (Box 1979, p. 202) in analyzing certain issues in financial economics; and (2) the empirical evidence reported below is more to be likened to the stylized example presented in Chapter 11 in that it attempts to illustrate certain implications of our input/output-sharing theory of aggregate supply. With these caveats duly noted the empirical experiments—both the successful and the unsuccessful—will be presented in the following section. Our own prior expectation is that the support for the implications of the theory will be weak, primarily because the institutional arrangements that govern supply adjustments at the individual firm level (namely, various covenants in the bond contract) are somewhat indirect, and therefore their effects on the pricing, production, and financing decisions in the economy will be remote. Nevertheless, as it turns out, our prior expectation in this regard is somewhat overly pessimistic, as we will see below.

Some Empirical Evidence on Supply Adjustments

Introduction

What are the empirical implications of our contracting theory of supply adjustment? The observable implications would seem to fall into three interrelated categories. The first implication is that expansions in employment and real output are financed with equity while contractions are financed with debt. In other words the contracting hypothesis suggests that financial leverage and dividend payouts—the vehicles by which the risks of financing production in the economy are adjusted in our model—should be negatively related to the level of business activity. The second and related implication is that the share of corporate income going to bondholders and stockholders should follow the same path over time as their respective shares in the financing of productive activity. Thus, when business activity is depressed, bondholder-type claimants receive a relatively large share of corporate income; on the other hand, when activity is buoyant, the bond contract is designed to provide them with a relatively small share of corporate income. The other side of this argument suggests that the stockholders' share in corporate income follows a procyclical path. Finally, the third broad implication of the contracting theory of supply adjustment is that financial leverage should be negatively related to some measure of the ratio of risky assets to safe assets, and the latter ratio should be positively related to general business activity. These particular relationships were argued to evolve from the various protective covenants in the bond contract in an n-good and n-firm economy with imperfect diversification. In this kind of economy we suggested that an expansion in aggregate demand led firm managers to initiate a speculative business strategy which in this model takes the form of raising the level of output and output prices and increasing the level of speculative inventories. When this business strategy is implemented the covenants in the bond contract require the stockholders to finance the expansion in production and speculative inventories, thereby shifting risk at the margin from bondholders to stockholders. Conversely, a reduction in aggregate demand is the signal for firm managers to implement a safe and conservative business strategy which takes the form of price and output reductions. These decisions will tend to reduce the level of speculative inventories and increase the level of relatively safe assets held by the firm. Now the bond contract allows stockholders to partially liquidate their investment in the firm, if not by share repurchases, then at least with relatively high dividend payouts. In this way financial leverage is negatively related to the ratio of risky to riskless assets, and the ratio of risky to riskless assets is positively related to economic activity.

We will now begin our empirical assessment of the contracting theory of firm behavior by examining the cyclical path of the risk or financing adjustments that occur in an economy where production is financed with bonds and stocks.

Risk Sharing: An Empirical Investigation of Corporate Financing Decisions Over the Business Cycle

As we mentioned above our contracting theory of supply adjustment implies that corporate financing decisions will be systematically related to employment, output, and pricing decisions of firms as the economy passes through various stages of the business cycle. Consider, then, an unexpected expansion in the money supply. When the economy adjusts its aggregate supply upward in terms of higher employment, output, and prices, firms in the aggregate will tend to finance the expansion at the margin with equity (either through new share issues or retained earnings) and thereby reduce the risk confronting the bondholders.[2] Similarly, in response to a money-induced contraction in employment, real output, and prices, we would expect the firms in the system to return the funds released from production to the stockholders, thereby raising the financial leverage in the economy, and shifting the risk of financing production toward bondholders.[3] Consequently, we have two closely related empirical hypotheses regarding the relationship between financing and production decisions: (1) the debt-equity ratio should be negatively related to general economic activity; and (2) the dividend-payout ratio (the ratio of dividends paid to the after-tax earnings of firms) should also be negatively related to general business activity. We will now test these empirical propositions with correlation techniques using a variety of surrogates for financing and production decisions.

Our first test will be to relate the leverage associated with new financing to a suitable measure of employment and real output.[4,5] The choices for labor inputs, N, and real output, Q, seem relatively straightforward, and in this experiment they will be taken from the Business Sector Accounts in the U.S. For labor inputs we chose the series: Hours of All Persons Employed in the Business Sector, 1977 = 100. For our measure of physical output we chose the related series: Gross Domestic Product Originating in the Business Sector, 1977 = 100.

The choice of a proxy for financial leverage is somewhat less straightforward and therefore requires some further discussion. To begin with, our contracting theory of supply adjustment was developed within the framework of a long-term partnership relationship between bondholders and stockholders. Their initial investment decisions were presumed to be based on their relative risk aversions along with the long-run prospects of the industry in which their particular firm happens to be a member. As such their short-run problem was seen to revolve around the contracting for shares of risk and return in the firm at different stages in the business cycle, the occurrence of which they were unable or unwilling to forecast. It would then seem natural that our measures of leverage should reflect the permanent nature of this partnership between bondholders and stockholders. Therefore, to accommodate the empirical experiments to the theory we will define financial leverage in this study to be the ratio of some appropriate measure of long-term debt financing to new debt and equity financing. Three specific measures of financial leverage will be used in this section. The first measure, L_1, is taken from the balance sheets published by the Federal Reserve System for the corporate nonfinancial sector, and is defined to be the ratio of the year-to-year change in long-term bonds and mortgages to the change in long-term bonds and mortgages plus changes in net worth. The second measure of leverage, L_2, is also obtained from the balance sheets for the nonfinancial sector, but here the change in long-term bonds and mortgages is divided by the changes in total liabilities (including short-term liabilities) and net worth. This measure of leverage includes short-term debt in the denominator. Finally, the third measure of leverage, L_3, used in the experiments presented below is the ratio of new issues of corporate bonds and notes to the sum of the new issues of corporate bonds and notes, preferred stock, common stock, and the retained earnings generated in the corporate sector. The first point to make in this connection is that all three measures of financial leverage attempt to proxy the new long-term financing decisions of all firms in the nonfinancial business sector. Moreover, the first two measures of leverage, L_1 and L_2, reflect changes in balance-sheet items in the nonfinancial sector; whereas the third measure, L_3, measures new issues of long-term securities for the entire corporate sector. Our strategy is to loosely experiment with all three measures of financial leverage in order to reduce the probability that our statistical results depend upon any one measure of leverage.

Consider next the dividend-payout ratio which in our model economy also represents a risk-adjustment decision taken by firm managers. We will experiment with two proxies which are conceptually the same but differ in terms of the types of firms included. Our first measure of dividend payout, DPR_1, is the broadest in coverage and is defined to be the ratio of dividends paid out to all stockholders in the economy to the after-tax earnings of all firms in the economy. The data are taken from the U.S. National Income and Product Accounts. The second measure of dividend policy, DPR_2, is defined in the same way as DPR_1, but only includes those firms engaged in manufacturing activities.

The results of our first statistical experiment are reported in Table 12.1. In Part A of this table we present the correlations between our L_1 and L_2 measures of leverage and employment, N, along with real output, Q, in the nonfinancial corporate sector over the 1961–1981 period. In Part B we exclude the years 1971–1974 (a period of government-mandated price and financial controls) from the time sample. In a number of our experiments with U.S. data we exclude this period on the grounds that firms were not completely free to use pricing and financing decisions (e.g., dividend policy) to adjust returns with risk. Recall, then, that our risk-return-sharing theory of

Table 12.1.   Simple Correlations Between Leverage, and Employment and Output in the Business Sector (correlation coefficients are reported in the body of the table)

A. 1961–1981 Annual	N	Q
L_1	$-0.785*$	$-0.804*$
L_2	$-0.747*$	$-0.746*$
B. 1961–1981 Annual, delete 1971–74	N	Q
L_1	$-0.818*$	$-0.832*$
L_2	$-0.778*$	$-0.771*$

*Indicates the correlation coefficient is statistically significant at the 1 percent level.

Definitions:

L_1: The change in long-term bonds and mortgages in the nonfinancial corporate business sector divided by the change in long-term debt and equity in the nonfinancial corporate business sector.

L_2: The change in long-term bonds and mortgages divided by the change in total liabilities and net worth in the nonfinancial corporate business sector.

N: Total hours worked in the nonfinancial corporate business sector, 1977 = 100.

Q: Gross domestic product originating in the nonfinancial corporate business sector in 1972 dollars, 1977 = 100.

supply adjustments suggests that financial leverage in the business sector should be negatively correlated with employment and real output. In other words, expansions are financed with equity while contractions are supported with debt. As can be seen in the body of Table 12.1 this hypothesis cannot be rejected, at least with the financing and product market data we have used from the nonfinancial corporate sector.[6] In all eight cases financial leverage is negatively related to a production variable, and this negative relationship is highly significant in the statistical sense.

In Table 12.1 we focused attention on the risk-sharing adjustment that links financing decisions to production decisions in the corporate sector. There we observed that an expansion (contraction) in employment and output in the economy was associated with a reduction (expansion) in the marginal leverage, and this relationship is certainly consistent with one part of our contracting hypothesis. We now wish to broaden our study of the risk adjustment *qua* financing and production decisions that occur in a contract economy over time. Toward this end we will next explore the relationship between financing decisions, on the one hand, and some measures of nominal GNP growth. Nominal GNP and GNP growth not only incorporate an output (employment) decision on the part of firms in the economy, but also a pricing decision. Our risk-and-return-sharing hypothesis implies that financing decisions will be systematically related to the rate of growth of nominal GNP.

Table 12.2 presents some information on this hypothesized relationship. In this table (listed across the top) we use three measures of GNP growth: (1) the percentage rate of growth of nominal gross national product, $\dot{Y}/Y$; (2) the natural logarithm of the growth rate of nominal GNP, $\ln(\dot{Y}/Y)$; and (3) the cyclical deviation from the linear trend of the growth rate of nominal GNP, $(\dot{Y}/Y - \dot{Y}/Y)$. For our measures of financial policy we proxy the debt-equity decision in Part I of the table with L_1, L_2, and L_3. In Part II of the table we proxy dividend policy with DPR_1 and DPR_2. The sample time period is again 1961–1981/82—which is reported in Part A—and 1961–1981/82, deleting the period of price and dividend controls in 1971–1974. The 30 correlation coefficients reported in the body of Table 12.2 all indicate that the debt-equity ratio and the dividend-payout ratio are negatively related to our three measures of nominal GNP growth, and these negative relationships are very significant in the statistical sense. Expansions in nominal GNP growth (as well as positive deviations from the linear trend) are associated with relative expansions in equity financing, contractions in the rate of growth of GNP with a relative growth in debt financing.[7] These results are also consistent with the risk-and-return-sharing theory advanced in Chapter 11.

Is the countercyclical movement of financial leverage unique to the U.S. economy? To shed some light on this question we present in Table 12.3

Table 12.2.   Financial Policy and General Economic Activity
(correlation coefficients are reported in the body of the table)

I. Leverage

A. 1961–1981 Annual	$\dot{Y}/Y$	$\ln(\dot{Y}/Y)$	$(\dot{Y}/Y - \dot{Y}?Y)$
L_1	−0.756*	−0.775*	−0.589*
L_2	−0.797*	−0.801*	−0.694*
L_3	−0.643*	−0.583*	−0.706*
B. 1961–1981 Annual, delete 1971–74	$\dot{Y}/Y$	$\ln(\dot{Y}/Y)$	$(\dot{Y}/Y - \dot{Y}?Y)$
L_1	−0.796*	−0.812*	−0.622*
L_2	−0.828*	−0.843*	−0.720*
L_3	−0.647*	−0.597*	−0.717*

II. Dividend Payout

A. 1961–1982 Annual	$\dot{Y}/Y$	$\ln(\dot{Y}/Y)$	$(\dot{Y}/Y - \dot{Y}?Y)$
DPR_1	−0.804*	−0.796*	−0.782*
DPR_2	−0.847*	−0.847*	−0.750*
B. 1961–1982 Annual, delete 1971–74	$\dot{Y}/Y$	$\ln(\dot{Y}/Y)$	$(\dot{Y}/Y - \dot{Y}?Y)$
DPR_1	−0.832*	−0.820*	−0.820*
DPR_2	−0.922*	−0.915*	−0.828*

*Indicates the correlation coefficient is statistically significant at the 1 percent level.

Definitions:

L_1: See Table 12.1;
L_2: See Table 12.1;
L_3: New issues of long-term bonds and notes divided by new issues of long-term bonds, notes, preferred stock, common stock, and retained earnings for the corporate sector.
DPR_1: Corporate dividends divided by corporate profits after taxes;
DPR_2: Dividends paid in the manufacturing corporate sector divided by after-tax profits in the manufacturing corporate sector;
$\dot{Y}/Y$: The annual percentage rate of change of nominal GNP in the United States;
$(\dot{Y}/Y - \dot{Y}?Y)$: The deviation form linear trend of the percentage rate of change in nominal GNP

the same kinds of correlations that were presented in Part I of Table 12.2 for a group of seven OECD countries including the United States.[8] Similar types of leverage measures were obtained from balance sheets (e.g., L_1 and L_2) and sources and uses of funds statements (e.g., L_1^* and L_2^*) for the nonfinancial corporate sectors in these countries. The sample period varied considerably in length all the way from 1966–1981 for the United States to 1974–1980 for Japan. As can be seen from Table 12.3 the correlations are negative for the

Table 12.3. Simple Correlations Between Leverage and the Rate of Change of Nominal GNP for Various Countries Over Various Time Periods (correlation coefficients are reported in the body of the table)

I. Balance-Sheet Measures of Leverage

A. L_1		$\dot{Y}/Y$	$\ln(\dot{Y}/Y)$	$(\dot{Y}/Y - \dot{Y}/Y)$
West Germany	1966–1979	NA	NA	NA
Canada	1969–1981	NA	NA	NA
United States	1967–1981	−0.480[a]	−0.494[a]	−0.257
France	1971–1980	0.017	0.003	0.221
Italy	1970–1980	−0.377	−0.480[b]	−0.176
Japan	1974–1980	0.405	0.429	−0.442
United Kingdom	1968–1977	−0.628[a]	−0.750[a]	−0.017

B. L_2		$\dot{Y}/Y$	$\ln(\dot{Y}/Y)$	$(\dot{Y}/Y - \dot{Y}/Y)$
West Germany	1966–1979	−0.654[a]	−0.884[a]	−0.648[a]
Canada	1969–1981	NA	NA	NA
United States	1967–1981	−0.685[a]	−0.706[a]	−0.504[a]
France	1971–1980	−0.055	−0.055	0.106
Italy	1970–1980	−0.651[a]	−0.713[a]	−0.498[b]
Japan	1974–1980	0.164	0.161	−0.503
United Kingdom	1968–1977	−0.530[b]	−0.607[a]	0.130

II. Sources and Uses of Funds Measures of Leverage

A. L_1^*		$\dot{Y}/Y$	$\ln(\dot{Y}/Y)$	$(\dot{Y}/Y - \dot{Y}/Y)$
West Germany	1966–1979	NA	NA	NA
Canada	1969–1981	0.061	−0.035	0.004
United States	1966–1981	−0.689[a]	−0.686[a]	−0.627[a]
France	1970–1980	−0.235	−0.255	0.032
Italy	1969–1980	−0.324	−0.356	−0.472[b]
Japan	1973–1980	0.366	0.365	−0.210
United Kingdom	1967–1977	−0.673[a]	−0.729[a]	−0.030

B. L_2^*		$\dot{Y}/Y$	$\ln(\dot{Y}/Y)$	$(\dot{Y}/Y - \dot{Y}/Y)$
West Germany	1966–1979	NA	NA	NA
Canada	1969–1981	−0.342	−0.363	−0.358
United States	1966–1981	−0.843[a]	−0.842[a]	−0.844[a]
France	1970–1980	−0.237	−0.247	−0.024
Italy	1969–1980	−0.515[a]	−0.539[a]	−0.594[a]
Japan	1973–1980	−0.032	0.014	−0.519[b]
United Kingdom	1967–1977	−0.612[a]	−0.686[a]	0.022

[a]Indicates the correlation coefficient is statistically significant at the 5 percent level.
[b]Indicates the correlation coefficient is statistically significant at the 10 percent level.

Definitions:

NA: Data not available;
L_1: See Table 12.1;
L_2: See Table 12.2;
L_1^*: Defined as L_1 but data obtained from Sources and Uses of Funds Accounts;
L_2^*: Defined as L_2 but data obtained from Sources and Uses of Funds Accounts;
$\dot{Y}/Y$: See Table 12.2;
$(\dot{Y}/Y - \dot{Y}/Y)$: See Table 12.2.

most part, and statistically significant at the 10 percent level or better in approximately 45 percent of the cases. The general impression conveyed is that the risk-sharing hypothesis regarding the countercyclical movement of financial leverage comes closest to being consistent with the data for West Germany, the United States, Italy, and the United Kingdom. There appears to be little or no support for the hypothesis in France or Japan. In any event, while these correlations are perhaps interesting, the limitations of the data and the shortness of the sample period suggest a very cautious interpretation of this evidence insofar as our hypothesis is concerned.

Up to this point our correlation experiments have focused attention on the risk adjustments firms seem to make over time and the business cycle. In Table 12.1 we explored this risk adjustment in terms of the link between financing decisions and employment and production decisions in the nonfinancial business sector. In Tables 12.2 and 12.3 we studied the relationship between financial policy and various measures of the growth rate of nominal GNP. There it was observed that GNP growth not only incorporates an output component but also a price component; and as we suggested on a number of occasions, the pricing decisions of firms is the mechanism by which real returns are altered between bondholder- and stockholder-type claimants. In other words, when firms alter prices in partial response to a monetary shock (thereby adjusting returns between bondholders and stockholders), the implicit and explicit covenants in the bond contract call upon firm managers to adjust production and the financing of production in a corresponding manner. The testable implication, then, is that financial policy should be systematically related to both prices and real output. Thus monetary expansions that lead to higher prices, employment, and real output should also be accompanied by a reduction in the debt-equity ratio and dividend-payout ratio. The converse would be expected in a general economic contraction.

These hypothesized relationships between financing and production decisions (the risk adjustment), and pricing decisions (the return adjustment) are analyzed in Table 12.4. Our proxies for the financial decisions of all firms in the economy (i.e., L_1, L_2, L_3, DPR_1, and DPR_2) are the same as those used in Table 12.2. On the product market side the pricing and real output decisions of firms are proxied by the percentage rate of change of the GNP deflator, $\dot{P}/P$, and the growth rate of GNP in 1972 dollars, $\dot{y}/y$. In the body of Table 12.4 we present the partial correlation coefficients between a financial policy variable, on the one hand, and the inflation rate and growth rate in real output for the U.S. economy. From our risk-return-sharing theory of supply adjustment we infer that these partial correlation coefficients will be negative. As can be seen, all 20 partial correlations are negative and statistically significant at the 1 percent level. Rising prices and higher levels of real output are associated with lower dividend payouts and falling lever-

Table 12.4.   Correlations Between Financial Policy, Inflation, and the Rate of Growth of Real Output (partial correlation coefficients are reported in the body of the table)

I. Leverage		
A. 1961–1981 Annual	$\dot{y}/y$	$\dot{P}/P$
L_1	−0.590*	−0.844*
L_2	−0.684*	−0.819*
L_3	−0.696*	−0.587*
B. 1961–1981 Annual, delete 1971–74	$\dot{y}/y$	$\dot{P}/P$
L_1	−0.607*	−0.857*
L_2	−0.705*	−0.837*
L_3	−0.735*	−0.618*
II. Dividend Payout		
A. 1961–1982 Annual	$\dot{y}/y$	$\dot{P}/P$
DPR_1	−0.753*	−0.773*
DPR_2	−0.784*	−0.866*
B. 1961–1982 Annual, delete 1971–74	$\dot{y}/y$	$\dot{P}/P$
DPR_1	−0.805*	−0.796*
DPR_2	−0.882*	−0.916*

*Indicates the partial correlation coefficient is statistically significant at the 1 percent level.

Definitions:

L_1:   See Table 12.1;
L_2:   See Table 12.1;
L_3:   See Table 12.2;
DPR_1:   See Table 12.2;
DPR_2:   See Table 12.2;
$\dot{y}/y$:   The percentage rate of change of GNP in 1972 dollars;
$\dot{P}/P$:   The percentage rate of change of the GNP deflator.

age. This evidence is also consistent with our contracting theory of the business cycle.

Table 12.5 presents these same partial correlation experiments for the seven OECD countries analyzed in Table 12.3. The surrogate measures for the debt-equity decision are L_2 and L_2^*. In all 24 cases the partial correlation coefficients are negative, and in 5/8 of the cases the negative correlation coefficients are statistically significant at the 10 percent or better level. As before, West Germany, the United States, and Italy provide the strongest sup-

Table 12.5. Correlations Between Leverage, Inflation, and the Rate of Growth of Real Output for Various Countries Over Various Time Periods (partial correlation coefficients are reported in the body of the table)

I. Balance-Sheet Measure of Leverage

A. L_2

		$\dot{y}/y$	$\dot{P}/P$
West Germany	1966–1979	-0.566^a	-0.591^a
Canada	1970–1981	NA	NA
United States	1967–1981	-0.660^a	-0.652^a
France	1971–1980	-0.159	-0.001
Italy	1970–1980	-0.526^b	-0.586^a
Japan	1974–1980	-0.695^b	-0.571
United Kingdom	1968–1977	-0.075	-0.496^b

II. Sources and Uses of Funds Measure of Leverage

A. L_2^*

		$\dot{y}/y$	$\dot{P}/P$
West Germany	1966–1979	NA	NA
Canada	1970–1981	-0.327	-0.437^b
United States	1966–1981	-0.879^a	-0.744^a
France	1970–1980	-0.063	-0.054
Italy	1969–1980	-0.836^a	-0.467^b
Japan	1973–1980	-0.577^b	-0.057
United Kingdom	1967–1977	-0.042	-0.589^a

[a]Indicates the partial correlation coefficient is statistically significant at the 5 percent level.

[b]Indicates the partial correlation coefficient is statistically significant at the 10 percent level.

Definitions:

NA: Data not available;
L_2:   See Table 12.3;
L_2^*:   See Table 12.3;
$\dot{y}/y$:   See Table 12.4;
$\dot{P}/P$:   See Table 12.4.

port for the risk-return-sharing theory of supply adjustment; France, on the other hand, provides the least support. Now, however, Japan and the United Kingdom present a more mixed result. Compared to Table 12.3, there is somewhat more support for the risk-return-sharing hypothesis, although again the relatively small sample size suggests a very cautious interpretation of this particular experiment.

Return Sharing: An Empirical Analysis
of the Cyclical Distribution of Income

Previously we have empirically analyzed the risk or financial adjustments firms make in response to changes in the level of business activity. We observed that the data were by and large consistent with the view that expansions were financed with equity and contractions with debt. Now we will focus our attention on the return adjustment that accompanies the risk or financing adjustment, since this is yet another way of empirically analyzing the contracting theory of supply advanced in Chapters 9–11.[9] In our discussion in those chapters it was duly noted that the contractual arrangements among the cooperating factor input contributors were such that the fixed priority claimants received a relatively large share of the firm's income when economic conditions were depressed and a relatively small share when economic activity was buoyant. Similarly those input contributors who took a variable residual claim in exchange for their factor service obtained a relatively small share of the firm's income when business conditions were depressed and took a relatively large share when the economy expanded. In other words, the income shares for both types of claimants would be expected to follow their share in the financing of productive activity over the business cycle. Thus the second principal implication of our contract theory of supply adjustment is that the distribution of corporate income shifts toward bondholders in times of contraction and toward stockholders during periods of expansion.

In Table 12.6 these propositions are tested with data from the non-financial business sector in the United States. Toward this end it will first be useful to define the variables used in the experiments. The income claims of bondholders will be proxied with interest payments on corporate debt, rD. A more comprehensive measure of fixed priority claims would also include wages, salaries, and supplements ($W + S$), for they, too, in large measure represent the fixed claims to the produced output. Next the income claims of stockholders will be proxied with dividend payments, Div, and retained earnings, RE. Again it must be remembered that these variables are no doubt rather crude proxies for the model variables discussed in Chapters 9–11. For example there are a host of labor income claims, such as commissions and bonuses, that are more like our stocklike claim to income, and therefore do not belong in the fixed priority classification to which they have been assigned in this experiment. Nevertheless, if we observe the hypothesized relationships with these crude proxies, then it would also be likely that the relationships would be observed with variables that more closely correspond to those discussed in the theory.

Table 12.6. Simple Correlations Between Various Income Shares in the Nonfinancial Business Sector and Various Measures of Economic Activity (correlation coefficients are reported in the body of the table)

I. Manufacturing Capacity Utilization, C.U., as a Measure of Economic Activity: 1961–1982

	C.U.
$rD/(rD + RE + Div)$	-0.636[a]
rD/Y_b	-0.555[a]
$(W + S + rD)/Y_b$	-0.637[a]
$(RE + Div)/(rD + RE + Div)$	0.642[a]
$(RE + Div)/Y_b$	0.624[a]

II. The Growth Rate of Real GNP, $\dot{y}/y$, as a Measure of Economic Activity: 1961–1982

	$\dot{y}/y$
$rD/(rD + RE + Div)$	-0.628[a]
rD/Y_b	-0.595[a]
$(W + S + rD)/Y_b$	-0.660[a]
$(RE + Div)/(rD + RE + Div)$	0.633[a]
$(RE + Div)/Y_b$	0.470[b]

[a]Indicates the correlation coefficient is statistically significant at the 1 percent level.
[b]Indicates the correlation coefficient is statistically significant at the 2 percent level.

Definitions:

Y_b: Domestic income originating in the nonfinancial corporate business sector;
rD: Net interest paid by the nonfinancial corporate business sector;
W: Wages and salaries paid in the nonfinancial corporate business sector;
S: Wage and salary supplements paid in the nonfinancial corporate business sector;
C.U.: Capacity utilization in manufacturing;
$\dot{y}/y$: The rate of change of GNP in 1972 dollars;
RE: Retained earnings in the nonfinancial corporate business sector;
Div: Dividends paid by the nonfinancial corporate business sector.

Our procedure will be to take the ratio of these various input claims (classified on a fixed-versus-variable basis) to both the net operating income (defined to be $rD + RE + Div$) and total domestic income generated in the nonfinancial business sector, Y_b, and then correlate these ratios first with the Federal Reserve Board Index of Capacity Utilization in Manufacturing, CU, and then the growth rate in real GNP, $\dot{y}/y$. Our expectation is that $rD/(rD + RE + Div)$, rD/Y_b, and $(rD + W + S)/Y_b$ will be negatively correlated with CU and $\dot{y}/y$. By the same token $(RE + Div)/(rD + RE + Div)$ and $(RE + Div)/Y_b$ will be positively correlated with CU and $\dot{y}/y$. The results of these correlations are presented in the body of Table 12.6 for the years 1961–1981. As can be seen, all 10 correlations have the correct sign and are highly significant in the statistical sense. This evidence, like the other correlations presented earlier, is consistent with the view that return sharing between bondholder- and stockholder-type claimants follows the same cyclical path as risk sharing measured in terms of the debt-equity ratio and the dividend-payout ratio. The next thing we must do to strengthen this line of reasoning is to more closely examine the actual mechanisms by which this risk and return sharing occurs in a decentralized financial system and economy.

Bond Covenants, Balance-Sheet Matching, and the Business Cycle

In the development of our contracting theory of supply adjustment for an n-good and n-firm economy in Chapter 10, we discussed how a combination of asset and liability constraints linked together in the bond contract could, in principle, produce the cyclical path of risk and return sharing implied by the theory and found above to be consistent with certain bodies of aggregate data. Here we will develop this micro account of contracting in somewhat greater detail, and also present some additional statistical evidence that is consistent with this micro view.

The micro theory of supply adjustment presented in Chapter 10 was seen to be based on the fundamental conflict that is presumed to exist between bondholder- and stockholder-type claimants concerning the future business strategy to be followed by the firm once the factor inputs have been collected and productive activity initiated. Recall from our earlier discussion that stockholders—by virtue of their diminished risk aversion—were relatively more inclined to favor a risky business strategy, which in this model economy takes the form of raising prices, increasing output, and accumulating speculative inventories. This strategy is risky because neither stockholders nor bondholders can be sure that the greater volume of higher-priced output can be sold in the future, thereby justifying the higher level of current investment in the firm. Bondholders, on the other hand, are more inclined to vote for a relatively safe business strategy, which in this economy is represented by the decision to reduce prices and production, and convert speculative inventories into relatively safe and liquid assets. This strategy is considered safe because it tilts the asset structure of the firm toward relatively safe assets which can easily be converted into general purchasing power and returned to investors.

The solution we proposed for the reconciliation of this conflict in Chapter 10 took the form of an agreement which in effect stipulated that whenever the firm pursued a risky pricing and production strategy, stock-holders would be required to finance the ensuing expansion in speculative inventories. Conversely, when the firm pursued a relatively safe strategy of reducing prices and the level of production (which in turn converted risky inventories into relatively safe assets), the agreement called upon bond-holders to finance a larger proportion of the firm's assets. This proposed solution suggests that when setting up the firm, bondholders and stock-holders attempt to match certain types of assets to the debt and equity of the enterprise, not necessarily on a one-to-one basis, but in the general direction of requiring stockholders to finance the risky assets and bondholders the safe assets. This kind of matching could easily be achieved in principle by placing certain asset and debt-equity related covenants in the bond contract. For ex-ample, as we mentioned in Chapter 10, a debt-equity constraint linked to a safe-risky asset constraint could achieve the approximate intention of this desired matching. Thus, during expansions, when businesses are optimistic, the business strategy pursued will be more speculative as firms raise output prices, expand production, and accumulate risky inventories. The result of these decisions is a redistribution of firm income from bondholders to stock-holders. A model bond contract would then require the stockholders to rein-vest their inflationary gain to support the higher level of production and in-vestment in inventories, and thereby shift the risk of financing the firm from bondholders to stockholders. Cyclical expansions are then characterized by: rising prices, higher levels of production, the accumulation of inventories at a faster rate than safe assets, and a reduction in the debt-equity ratio, all of which shift risk and return at the margin toward stockholders. A similar line of reasoning suggests contractions are characterized by: falling prices, lower levels of output, the conversion of inventories into safe assets, and an in-crease in the debt-equity ratio. In this case risk and return are shifted toward bondholders. We would now like to see empirically whether this balance-sheet matching is observable in the data and whether it is systematically re-lated to general economic activity.

Some empirical evidence on balance-sheet matching and its relation-ship to business activity is presented in Tables 12.7 and 12.8. Consider first the simple correlations presented in Table 12.7. In Part A of this table we first correlate several measures of financial leverage to both the growth rate in nominal GNP and the inflation rate. The second thing we do in Part A is to correlate these measures of leverage with such asset ratios as inventories to total assets and inventories to liquid assets for all firms in the nonfinancial business sector. In the body of Table 12.7 we can see that our L_1 and L_2 mea-sures of financial leverage are negatively correlated with the growth rate in nominal GNP, $\dot{Y}/Y$, and the rate of growth of the GNP deflator, $\dot{P}/P$. The negative correlations indicate that when the economy is cyclically expanding

Table 12.7.   Balance-Sheet Matching and Economic Activity (correlation coefficients are reported in the body of the table)

A. Simple Correlations Between Leverage, Asset Ratios, Nominal GNP Growth, and Inflation Rates: 1961–1981 Annual

	$\dot{Y}/Y$	$\dot{P}/P$	Inv/TA	Inv/LA
L_1	-0.756*	-0.762*	-0.744*	-0.789*
L_2	-0.797*	-0.619*	-0.650*	-0.669*

B. Simple Correlations Between Asset Ratios, Nominal GNP Growth, and Inflation Rates: 1961–1981 Annual

	$\dot{Y}/Y$	$\dot{P}/P$
Inv/TA	0.634*	0.633*
Inv/LA	0.877*	0.940*

*Indicates the correlation coefficient is statistically significant at the 1 percent level.

Definitions:

L_1:   See Table 12.1;
L_2:   See Table 12.1;
$\dot{Y}/Y$:   See Table 12.2;
$\dot{P}/P$:   See Table 12.5;
Inv/TA: The ratio of inventories to total assets in the nonfinancial corporate business sector;
Inv/LA: The ratio of inventories to liquid assets in the nonfinancial corporate business sector.

and firms are pursuing a speculative strategy of raising prices and expanding production, they are also in the process of reducing the financial leverage in the system, and thereby shifting the risk of financing production toward stockholders who in turn are benefiting from the cyclical expansion in the inflation rate. In Part A of the table we can also observe the balance-sheet matching discussed above. There we can see that our two leverage measures are negatively correlated with such asset items as the ratio of inventories to total assets and the ratio of inventories to liquid assets. Part A of Table 12.7 is consistent with the view that the pricing and production decisions of firms alter the composition of their assets, and this alteration is matched to a certain extent with a corresponding change in financial leverage. In Part B of the table we complete the picture by presenting the positive and statistically significant correlations that run between our two asset management ratios and GNP growth or inflation.

Taken together the correlations in Parts A and B of Table 12.7 indicate that improving business conditions are associated with the relative accumulation of risky inventories, and in turn this increase in inventory investment is associated with a reduction in financial leverage. While these 12 statistically significant correlations do not prove the causal ordering suggested by our contract theory of supply adjustment, they are certainly consistent with this theory in that the balance-sheet matching we observe is systematically related to general business conditions.

Table 12.8 reinforces the general picture presented in Table 12.7. Here the balance-sheet matchings are combined together with fluctuations in business activity. In the body of Table 12.8 the partial correlations between leverage and nominal GNP growth, and leverage and the ratio of inventories to other types of assets are both negative and statistically significant in seven out of the eight possible cases.[10] This evidence is consistent with our micro account of how risk and return are shared in an n-good and n-firm economy; and this micro account is the foundation for our contract theory of supply adjustment.

Table 12.8.   Correlations Between Leverage, Nominal Income Growth, and Two Asset Ratios: 1961–1981 Annual (partial correlation coefficients are reported in the body of the table)

I.	$\dot{Y}/Y$	Inv/TA
L_1	-0.584^a	-0.581^a
L_2	-0.656^a	-0.310
II.	$\dot{Y}/Y$	Inv/LA
L_1	-0.518^a	-0.615^a
L_2	-0.650^a	-0.352^b

[a]Indicates the correlation coefficient is statistically significant at the 1 percent level.
[b]Indicates the correlation coefficient is statistically significant at the 7½ percent level.

Definitions:

L_1:	See Table 12.1;
L_2:	See Table 12.1;
$\dot{Y}/Y$:	See Table 12.2;
Inv/TA:	See Table 12.7;
Inv/LA:	See Table 12.7.

Summary and Conclusions

In this chapter we have performed a host of preliminary statistical experiments to determine whether there is any support for the view that risk and return are adjusted together as aggregate supply in the economy adjusts to changes in aggregate demand. From the macro prospective, pricing decisions alter the distribution of real income among bondholder- and stockholder-type claimants, while the associated production and financing decisions redistribute the risks in the system. A rational supply adjustment—one that does not confer all the benefits or costs of the adjustment to any single group of participants in production—will therefore be characterized by a systematic relationship between product market decisions and financing decisions. These hypothesized relationships were argued to evolve from the localized conflicts among bondholder- and stockholder-type claimants over the riskiness of the business strategy to be pursued once the capital resources have been invested and the individual enterprise created. These conflicts were seen to be partly resolved through an elaborate set of contracts that in effect required stockholders to finance expansions and bondholders to finance contractions. Our empirical tests focused on these hypothesized relationships and were divided into three sets of experiments.

The first set of statistical experiments were performed and the results presented in Tables 12.1–12.5. The general purpose of these experiments was to describe the relationship between financing decisions (the risk adjustment) and production decisions in various ways. In Tables 12.1 through 12.3 simple correlation techniques were used to test the strength of these relationships in the United States and a number of other OECD countries. For the United States, these correlations between financial leverage and dividend payouts, on the one hand, and such measures of business activity as employment, real output, and various measures of GNP growth, on the other hand, were negative and statistically significant. In other words, the financing of production shifted toward bondholders during periods of contraction and toward stockholders during periods of expansion. For other OECD countries the results were mixed. West Germany, Italy, and the United Kingdom were found to conform to the implications of our contracting theory of supply. France and Japan, on the other hand, provided little support for the view that leverage is negatively related to general business activity. Tables 12.4 and 12.5 extended the empirical inquiry by breaking up the growth rate in GNP into an inflation component and real output component. Table 12.4 described the results for the United States. There we saw that the partial correlations between our two measures of the risk adjustment (i.e., financial leverage and dividend payouts), and both the inflation rate and real output growth were negative as implied by the theory, and statistically significant. Table 12.5 presented the same partial correlations for our sample of OECD countries, and like the results in Table 12.3, the evidence was mixed. Again West Germany and Italy provided the strongest support for our contracting theory, and France the least. In summarizing these results it would seem that the statistical relationships between financing decisions and economic activity are very strong in the United States. They are also very strong in West Germany and Italy. For the other OECD countries the evidence is mixed at best, and at worst nonexistent. It would therefore seem that our international comparisons raise more questions than they answer. In terms of future research they suggest more attention be directed toward the analysis of price-output-financing decisions of public enterprises in mixed economies such as France and the United Kingdom. A second research area would seek an explanation of the optimal risk-and-return-sharing arrangements that underlie factor input cooperation in societies like Japan where for cultural reasons the coalescing process may well be different than it is in the United States, West Germany, and Italy.

The second set of experiments were carried out and the results presented in Table 12.6. The general objective here was to explore the cyclical path of return sharing between bondholders and stockholders, which, along with the risk sharing discussed previously, forms the core of our contract theory of the firm. Since it was observed that stockholders finance expansions and bondholders finance contractions, our theory suggests that stockholders receive a relatively large share of corporate income during expansions and bondholders a relatively large share during contractions. In Table 12.6 we presented some evidence on the cyclical distribution of corporate income between bondholder- and stockholder-type claimants. There it was found that each claimant's share of income varied with its share in the financing of production; in other words, the bondholder's share in corporate income was negatively related to general economic activity (e.g., capacity utilization and the growth rate of real GNP) as was their share in the financing of production, while the stockholder's share was positively related to economic activity, which also matched their share in the financing of productive activity. All correlations were statistically significant.

The third and final set of experiments was conducted and the results presented in Tables 12.7 and 12.8. These experiments were directed toward the balance-sheet matching and its relationship to business activity, which underlies our micro account of firm behavior over the business cycle. Among other things this micro account of firm behavior suggested that pricing and production decisions could be expected to alter the risk structure of the firm's assets, and a change in the risk structure of a firm's assets would in turn change the debt-equity mix of new financing. In Table 12.7 we observed with simple correlation techniques that the debt-equity ratio was negatively related to the ratio of inventories (our proxy for risky assets) to other assets, and that this particular asset ratio was positively related to economic activity. These statistically significant correlations were consistent with the view that the firm follows a speculative business strategy during expansions and that this speculation is financed with equity. In periods of contraction the firm would tend to follow a relatively safe business strategy, which in turn would be financed at the margin with debt. Finally, the results in Table 12.7 regarding the hypothesized relationship between balance-sheet matching and business activity were corroborated with partial correlation techniques in Table 12.8.

All in all it would appear that the various pieces of evidence gathered in this chapter are consistent with a risk-and-return-sharing theory of supply adjustments in a contract economy when aggregate demand deviates from its long-run trend value. No one experiment or set of experiments presented here establishes the case, but taking all of the correlation experiments together a stronger case can be made that the data reported here do not reject the contracting hypothesis of supply adjustment. Nevertheless, tiring as it may seem, Black (1982) and Leamer (1983) are perfectly correct in reminding us that correlation does not prove causation; and it is causation that would seem to be of primary interest to the social scientist and policymaker. In this sense our theory or description of supply adjustments over the business cycle may be incomplete since it does not speak to the issue of whether the risk adjustment causes the return adjustment, or whether the reverse is true. All our analysis suggests is that rational behavior in a contract economy requires the two to move together over time, and this is what we have tried to test in this chapter. Thus, in closing we would like to reiterate that the objective of this chapter and Chapters 9–11 will be accomplished if the reader is motivated—either from agreeing or disagreeing with the views set forth in this book—to reconsider the coordinating role of a financial contract system over the business cycle.

Notes

1. We use the term empirical experiment somewhat loosely to include the host of nonexperimental correlation studies that have typically been conducted by economists and will also be carried out in this chapter.

2. In a decentralized n-firm and n-good economy it was argued in Chapter 10 that this relationship between financing and production decisions evolved from the balance-sheet covenants built into individual bond contracts. During periods of expansion managers acting as agents for stockholders were argued to follow a risky business strategy, which in turn reduced the safety and liquidity of the firm's assets as more of the increased (and higher-priced) output finds its way into inventories. The covenants in turn require the firm to finance this expansion in risky assets with equity. If liabilities and equities were perfectly matched to safe and risky assets, the new production and increased level of inventories would be financed dollar for dollar with equity, as was the case in the stylized numerical example presented in Chapter 11. In reality the covenants in the bond contract do not proscribe dollar-for-dollar adjustments in financing in response to a change in the composition of the firm's assets during expansions, but they do push the firm in this general direction, as we will see below.

3. In this case a contraction gives rise to a conservative business strategy which takes the form of a reduction in production (including the price of output) and inventories. Thus the covenants allow the firm to have a higher level of financial

leverage in response to the reduced level of risky assets during periods of recessed economic activity.

4. We choose to measure leverage in terms of new financing, rather than new and old financing, for several reasons. To begin with, the contracting theory presented above addresses the issue of new financing, in other words, the financing associated with changes in the level of production. Second, old financing must be valued, and, unfortunately, accounting book values are still the most readily available information at our disposal even though market valuations would be preferable. Moreover, if the implications of our contracting hypothesis are not observable on new financing, then it is very doubtful that they will be observable for the total financial mix of the firm.

5. The data used in the experiments reported in this chapter are described more completely in the Appendix dealing with data sources.

6. Using the flow leverage measure for the entire corporate sector, these correlations, while negative, are greatly reduced. They are, respectively:

(i) $R(L_3, N)$ = -0.407 (1961–1981);
(ii) $R(L_3, Q)$ = -0.346 (1961–1981);
(iii) $R(L_3, N)$ = -0.401 (1961–1981, delete 1971–74);
(iv) $R(L_3, Q)$ = -0.341 (1961–1981, delete 1971–74)

where R represents the correlation coefficient. The correlations between L_3 and N are statistically significant at the 5 percent level, while the correlations between L_3 and Q are significant at the 7½ percent level.

7. The correlations between L_1 and L_2, and the Federal Reserve Index of Capacity Utilization, while negative, are statistically insignificant. On the other hand, the correlation between L_3 and capacity utilization is significant at the 2½ percent level. Finally the correlation between L_1 and the ratio of inflation to GNP growth (i.e., $\dot{P}/P/\dot{Y}/Y$) was negative and significant at the 1 percent level.

8. The seven-country sample (West Germany, Canada, United States, France, Italy, Japan, and the United Kingdom) was obtained by collating those countries for which the OECD had balance sheets or sources and uses of funds statements for the nonfinancial corporate sector to those countries for which the Federal Reserve Bank of St. Louis had data on GNP growth and inflation rates.

9. One test of this proposition is to correlate the share of interest payments in the net income of firms to the ratio of the stock of all debt-paying interest to the total assets for a given sample of firms. The theory suggests that this correlation will be positive. Thus, as firms increasingly finance their operations with debt, a larger share of the net income will be taken up in interest payments. For the 1961–1981 period this correlation is positive; namely:

$$R(rD/X, CMD/TA) = 0.861$$

where

R = the correlation coefficient;
rD = interest payments in the nonfinancial business sector;

X =   the sum of interest payments, retained earnings, and dividends paid in the nonfinancial business sector;

CMD =   the stock of credit market debt outstanding in the nonfinancial business sector;

TA =   total assets in the nonfinancial business sector.

The correlation coefficient is statistically significant at the 1 percent level.

10. When the inflation rate, $\dot{P}/P$, is substituted for nominal GNP growth, the partial correlations are both negative but no longer statistically significant.

—13—

Some Concluding Thoughts
on the Financial Economics
of a Positional Society

Input Sharing, Output Sharing, and the Positional Economy

Finance theory in its micro and macro versions begins with the works of Irving Fisher and John Maynard Keynes. Fisher's micro contribution revolved around the insight that when capital markets are perfect, individual consumption decisions could be separated from individual productive investment decisions. This important contribution was a straightforward extension of Adam Smith's observation that in a timeless economy we should specialize in production on the basis of comparative advantage and then trade with one another in the marketplace to attain our desired bundle of consumption goods.[1] In terms of understanding the role of the financial system in a capitalist economy, separation is an important property of financial markets in that it has been shown to imply, under certain circumstances, that business decisions heretofore thought to be important in the actual conduct of business affairs (e.g., financial structure, dividend payout, and the merging of two or more firms) are in principle irrelevant. Here then is something the market can do as well as the firm, and academic insights in the 1960s and 1970s seemed to be measured in terms of the number of firm-related decisions that can directly be resolved by markets. We have gone over some of these propositions in Chapters 2 and 4 and found that one of the key requirements for a perfect capital market is that a portfolio investor's rational expectations of the capital market income of a firm (measured in terms of dividends paid over a given time period plus changes in the price of the firm's securities over that same time period) must be identical to the firm's actual product market income (measured in terms of sales revenues minus costs). When this is the case it is clear that financial policy at the firm level is irrelevant.

Keynes, too, was impressed with separation—separation of consumption and investment decisions, and separation of savings and portfolio decisions—but felt that, with imperfect markets and increasing returns, it was the root cause of what he called involuntary unemployment. How can we be sure, he wondered, that the separated consumption and investment spending of all individuals and firms will be perfectly coordinated by the price system, and provide work for all those who want to work at some institutionally given wage rate in an uncertain environment. Unlike Fisher's micro theory of finance constructed on the foundations of perfect markets, the macro theory advanced by Keynes accorded an important role to discretionary financial policy; in other words, monetary and fiscal policy, unlike company financial policy, was very relevant.

It is curious that both of these great economists, who were so impressed with one kind of separation or another, chose not to develop their own analyses from the points of view of the separated interests of the different input contributors in a society. In our opinion this was unfortunate, for much of the economic behavior of input contributors in an uncertain world seems to be governed by position: position in the distribution of income or position along some other economic or noneconomic dimension. In terms of individual behavior, market economies tend to be comparing societies. Moreover there would seem to be much in the economic history of Western-type societies that suggests in a number of different ways that issues centering around position of one sort or another assume a greater economic significance when the rate of economic progress diminishes in a country. In this connection the prospects for an increasing standard of living as we presently know it in the West are not particularly bright, and for this reason the positional aspects of economic behavior may well become more important in the future.

The focus of attention in this book has been on the output-sharing rules and the positional aspects of economic organization as they are reflected in financial contracts. This theme has been woven around a number of micro and macro financial policy issues, and forms the basis for the integrative approach taken in this book. While we will not provide a comprehensive review of all that has passed within these pages, some of these issues will now be summarized.

Our study began in Chapter 2 with a description of Fisher's micro model of intertemporal consumption in a perfectly certain world with perfect exchange markets. This model was then extended in Chapter 3 to provide a general equilibrium description of the entire economy. In this model the young were endowed with time and the old with capital. With these productive factors they joined together as partners in the firm to create an output which in the end they will share in some way. The output-sharing rules or financial contracts in this world were proportional equity sharing rules based on the marginal productivities of the two factor inputs, labor and capital. Since the environment was assumed to be certain, risk played no role in the distribution of income nor the rate of return earned on human and nonhuman capital. With this model we were able to describe with an extraordinarily simple geometry the general equilibrium for this artificial economy. Starting with immutably fixed endowments and tastes known to all participants in the economy, the model generated: (1) the current consumption of leisure by the young, (2) the consumption of goods by the old, (3) the supply of labor services by young workers, (4) the supply of capital services by retired workers or capitalists, (5) the produced output for the next period, (6) the distribution of that output between active and retired workers, and (7) the rate of return on human and nonhuman capital. While this Fisher-inspired model represents an oversimplification of all economic aspects of life in reality, it does point to some important and practical economic truths; namely, the retirement consumption and bequests of the parent generation of workers depend upon the magnitude and productivity of the capital they contribute to the production process. Moreover the model clearly illustrates the pre-Keynesian or classical proposition that when starting from some initial equilibrium, any attempt to peg the rate of return on human capital above the level given by its marginal productivity will reduce the level of employment and output from their Pareto efficient levels.

When the environment is uncertain, the questions and issues centering around output sharing and economic position become more complex. We eased into this subject by first considering the simple capital asset pricing model of resource allocation and the associated distribution of income and risk. The securities or output-sharing rules in this model consisted of stocklike claims to the unknown future output in the risky sector and stocklike/bondlike claims to the known future output in the riskless sector. With the assumption set of this model we were able to simplify each household's resources allocation or portfolio decision problem to one of investing their factor input (generally taken to be a capital input) in one or both of two mutual funds. One of the funds specialized in financing productive opportunities in the risk-free sector of the economy and generated a risk-free rate of return denoted by R_F. The other mutual fund financed productive opportunities in the risky sector and generated an expected rate of return $E(\tilde{R}_M)$ on its portfolio as well as a risk measured by the standard deviation of the portfolio return or $\sigma(\tilde{R}_M)$. In both mutual funds the share of income or output distributed to each household was proportional to the share of capital inputs contributed to each fund, and in this sense, at any rate, there would be little conflict between the different input contributors once the initial endowments were fixed. Here, again, we would remind the reader that the focus of analysis is directed toward the market structure characterizing this artificial economy, and not the institutional characteristics of the individual firms that actually carry out productive activity in this economy. Firms are not very relevant or interesting when they are infinitesimally small or when it does not make any difference whether they are small or large. In any event one of the key insights provided by this model description of allocation under uncertainty was the formulation of an explicit expression for the economy-wide trade-off between risk and return, which took the relatively simple form of $[E(\bar{R}_M) - R_F]/\sigma(\bar{R}_M)$. This trade-off between risk and return or market price of risk reduction was found to be useful in empirically assessing the probable effects of government intervention in the capital market, a topic that was studied in Chapter 6. Moreover, in Chapter 4 it was observed that the assumptions of the model implied that company financial policy was irrelevant; while in Chapter 5 these same assumptions implied that the distribution of investment in the economy was Pareto efficient.

In retrospect and for certain purposes the capital asset pricing model turned out to be a useful way to model an artificial economy subject to exogenous shocks that follow a particular class of probability laws. Unfortunately, in order to answer certain questions in this environment, the model was developed with a specific set of assumptions that seemed to preclude an examination of other, and perhaps equally interesting, questions. For example it would seem difficult to motivate the economic problem of involuntary unemployment (if such unemployment can exist) within the capital asset pricing model framework, since, among other things, the model assumes that output is produced under conditions of constant returns to scale by infinitesimally small enterprises. Since there are no barriers to entry in this world, an agent can fully invest his or her human or nonhuman resources in the risk-free and risky sectors subject only to the endowment constraint. For an individual agent, investing resources in a vineyard in the backyard is no better or worse than investing with others on a larger property, say Chateau Palmer. And yet who can deny that occasionally the actual underemployment of productive resources (even in Bordeaux) is perceived to be a serious social problem in actual market economies? Furthermore a pure change in monetary units or inflation would be of little consequence within the framework of this model of resource allocation because of the zero-degree homogeneity requirement for equilibrium and the fact that every household in the system exchanges their productive resources for equity-type claims in both the risk-free and risky sectors. Again, who can deny that inflation is perceived to be a disruptive force in actual market economies? Finally, if there were any good reasons to study the pricing, output (employment), and financing decisions of firms as part of a unified business strategy, this would have to be done within a different framework of analysis, since by assumption the capital asset pricing model separates these decisions. It would then seem that in order to study these kinds of issues and problems it will be necessary to consider alternative artificial economies rather than the ones posed by Fisher and the capital asset pricing model.

No doubt it was the apparent inability of these conventional general equilibrium-type models (with their heavy reliance on perfect markets and the coordinating role of the price system) to explain away the high and prolonged levels of unemployment in and around the 1930s that motivated Keynes to develop the demand-oriented income-expenditure model reviewed in Chapter 7. There we saw that Keynesian macroeconomics represented a sharp break from the tradition followed by conventional economics of the kind discussed in Chapters 2, 3, and 4. As we have seen in these chapters the traditional approach is to derive positive and normative propositions from economic equilibrium in a step-by-step process beginning with the endowments, preferences, and technologies available to agents. Keynes, on the other hand, seemed to have an intuitive vision of how capitalist economic systems worked in practice, and from this vision developed certain positive and normative implications from a set of loosely connected interrelationships between the product, factor, money, and bond markets. While there was a certain degree of plausibility attached to the interrelationships between these markets that underly the IS-LM version of his model, they were not derived from the more basic endowments, tastes, and technologies, which in turn represented the starting point for classical economic theory. However, it did not take long before other more conventional economists were trying to derive his basic macroeconomic propositions from the more traditional approach of general equilibrium.[2]

At first Keynes' methodological revolution enjoyed great success, since his set of macroeconomic interrelationships were evidently more amenable to empirical verification than were the propositions advanced by the general equilibrium analysis of that time. However, eventually the popularity of the methodology began to wane, partly because inflation replaced unemployment as the major perceived economic problem in the 1970s (and Keynesian macroeconomics had relatively little to say about that problem), and partly because of the rebirth of interest in the formulation and empirical testing of certain propositions (e.g., the trade-off between unemployment and inflation, supply adjustments during the business cycle, and the effectiveness of government financial policy) derived from more classical general equilibrium models. This transition in economic thinking was summarized in Chapter 8.

As might be expected this rebirth in classical modes of economic reasoning did nothing to unify professional opinion. How changes in nominal GNP are divided between changes in prices and real output, and whether government financial policy could be used to systematically influence any of the variables, continues to divide economists just as sharply as they did in Keynes' day.

Chapters 9, 10, and 11 offered still another theory that accounts for cyclical movements in prices, employment, and output: a theory based more on certain financial principles emphasized throughout this work, albeit somewhat unorthodox financial principles. One important difference between our own account of the trade cycle and those presented by others is centered around the nature of the firm, in particular, the input/output-sharing arrangements that bind different agents to the firm. The basic idea of input sharing and output sharing is, perhaps, most easily described in terms of the different kinds of financial contracts that tend to emerge in capitalist economies when the environment is uncertain. This is the path we followed, and accordingly the supply adjustments described in Chapters 9–11 for the entire economy were analyzed from the point of view of: (1) bondholders as they proxy for all input contributors who hold a fixed priority claim to the end-of-period income; and (2) stockholders as they proxy for those input contributors who hold the variable residual claim to the social output. The objective was then to find a combination of pricing, output (employment), and financing decisions by firms that would coalesce the interests (in terms of returns and risk) of the joint partners in the firm during the supply adjustment process. Within this framework of input and output sharing as they are represented in bondlike and stocklike contracts, we were able to account for a rational adjustment in aggregate supply in terms of prices, employment, output, and financing over the business cycle. Moreover, the adjustments were accomplished in such a way that the various partners or cooperating input contributors would willingly join together in the firm to initiate productive activity.[3] In one empirically relevant supply adjustment, it was observed that bondholder-type claimants contract for a larger share of the expected output during periods of recessed economic activity, but the same contract obliges them to absorb a larger share of the risks associated with the financing of production. On the other hand, during periods of expansion their share in the social output declines along with their share in the financing of the inputs. The reverse was postulated for stockholder-type claimants in this particular supply adjustment scheme. The important lesson in this exercise was that the cyclical distribution of income between bondlike and stocklike claimants was linked to their share in the distribution of risk measured in terms of their input contribution, and that both of these dimensions of investment and employment activity are effectively contracted for in advance by rational agents when initiating productive activity within the firm.[4] In Chapter 12 we carried out a host of correlation experiments designed to shed some light on the interdependent nature of pricing, production, and financing decisions. These are the decisions that facilitate the cyclical sharing of risk and return within the firm, called for by the contract between bond-holder- and stockholder-type claimants. In the vast majority of cases we were unable to reject the hypothesis that pricing, production, and financing decisions were statistically related to each other, as suggested by our contracting theory of supply adjustment.

In putting these ideas into perspective let us compare and contrast the description of a money-induced supply adjustment as set forth in Chapters 9–11 to the supply adjustment proposed by the equilibrium school of thought, which, as we observed in Chapter 8, is built on the twin foundations of continuous market clearing and rational expectations.[5] Toward this end consider an economy just after the monetary authority has unexpectedly increased the purchasing power in the system, which according to the equilibrium school leads to an increase in prices throughout the economy. The crucial question for this school of thought is how will the price increases in each market be perceived by individual rational agents? If they are perceived to be part of a general inflation (correctly, as it turns out in this case), then nothing will be done if these agents were in equilibrium with respect to employment and production before the monetary injection. Suppose, on the other hand, that each agent perceives the price increase to be unique to his or her particular product line, possibly reflecting a change in consumer preferences. Then our rational agent is presumed to ask an additional question; namely: Is the price rise transitory, possibly reflecting a fad, or is it permanent? If it is perceived to be permanent then the agent will want to make an increased investment in tangible capital in order to accommodate the increased demand for his products. It might be noted at this point that an expansion in investment during cyclical upswings is one of the stylized facts of business cycles, and thus the theory is consistent with economic reality.[6] Moreover, it would also seem that these agents would want to hire additional workers to run the machines in order to accommodate the higher demand, and to attract the additional workers would therefore offer to pay a wage rate higher than that which prevailed in the sector before the monetary expansion. However, wage rates, too, are prices, and we must therefore ask how workers *qua* agents will perceive the offer of higher wages along the permanent/transitory scale. Now evidently another stylized fact of economic reality is that when wage increases are perceived to be permanent by workers, there will be no increase (and perhaps a small decrease) in labor supplied to the marketplace. We are now confronted with a seemingly minor dilemma: the stylized facts of business cycles require an expansion in employment, and yet other and equally important facts suggest that permanently perceived wage rates will not bring forth the additional labor inputs. This dilemma would be eliminated, according to the equilibrium school of thought, if employer-type agents could make the wage increases seem transitory to worker-type agents (e.g., temporary overtime rate), for there evidently is some evidence that indicates that transitory wage increases will call forth an increase in labor supply.[7] Thus, in order for the theory to be consistent with a broad range of stylized facts, we must have workers perceiving their wage increases as transitory in nature, while at the same time their employers perceive product price increases as permanent. This immediately raises the following question: Why is it that these two closely related price changes are so differently interpreted by the cooperating factors of production? Lucas (1977, p. 230) answers this question—as well as the more general question of why individual agents cannot see that the monetary expansion that raises prices in their market is raising prices in all markets—in the following way.

> In the reality of a multi-commodity world, however, no one would want to observe all prices every day nor would market traders find published price indices particularly useful. An optimizing trader will process those prices of most importance to his decision problem more frequently and carefully, those of less importance less so, and most prices not at all.

It would seem that informational gaps of this kind are bound to occur when the focus of the analysis is to study the supply decisions of individual agents in markets for inputs and outputs, and capital markets are ignored. Agents in this world are made to seem as if they are operating on islands or in closets and separated from their fellow agents. The markets they operate in are indistinguishable from auction markets. What seems to be lacking—at least in our opinion—is a careful description of the firm and its role in organizing and coordinating productive activity, as well as serving as the vehicle by which the produced output or monetary value of that output is distributed among the input contributors. Perhaps this oversight stems from the view that firms are black boxes or fictional entities—so why filter economic activity through them rather than seeking explanations of economic phenomena directly in factor and product markets? And yet the very existence of firms implies an incompleteness in the market's ability to coordinate economic activity by itself. Thus, because productive activity in modern societies is actually organized around the firm, the concept itself might prove to be useful when attempting to account for fluctuations in economic activity.

A firm, as we emphasized in Chapters 9–11, is nothing more than a set of agreements or contracts that defines the basis for cooperation among various input contributors.[8] Among other things, these agreements define how the different inputs will be combined in the production process, and how the income of the firm will be divided between the cooperating agents. It was this latter observation that led us to place great emphasis on the risk-and-return-sharing agreements embedded in financial securities, since financial securities represent marketable claims to the future income generated by the firm. The market prices of these securities, in turn, will reflect all the information that is known to exist in the market for inputs and outputs so assiduously studied by the new classical macroeconomics; and these security prices will tell agents whether the price changes in factor and product markets are part of an inflationary process, and whether any changes in relative prices are permanent or transitory. How then do fluctuations in real output and employment arise, for as Lucas (1975, pp. 1137–1138) has observed, too much information of the type contained in capital market prices precludes monetary disturbances from having any effect on real output and employment when agents behave in a rational manner.

In Chapters 9–11 our answer to this question had to be quite different from the explanation offered by the new classical view. We began with rational agents but not rational expectations. It was assumed instead that agents in the economy faced Knightian uncertainty. In this model comparative advantage and incompleteness of markets brings different factor contributors together to jointly cooperate and manage productive activity within the contractual framework of the firm.[9] Our agents are more like joint partners who actively participate in the management of the enterprise than the hired inputs envisioned in traditional economics. When setting up the firm these agents know in a general way that future demand for their products will change and that supply will have to adjust to the new demand. Nevertheless they are unsure of the timing (who can predict future central bank policy?) as well as the magnitude of the change in demand; but what separates our theory from conventional theory is that our agents make little or no attempt to forecast these short-run fluctuations. Moreover, these agents are different from one another in terms of preference orderings over consumption in different states of the economy and in terms of risk aversion. Accordingly, for these and other reasons, our agents find it efficient to resolve the uncertainties in capitalist production by fashioning contracts with one another that define the output-sharing rules that will govern the basis for their cooperation in the firm. One group of agents chooses to take a fixed priority nominal claim to the future income of the firm in exchange for their factor service, another group takes the variable residual. These claims or contracts define the rights and privileges of the various input contributors within the firm, and since the rights and privileges of one group often conflict with the economic interests of some other group (particularly after the inputs have been invested), there must be some agreement as to how the firm will be managed. The right to manage a firm is an important right which must be limited by contract or custom if different input contributors hold different output-sharing agreements with the firm. This is the case because an unconstrained manager could manage the firm in such a way as to systematically exploit one group of input contributors for the benefit of some other group and thereby rob factor cooperation in production of all rationality.[10] Consequently, whether managerial behavior is described by constrained wealth maximization, or satisficing, or coalescing is unimportant just so long as it is recognized that the agreements or contracts that bind together factor cooperation shape the management of the firm in general and the supply adjustment over the business cycle in particular. The specific mechanisms by which the contracts shape the supply adjustment were discussed in Chapters 9–12 in terms of a balance-sheet matching requirement that pushed firms in the direction of financing risky assets (e.g., such as inventories) with equity, and relatively safe assets (e.g., cash and marketable securities) with debt. The end result is that firms tend to respond to a positive monetary shock in the system with a speculative business strategy, which in our short-run model takes the form of raising prices, increasing production, and shifting the composition of their assets more toward risky inventories.[11] These speculative decisions not only increase the riskiness of firms in the economy, but also shift expected returns from bondholders to stockholders. Our model covenants in the bond contract would then require firms to finance this risky expansion with equity, which in turn reduces the risk of bondholders, thereby providing the protective equity cushion that enables firms to survive subsequent and inevitable contractions in economic activity. Thus, during cyclical expansions our coalescing managers give each type of input contributor something they desire (increased income for residual claimants, and increased safety for fixed priority claimants) and something they would prefer to avoid (reduced real income for fixed priority claimants, and an enlarged share of the input contribution for the residual claimants). In this way both claimants share the benefits and the costs of the supply adjustment. It was also observed that in the case of a money-induced recession the benefits and costs of the adjustment are reversed for the two different types of claimants in the economy. When firms are managed in this way, bondlike and stocklike claims will continue over time to form the contractual basis for factor cooperation in the firm.

In the past several paragraphs and throughout this book we have compared and contrasted several views regarding the causes and processes by which real output, employment, and prices fluctuate over time and in response to monetary shocks. We have offered these comparisons not so much to try to convince the reader which view might be more correct, whatever that might mean, but rather to illustrate the different approaches that might be taken to account for certain perceived stylized facts that tend to recur over and over again in capitalist economies. Keynesian and classical theories have been articulated by very intelligent economists, and their insights into the causes and processes of business fluctuations are extremely valuable. From the Keynesian school we gain an understanding of the link between money and output (employment) via interest rates, financing, investment, and induced consumption; from the new classical school, we gain an understanding of the link between money and output via prices, the marginal efficiency of investment, and investment. In Chapters 9–11 we have called attention to still another financial dimension of business fluctuations; namely, how different groups of agents share the benefits and costs associated with adjusting production in response to monetary disturbances. This question, too, is important, for it helps us understand why certain contractual forms tend to be used over and over again to unite different factor contributors within the firm. In one sense our approach represents a return to a new form of institutionalism, and by and large this approach has not been applied to the study of business fluctuations. Nevertheless the state of contentiousness in business cycle research suggests that no one methodological approach enjoys or deserves a monopoly in the study of this complex subject.

Positional Economics and the Social Order

But what about the system of output sharing we live with in the West today? Invariably the question is asked—and should be asked—as to whether economic position in terms of money income is a socially legitimate avenue in which to distinguish one individual from another. In answer to this question Keynes (1936, p. 374) was probably close to the truth when he reminded us that: "It is better that a man should be tyrannic over his bank balance than over his fellow citizens; and whilst the former is sometimes denounced as being but a means to the latter, sometimes at least it is an alternative." Keynes, however, went on to say that in his opinion the economic game of chance could be played for more modest stakes than those that prevailed in his time. Nevertheless, as financial economics continually reminds us, these rewards cannot be taken as independent of risk since there would seem to be nothing in the development of the human condition that suggests a man is any more willing today to risk going from the always comfortable upper middle class to the poverty level in pursuit of economic gain than he was in some former period.

In the 1980s individual distinction in financial management—and probably management in general—is at a low ebb in the United States. It was not always so. In the 1950s and 1960s investment managers advertised their skillful management of investment funds in a sharply rising stock market to an eager and optimistic investing public. Critical academic scrutiny of these claims and the collapse of the stock market in the 1970s considerably assuaged these somewhat immodest proclamations. There was, at the time, a malaise creeping over the country, brought on in considerable measure by the national disasters of Vietnam, Watergate, Iran, and Lebanon. The investment industry at first patriotically tried to stem the tide of growing pessimism, but then accommodated the mood with what was then thought to be prudent investment advice for the times. Patriotism can never be the last refuge of a business enterprise that hopes to survive in a competitive market economy, even though it seemed in the 1970s and 1980s that more were being managed by scoundrels as real as those in Samuel Johnson's time. Nowhere was this drama so amusingly portrayed than in the television advertisements of a prominent brokerage house when in the early 1970s the investing and football-watching public were counseled to be bullish on America. The subsequent decline in real values in the stockmarket and the growing inflation soon changed the theme of this advertisement to one of the bull himself forlornly seeking shelter from the ravages of an inclement economy as the audience became more football watching and less interested in investing during the decade. It was also during this period that we observed the growth and development of the so-called index fund that approximates the market portfolio of the capital asset pricing model. Such an investment vehicle, rightly or wrongly, would have been regarded with contempt during the 1950s. But times were quickly changing. There was a growing feeling that successful management of financial and physical assets was more a matter of luck, and practicing managers were increasingly coming to agree, particularly those whose performances were among the less enviable. There also was a growing feeling at the same time that U.S. workers and managers were becoming inherently less capable than their counterparts in Europe and Japan. We were now asking whether it was possible for Americans to emulate Japanese managerial techniques in order to shore up an economy that was becoming increasingly battered by foreign competition. There is much irony in all of this, since only two-and-a-half decades ago some economists were attempting to explain the Leontief paradox in terms of the inherent superiority of U.S. workers, and U.S. managerial talent was so respected and feared abroad that special barriers were imposed against U.S. direct investment in order to blunt what Servan-Schreiber called the American Challenge.

As the decade of the 1980s unfolds, the pessimism in the West in general, and the United States in particular, continues. Journalists seem to tell us every day that like lemmings we are marching (or worse yet, being marched) into a sea of unemployment and inflation. Like the Great Depression this era has brought forth its share of nonconventional remedies to the economic problems of the day, and some of these remedies are now in the process of being implemented and (as usual) rejected as government policy. One of the themes of this work has been that unemployment and inflation are the manifestations of a positional struggle between input contributors within a society, a struggle that is resolved by administrative order in a socialist economy, and by contracts (including financial contracts) in a market economy. In this work these struggles have been studied as a domestic economic conflict among input contributors holding different output-sharing contracts, but as the huge foreign debts of the Third World and socialist countries now remind us, the conflict can take on an international dimension. In the past the financial contract system has played an important role in partially blunting and accommodating these positional struggles—so often the result of changes in tastes, technologies, and endowments—and no doubt in some instances has substituted for a more violent solution; there is hope that it will continue to do so in the future.

Notes

    1. The inability of agents to trade (in inputs and output markets) to their optimal consumption bundle for whatever reasons plays an important role in disequilibrium accounts of unemployment and the existence of non-Walrasian equilibriums. For a review of this strand of post-Keynesian thought see the survey by Drazen (1980).

    2. For a survey of this restatement, as well as a comparison with the classical system, see the reviews contained in Sargent (1979, chaps. 1 and 2), Drazen (1980), and Azariadis and Stiglitz (1983).

    3. In our description of a market economy all input contributors are in effect partners in the firm and all participate in future management decisions, even though some contributors hold different types of claims than others. Thus, our emphasis is on the cooperative aspects of business management and decision rules. The conventional view is that some input contributors (e.g., stockholders) hire others (e.g., workers) on a competitive market for a given remuneration, and then manage the firm in their own interest. In this set-up business management and decision rules represent conflicts between the different input contributors.

    4. How different this view is from that summed up by Keynes (1936, p. 372): "The outstanding faults of the economic society in which we live are its failure to provide for full employment and its arbitrary and inequitable distribution of wealth and incomes." In our theory the cyclical distribution of income is not arbitrary. If it were, it would be difficult to rationalize cooperation in production and we would not observe the kinds of input/output-sharing arrangements that have long been part of our institutional framework. It would therefore seem useful to develop something along the lines of a Lorenz curve for risk bearing to accompany the Lorenz curves we now have for income sharing, for then we should be in a better position to pass judgment on the distribution of income in a particular society.

    5. At a very general level rational expectations merely suggests that individual agents use all the information at their disposal to predict a certain economic variable or event. A somewhat more specific expression of this general idea is that the forecast of the agent is equivalent to the equilibrium solution of the true model, or that the subjective distribution used by the agent is equivalent to the objective distribution that actually generates the variable or event in question. The distinction that is often drawn in these discussions is between what Knight (1921) would call situations of risk and uncertainty. The outcome of most economic decisions are unknown, but some are more unknown than others, partly because of our past experiences (or lack thereof) in making similar kinds of decisions. Those decisions for which we have

much experience and are recurrent in nature, Knight classified as risk situations and were thought to be amenable to statistical analysis. Lucas (1977) (1980) suggests that this is the case for many economic variables during business cycles. However, there are some decisions (e.g., introducing a new product or adapting a new technology) for which agents have no past experience, and hence these kinds of decisions are less amenable to probability statements and statistical analysis. Knight called these situations uncertainty. The literature in financial economics has largely discarded this view of Knight that would draw a distinction between recurrent and nonrecurrent events, and now more or less assumes that agents are rational Bayesian decision makers and that the relevant probabilities are subjective. Yet we must be careful here, for as Lucas (1977) reminds us, even psychotic behavior can be understood as rational if by rational behavior all we mean is decision making based on any (informed or uninformed) subjective probability distribution.

6. The stylized fact is that production of investment goods is procyclical and has a greater amplitude than output in general. The theory suggests that price fluctuations induce output fluctuations. It would then seem that another stylized fact should be that the price of investment goods will fluctuate more sharply than prices in general. This is not clearly borne out by the data for what they are worth. For example the standard deviation and the coefficient of variation for the implicit price deflator on the durable goods component of consumption is much smaller than the standard deviation and coefficient of variation for the implicit price deflator on GNP for the 1956–1978 period. Moreover these two statistics for the fixed investment component of gross private domestic investment are almost identical to those for GNP in general. Since quality changes in investment goods are hard to measure, it is quite possible that the reported prices overstate the inflation that has actually occurred in the investment goods industry. If this is the case then the fact that investment expenditures have a greater procyclical amplitude is not necessarily borne out by the fact that output changes are induced by price changes, unless there is something peculiar about the investment goods industries versus industry in general that diminishes the response of output variation to price variation.

7. See Ghez and Becker (1975).

8. This point, in a different connection, is also made by Fama (1980).

9. In this set-up agents are assumed to make an initial career or investment decision in some industry in the economy and then invest their human and/or nonhuman resource in that sector. How these career decisions are made is a complicated question which incorporates economic and noneconomic factors, all of which are outside the scope of this inquiry. Once having made this decision, however, they insist on participating in the management's decisions that will have a bearing on the risk and return sharing they will experience in the future.

10. Jensen and Meckling (1976) have explored some of the constraints imposed on owner/managers by external owners that limit the perquisites of managers. Without these constraints managers/owners would tend to increase their on-the-job consumption, which could only come at the expense of external owners.

11. This speculative strategy is the firm's response to a perceived improvement in the general economic environment which in turn shifts the *BB* and *SS* schedules described in Chapters 10 and 11. Thus, in Chapter 11 an expansion in the money

supply was seen to shift the equilibrium bond market and stock market schedules reflecting the perceived improvement in the economic environment. Managers in our artificial economy responded to this signal from the capital market by pursuing a risky business strategy of raising prices and the level of production, policies which could be expected to raise the level of risky assets carried by firms. Covenants in the bond contract would then require firms to finance the expansion with equity. In the new product and capital market equilibriums stockholders end up with a larger real income while bondholders end up with a reduction in risk.

Appendix: Data and Sources

Financial Data, Definitions, and Sources

Financial Leverage

1. L_1: The change in long-term bonds and mortgages in the nonfinancial corporate business sector divided by the change in long-term bonds, mortgages, and net worth. For the United States the data was obtained from the *Balance Sheets for the U.S. Economy*, Division of Research and Statistics, Board of Governors of the Federal Reserve System, 1982. For the other OECD countries the data was obtained from the *Non-Financial Enterprises Financial Statements*, OECD Statistics Part 3, 1982.
2. L_2: The change in long-term bonds and mortgages divided by the change in total liabilities and net worth in the nonfinancial corporate business sector. Data sources for the United States and other OECD countries are the same as in 1.
3. L_3: New issues of long-term bonds and notes divided by new issues of long-term bonds, notes, preferred stock, common stock, and retained earnings of the corporate sector. This data was obtained from Table B-21, p. 187, and Table B-91, p. 266 in *Economic Report of the President*, Washington, D.C.: United States Government Printing Office, 1983.
4. L_1^*: New issues of long-term bonds, notes, and mortgages divided by new issues of long-term debt, stock, and retained earnings. These sources and uses of funds data were obtained from the *Non-Financial Enterprises Financial Statements*, OECD Statistics Part 3, 1982.
5. L_2^*: New issues of long-term bonds, notes, and mortgages divided by total sources of new funds in the nonfinancial sector. Data source is the same as in 4.

Dividend Payout

1. DPR_1: Corporate dividends divided by corporate profits after taxes. This data was obtained from Table B-21, p. 187 of the *Economic Report of the President*, Washington, D.C.: United States Government Printing Office, 1983.

2. DPR_2: Dividends paid by manufacturing firms divided by profits after taxes in the manufacturing sector. This data was obtained from *Business Statistics: The Biennial Supplement to the Survey of Current Business, 1979*, U.S. Department of Commerce; and various issues of the *Survey of Current Business*, U.S. Department of Commerce.

Product Market Data, Definitions, and Sources

1. N: Hours of all persons employed in the business sector. This data was obtained from Table B-40, p. 208 of the *Economic Report of the President*, Washington, D.C.: United States Government Printing Office, 1983.
2. Q: Output in the business sector. Data source is the same as 1.
3. $\dot{Y}/Y$: The annual percentage rate of growth of nominal GNP. This data for the United States and the other OECD countries used in this study was obtained from *International Economics Conditions, Annual Data 1960–1981*, prepared by the Federal Reserve Bank of St. Louis, July 1982.
4. $\dot{P}/P$: The annual percentage rate of growth of the GNP deflator. This data was obtained from the same source as 3 above.
5. $\dot{y}/y$: The annual percentage rate of growth of real GNP. For the United States the base year is 1972. For the other OECD countries the base date varies from country to country. Data source is the same as in 3.
6. C.U.: The Federal Reserve Board index of capacity utilization in manufacturing. This data is found in Table B-45, p. 213 of the *Economic Report of the President*, Washington, D.C.: United States Government Printing Office, 1983.

Factor Income in the Nonfinancial Corporate Business Sector

1. W: Wages and salaries. This data was taken from Table 1.13 in various issues of the *Survey of Current Business*, U.S. Department of Commerce.
2. S: Supplements to wages and salaries. The data source is the same as in 1.
3. rD: Net interest payments. The data source is the same as in 1.
4. RE: Undistributed profits. The data source is the same as in 1.
5. Div: Dividend payments. The data source is the same as in 1.
6. Y_b: Net domestic product. The data source is the same as in 1.

Selected Asset Items in the Nonfinancial Corporate Business Sector

1. LA: Liquid assets. These assets include cash and short-term marketable securities. This data was taken from the *Balance Sheets for the U.S. Economy*, Division of Research and Statistics, Board of Governors of the Federal Reserve System, 1982.
2. Inv: Inventories. The data source is the same as in 1.
3. TA: Total assets. The data source is the same as in 1.

Bibliography

Alberro, J. 1981. "The Lucas Hypothesis on the Phillips Curve: Further International Evidence." *Journal of Monetary Economics* 6: 239–250.

Alchian, A. and H. Demsetz. 1972. "Production, Information Costs, and Economic Organization." *American Economic Review* 62: 777–795.

Amihud, Y. and V. Lev. 1981. "Risk Reduction as a Managerial Motive for Conglomerate Mergers." *Bell Journal of Economics and Management Science* 12: 605–617.

Arrow, K. 1964. "The Role of Securities in the Optimal Allocation of Risk Bearing." *Review of Economic Studies* 31: 91–96.

———. 1965. *Aspects of the Theory of Risk Bearing.* Helsinki: Academic Bookstore.

———. 1970. *Essays in the Theory of Risk Bearing.* Amsterdam: North-Holland.

———, H. B. Chenery, B. Minhas, and R. M. Solow. 1961. "Capital-Labor Substitution and Economic Efficiency." *Review of Economics and Statistics* 43: 225–250.

Azariadis, C. 1975. "Implicit Contracts and Unemployment Equilibria." *Journal of Political Economy* 83: 1183–1202.

——— and J. Stiglitz. 1983. "Implicit Contracts and Fixed Price Equilibria." *Quarterly Journal of Economics* 98: 1–22.

Bailey, M. J. 1962. *National Income and the Price Level.* New York: McGraw-Hill.

Baily, M. N. 1974. "Wages and Employment Under Uncertain Demand." *Review of Economic Studies* 41: 37–50.

Barro, R. J. 1974. "Are Government Bonds Net Wealth?" *Journal of Political Economy* 82: 1095–1117.

———. 1977. "Unanticipated Money Growth and Unemployment in the United States." *American Economic Review* 67: 101–115.

———. 1978. "Unanticipated Money, Output, and the Price Level in the United States." *Journal of Political Economy* 86: 549–580.

———. 1981. *Money, Expectations and Business Cycles.* New York: Academic Press.

——— and H. I. Grossman. 1971. "A General Disequilibrium Model of Income and Employment." *American Economic Review* 61: 82–93.

—— and M. Rush. 1980. "Unanticipated Money and Economic Activity." In *Rational Expectations and Monetary Policy*, edited by S. Fischer, pp. 23–48. Chicago: University of Chicago Press.

Baumol, W. J. 1952. "The Transaction Demand for Cash: An Inventory Theoretic Approach." *Quarterly Journal of Economics* 66: 545–556.

Black, F. 1972. "Capital Market Equilibrium with Restricted Borrowing." *Journal of Business* 45: 444–454.

——. 1982. "The Trouble With Econometric Models." *Financial Analysts Journal* 38: 3–11.

—— and M. Scholes. 1973. "The Pricing of Options and Corporate Liabilities." *Journal of Political Economy* 81: 637–659.

Blinder, A. 1980. "Comment on Barro and Rush." In *Rational Expectations and Monetary Policy*, edited by S. Fischer, pp. 49–54. Chicago: University of Chicago Press.

—— and R. M. Solow. 1974. "Analytical Foundations of Fiscal Policy." In *The Economics of Public Finance*, edited by A. Blinder and R. M. Solow, pp. 3–115. Washington, D.C.: The Brookings Institution.

Bosshardt, D. 1983. "Spanning, Pareto Optimality, and the Mean-Variance Model." Unpublished Manuscript, State University of New York at Buffalo.

Box, G. E. P. 1979. "Robustness in the Strategy of Scientific Model Building." In *Robustness in Statistics*, edited by R. L. Launer and G. N. Wilkinson, pp. 201–236. New York: Academic Press.

Buiter, W. H. and J. Tobin. 1980. "Debt Neutrality: A Brief Review of Doctrine and Evidence." In *Social Security Versus Private Saving*, edited by G. M. Von Furstenberg, pp. 39–63. Cambridge, Mass.: Ballinger.

Cass, D. and M. E. Yaari. 1966. "A Re-Examination of the Pure Consumption Loans Model." *Journal of Political Economy* 74: 353–367.

Chua, J. H. and R. S. Woodward. 1983. "J. M. Keynes' Investment Performance: A Note." *Journal of Finance* 38: 232–235.

Clower, R. 1965. "The Keynesian Counter-Revolution: A Theoretical Appraisal." In *Theory of Interest Rates*, edited by F. H. Hahn and F. P. R. Brechling, pp. 103–125. London: MacMillan.

Darby, M. R. 1976. "Three-and-a-Half Million U.S. Employees Have Been Mislaid: Or, an Explanation of Unemployment, 1934–1941." *Journal of Political Economy* 84: 1–16.

Debreu, G. 1959. *Theory of Value*. New York: John Wiley and Sons.

Diamond, P. A. 1965. "National Debt in a Neoclassical Growth Model." *American Economic Review* 55: 1126–1150.

Drazen, A. 1980. "Recent Developments in Macroeconomic Disequilibrium Theory." *Econometrica* 48: 283–306.

Dreze, J. H. and J. A. Mirrlees. 1974. *Allocations Under Uncertainty: Equilibrium and Optionality.* London: MacMillan.

Dunning, J. H. 1969. *The Role of American Investment in the British Economy.* London: P. E. P.

Ekern, S. and R. Wilson. 1974. "On the Theory of the Firm in an Economy With Incomplete Markets." *The Bell Journal of Economics and Management Science* 5: 171–180.

Fair, R. C. 1979. "An Analysis of the Accuracy of Four Macroeconometric Models." *Journal of Political Economy* 87: 701–718.

Fama, E. F. 1970. "Multiperiod Consumption-Investment Decisions." *American Economic Review* 60: 163–174.

———. 1972. "Perfect Competition and Optimal Production Decisions Under Uncertainty." *Bell Journal of Economics and Management Science* 3: 509–529.

———. 1976. *Foundations of Finance.* New York: Basic Books.

———. 1980. "Agency Problems and the Theory of the Firm." *Journal of Political Economy* 88: 288–307.

——— and M. H. Miller. 1972. *The Theory of Finance.* Hinsdale, Ill.: Holt, Rinehart and Winston.

Feldstein, M. S. 1974. "Social Security, Induced Retirement and Aggregate Capital Accumulation." *Journal of Political Economy* 82: 905–926.

———. 1976. "Temporary Layoffs in the Theory of Unemployment." *Journal of Political Economy* 84: 937–957.

Fischer, S. 1977. "Long-Term Contracts, Rational Expectations, and the Optimal Money Supply Rule." *Journal of Political Economy* 85: 191–210.

Fisher, I. 1907. *The Rate of Interest.* New York: MacMillan.

———. 1930. *The Theory of Interest.* New York: MacMillan.

———. 1973. "A Statistical Relation Between Unemployment and Price Change." Reprinted in *Journal of Political Economy* 81: 496–502.

Friedman, B. 1979. "Optimal Expectations and the Extreme Information Assumptions of Rational Expectations Macromodels." *Journal of Monetary Economics* 5: 23–43.

Friedman, M. 1968. "The Role of Monetary Policy." *American Economic Review* 58: 1–17.

———. 1974. "A Theoretical Framework for Monetary Analysis." In *Milton Fried-*

man's Monetary Framework, edited by R. J. Gordon, pp. 1–62. Chicago: University of Chicago Press.

———. 1977. "Nobel Lecture: Inflation and Unemployment." *Journal of Political Economy* 85: 451–472.

Galai, D. and R. Masulis. 1977. "The Option Pricing Model and the Risk Factor of Stock." *Journal of Financial Economics* 4: 53–82.

Ghez, G. R. and G. S. Becker. 1975. *The Allocation of Time and Goods Over the Life Cycle.* New York: National Bureau of Economic Research.

Goldsmith, R. W. 1958. *Financial Intermediaries in the American Economy Since 1900.* Princeton: Princeton University Press.

Gordon, D. F. 1974. "A Neoclassical Theory of Keynesian Unemployment." *Economic Inquiry* 12: 431–459.

Gordon, M. 1962. *The Investment, Financing and Valuation of the Corporation.* Homewood, Ill.: Richard D. Irwin.

Gordon, R. J. 1980. "Comment on Barro and Rush." *In Rational Expectations and Monetary Policy,* edited by S. Fischer, pp. 55–63. Chicago: University of Chicago Press.

———. 1981. "Output Fluctuations and Gradual Price Adjustment." *Journal of Economic Literature* 19: 493–530.

Gorman, W. 1953. "Community Preference Fields." *Econometrica* 21: 63–80.

Grossman, S. and O. Hart. 1979. "A Theory of Competitive Equilibrium in Stock Market Economies." *Econometrica* 47: 293–329.

——— and ———. 1980. "Takeover Bids, The Free-Rider Problem, and the Theory of the Corporation." *Bell Journal of Economics* 11: 42–64.

——— and ———. 1983. "Implicit Contracts Under Asymmetric Information." *Quarterly Journal of Economics* 98: 123–156.

——— and J. Stiglitz. 1977. "On Value Maximization and Alternative Objectives of the Firm." *Journal of Finance* 32: 389–402.

——— and L. Weiss. 1982. "Heterogeneous Information and the Theory of the Business Cycle." *Journal of Political Economy* 90: 699–727.

Gurley, J. G. and E. S. Shaw. 1955. "Financial Aspects of Economic Development." *American Economic Review* 45: 515–538.

——— and ———. 1956. "Financial Intermediaries and the Saving-Investment Process." *Journal of Finance* 11: 257–266.

Hall, R. E. 1970. "Why Is the Unemployment Rate So High at Full Employment?" *Brookings Papers on Economic Activity* 1: 369–402.

Hamada, R. S. 1969. "Portfolio Analysis, Market Equilibrium and Corporation Finance." *Journal of Finance* 24: 13–31.

Harris, M. and A. Raviv. 1979. "Optimal Incentive Contracts With Imperfect Information." *Journal of Economic Theory* 20: 231–296.

Harrod, R. 1951. *The Life of John Maynard Keynes.* London: MacMillan.

Herring, R. and T. Willett. 1972. "The Capital Control Program and U.S. Investment Activity Abroad." *Southern Economic Journal* 34: 58–71.

Hicks, J. R. 1937. "Mr. Keynes and the Classics: A Suggested Interpretation." *Econometrica* 5: 147–159.

Higgins, R. C. and L. D. Schall. 1975. "Corporate Bankruptcy and Conglomerate Mergers." *Journal of Finance* 30: 93–113.

Hirschleifer, J. 1958. "On the Theory of Optimal Investment Decisions." *Journal of Political Economy* 66: 329–352.

————. 1970. *Investment, Interest and Capital.* Englewood Cliffs, N.J.: Prentice-Hall.

Holmstrom, B. 1979. "Moral Hazard and Observability." *Bell Journal of Economics and Management Science* 10: 74–91.

Intriligator, M. D. 1971. *Mathematical Optimization and Economic Theory.* Englewood Cliffs, N.J.: Prentice-Hall.

Jedamus, P. and R. Frame. 1969. *Business Decision Theory.* New York: McGraw-Hill.

Jensen, M. C. 1972. "Capital Markets: Theory and Evidence." *Bell Journal of Economics and Management Science* 3: 357–398.

———— and J. Long. 1972. "Corporate Investment Under Uncertainty and Pareto Optimality in the Capital Markets." *Bell Journal of Economics and Management Science* 3: 151–174.

———— and W. Meckling. 1976. "Theory of the Firm: Managerial Behavior, Agency Costs, and Ownership Structure." *Journal of Financial Economics* 3: 305–360.

Kemp, M. C. 1961. "Foreign Investment and the National Advantage." *Economic Record* 28: 56–62.

Keynes, J. M. 1936. *The General Theory of Employment, Interest and Money.* New York: Harcourt Brace.

————. 1956. *Essays and Sketches in Biography.* New York: Meridian Books.

Knight, F. H. 1921. *Risk, Uncertainty and Profit.* New York: Houghton Mifflin.

Krainer, R. E. 1967. "The Structure of Foreign Investment: Reply." *Journal of Finance* 22: 655–656.

————. 1969. "Liquidity Preference and Stock Market Speculation." *Journal of Financial and Quantitative Analysis* 4: 89–97.

————. 1974. "Firm Adjustment and Macroeconomic Equilibrium." Unpublished Manuscript, University of Wisconsin.

————. 1977. "Interest Rates, Leverage, and Investor Rationality." *Journal of Financial and Quantitative Analysis* 12: 1–16.

————. 1978. "On the Role of a Capital Market in the Determination of Macroeconomic Equilibrium." Unpublished Manuscript, Oxford Centre for Management Studies, Management Research Papers 78/17.

Lange, O. 1935. "Marxian Economics and Modern Economic Theory." *Review of Economic Studies* 2: 189–201.

Leamer, E. 1983. "Let's Take the Con Out of Econometrics." *American Economic Review* 73: 31–43.

Leijonhufvud, A. 1968. *On Keynesian Economics and the Economics of Keynes.* London: Oxford University Press.

Leland, H. E. 1974. "Production Theory and the Stock Market." *The Bell Journal of Economics and Management Science* 5: 125–144.

Leontief, W. 1953. "Domestic Production and Foreign Trade: the American Capital Position Re-Examined." *Proceedings of the American Philosophical Society* 97: 331–349.

Levy, H. and M. Sarnat. 1970. "Diversification, Portfolio Analysis and the Uneasy Case for Conglomerate Mergers." *Journal of Finance* 25: 795–802.

Lewellen, W. G. 1971. "A Pure Financial Rationale for the Conglomerate Merger." *Journal of Finance* 26: 521–537.

Lintner, J. 1965. "Security Prices, Risk, and Maximal Gains from Diversification." *Journal of Finance* 20: 587–615.

————. 1971. "Expectations, Mergers and Equilibrium in Purely Competitive Securities Markets." *American Economics Review* 61: 101–111.

Lipsey, R. G. 1960. "The Relation Between Unemployment and the Rate of Change of Money Wage Rates: A Further Analysis." *Economica* 28: 1–31.

Lorie, J. H. and L. J. Savage. 1955. "Three Problems in Rationing Capital." *Journal of Business* 28: 56–66.

Lucas, R. E. 1972. "Expectations and the Neutrality of Money." *Journal of Economic Theory* 4: 13–34.

————. 1973. "Some International Evidence on Output-Inflation Tradeoffs." *American Economic Review* 63: 326–334.

————. 1975. "An Equilibrium Model of the Business Cycle." *Journal of Political Economy* 83: 1113–1144.

————. 1976. "Some International Evidence on Output-Inflation Tradeoffs: Errata." *American Economic Review* 66: 985.

————. 1977. "Understanding Business Cycles." In *Stabilization of the Domestic and International Economy*, edited by K. Brunner and A. Meltzer, pp. 7–29. Carnegie-Rochester Conference Series on Public Policy. New York: North-Holland.

————. 1978. "Unemployment Policy." *American Economic Review* 68: 353–359.

————. 1980. "Methods and Problems in Business Cycle Theory." *Journal of Money, Credit, and Banking* 12: 696–715.

———— and L. A. Rapping. 1969. "Real Wages, Employment, and the Price Level." *Journal of Political Economy* 77: 721–754.

MacDougall, G. D. A. 1960. "The Benefits and Costs of Private Investment from Abroad: A Theoretical Approach." *Economic Record* 26: 13–35.

Malinvaud, E. 1977. *The Theory of Unemployment Reconsidered*. Oxford: Basil Blackwell.

Mandelker, G. 1974. "Risk and Return: The Case of Merging Firms." *Journal of Financial Economics* 1: 303–335.

Markowitz, H. 1952. "Portfolio Selection." *Journal of Finance* 7: 77–91.

————. 1959. *Portfolio Selection: Efficient Diversification of Investments*. New York: John Wiley and Sons.

Marx, K. 1961. *Capital*, Vol. I. Moscow: Foreign Language Publishing House.

Merton, R. C. 1973. "An Intertemporal Capital Asset Pricing Model." *Econometrica* 41: 867–887.

———— and M. Subrahmanyam. 1974. "The Optimality of a Competitive Stock Market." *Bell Journal of Economics and Management Science* 5: 145–170.

Miller, M. H. 1977. "Debt and Taxes." *Journal of Finance* 32: 261–275.

———— and F. Modigliani. 1961. "Dividend Policy, Growth, and the Valuation of Shares." *Journal of Business* 34: 411–433.

———— and ————. 1966. "Some Estimates of the Cost of Capital to the Electric Utility Industry, 1954–57." *American Economic Review* 56: 261–297.

———— and M. Scholes. 1972. "Rates of Return in Relation to Risk: A Re-examination of Some Recent Findings." In *Studies in the Theory of Capital Markets*, edited by M. C. Jensen, pp. 47–78. New York: Praeger.

———— and ————. 1978. "Dividends and Taxes." *Journal of Financial Economics* 6: 333–364.

———— and C. W. Upton. 1974. *Macroeconomics: A Neoclassical Introduction*. Homewood Ill.: Richard D. Irwin.

Mirrlees, J. A. 1976. "The Optimal Structure of Incentives and Authority Within an Organization." *Bell Journal of Economics and Management Science* 7: 105–131.

Modigliani, F. and M. H. Miller. 1958. "The Cost of Capital, Corporation Finance, and the Theory of Investment." *American Economic Review* 48: 261–297.

——— and ——— . 1959. "The Cost of Capital, Corporation Finance, and the Theory of Investment: Reply." *American Economic Review* 49: 655–669.

——— and ——— . 1969. "Reply to Heins and Sprenkle." *American Economic Review* 59: 592–595.

Mossin, J. 1966. "Equilibrium in a Capital Asset Market." *Econometrica* 34: 768–783.

——— . 1973. *Theory of Financial Markets.* Englewood Cliffs, N.J.: Prentice-Hall.

——— . 1977. *The Economic Efficiency of Financial Markets.* Lexington, Mass.: D. C. Heath.

Mundell, R. A. 1962. "The Appropriate Use of Monetary and Fiscal Policy for Internal and External Stability." *IMF Staff Papers* 9: 70–79.

Muth, J. 1961. "Rational Expectations and the Theory of Price Movements." *Econometrica* 29: 315–333.

Phelps, E. S. 1967. "Phillips Curve, Expectations of Inflation and Optimal Unemployment Over Time." *Economica* 34: 254–281.

——— . 1970. "Money Wage Dynamics and Labor Market Equilibrium." In *Microeconomic Foundations of Employment and Inflation Theory*, edited by E. S. Phelps, pp. 124–166. New York: Norton.

——— and J. B. Taylor. 1977. "Stabilizing Powers of Monetary Policy Under Rational Expectations." *Journal of Political Economy* 85: 163–190.

Phillips, A. W. 1958. "The Relationship Between Unemployment and the Rate of Change of Money Wage Rates in the United Kingdom, 1861-1957." *Economica* 25: 283–299.

Roll, R. 1977. "A Critique of the Asset Pricing Theory's Tests." *Journal of Financial Economics* 4: 129–176.

Ross, S. A. 1973. "The Economic Theory of Agency: The Principal's Problem." *American Economic Review* 63: 134–139.

——— . 1977. "The Determination of Financial Structure: The Incentive-Signalling Approach." *Bell Journal of Economics* 8: 23–40.

Rubenstein, M. E. 1973. "A Mean-Variance Synthesis of Corporate Financial Theory." *Journal of Finance* 28: 167–181.

Ruttenberg, S. 1971. *Needed: A Constructive Foreign Trade Policy.* Washington, D.C.: AFL-CIO, Industrial Union Department.

Samuelson, P. A. 1956. "Social Indifference Curves." *Quarterly Journal of Economics* 70: 1–22.

———. 1958. "An Exact Consumption-Loan Model of Interest With or Without the Social Contrivance of Money." *Journal of Political Economy* 56: 219–234.

———. 1969. "Presidential Address." In *International Economic Relations, Proceedings of the Third Congress of the International Economic Association*, edited by P. A. Samuelson, pp. 1–11. London: MacMillan.

———. 1970. "The Fundamental Approximation Theorem of Portfolio Analysis in Terms of Means, Variances and Higher Moments." *Review of Economic Studies* 37: 537–542.

Sandmo, A. 1969. "Capital Risk, Consumption, and Portfolio Choice." *Econometrica* 37: 586–599.

———. 1970. "The Effects of Uncertainty on Saving Decisions." *Review of Economic Studies* 37: 353–360.

———. 1974. "Two-Period Models of Consumption Under Uncertainty: A Survey." In *Allocations Under Uncertainty: Equilibrium and Optimality*, edited by J. H. Dreze and J. A. Mirrlees, pp. 24–35. London: MacMillan.

Santomero, A. and J. Seater. 1978. "The Inflation-Unemployment Trade-off: A Critique of the Literature." *Journal of Economic Literature* 16: 499–545.

Sargent, T. 1971. "A Note on the 'Accelerationist' Controversy." *Journal of Money, Credit, and Banking* 3: 721–725.

———. 1973. "Rational Expectations, the Real Rate of Interest and the Natural Rate of Unemployment." *Brookings Papers On Economic Activity* 2: 429–479.

———. 1976. "A Classical Macroeconometric Model for the United States." *Journal of Political Economy* 84: 207–237.

———. 1979. *Macroeconomic Theory*. New York: Academic Press.

——— and N. Wallace. 1975. "Rational Expectations, the Optimal Monetary Instrument, and the Optimal Money Supply Rule." *Journal of Political Economy* 83: 241–254.

Sharpe, W. F. 1964. "Capital Asset Prices: A Theory of Market Equilibrium Under Conditions of Risk." *Journal of Finance* 19: 425–442.

Sims, C. A. 1972. "Money, Income, and Causality." *American Economic Review* 62: 540–552.

Small, D. H. 1979. "A Comment on Robert Barro's Unanticipated Money Growth and Unemployment in the United States." *American Economic Review* 69: 996–1003.

Smith, C. W. and J. B. Warner. 1979. "On Financial Contracting." *Journal of Financial Economics* 7: 117–161.

Solow, R. M. 1969. *Price Expectations and the Behavior of the Price Level*. Manchester: Manchester University Press.

————. 1971. "Some Implications of Alternative Criteria for the Firm." In *The Corporate Economy*, edited by R. Marris and A. Wood, pp. 318–342. Cambridge, Mass.: Harvard University Press.

Stevens, G. V. G. 1972. "Capital Mobility and the International Firm." In *The International Mobility and Movement of Capital*, edited by F. Machlup, W. Salant, and L. Tarshis, pp. 323–353. New York: National Bureau of Economic Research.

Stiglitz, J. 1972. "On the Optimality of the Stock Market Allocation of Investment." *Quarterly Journal of Economics* 86: 25–60.

————. 1974. "On the Irrelevance of Corporate Financial Policy." *American Economic Review* 64: 851–866.

Taylor, J. B. 1980. "Aggregate Dynamics and Staggered Contracts." *Journal of Political Economy* 88: 1–23.

Thurow, L. C. 1980. *The Zero-Sum Society: Distribution and the Possibilities for Economic Change*. New York: Basic Books.

Tinbergen, J. 1952. *On the Theory of Economic Policy*. Amsterdam: North-Holland.

Tobin, J. 1956. "The Interest-Elasticity of Transactions Demand for Cash." *Review of Economics and Statistics* 38: 241–247.

————. 1958. "Liquidity Preference as Behavior Towards Risk." *Review of Economic Studies* 26: 65–86.

————. 1974. "Friedman's Theoretical Framework." In: *Milton Friedman's Monetary Framework*, edited by R. J. Gordon, pp. 77–89. Chicago: University of Chicago Press.

————. 1975. *Essays in Economics: Consumption and Econometrics*. Amsterdam: North-Holland.

Treynor, J. 1961. "Towards a Theory of the Market Value of Risky Assets." Unpublished Manuscript.

Walters, A. A. 1963. "Production and Cost Functions: An Econometric Survey." *Econometrica* 31: 1–66.

Weintraub, R. 1980. "Comment on Barro and Rush." In *Rational Expectations and Monetary Policy*, edited by S. Fischer, pp. 63–70. Chicago: University of Chicago Press.

INDEX

Adaptive expectations, *see*
 Expectations, Adaptive
Agency theory, 181, 305
Alberro, J., 174
Alchian, A., 202
Allocational efficiency, 1–2, 5–6.
 See also Capital markets, efficiency
 of; Pareto efficient in a certain
 environment, 85–88, 127
 in the capital asset pricing model,
 88–100, 295
Amihud, Y., 205
Arrow, K., 36, 62, 78, 80, 108
Assignment rule, 199–200, 215, 219,
 222, 225
Azariadis, C., 203, 304

Bailey, M. J., 140
Baily, M. N., 203
Balance sheet matching,
 empirical evidence of, 283–286
 theory of, 218–221, 283–286
Bankruptcy, 71–74, 83, 84
 costs of, 73–74
Barro, R. J., 50, 129, 165–167, 173,
 174, 238
Baumol, W. J., 148
BB-SS equilibrium, 192–194, 203, 204,
 214, 236
 numerical computation of, 267
Becker, G. S., 169, 305
Bequest, 35, 59–60
Black, F., 84, 120
Blinder, A., 129, 143, 149, 151, 174,
 239
Bond market
 equilibrium in financial contracting
 model, 189–193, 203, 204
 equilibrium in IS-LM model, 132,

135–137, 138, 148
Bosshardt, D., 93, 98, 101
Box, G. E. P., 271
Buiter, W. H., 50
Business cycle, 7. *See also* Supply,
 adjustment over business cycle in
 financial contracting model,
 207–225, 299–301
 in Keynesian model, 167, 171
 in rational expectations model,
 167–171, 179–180, 298–299
Business strategy
 in financial contract model, 196–201,
 208–234, 267, 289, 305
 in rational expectations model, 168,
 175, 176

Canada, 276, 280
Capital
 human compared to financial,
 201–202
Capital accumulation
 Fisher motive, 13–14, 26, 27
 Marxian motive, 13, 27, 28
Capital asset pricing model (CAPM),
 5–6, 58
 allocation of investment. *See*
 Allocational efficiency, in the
 capital asset pricing model
 assumptions, 62–63, 104–105
 bankruptcy in, 71–74, 83
 compared to liquidity preference
 theory, 80, 135–137, 145.
 See also Portfolio theory,
 Keynesian compared to capital
 asset pricing model
 decentralized decision-making in,
 93–94, 97
 diversification in, 6, 66, 73, 76,

319

About the Author

ROBERT E. KRAINER is Professor of Business at the University of Wisconsin-Madison where he teaches courses in corporate finance and financial markets. He holds a B. S. degree from the University of Wisconsin and M. B. A. and Ph. D. degrees from the University of Michigan. After receiving his Ph. D. he spent one year on a postdoctoral fellowship at Harvard University. He has taught courses in financial economics at the University of Michigan and Oxford University.

Professor Krainer has published numerous articles in the areas of financial institutions, corporate finance, capital markets, macroeconomics, and international finance. His articles have appeared in a number of scholarly journals including the *Canadian Journal of Economics, Journal of Business, Journal of Finance, Journal of Financial and Quantitative Analysis, Journal of Money, Credit and Banking, Journal of Political Economy,* and *Oxford Economic Papers* among others. His current research is in the area of the interrelationship between production and financing decisions of firms over the business cycle.